winning women's **votes**

:

*Propaganda and Politics
in Weimar Germany*

Julia Sneeringer

The
University *of*
North Carolina
Press

CHAPEL HILL
& LONDON

copyright © 2002 | the university of north carolina press

Designed by Julie Spivey
Set in Bembo and Goudy Sans
by Tseng Information Systems, Inc.

*The paper in this book meets the guidelines
for permanence and durability of the Committee
on Production Guidelines for Book Longevity
of the Council on Library Resources.*

Library of Congress Cataloging-in-Publication
Data
Sneeringer, Julia.
Winning women's votes : propaganda and
politics in Weimar Germany / Julia Sneeringer.
p. cm.
Includes bibliographical references and index.
ISBN 0-8078-2674-x (cloth : alk. paper) —
ISBN 0-8078-5341-0 (pbk. : alk. paper)
1. Women—Germany—History.   2. Women
—Suffrage—Germany.   3. Women's rights—
Germany.   4. Germany—Politics and
government—1918–1933.   I. Title.
HQ1623.S595   2002
305.4'0943—dc21   2001053243

06   05   04   03   02   5   4   3   2   1

contents

illustrations

After over ten years of work on this project, it is a task both daunting and pleasurable to acknowledge the people and institutions that made its completion possible. I have been fortunate to have received support from so many quarters.

Nothing happens without funding, so my thanks to the organizations that granted financial support at various stages of this work: the Fulbright Commission, the National Endowment for the Humanities, the German Academic Exchange Service, and the Andrew W. Mellon Foundation. Their assistance made possible archival research at Bundesarchiv branches in Koblenz, Berlin, and Potsdam; the Geheimes Staatsarchiv Preussischer Kulturbesitz in Berlin-Dahlem; the Landesarchiv Berlin; the Hoover Institution Archives; and both houses of the Staatsbibliothek Preussischer Kulturbesitz in Berlin. Many thanks to the knowledgeable staffs of these archives and libraries, especially Herr Fischer at the Bundesarchiv Koblenz, as well as the reference staff at Van Pelt Library at the University of Pennsylvania, especially Stephen Lehmann. Thanks also to Dean David Burrows at Beloit College for a publishing subsidy.

I would have never come this far intellectually without the guidance of some great teachers. I was very lucky to land in the graduate history program at Penn, where Tom Childers helped me conceptualize this study and then convinced me that I could do it. I will be forever grateful for his insights and understanding. Jane Caplan opened up the field of gender and women's history to me, and her continued support has been more affirming than she will ever know. Lynn Hunt gave me the intellectual tools to do justice to my sources and taught me to be a better teacher. I owe a large debt of gratitude to members of Penn's history department for their sustained support, especially Lynn Lees, Drew Faust, Walter Licht, and Jeff Fear. And my sincere thanks to Betty Richards and Tim Corrigan for mentoring this Temple undergrad at a crucial stage.

Penn surrounded me with a cohort of wonderfully warm and vital classmates. For their comradeship I thank Steve Conn, Marc Stein, Jay Lockenour, Alison Isenberg,

Lara Iglitzin, Abby Schrader, Ingrid Schenk, and Mike Allen. Maria Höhn in particular has always been ready with an encouraging word or a beer to cry in; she is a remarkable spirit.

In Berlin I met some scholars of Germany who remain treasured friends and colleagues. Brigid Doherty, Lynne Frame, and Paul Lerner taught me a great deal about Weimar, and I hold their friendship dear. My warmest thanks also to Barbara Solbach, who put me up—and put up with me—time and again, with love and good humor.

Other members of the German studies community graciously shared their time and insights in ways that have enhanced this work. I am grateful to Larry Jones for his encouragement and advice. He and the other reader for the University of North Carolina Press offered most useful, detailed criticism of this manuscript, and I truly appreciate their comments. Thanks also to Kathleen Canning, Geoff Eley, Raffael Scheck, Eric Weitz, and the participants at the always stimulating Midwest German History Workshops. For their comradeship, I also thank Paul Jaskot and Maria Mitchell.

Since I have been at Beloit College, I have benefited from the support of several people. Dean David Burrows granted me some scheduling flexibility that sped this project along. Thanks also to everyone in the history department, especially chair Bob Hodge, for being colleagues in the truest sense of the word. Georgia Duerst-Lahti, Sonja Darlington, and everyone in women's studies also offered valuable support. Many of my students have been a source of inspiration. And my thanks to Arno Damerow and Al Tolu-Honary for able, friendly technical assistance.

Everyone at the University of North Carolina Press has been a pleasure to work with. Lewis Bateman first took on this project, and I appreciate his confidence in me and this book. Charles Grench helped see it through to completion, along with Paula Wald, Ruth Homrighaus, Glenn Perkins, and Alison Waldenberg. I thank them all.

Before I was a historian, I was the ninth child of Joseph and Norma Sneeringer. I could not have done any of this without the love and support of my mother and the Sneeringer clan—thanks for making me laugh and keeping me sane. My late father imparted to me an interest in politics and the world; his influence on me has been profound. I owe a special debt of gratitude to my brother-in-law, Peter Gannone, for sharing a love of history and to my sister, Ann Wilson, for staying close through it all. Thanks also to Stuart Lacey and Jessica Reed, friends who have been like sisters for many years.

Above all, my deepest thanks to Agustin Bolanos—for tea and sympathy, stimulating conversation, pleasant diversions, and a happy home; for being the most supportive partner I could ever hope for; and for his abiding love. This book is dedicated to him.

BDF	League of German Women's Associations
BVP	Bavarian People's Party
DDP	German Democratic Party
DHV	German National Shop Clerks Association
DNVP	German National People's Party
DSP	German State Party
DVP	German People's Party
FRS	Frauenreichssekretariat (KPD women's organization)
IAH	International Workers' Aid
KFD	Catholic Women's League of Germany
KPD	German Communist Party
NSDAP	National Socialist German Workers Party
NSF	National Socialist Women's Organization
PAV	Personnel Retrenchment Decree
RFMB	Red Women's and Girls' League
SA	Sturmabteilung (Nazi Party "storm front")
SPD	Social Democratic Party
SS	Schutzstaffel (Nazi paramilitary organization)
USPD	Independent Social Democratic Party
ZK	Central Committee (of Communist Party)

winning women's **votes**

Introduction

:

The Political Mobilization of Women

November 1918 witnessed two political revolutions in Germany: the proclamation of the republic and the enfranchisement of women. Female suffrage forever changed the landscape of German political life as women became the majority of voters in one fell swoop. Political parties found themselves (often reluctantly) addressing women as political actors for the first time and, as a result, sought to define their interests and characteristics—indeed, women's "nature"— to tap their votes over the course of ten national and dozens of regional elections between 1919 and 1932. As such, the parties were perhaps the most visible, sustained participants in a far-reaching public discourse on women. Despite the mushrooming scholarship on women in the Weimar era, scant attention has been paid to how they were mobilized for politics.

Much of the scholarship on their political participation in Weimar has focused on *how* women voted or their relationship to individual parties, particularly the Nazi movement, while partisan tactics and mobilizing strategies have been barely explored.[1] The struggle to draw women into electoral politics was but one reflection of how political turmoil, economic shifts, new attitudes about sexuality, and mass culture were changing women's position, yet it was certainly one of the most dramatic reflections and reveals a great deal about the larger issue of how attitudes and anxieties concerning women's roles evolved throughout the Weimar period—concerns central to postwar Germany's cultural and political self-definition.

Focusing on attempts by the major parties—from left to right, the Communists (KPD), Social Democrats (SPD), Democrats (DDP), German People's Party (DVP), Catholic Center Party, German National People's Party (DNVP), and the National Socialists (NSDAP)—to mobilize female voters through propaganda, this work explores the effects of women's changed political status on the debate about their public and private roles during Weimar. Using the national elections between January 1919 and November 1932, this study compares party appeals issued across the political spectrum, both within campaigns and across time, to examine how propaganda constructed women as political actors. Its focus is propaganda created explicitly for female voters, something the parties produced on a significant scale only after 1918. This study also considers how the idea of the political woman appeared in appeals to mixed-sex or implicitly male audiences, sites where parties had to confront tensions between concerns of gender versus those of class and economic interest. The addition of women to the polity expanded the range of issues that surfaced during elections. Acting on the assumption that women were different politically from men, all parties sought to articulate what they assumed to be female voters' interests by invoking a set of "women's issues"—political and economic rights, maternity, religion, social welfare, and so on—a process that simultaneously anchored these themes in German political discourse in new ways. At the same time as it constructed political identities for women, propaganda revealed how each party conceptualized democracy, the war, revolution, class, the state, and culture. Examining the symbolic terrain of politics—the languages that marked the boundaries of what could be articulated and accepted in the public sphere—can illuminate how women's entry as formal participants changed the political and offers one way to write women back into German political history.

To better understand how these discourses on women evolved during the turbulent Weimar Republic, this study analyzes propaganda materials produced by the major parties to attract women as voters and members. Such materials were largely produced in-house, often in an ad hoc manner by party workers (professional advertising writers played but a small part in this process before the 1930s). These materials include pamphlets, party publications, and, above all, campaign flyers, which parties relied upon most heavily to reach voters in an age before the dominance of electronic media.[2] These items were handed out at busy intersections or train stations, plastered on walls and advertising kiosks, tossed from trucks, distributed during lectures and house visits, disseminated at rallies and recruiting drives, and mailed to private homes during drives that targeted potential sympathizers by occupation or social status.[3] Posters comprised another element in Weimar's war of symbolic images that parties used to communicate in bold visual terms what and whom they represented.[4] This study also uses evidence from eight major newspapers,[5] some of which were party mouthpieces and all of which open a window on how images of women were constructed and contested by writers and readers in the powerful daily press. These materials not only propagated ideas but also helped mobilize the loyalties, emotions, and dreams of the public through the street-level rituals of election campaigns. Their quantity and quality make them invaluable sources through which to explore the preoccupations of mass politics in these crisis years of German modernity.[6]

Interest in what Thomas Childers has called "the everyday language of politics" has grown steadily since historians such as Gareth Stedman Jones and William Sewell called for a "mapping out" of political discourses as a way to understand class formation.[7] Childers has applied this methodology to the study of German political culture, demonstrating what Weimar-era partisan literature targeted at occupational groups reveals of parties' working assumptions about the interests and values of those constituencies.[8] But the gendered dimensions of political mobilization have remained largely invisible in German historiography, leaving one to wonder how seamlessly women were incorporated into political life after the introduction of female suffrage (indeed, a great deal remains to be written about life after suffrage in other countries as well). Several German histories have taken up Joan Scott's call for attention to the gendered dimensions of language and its work of constructing social identity and perception, including Kathleen Canning's work on the gendering of class and Eric Weitz's rereading of German communism.[9] Most studies in this vein illuminate how language operates within a political field, broadly defined as any contest for power within which identities are created, including those in the private sphere, but no one has yet investigated across class or party lines how gender operated to create subjects within a politics more traditionally defined as the arena of formal participation in government or the state.[10] Because the Weimar parties relied so heavily on printed propaganda to do the work of grassroots mobilization, a reading of these texts that attends to the ways they constructed gender identities—in this case, for women—can take us one step closer to formulating a general account of German politics in this crucial period that does not systematically or unconsciously exclude women.[11]

All German women over the age of twenty attained franchise on equal terms in national, state, and communal elections through a 12 November 1918 decree of the Council of People's Deputies, which was comprised of SPD and Independent Social Democratic (USPD) delegates. The move came as something of a shock since most states had legalized women's participation in political organizations only in 1908. Germany's prewar suffragist movement had also been weak, in part because the women's movement was dominated by moderates for whom suffrage was a relatively low priority, viewed not as the gateway to equality but as the crowning recognition of women's indispensability to public life.[12] Ultimately, woman suffrage in Germany was the fruit not of a suffragist campaign but of the revolution, which spoiled it in the eyes of many who opposed the new regime, both male and female. Because the Left had been the prime mover behind the introduction of female suffrage (as late as October 1918 all nonsocialist parties had rejected it), the great debate in the first election in which women participated was whether they would express their "thanks" by voting Socialist. While many did in January 1919, their pattern of voting during Weimar would become one of consistent support for parties of a conservative, confessional bent. Those that openly pledged support for female emancipation—the socialist parties and the liberal Democrats—did not generally fare as well with female voters.

Statistics on female voting patterns exist thanks to a provision of the 1918 Wahlverordnung that allowed (but did not mandate) districts to separate ballots by sex. This was usually done by distributing different colored slips or erecting separate voting urns. Both methods, however, caused so much extra work and expense that sex-segregated balloting was conducted nationwide only for the elections to the 1919 National Assembly and the 1930 Reichstag. Many local communities sporadically tabulated votes by sex; only the city of Cologne did so consistently from 1919 to 1932. Gabriele Bremme's 1956 study of female voting patterns, still the standard reference, is based on tallies from seventy-three electoral districts from 1919 to 1930; supplemented by Helen Boak's calculations for 1930–32 and figures compiled by Jürgen Falter's team, the record permits certain general conclusions.[13]

Measured in terms of turnout, women apparently took suffrage seriously, particularly in 1919 when they cast more ballots than men (an imbalance also attributable to women's demographic preponderance after the war). Female voting rates subsequently declined from this peak (as did male), sliding after 1920 but rebounding during the hotly contested races of the early 1930s. The sexes also resembled each other in that both turned out more enthusiastically for national races than for state or communal ones. Women, however, were less likely than men to vote in "routine" elections and more likely to vote during times of national crisis. Figures suggest that women in higher status occupations such as teaching, civil service, or white-collar work had higher participation rates; domestic servants had the lowest. Rates for working-class women could be either very low or very high, depending on the politicization of their neighborhood. The oldest and youngest women were less likely to vote, as were divorced women. Married and urban women turned out more often than rural ones. Although female turnout generally lagged only a few points behind male, contemporaries routinely pegged women as politically apathetic.[14]

Political sociologists have established not only which women voted but how. Women's preferences, like men's, were highly determined by class and religion. Working-class women generally chose Marxist-socialist parties (the SPD, KPD, or USPD until 1922), while their middle- and upper-class sisters stuck to the bourgeois camp (the DDP, DVP, DNVP, or, as the political middle collapsed in 1924–30, single-issue splinter parties). Catholics—especially women—tended to back the Center, while Jews were overrepresented in the liberal parties. Two rules characterize Weimar women's political behavior: women showed strong support for parties with a religious cast, and they chose the least radical alternative within their respective class milieu. For example, proletarian women preferred the reformist SPD to the more polemical KPD.[15]

In terms of sheer numbers, the most female votes went to Weimar's largest party until July 1932, the SPD. But contemporaries measured a party's success with female constituents by the *percentage* of its vote that came from women, as a gender gap cost a party seats under Weimar's system of proportional representation. Percentagewise, the Center Party benefited the most from female suffrage. Women consistently comprised about 60 percent of Center voters; numerically, this translates to between 8 and 17 percent of all votes cast by women between 1919 and 1933. Next in order of popularity came the conservative DNVP, then the national-liberal DVP—both parties with solid female support in Protestant Germany. Moving left on the political spectrum, one crosses a line beyond which women constituted less than 50 percent of a party's voters. Here we find the left liberal DDP, whose voters were more likely to be male, though not by a margin much higher than 1 percent. We also find the SPD, whose gender gap ranged between 5 and 10 percent but steadily narrowed through the late 1920s for various reasons, not least of which was the growing Communist and Nazi challenge. Throughout Weimar women categorically rejected the KPD, despite (or perhaps because of) its argument that gender equality was a central part of its larger revolutionary agenda. Outside of a handful of districts, women also largely shunned the NSDAP through 1930; it was only in Weimar's last years that a combination of the depression and new tactics triggered the Nazis' national breakthrough with women, particularly in Protestant regions.[16]

These figures represent the most accurate rendering of female voting preferences we have. To provide a clearer picture of the context in which the parties vied for female votes, a brief stroll through the Weimar political landscape is in order. The republic's architects devised a system of proportional representation that awarded a Reichstag seat for every 60,000 votes a party polled in a given district.[17] This spawned a profusion of competing parties, from national heavyweights like the SPD to small fry like the Mecklenburg Village League. Furthermore, since its origins in the 1860s the German party system was structured along cleavages of class, religion, and region. Parties mobilized constituencies within these boundaries by targeting and cultivating specific groups (workers, Catholics, Bavarians, etc.), rather than seeking to win the electorate as a whole. This structure combined with another legacy from the Empire, which denied parties the right to actually govern, to produce campaigns oriented around sweeping ideological pronouncements rather than concrete proposals. During Weimar such tactics increased the special-interest nature of politics, promoted negative campaigning and infighting, and thwarted the formation of stable governments (there were eighteen cabinet changes between February 1919 and January 1933). Because Germans voted for party lists rather than individual candidates, they were further removed from their representatives, making voting increasingly an expression of protest guided less and less by consideration as to who might actually govern. The growing clout of trade unions and occupational organizations also promoted intense competition, as the bourgeois parties in particular jockeyed for the favor and financial contributions of economic interest groups, routinely at the expense of women. In short, Weimar politics was combative and theatrical; the successive jolts of inflation, a harsh stabilization, and the depression made it combustible.[18]

The fault lines in Weimar's political terrain set the ways parties pitched appeals to voters. The bourgeois and confessional parties targeted their appeals primarily to occupational groups such as civil servants, farmers, or white-collar employees.[19] Marxist parties favored a sweeping address to workers. All parties addressed cross-class groupings such as soldiers, pensioners, youths, and women. Women were numerically the largest such category, targeted in at least 10 and sometimes up to 25 percent of a party's appeals in a given campaign, especially during 1919–20 and again in the early 1930s.[20] Yet the parties did not quite know how to speak to women. Could they appeal to them on the basis of material interest like occupational groups? Were women a *Stand*, a unified economic and social group with particular values and norms? Were "private" issues such as reproduction appropriate content for political propaganda? How could women's identification with the spiritual be transposed into what so many regarded as the base world of political horse trading? Was there even such a thing as the women's vote?

Women activists often reminded their parties of the fluidity of female identities, arguing that propaganda had to address women's material interests as workers or housewives, but also insisting that their "nature" and roles made them more than a special-interest group that could simply be appealed to on the same terms as men. Lived identities of gender, class, ethnicity, age, and so on are inherently unstable and constantly in competition, existing in a kind of overlapping simultaneity. But political discourse flattened out such complexity—it was almost as if the parties could only begin to address women by imagining them as possessing uncomplicated, unified identities emanating from some universal female essence. Ironically the turmoil of Weimar itself muddled any attempt to neaten gender boundaries, propelling the parties into a contradictory cycle of trying to stabilize identities for their political purposes and, at the same time, reshape them in the context of a rapidly changing political climate. Examining the parties' repeated attempts to imagine and address the woman voter can reveal the political operations of gender—its constructedness as well as its relational aspects as seen, for example, in the ways parties contrasted female voters to male.

To understand fully these prescriptive portrayals of women, we should not overlook the organizers of party mobilization—those who made propaganda. While it is often difficult to determine exactly who created specific appeals, we do know that throughout the Weimar era, parties tended to relegate the work of recruiting female support to their women's committees (*Frauenausschusse*). By 1921 all major parties had formed *Frauenausschusse* charged with creating and distributing women's propaganda and periodicals, running political education courses and social gatherings, suggesting female candidates for electoral ballots, monitoring the mood of female voters, and advising the party on policy issues relevant to women. A party's national women's committee was usually an executive branch alongside those for other occupational or social target groups, with local branches linked in a chain of command. It was staffed and operated by a handful of paid workers in Berlin, supported by a nationwide network of volunteers who were typically all female, except where no women could be recruited. When interpreting party propaganda aimed at or describing women, it is crucial to keep in mind women's close involvement in the process of constructing these appeals, an involvement that occurred by default because no party really treated agitation among women as an affair of the party at large. As these writers publicly struggled to articulate what they thought women wanted to hear—and in the process worked to construct "proper" roles for them—what they could say was limited by the political languages that were available, the ideological frameworks of the parties to which they were loyal, and the opposition or blank indifference they encountered from party men. This last element, which relates to female activists' relationships with their parties, is something this study weaves into its narrative, where sources permit.[21]

How various parties established and treated their women's committees sheds light on how they valued female activists and, by extension, voters. For example, the SPD, whose main audience was the skilled working class, had demanded female suffrage in its 1891 program at the insistence of August Bebel, who made the first argument for votes for women on the floor of the Reichstag in 1895. It had the oldest women's party organization and a female presence in the proletarian milieu that undoubtedly enhanced the SPD's strength during the Wilhelmine era.[22] Both the SPD and its breakaway rival, the KPD, whose support by Germany's most dispossessed proletarians would make it the most powerful Communist party outside Russia, preached the need to incorporate women and their agitation into all facets of party work while maintaining separate women's organizations. However, both parties failed during Weimar to integrate women and their concerns in practice. The KPD, for example, was slow to set up a network of women's committees after its founding in late 1918. Revolutionary battles, organizational confusion, and a lack of able women contributed to the lag, though distrust and outright hostility toward women also played a huge role, despite Lenin's dictum that women were indispensable to the class struggle. Auxiliary organizations such as the Red Women and Girls' League eventually attracted thousands but never yielded the mass female support the KPD desired. The women's organizations of both the KPD and the SPD maintained a strict distance from the bourgeois feminist movement, stressing class over gender solidarity.

The bourgeois parties, for their part, kept their women's organizations largely segregated within the organization. An extreme example of this was the NSDAP (whose appeal crossed into the working classes), which barred women from the directly political side of party work and never had a female representative on any governing body. Women's work in the bourgeois parties included fund-raising, writing materials for female audiences, and staging meetings, courses, and socials with speeches and entertainment. The two liberal parties had ties to the League of German Women's Associations (BDF), the umbrella organization for bourgeois women's groups. The forebears of the left liberal DDP had had female members since the 1908 reform of the Law of Associations; the DDP itself quickly attracted prominent BDF members during Weimar. In contrast the DVP, which was less enthusiastic about the republic, had been reluctant to embrace women's entry into politics for fear that it would "confessionalize" them. This party, which appealed primarily to business and civil service interests, set up a women's organization with loose ties to the BDF upon its founding in December 1918. Female activists in both liberal parties, who defined themselves (often uneasily) as feminists, strove to create a new model of female citizenship anchored in equal rights but imbued with notions of "social motherhood," women's purported ability to bring unique, maternal qualities to the nation's service.[23]

The two parties most successful with women voters ironically had weaker women's committees, relying instead on existing organizations to mobilize female support. The DNVP, which demanded the restoration of monarchy and empire, never fully integrated women into the party and counted on Evangelical Protestant women's groups to anchor female support. This was even more true for the Center, a mass party that assembled Catholics across class lines. Previously opposed to female suffrage, it relied on the Catholic Women's League (KFD) to reach women until it founded its own women's group in 1921. Both parties tapped the power of the pulpit and church organizations to mobilize women around a conservative, Christian cultural agenda.

The decree that granted female suffrage also allowed women to be elected to office. In 1919, 9.6 percent of those elected to the National Assembly were female, the highest representation in any country at the time and a figure West Germany only surpassed in the 1980s. Women initially benefited from a system in which voters elected party lists. Each party earned a number of seats proportional to the amount of votes it won and distributed its seats based on its own ranking of its candidates. This method focused less attention on individual personalities, helping female candidates who were relative unknowns. Increasingly, however, the system worked to women's disadvantage as the novelty of suffrage wore off and parties felt less compelled to place women near the top of their candidate lists, thus diluting their election prospects. Already in 1920 women fell to 8 percent of Reichstag delegates and 5.7 in 1924. This was partly attributable to the fact that the parties with consistently high numbers of women candidates, the SPD and DDP, were losing votes. Roughly 10 percent of SPD delegates were female, a figure matched by the short-lived USPD in 1919–20; the DDP hovered around 8 percent. Fifty percent of KPD representatives were female in 1920 (it had only two seats that year), but female representation otherwise stood at around 6 percent until 1930 when the ratio jumped to 17 percent. The remaining parties hovered between 4 and 5 percent. During Weimar no woman ever sat in the Reichsrat (the upper legislative chamber) or held a cabinet post. At the local level, female participation in government was stronger where the Left was strong.[24]

Women's lack of influence within the parties would fuel talk throughout the Weimar period of alternative ways to strengthen their clout. The BDF lobbied parties before each election to put forth more female candidates. Katharina von Kardorff, Anita Augspurg, and Lida Gustava Heymann at various times each floated the idea of a women's party, though this never took off. Even if female activists could have bridged their divisions, a women's party would have lacked a firm base, as potential leaders and voters had already allied themselves with existing parties. Cross-party ballots assembling female candidates onto one ticket materialized occasionally at the local level during elections but never coalesced into enduring structures.

Women politicians spoke less on the floor of the Reichstag than in committee. Though Clara Zetkin, Toni Sender, and Gertrud Bäumer all spoke on foreign affairs, women's main parliamentary activities were in the realm of social welfare.[25] Historians have debated whether this constituted ghettoization or progress for women. Helen Boak, for example, depicts a situation in which men, anxious to thwart female challenges to their leadership, let inexperienced women relegate themselves to "women's issues." While it is true that men gladly left lower-status social policy work to women, Boak's picture tends to downplay women's achievements and overlooks their own preferences. Moderate feminists had argued for decades that since public institutions had taken over many family functions, women had to secure a strong presence in the social realm—indeed, a healthy and balanced state required it.[26] Marion Kaplan interprets prewar social service activism as a form of female politics at a time when women were barred from the parties and voting. Other historians, noting that the new republic placed a "women's realm"—welfare—at its heart, have called us to rethink the implications of women's identification with the social for their access to power.[27] Any evaluation of the ways political discourse constructed women's roles must be attentive to how women and men of the day envisioned appropriate spheres of activity for women.

Historians of Weimar Republic women have long wrestled with the disparity between the promise of liberation, symbolized by the New Woman, and women's lived experience. Contemporaries often read the legal equality formalized by article 109 of the Weimar constitution, which states that "men and women have basically the same civil rights and duties," and women's greater visibility in public life as signs that female emancipation had arrived. Historians, in contrast, have argued that emancipation was more appearance than reality. Renate Bridenthal's germinal scholarship on Weimar women has argued that continuities in patriarchal social, economic, and legal structures diminished the impact of women's new political freedoms, leading many women to conclude that emancipation—and the republic associated with it—was a fraud.[28] Similar arguments have been advanced by historians who stress liberal feminism's failure to win tangible social or political gains for women,[29] as well as those seeking to explain why women consistently chose parties that rejected gender equality in favor of "separate spheres."[30] Unlike the popular culture image of the modern, sexually liberated New Woman, most German women still became wives and mothers. In fact, the war's decimation of a generation seemingly heightened the allure of marriage for the 2 million "surplus women" whose potential husbands fell in Flanders's fields. Despite public interest in the sex reform movement, abortion was still illegal and contraceptives difficult to obtain. Most women who worked for wages did so in low-paying, unskilled jobs, juggling the multiple burdens of work, housework, childrearing, and household consumption. Even the new breed of highly visible white-collar women worked long hours with few prospects for promotion. Despite the fact that women constituted over 35 percent of the workforce by 1925, work was still considered a way station before marriage; careers were acceptable only for single women. As Bridenthal has argued, most women, besieged economically and psychologically by the crises and dislocations of the Weimar years, rejected New Womanhood for ideologies and organizations that promised to defend their embattled domestic territory.

This wave of historiography emphasizes Weimar's failure to improve women's lives. Yet while continuities of repression are undeniable, our picture of Weimar would be incomplete if we overlooked the degree of change that did occur, such as the widespread acceptance of an interval of independence between school and marriage for young women. Subsequent research has shifted attention to Weimar's possibilities and struggles —some successful, some not—for change, including Atina Grossmann's work on the sex reform movement and Cornelie Usborne's account of efforts to reform reproductive law.[31] Other studies spanning the Wilhelmine and Weimar eras question models that stress German feminism's deviation from some healthy Western norm of liberal individualism, attempting to understand bourgeois and even conservative feminisms on their own terms.[32]

Investigation has also focused on representations of women in a media savvy era that was rife with gender anxiety, sentiments encapsulated in one man's 1931 letter to the *Deutsche Allgemeine Zeitung*: "In our time of confusion, one thing is most important—clearness about the positions and tasks of man and woman."[33] In other national contexts, scholars of the postwar period have produced works examining representations of gender, particularly femininity, as markers of larger cultural conflict, including Susan Kingsley Kent's charting of Britain's "sex war" and Mary Lou Roberts's study of French discourses on population decline and female sexuality. Work on gender representations during Weimar has often come from the literary criticism or art history camp, such as Patrice Petro's examination of women and melodramatic form in the cinema or a recent collection on women in the metropolis.[34]

The present study situates itself within the study of representations, as well as the broader fields of women's history, gender history, and political history. It takes seriously Weimar's preoccupation with women's changing roles, which stemmed from real social upheavals such as women's growing presence in the labor force since the nineteenth century. The war in particular burdened Weimar with tremendous social dislocations, dramatically realigning public and private through mass mobilization and mass privation, in ways that both enhanced women's power and fed resentment against them.[35] Women's enfranchisement in 1918 lent these tensions a new political salience. This study focuses on the ways these anxieties were enacted on the stage of party politics, countering the tendency of the historiography of German parties and elections to overlook women by illuminating the gendered dimensions of the most far-reaching collective acts of political articulation—voting and campaigning.[36] This work also aims to reintroduce a political dimension often missing from the study of gender and representations, something indispensable to understanding a historical context in which all of life became highly politicized. Political languages, and the exploding mass culture of which they were a part, furnished symbols and stereotypes people used in order to think and act in the world.[37] Thus discourse—defined as the complex of statements, signs, texts, and practices attached to a concept and dispersed across different public sites—is the focus of this study. However, it does not treat discourse as the sole producer of reality or experience. Rather it accepts that discourses position historical subjects, who in turn mediate, challenge, accept, and transform discourses as they strive to make sense of their experiences and define their own identities. Methodologically, this means situating discourse in its context by attempting to link propaganda with women's (and often men's) experience—after all, material relations do exist and set limits on the range of meanings historical subjects can assign to their world. In the case of Weimar, the discourses produced by women's rising visibility and enfranchisement were not simply an imaginary product in the minds of writers or politicians. As Canning argues, the meanings men and women assigned to prevailing discourses shaped the political order, producing moralizing and regulative effects with tangible impacts on women's bodies, economic and educational options, family relations, ability to act collectively, and access to political life.[38] That fact makes studying gender discourses in the formal political realm a project worth undertaking.

Agency is easier to locate for those historical actors who participated directly in the process of mobilizing women through propaganda. Reading appeals devised by female activists can illuminate how those actors constructed their own political identities. It is more difficult to pinpoint agency for the mass of female voters or to link what we know about how women voted with theories about what motivated their choices. Even if an exhaustive poll on female political opinion were to surface in some forgotten archive, it could never tell us exactly why so many women preferred the Center or pinpoint which of their constantly shifting identities compelled them to check one box over another. But we do know that propaganda only resonated with audiences when it corresponded on some level to their needs and desires. The ways women responded with their votes can allow us to speculate about how their lived experience of modernity shaped their readings of the everyday language of politics, which of their identities drove their political choices, and the centrality of gender to the formation of political and social consciousness. This study cannot definitively state why women preferred certain parties, nor is this its aim. Rather it seeks to uncover which "women" could be represented in Weimar political discourse, moving beyond the question of whether suffrage emancipated women to the question of what impact female suffrage had on Weimar political culture.[39] Knowing which models of femininity could attain political expression—and which were knowingly or unwittingly suppressed—can also reveal something about which models of femininity could be publicly lived or at least desired by masses of women.

The discourses on women were not static, especially in a context in which the terms could shift dramatically from one year to the next. To provide a sense of this change, this study charts chronologically how political constructions of "woman" evolved across the key elections of the Weimar period. Chapters cover 1918–20 and women's first mass electoral participation; 1924, when two national elections followed on the heels of several coup attempts and devastating inflation; 1925–28, Weimar's relatively stable "golden" period; 1930, which saw the advent of both the depression and the Nazis' national rise; and 1932, when soaring unemployment fueled polarization and an all-out war of political symbols over five major elections. Among other things, this study asks how elections altered propaganda aimed at or invoking women; what issues dominated in election as opposed to nonelection years; how specific economic and political crises affected gender discourse; and whether events of direct import to women, such as the 1931 abortion rallies, emerged as themes in campaign propaganda.

Berlin forms the implicit geographic focus for this study because, as Germany's center of mass media, it was central to the process of image creation for the entire nation. In addition to a burgeoning advertising industry, the city housed Germany's major publishing concerns and supported over 800 daily, weekly, and monthly newspapers. As the capital, it was the center from which parties disseminated campaign material and operated wire services, providing information to local groups and the press nationwide. Finally, Berlin set the tone for Weimar culture and the modernity it embodied, including the New Woman. While this study focuses on Berlin, where sources permit, it also discusses variations in local appeals.

This work will show that despite their well-documented ideological differences in other areas, the Weimar parties shared many basic assumptions about women's political role. All discouraged a female solidarity that could transcend class or religious lines. The liberal parties in particular vehemently denounced the idea of a women's party, not so much as a tactical threat but as an "abomination" that violated the unwritten rules that allowed women to participate in politics. At the same time as the parties sought to undermine gender as a rallying point for political action, they all characterized women first and foremost by gender. Party propaganda portrayed women as ultimately capable only of political action consistent with "female nature" (a "politics of the heart"), while simultaneously discouraging them from deploying that femininity in ways that could seriously challenge the status quo.

This work also charts the ways propaganda refashioned existing discourses to construct the female citizen. In Weimar's first elections all parties raced to claim that they had always supported women's right to a public role. The parties that most openly embraced the republic, the DDP and SPD, were also most prone to address women as equal citizens whose new rights gave them both the opportunity and the duty to help shore up the foundations of democracy. The USPD and later the KPD preached female equality as integral to a just society, but because of their conviction that democracy was a sham, they constructed an image of the political woman who was less a citizen of the nation than a loyal fighter in the proletarian front. While every major party rhetorically embraced women's rights, all exhorted women to act politically on behalf of others—their children, the *Volk*, the working class—and only rarely for themselves. The most socially conservative parties, the DNVP and Catholic Center, in fact spoke to women exclusively in the language of "separate spheres," assigning them to neatly defined, gender-based forms of activity and representation. But they were not alone in ascribing to women a "natural" propensity to act along maternal lines—all parties from left to right invoked at one time or another certain "unique feminine traits" that women brought to the greater community. Female activists themselves routinely invoked difference to justify women's right to a political role, something they inherited from the German women's movement.

As stated above, the parties based their general appeals on occupation, an implicitly masculine category. Women, in contrast, were addressed first and foremost on the basis of their gender, which trumped occupation or class. Instead of material concerns, all parties believed that women were more effectively mobilized by appeals to cultural or social issues—religion, children's education, welfare, and so on. The rare occupation-based appeal to women routinely couched issues of economic interest to female workers in cultural terms, devoting little attention to specific problems women workers faced on the job or at home. Women were considered to be above the dirty business of politics in light of their "essence" and special role as mothers. The parties assumed that women acted politically on the basis of their domestic roles as nurturers and "culture bearers," unlike men, who acted primarily out of economic interest. Consequently, parties routinely used appeals to women to discuss their own "cultural mission," which both gave women an expanded public role and circumscribed that role within limits dictated by female nature.

The intensity of debate over women's public and private roles corresponded to general levels of anxiety about the nation's future. As subordinate members of society, women had for centuries been a convenient screen onto which national fears and aspirations could be projected. But their political enfranchisement combined with long-term changes in their economic, sexual, and social status and the upheavals caused by the war to construct femininity as a "problem" eternally in search of a solution. During the republic's most crisis-ridden years (1918–23 and 1930–33), the political debate over women took on the greatest urgency and shrillest tones as women were portrayed both as Germany's last salvation and as potential traitors. Whether or not they favored equal rights for women, all parties believed that women's highest goal was motherhood; maternal, not sexual, desire functioned as their main political motivator. Recurring images of motherhood were intended to create some sense of stability in a republic marked by acrimonious politics, dizzying social change, and economic trauma. Propaganda also addressed male fears of instability and worries about Germany's future. Poster imagery in particular attempted to create new men who were strong in the face of a republic that its enemies on both left and right portrayed as an emasculating force. Indeed, desire for clear gender boundaries emerged among both sexes, particularly during Weimar's last years, when the parties and political figures most prone to produce nuanced images of women had been severely weakened.

The results of this research constitute an analysis of the intersection of the political, social, and economic concerns of the major parties and ideas concerning the proper roles of women as expressed through propaganda. These issues are of vital concern to historians studying any period of history but are particularly salient in an era when changing gender roles were the subject of such intense, sustained debate. While we can never know precisely how women and men interpreted the symbols conveyed in competing political languages, such symbols sought to establish norms of behavior by dramatizing ideals with tremendous emotional impact. By examining the language of propaganda, this work aims to integrate this aspect of the history of women and gender into the story of Weimar Germany and its political dynamics. Political culture cannot be fully understood without attention to the system of signs and symbols that delineated what could be said and accepted in the public sphere. Our analysis of political culture must account for the process through which historical actors constructed women's place in the public sphere as it expanded to include women.

I

Onward, My Sisters!
:

Winning Women for Politics,
1918–1920

Amid the tumult of the November Revolution, the Council of Peoples' Deputies passed a law that allowed all women over the age of twenty to vote, starting with the January 1919 National Assembly election. Henceforth, German political culture was forever changed, as women became the majority of eligible voters. All political parties—including those that had opposed female suffrage—had to confront women as political actors for the first time. Recognizing women's numerical power, they vigorously set out to win their vote. But uncertainty over how women would behave politically led parties in the immediate postwar years to bombard women with often contradictory messages as they searched for the key to unlock this new constituency.

Bombardment is an apt metaphor here, as political campaigns had been likened to battles since the 1870s. This was even more the case after the revolution, which utilized the streets as a public forum like never before in Germany. Public space became the staging ground for the "propaganda wars" that became the *Alltag*, or everyday life, of Weimar politics.[1] Between November 1918 and late 1920, the parties faced off in three major campaigns: the National Assembly contest of 19 January 1919, state elections in Prussia (which comprised three-fifths of the Reich) on 26 January 1919, and the Reichstag election of 6 June 1920. In this period, Germany was reeling from a military defeat for which the public had been wholly unprepared. The cease-fire terms kept a blockade in place until July 1919, stoking a black market and inflation that would burst into hyperinflation by 1923. These conditions bequeathed a crisis of legitimacy to the republic, and eventually, the parties identified with the new form of state. Despite some initial enthusiasm, such as that conveyed in the remarks of eighty-five-year-old feminist Hedwig Dohm, this republic would find few friends, coming under attack from both the Right and the radical Left, who treated it like an unwanted stepchild.

In these early years, broad national issues such as the peace settlement and continuing revolutionary unrest weighed heavily on the minds of all voters. Women, for their part, faced the particular problems of climbing consumer prices, the loss of their men in the war, and the uneasy reintegration of those who did return from the front. Women, whose waged work in "male" sectors such as transport and heavy industry had mushroomed during the war, found themselves unwanted competitors as the men came home. This resentment was codified in the March 1919 demobilization decree, which demanded working women's dismissal in favor of returning veterans, starting with married women and eventually including all female workers (though the industrial resurgence of the early 1920s would prevent the order being carried this far). Thousands lost their jobs in transportation, civil service, the metal and chemical industries, and even the restaurant business. These firings were already envisioned in the November 1918 Stinnes-Legien accord between labor and management and had broad support, not least among the working class. Few women openly protested the measure, and many in fact joined the postwar marriage boomlet, voluntarily leaving jobs many had seen as only temporary. But the issue of gender competition for jobs—one of "the wars after the war"—would continue to smolder, reigniting in times of economic crisis throughout the Weimar period.[2]

In 1918–20 women faced new political rights, shifting economic roles, and social dislocation. The promise and the shock of the new sparked an unprecedented flurry of political activity nationwide; women too set out to find their place in this new Germany. The parties for their part had to reorient themselves to a new regime in which women's interests would be impossible to ignore. How would parties process these considerations into propaganda that could resonate with the masses? Would the brave new postrevolutionary world dissolve inherited gender assumptions, or would fears of chaos promote the invocation of seemingly eternal notions of female nature? As the parties reached out to women by addressing issues such as their legal and economic rights, motherhood, religion, and culture, they worked to construct the woman voter herself. Through this process they also articulated their visions of the greater political and social order. During 1918–20 this meant giving meaning to democracy, the revolution, the welfare state, and women's place in all of them.

To reach the masses of new female voters, parties had to build mobilizing organizations. The socialist movement already had decades of experience including women in the business of mass politics; other parties had to catch up quickly. During the republic's first days, these other parties often relied on existing women's groups while their own women's committees (*Frauenausschusse*) were being set up.[3] By 1919 all major parties but the Catholic Center had founded *Frauenausschusse* headed by female notables and usually installed as a branch of the party executive (*Vorstand*) alongside committees for civil servants, employees, the *Mittelstand*, farmers, industry, white-collar workers, small business, and youth. Parties quickly added women to their larger national committees (*Reichsausschusse*), of which they tended to comprise roughly 10 percent of members. To varying degrees, members of the executive and the heads of interest group committees comprised a party's nominal leadership, but a party's most powerful body tended to be its executive board (*Geschäftsführende Ausschuss*). Women were infrequently represented on this or other committees not seen as directly related to "women's issues." The process of naming women to the executive was the one (and sometimes only) occasion during Weimar where party organizations showcased women and touted their political importance. As one DVP man put it, to have no woman on the executive would not be a crime, but it would be a blunder.[4] It would subsequently be incumbent upon female activists to remind their parties of commitments made on those occasions to political work among women.

What were the women's committees' responsibilities?[5] Largely run by women for women but financed by the *Vorstand*, their task was to win female voters and enroll new members. They were to educate and recruit through personal contact and mass propaganda. The bourgeois parties in particular saw social gatherings such as teas and family evenings as more likely to attract women than "strictly political" meetings; this view also penetrated SPD thinking in the 1920s. The committees also reported to the party on the morale of female voters and on "women's issues." They were largely responsible for writing propaganda for women,[6] as well as newsletters or "women's pages" in party journals. Naturally, the content of these had to dovetail with the general party line—no party wanted to win female votes at the expense of men's. This literature was offered to regional branches to distribute or tailor to local conditions. Circulation of major campaign flyers regularly reached 100,000 or more. The production of propaganda for women was most intensive in Weimar's first major campaigns: the DNVP produced at least forty-four flyers and posters for women between late 1918 and 1920, the DDP fifty-three, the DVP twenty-seven, and the Center twenty.[7]

Socialist organizations differed slightly in form. While there were variations between the SPD, USPD, and Communist Party (the latter will be examined more closely in chapter 2), each established a women's bureau charged with recruitment, agitation, coordination of local women's groups, and education in theory and praxis. In addition to propaganda through rallies, courses, house visits, and film or slide shows, a steady stream of pamphlets, flyers, posters, and publications for women appeared. More than the bourgeois parties, socialists presented women's mobilization as a concern of the party at large, in accord with the Marxist dictum that women's emancipation was integral to that of the entire proletariat. Organizational statutes ordered women's inclusion in leadership at all levels, from national executive to district cell. However, the Marxist parties also believed that centuries of women's exclusion from politics necessitated unique tactics as well. Party dues, which were pegged to a worker's hourly wage, were reduced for female members. Different forms and content for their political schooling were also mandated. For example, in addition to factory agitation, housewives were to be reached

with events on consumer issues, housing, and welfare, the last seen particularly by the SPD as a "natural" area for female activism and recruiting.[8]

Another key function of all parties' women's bureaus was nominating
female candidates, as the same law that granted women suffrage also allowed them to seek office. Largely ignorant of the world of female activism, parties relied on their women's committees to supply women fit to
tackle political office, especially in 1919 and 1920, when they hoped to lure
women voters by putting female candidates high on the party slate. This
coincided with the bourgeois parties' postrevolution forays into populism, in which they put forth candidates from a wide variety of occupations, establishing a trend that would force women to jockey with these
groups for favorable list spots. A party's stance on whether women should
be treated like occupational or other groups informed the ways they appealed to female voters, as did the debate over whether parties could
most effectively appeal to women through their material and personal interests—jobs, reproduction, legal status—or through invocation of their
female essence.

The issues parties invoked in their first propaganda blitzes to female
voters would remain staples of Weimar political discourse. But the tenor
of the republic's first campaign, the election of delegates to the constitutional National Assembly, would never be matched for its sense of possibility and the optimism promoted, especially by the parties allied with
the new democracy. That hopefulness had everything to do with the ex-
citement—and anxiety—caused by women's debut as full-fledged participants on the political stage.

The German Democratic Party (DDP) was formed in late 1918 as the successor to the left liberal Progressives. In 1919 the financially strong party
distributed 15.5 million flyers to a broad range of groups, promoting free
democracy and republicanism.[9] More than any other non-Marxist party
in 1918–20, the DDP made support for women's new constitutional rights
the focus of its appeals to them. It addressed them as "equal citizens"
and scorned parties that had previously blocked female suffrage (omitting
the Progressives' own opposition as late as October 1918). DDP appeals assumed that women greeted the republic for the "gifts" it brought them
and strove to reach progressive-minded women whose bourgeois identity alienated them from socialism. They sought to educate women in
the exercise of their rights and pledged to defend the economic, political,

and cultural demands of all women.[10] This stress on equal rights (*Gleich-berechtigung*), however, was shot through with talk of women's "special duties and nature," reflecting bourgeois feminist notions of citizenship rooted in the idea of "social motherhood."[11] The women who wrote these appeals did not limit their vision to a female citizenship rooted solely in maternal values but tried to reconcile the implications of women's new power in the "masculine" world of politics with prevailing notions of the feminine.

Perhaps the most striking demonstration of the DDP's campaign commitment to civil emancipation was its adoption of the "party of women" (*die Partei der Frauen*) slogan in its 1919 women's propaganda.[12] The DDP hoped to capitalize on the fact that it had attracted nearly all the leaders of the bourgeois feminist movement, among them Dr. Marie-Elisabeth Lüders and Agnes von Zahn-Harnack, who coordinated female labor during the war; social work pioneer Alice Salomon; education reformer Helene Lange; and her companion Gertrud Bäumer, disciple of DDP founder Friedrich Naumann.[13] These women figured prominently as both authors and subjects of women's flyers, indicating that the party expected female voters to follow their "leaders" into the DDP. Clearly, the DDP assumed that enough women identified their own goals with those of the women's movement to make this a profitable campaign motif.

Another source of the DDP's belief that it could win female votes with a stress on equal rights lies in what Thomas Childers has called its bid to create a language of democracy for the young republic.[14] Pamphlets aimed at both sexes in 1919 consistently linked democracy with social reconstruction, freedom for all citizens, the right to work, a community of nations, and the civil equality of women.[15] Women were urged to support the DDP because its democratic agenda encompassed protection of the individual, career advancement based on merit, freedom of religion, and equality of all people's comrades (*Volksgenossen*). Women's new rights gave them not only the opportunity but also the duty to help build a "people's state" and end the conflict perpetuated by men (*Männergezank*).[16] "Women's rights are human rights. We women now embrace the great responsibility of citizenship—but our rights carry duties. Therefore, we choose the party that strives to build spiritually [*im Innern*], the DDP. This party calls us not merely to use our votes to boost their numbers—it truly recognizes that female cooperation is crucial at all times. *We women feel it, despite all the privations and chaos of our times: the epoch of humanity has dawned. Democracy is humanity!* Therefore give your vote to the DDP, the party of women!"[17] By equating women's rights with human rights, the DDP wished to convince women that the fortunes of their civil liberties rose and fell with those of the republic and its advocates. This linkage of gender and human rights, penned by a woman, also constitutes a response to critics who saw advocacy of women's rights as mere special-interest politics. Drawing on arguments advanced by the women's movement since the nineteenth century, DDP women presented civil rights not as mere tools for individual advancement but as the means to a greater female role in reforming the nation.[18]

To best serve the common good, women needed instruction in the use of their political rights. Like all major parties, the DDP produced special flyers (fourteen in all) outlining the new system and encouraging female activism. For example, a flyer signed "the women of the DDP" listed their Berlin office address and visiting hours, inviting women to drop by. Another women's committee pamphlet explained state functions and the implications of revolutionary changes for women. It instructed them to elect persons who would uphold democracy and portrayed the ballot as the building block of the future. Yet another committee flyer described women's right to run for office and the process of voting: "Your vote is completely autonomous, and no one, either in your family or workplace, may stop you from voting or order you to vote a certain way. . . . The campaign needs female *assistants, organizers, and speakers*—housewives and daughters as much as working women."[19] Such instructions were designed to instill a sense that women had a place in politics as well as to assuage fears about the secrecy of the ballot.[20] The marked degree to which women voted differently from men implies that this message was well taken.[21]

The DDP's message of gender equality extended to the economic sphere as well. Most impressively, this was not relegated just to propaganda for female voters. A Stuttgart poster for a mixed-sex audience included demands for legal reform to ensure women's claim to half the property acquired during marriage, while pieces for civil servants or workers called for equal gender representation on labor boards.[22] When speaking specifically to women, the DDP, more than any other bourgeois party in 1918–20, addressed many appeals to working women, even once calling itself the "party of working women."[23] While occupational appeals usually assumed a male audience, the DDP was unique in issuing a series of flyers to female white-collar employees, civil servants, and teachers. Usually produced by the women's committee, these raised concrete material issues such as equal pay, promotions, representation in professional organizations, and training.

The DDP's focus on equal rights reflected the strong presence of personalities and ideas from the women's movement as well as the party's acceptance of the realities of the revolution. Its open support for the new republic led it to cooperate with the SPD and to preach class reconciliation. But it was also at pains to assure the shaken middle classes that working with the SPD in no way signaled an endorsement of socialism. Indeed, rhetoric to all groups condemned the SPD as seeking a "one-sided dictatorship of the proletariat."[24] Anti-Socialist rhetoric was particularly pointed in materials for women because the DDP (like all parties) was deeply worried, especially in 1919, that women would reward the SPD for its role in delivering female suffrage. To ward off this threat, materials painted the SPD as the incompetent architect of inflationary policies that hurt working women and housewives. One even cast the SPD as part of a radical cabal aiming to nationalize industry and institute political litmus tests for civil servants, an issue of concern to the thousands of women seeking jobs in government and the burgeoning welfare sector.[25]

The most outrageous anti-Socialist attack appeared in the *Berliner Tageblatt*, one of the press organs on which the DDP heavily relied for publicity. A report, taken from the *London Times*, claimed that the Russian city of Saratov had "nationalized" women: all marriages were dissolved and women made the "communal property of the proletariat," reduced, in the article's words, to "breeding machines." This last phrase indignantly cast the Soviet system as degrading to women and aimed to deflate socialism's claim to be the only system that would liberate them. This fake story, which entered Weimar's anti-Socialist folklore, reveals the link made in bourgeois circles between revolution, socialism, and loose morals (*Verwilderung*). Even those who saw the Revolution as a source of some good were prone to fears that radical change in the social and political order would upend the sexual order.[26]

Resisting the SPD was made a test of women's political maturity, the message being that they should not elect a party solely for its stance on women's issues. For example, a flyer for female white-collar workers instructed them to "show that the Social Democrats' calculations are wrong, that your ranks are unified and you clearly see where fulfillment of your demands lies." The ranks the DDP had in mind were those of class, not gender, for, as the appeal continued, the new people's state could not be constructed only from the masses of manual laborers and women workers (*Handarbeiter und Arbeiterinnen*).[27]

A linkage of bourgeois solidarity with women's political maturity also marked the DDP position on *Frauenliste*, cross-party lists of female candidates designed to help more women get elected. In June 1920, the *Berliner Tageblatt* blasted Anna von Gierke's *Frauenliste* as the worst enemy of woman suffrage: "a representation of the female sex as such in political bodies is an absurdity [*Unding*]." Democratic women were expected to show "responsibility" and "discipline"; any woman who appeared on Gierke's list revealed herself as too immature for the right to vote. The newness of suffrage inflated the threat of women's lists—in reality, few ever got off the ground.[28] But men and women in the DDP were leaving nothing to chance. They told women in no uncertain terms that their interests were best represented by the established parties and, despite their own special appeals and organizations for women, stated that there were no differences between the interests of the sexes in the political arena. This message subtly threatened that the vote was a gift, not a right, that could be revoked if used "incorrectly."[29]

Strong antisocialism also marked DDP discussion of religion. Like the Left, the DDP favored separation of church and state but quickly distanced itself from politicians such as Adolf Hoffmann (USPD), who sought to ban religion in Prussian schools. The DDP portrayed itself as a bulwark against the *Religionsfeindlichkeit* of the Left—significantly, this angle appeared mainly in flyers for women, while those for other groups stressed religious tolerance.[30] At the same time, the DDP warned women that the proreligious parties (the Center and DNVP) violated the spirit of love by sowing hatred of *Volksgenossen* not of the Christian faith—a jab at DNVP anti-Semitism. It emphasized this intolerance to tar these parties with the brush of misogyny: "German women, don't forget that they greeted every attempt to pass female suffrage with derisive laughter! If they come to the helm, you have voted once and never again."[31] Yet the DDP had to be careful not to appear antireligion as it emerged that women strongly supported parties with a religious basis.[32] It argued that it objected not to religious instruction in schools per se but to religious coercion. The party also stressed its dedication to preserve Germany's cultural heritage and to recivilize the nation after the war and revolution, realms in which German women had "special tasks."

Here is where the DDP's professed commitment to female equality merged with an identification of women with the social and cultural arenas. The translation of this identification into political appeals came swiftly and was driven not least by bourgeois feminists, who in the DDP's case aspired both to equality as a democratic principle and to the deployment of "female traits" in areas that could benefit mothers and children. This can be seen in the way literature delineated female spheres of political activity. Women in government were there to represent not universal or occupational interests but the interests of women, as a flyer profiling Lüders declared. Another praised Agnes von Harnack as a defender of family life, religion in schools, working women, and youth and child welfare—all "women's issues" because they were extensions of the domestic domain. Although these were indeed areas where female politicians concentrated their efforts, their other activities, such as Bäumer's involvement in foreign policy, rarely surfaced in campaign literature from the DDP or other parties. DDP women's propaganda bore the distinct pedigree of bourgeois feminism, especially its moderate strain, which sought to instrumentalize spiritual motherhood as the basis of women's contribution to the greater good and the justification for their equal access to public life. It is evidence of how pervasive this view had become that both women and men in the DDP agreed that women, as "born representatives of the social conscience," were best suited to social and cultural policy and that invoking this would win female votes.[33]

This message of equal but different also emerged when flyers discussed "appropriate" spheres of female employment. DDP appeals invoked women's right of access to all careers and sought to represent the growing diversity of their occupations. Yet in the same breath came the assumption that women's work belonged in certain areas. A general audience flyer stated that the right to vote called women to work in public affairs, specifically poor relief and school administration.[34] A flyer by the women's committee similarly demanded "the distribution of work between the sexes according to strength and suitability."[35] Women's work outside the home was conceived as secondary to men's, as the National Assembly debate on demobilization illustrates. A brief submitted by six women from the Center, DDP, SPD, and DNVP protested the treatment of women workers after the war. They agreed that returning veterans had priority in the job market but felt that women's work also needed protection. Marie Baum (DDP) urged a restructuring of women's work that would not force those under economic pressure to work outside the home but also would not reinforce the cliché that "women belong in the home" because nothing should hinder "women's striving forward."[36] These women were outraged that women's economic needs had no bearing on whether they were allowed to keep their jobs, yet by agreeing that their right to work should be evaluated on a basis of need, they accepted the basic premise of demobilization—women's work outside the home had to be justified by some higher social function while men's did not.[37] Helene Lange's flyer put it most clearly: "Man represents primarily career interests; woman can and should, in contrast, guarantee stronger consideration of cultural and human interests."[38]

Lange, who had promoted moderate feminist positions since the early 1900s, became very influential within the DDP (she would in fact be named its only female honorary chair). Her call for women's public activity to become a "politics of the home, of mothers" was reflected in DDP materials to women in 1918–20, the majority of which addressed them as mothers. Reluctant to assign to women the kind of material motivations that were assumed to drive men's political choices, the party even appealed to working women on the assumption that they voted less to protect their own interests than their children's. As a Berlin women's committee flyer put it, "You vote not for yourselves, but . . . your family, for the *Volk*."[39] This suppression of interests particular to women constitutes an attempt to make them appear worthy of citizenship, which stands in opposition to particularistic forms of social commitment.[40] By identifying women's interests with those of family and then redefining the family as the national family—the *Volk* itself—female citizenship could be defended even against its most reactionary critics.

Regardless of their new rights, women were still assumed to be responsible for maintaining the household. A women's committee flyer instructed them on how to square the two by advising them to vote early or finish chores the day before the election—cooking Sunday dinner on Saturday, for example, would free up plenty of time to vote.[41] A flyer by Alice Salomon to "German family fathers" stated that women's new rights need not change relations in the home. Aimed at men hostile to female suffrage, it asked them not to shut their wives and daughters out of politics but to bring them in to boost the power of the bourgeoisie: "German father! You don't need to change your position in the domestic circle. Just remain who you were and who you are, but include your wife and daughters, strange as it may seem to you to speak politics with them. . . . Become their political teacher and leader."[42] Salomon, who wrote in 1908 that the woman question was at root a question of women's position within the family, had long fought to improve their domestic rights. But in trying to overturn the notion that female suffrage was unneeded because women were already represented by their husbands, her flyer unwittingly issues a reassurance that patriarchy in the private sphere—depicted here as benevolent—could remain intact. This was a message the party could live with, as it clearly wanted women's votes, but not at the cost of men's. The piece also illustrates how the changed context of women's enfranchisement promoted a reconstitution of the male voter through differentiating him from the female. Constructing the male voter as wise and seasoned threw into relief women's inexperience and the need for monitoring to ensure they voted "correctly."[43]

Ultimately, the DDP in this period tried to cover as many bases as possible in its message to women. Appeals did not simply defend female equality as a basic human right but invoked a citizenship consistent with "female nature" deployed in the service of the *Volk*. The DDP wanted to reach all women and worked harder than any other party to address the diverse conditions of their lives. In 1918–20 the "party of women," riding Germany's leftward drift immediately after the revolution, stressed a progressive agenda of equal rights, and in the 1919 National Assembly election, women voters, riding that same current, helped make the DDP the second strongest party, their share of its vote lagging only slightly behind men's. This soon changed, however, as the DDP's identification with the recent Versailles treaty and rising inflation more than halved its vote in 1920. Significantly, statistics show that women's vote for the party was falling faster than men's. This would impact future strategy and weaken the pronounced stamp that feminists could put on the DDP's message to both women and general audiences. Financial woes would mean fewer appeals with a less nuanced message to women than in Weimar's first heady campaigns. As we shall see, the strong equal rights message that set the DDP apart in 1918–20 would become all but buried under a more conservative rhetoric that made its women's appeals increasingly indistinguishable from its rivals'.

The German People's Party (DVP) in 1918–20 was openly ambivalent toward the republic. While this ambivalence would remain central to its self-presentation, the DVP gradually accepted that the empire was gone and Germany's present situation had to be managed until something better could replace it. This realpolitik was mirrored in the DVP's attitude toward female rights and suffrage. Both DVP men and women saw the vote as a "gift of the Revolution"—even though it had not come about the way they would have liked, it should be accepted and used to benefit both party and nation.[44] As liberals, the DVP claimed to accept and even embrace women's equality and right to free development but coupled this with a strong nationalism, which dictated that personal freedom remain within boundaries dictated by the greater needs of the *Volk*. These two strands of thought ran throughout the DVP's message to women in 1918–20, with the national thrust edging out the liberal.

The DVP presented itself in this period as an advocate of women's rights. During the National Assembly campaign, this claim appeared in materials aimed at both sexes. For example, number eight of the party's fourteen points read, "Equal rights for women in public and political life. Protection for new mothers and children." The "Ten Commandments of the DVP" declared, "Thou shalt have equal rights as a citizen, whether worker or civil servant, teacher or officer, man or woman."[45] As in DDP flyers, equality was linked to liberal individualism, but this was swiftly channeled into the notion that women's rights, while basic human rights, should be seen primarily as a tool to help fix Germany. More so than the DDP, DVP materials were drenched with images of a nation mired in defeat and chaos. Law and order had been strangled by black marketeers and strikers, while immorality spread like cancer.[46] All had a patriotic duty to repair this *Trümmerfeld Deutschland*, however distasteful its current government.[47] While all groups were exhorted to sacrifice for the nation, this was particularly central to DVP definitions of the role of women because it provided justification for their newly won—and often grudgingly accepted—political rights.

The DVP blamed the national catastrophe on the Socialists as well as on its liberal rivals, the DDP. A pointed language of class antagonism marked all DVP propaganda, including women's flyers, in 1918–20. It argued to female voters that SPD incompetence would reduce Germany to "Russian" economic conditions, endangering the jobs of working women. Morally, the SPD was not the great defender of women but the party of August Bebel, who wrote that marriage should be strictly a private contract and sex the fulfillment of a physical urge. SPD plans for women signified the greatest unhappiness, the deepest humiliation, the darkest stain on female honor. Furthermore, social democracy was the "enemy of our spiritual treasures" and the agent of irreligion, according to a flyer for "German women and girls." Like the Center and DNVP, the DVP explicitly made religion a central pillar of its women's program for the National Assembly election.[48] Unlike the DDP, which limited religion mainly to women's materials, the DVP made it a standard theme in flyers for both sexes, as part of a broader discourse linking the revolution to national and moral decline. Merging languages of class and sexuality with race, the DVP urged all voters to protect German culture and religion from foreign influence, a strategy that culminated in the 1920 Reichstag campaign, when the DVP styled itself as the leader of a bourgeois front to defend Europe from Asiatic Bolshevism.[49] Attacks on the DDP aimed to convince middle-class voters that the Democrats had abandoned this crusade for their new friends on the left, portraying them as effete cosmopolitans unrepresentative of the *Volk*.[50] A flyer to "all men and women of the bourgeoisie" listed what separated the DVP from the DDP: a refusal to work with the SPD and a commitment to *Kultur*, which it defined as preserving the church's state role.[51] This use of religion as a wedge issue, plus its hostility to the revolution, helped the DVP in this period win some support from rural pastors and Protestant women's groups.[52]

Another key facet of the DVP's attack on its rivals to the left was the need to discredit their image as champions of female emancipation. In this period, the DVP assumed and feared that women would rally to the SPD and DDP because of their early and vocal support for equal rights. To tarnish the SPD, the DVP claimed its opponent supported suffrage only to win female votes and urged bourgeois women to turn out en masse on election day to foil this scheme. The SPD "offered nothing" to middle-class women, materials claimed, and the DVP predicted a flight from the party once women got to know it.[53]

The DVP had fewer grounds on which to criticize the DDP women's program, whose mix of equal rights and social motherhood was similar to its own, so it deflected attention from the DDP's strong feminist message back to what the DVP portrayed as its insufficient national zeal. Clara Mende's 1919 pamphlet for women admitted that the DDP had attracted prominent feminist leaders but, swallowing her own BDF affiliation, said that women who supported the DDP for that reason alone were acting like sheep. Unlike the so-called party of women, the DVP did not need glib slogans to prove its commitment to women—it knew that their interests were best served by strengthening the fatherland.[54]

But the DVP did agree with its rivals that women should support a party not just for its message to women. It categorically rejected women's lists and a women's party as *Frauenrechtlerei*—the assertion of particular interests to the detriment of the whole, in this case the nation. Writings from both DVP women and men recognized that women as a group had certain unique and "justifiable" demands (these were not explicitly spelled out), but they argued that these would best be addressed by a larger body, not a fringe *Frauenpartei*. To prove that women and their concerns had real clout within the party, a 1920 flyer showcased the fact that a woman headed one DVP ballot in the Berlin communal races.[55] With friends like the DVP, women did not need their own party.

Such claims emanated from widespread anxiety over tense postwar gender relations. Women activists in particular stressed the theme of reconciliation between the sexes in DVP women's literature, analogous to larger party claims that it welcomed all faiths, estates (the term "class" was studiously avoided), and occupations. The most interesting formulation of this theme was Mende's call to revive the spirit of cooperation that allegedly had existed during the war, a sort of sexual *Burgfriede*: "Fear of annihilation and ruin of the fatherland . . . brought man and woman closer; shared views bound people together, and the difference between the sexes finally fell away."[56] Mende's attempt to rewrite the gender history of the war glossed over the stark tensions between men at the front and women at home, such as hostility toward women's waged work outside the existing gender division of labor or the "unpatriotic" sexual behavior of "war wives."[57] But her account is even more notable for once again invoking the themes of cooperation and sacrifice of individual desires to those of the community at a time when gender conflict raged across Germany's factory floors and bedrooms. At a time when the DVP claimed the fate of bourgeois culture was hanging in the balance, women's political cooperation with men in the fight to rescue the fatherland became a way to prove their political maturity.

Women could also prove their maturity in the economic realm. To ensure maximum utility in the project of national and moral reconstruction, each sex had to work in its proper sphere. The "equal but different" theme surfaced repeatedly in this period's DVP materials for women as well as for mixed-sex audiences: "What does the DVP want? . . . 6. Respect and care of German female nature [*Frauenart*] with equality of the sexes." Party writers seemed compelled to delineate job categories by gender, with women going into considerable detail on women's "natural" affinity for the socially and culturally oriented vocations. Translating moderate feminist principles into propaganda, they treated separate spheres not as a limitation but as a way to protect women's right to employment by making it indispensable. Clara Mende, the party's highest-ranking female, wrote that the center of a "true" woman's life was ideally not work but family; no woman whose husband could support her should work "for sport." But until economic realities changed, the state must protect women's right to work.[58]

Marie Bernays's speech at the October 1919 party conference, published as a pamphlet, neatly sums up this particular feminist agenda at the heart of the DVP's message to women. The family, she said, was the core of cultural life; all socially aware women must fight forms of work detrimental to the female organism and motherhood. But she recognized that a "man shortage" was depriving many women of the "highest goals" of marriage and motherhood. Thus, rights to equality and individual development must be extended to women—something the DVP supported, unlike the retrograde Conservatives. But democracy had its shortcomings, such as unfettered gender competition. A "reasonable" division of labor was needed to channel women into areas dealing with human life, such as nursing, education, and social welfare—occupations they could fill with the spirit of love. Men were the architects of culture, women the no less important nurturers of that culture.[59] Women could act as a bridge between family and state, between the sexes, just as the DVP saw itself as a bridge between the Left and Right. Like women in the DDP, those in the DVP sought to justify female citizenship by placing it in service of the greater good, albeit with a much more pronounced denial of women's personal or material interests.

Another difference between the two liberal parties, this one tactical, is that while DDP materials carried a strong voice from its women's committee, no group identity emerged from DVP women, who wrote instead as individuals. Without the stamp of the *Frauenausschuss*, authorship is difficult to determine for most DVP women's flyers. Furthermore, a significant part of the DVP's message to women appeared in flyers aimed at both sexes, likely authored by men.[60] Also, unlike the DDP, which used a host of pithy one-page flyers to reach women, the DVP relied on lengthy pamphlets whose readership was likely more limited.

When searching for reasons why one party produced fewer materials for women than another, one must consider female activists' status within the party. The DVP's early years were marked by members' unswerving loyalty to leader Gustav Stresemann and disdain for open conflict in the ranks; party and parliamentary records reveal that women shared these sentiments. When Clara Mende was nominated in April 1919 to the party executive's number two post, rather than open up debate, she deferred to

Oberpräsident von Richter, stating, "We women will be perfectly happy with position three." Women activists, who had a much lower public profile than the female notables in the DDP, constantly assured the party of their loyalty by rejecting *Frauenliste* and a women's party. They echoed the party's realpolitik stance on women's rights and harped on the need for gender cooperation, not competition. In 1920 Emma Stropp favorably contrasted the DVP with the SPD and DDP, whose women, she claimed, were disenchanted with their "kind but inadequate role." Unlike them, the DVP did not treat women like "vote cattle" (*Stimmvieh*). DVP women even tried to put a feminist spin on party history, claiming that the National Liberals had supported female suffrage early in November 1918.[61]

But if DVP women were accommodating, they were not entirely uncritical. Mende, for example, said that while female activists understood that a "people's party" could not always conduct *Frauenpolitik*, they did not want antiwoman tendencies to surface either. At the first DVP conference in 1919, women agreed with their party that female workers had a duty to vacate wartime jobs for returning veterans. But they also signed the National Assembly protest against the demobilization decree, demanding that women legislators have a say in how the process was handled.[62] Mende's postmortem of the June 1920 campaign in the party journal women's section bore a cynical tone rarely seen in DVP women's writings. She criticized how women had been tacked on to the list of target groups as if they were just another *Beruf* (occupational) category. She asked with mock "female modesty" how this squared with "male logic," as occupations were narrow interest groups while women were half of the populace. A more logical classification, she wrote, would address individual male *and* female occupations. Furthermore, she argued, these groups' claim that only one of their own could represent them because "only he knows where the shoe pinches" also held for women, who needed their own representation. Mende's piece is one of the few produced by anyone in any party that noted the parties' inconsistency in appealing to men through *Beruf* while treating women as less interested in material issues. Her comments reveal an awareness that masculinity and femininity were constructs, albeit ones to which Mende herself adhered.[63]

Mende reserved deeper criticism for the parties' maltreatment of female candidates, something she had personally experienced. On 26 April 1920, the DVP gave her the second spot on both the Potsdam district II and Reich ballots. One week later, a narrow majority awarded her

Potsdam spot to Siegfried von Kardorff, whose recent defection from the DNVP became a publicity coup for the DVP; Mende had to settle for a position on the indirectly elected Reich list.[64] She subsequently wrote that it was essential for all parties to send women to the Reichstag. Even if a deserving man did not win a seat, Parliament could function without him, but electing a woman was a clear boon, for she brought fresh ideas. Men, she continued, had long been able to ignore the women's movements and ideas: "There is still a great deal to learn until men and women really stand side by side and truly work together—men and women!"[65] While she remained committed to cooperation for the good of the party, her tone, mild as it was, was rare in DVP publications for conveying female activists' nascent frustration at the lip service paid to women's rights.

Despite the argument that equal treatment for women was both consistent with liberal principles and beneficial to the party by maintaining unity and even attracting disgruntled women from other parties, as Emma Stropp wrote,[66] the fact remained that women did not have an equal position within the DVP. Mende's treatment in 1920 was no aberration—the DVP from the start was beholden to occupational groups, especially civil servants, and would routinely pass women over to award candidacies to *Beruf* representatives. Dr. Kahl's comments in the National Assembly reveal how lightly these men regarded gender inequalities: "Yesterday we heard talk of the 'liberated woman'—you could positively hear the chains falling off her (laughter)."[67] Yet DVP women's writings excused men's attitudes. Unenlightened male reactions were to be expected, like growing pains. Mende said it was women's task to dispel hostility to women's rights (begging the question of who was at fault if male attitudes did not change). These women were negotiating the treacherous waters of politics for the first time, unsure of how to promote their demands within the party and on the larger playing field of government. They debated how women should act politically—should they use "feminine" ways of arguing, or did they have to "masculinize" when battling with radicals "who'd stop at nothing"?[68] They tended toward the former, preferring to believe that men would treat them fairly because it was the liberal thing to do. When they did protest, they kept their comments to publications read by few but themselves.

Significantly, after 1920 the DVP did relatively well with bourgeois women, their share of the party vote slightly surpassing men's. The DVP preached a message to women of rights in service of the national idea, but citizenship did not equal sameness. Anne-Lise Schellwitz-Ultzen proclaimed the dawn of a new female generation, different from the idle daughters of the rich or the bluestockings of the past. The ideal she and her sisters promoted was a femininity capable of uniting a progressive, maternal sensibility oriented toward the social with a truly German essence focused on the national—strands propaganda claimed were united in the DVP. In the end, however, the national took precedence, as women were urged to set aside "particularist" concerns to save German culture. Ironically, the DVP itself would prove unable to do this, pandering to the particularist occupational lobbies that financed it, to the detriment of women's position within the party.

Emblazoned across every campaign pronouncement of the Catholic Center Party were the ideals of Christianity, family, and morality—themes that also came widely to be seen as women's issues. The Center quickly became home to a large and loyal bloc of female voters, most of them Catholic. Its appeals to women stressed the "fundamental difference" between the sexes, calling on them to apply maternal self-sacrifice to the wounds of war and arrest the moral decline stemming from the blockade and revolution. Unlike the dour DVP or the secular DDP, the Center touted a new national beginning based on moral renewal defined in religious terms, bringing into Weimar the language it had long spoken to its almost exclusively Catholic constituency. This cross-class party strove to unite its conservative and left wings around a cultural agenda deemed more important than the diverging material concerns of its supporters.[69] Ironically, this focus on cultural issues seems to have been most effective in attracting women, whose enfranchisement the party had stubbornly resisted until it was a fait accompli.

In 1918–20 the Center set out to explain this opposition and welcome women into the party, even taking credit for getting them the vote. *Germania*, the party's Berlin daily, and other publications argued that the Center had opposed suffrage not out of contempt for women but out of respect for their virtue and a desire to shield them from the rawness of politics. Unlike its "unenlightened" opponents (i.e., the Conservatives), it now realized that democratization meant including women and welcomed them as advocates for family and youth. Women's war service had proven their willingness to serve the fatherland. The party also saw that as workers, women deserved a say in how their taxes were spent. Finally, accepting an argument the Catholic women's movement had pressed since 1904, the party now agreed that women could act as a political counterweight to men, their "instinct" bringing new insight to issues ill served by cool rationality.[70]

These early testaments to the Center's conversion on female political participation were penned by women, as were practically all propaganda materials for female audiences. Men were either silent on the subject or unenthusiastic about the new political woman. A 1919 pamphlet by the Prussian Center Party, in fact, blasted the SPD for introducing female suffrage, arguing that it pushed women from the home into the maelstrom of public life.[71] Women, the author declared, could only participate in public life insofar as it did not detract from their duties to husband and children. A deep resistance to women's politicization would remain in place for years to come, despite numbers showing that 60 percent of the Center's vote throughout the Weimar era came from women.

While assuming that women's hearts dictated their politics, the Center hedged its bets by providing them with some basic civic education, something neglected among Catholic women since the war halted Catholic Women's League (KFD) efforts in this area. In November 1918 the party called on the KFD, which just weeks earlier it had considered disbanding, to revive its mobilization efforts.[72] Female activists realized that the kinds of women most likely to vote Center—housewives, mothers, older women—were also more likely to avoid the polls because of time constraints, apathy, or fear. Thus, campaign flyers and the Catholic press implored women to shed their resistance to politics. While the "whirlpool of party politics" could harm the female psyche, they said, the fresh impulses women brought were needed to correct male politicians' cynicism and alienation from daily life.[73] Their unique gifts were needed to mend the nation's torn moral fabric in a time of crisis: "When hasn't a true woman, a mother, learned anew when it was time to heal and save?" As two KFD flyers put it, politics could not damage a noble soul in a noble cause— the fate of Germany's next generations. Center and KFD appeals aimed to redefine politics as a sphere with room for women. But in stark contrast to the triumphant tone of propaganda from the "party of women," Center women's appeals made the vote seem like a bitter pill that must be swallowed in the interest of national recovery.[74]

Party women argued that the Center had a very pragmatic reason for securing women's support—their influence in the home. These activists assumed that Catholic women identified themselves primarily by their domestic roles and set out to mobilize them on that basis, not least out of concern that politics would become dominated by single working women.[75] As housewives, women controlled household spending and thus needed to be informed of state policies' connection to their own economic fate. As mothers, they were children's first influence—they needed to learn that only the Center embodied politically the Christian ideals they cherished. Finally, wives could keep husbands and youths loyal to the Center, shoring up Catholic culture against Marxism, especially among the working classes.

These concerns made the SPD the primary target in all Center propaganda, both for women and for general audiences, despite the parties' partnership at the Reich and Prussian levels. Applying arguments used since the 1890s to the Weimar context, appeals presented the SPD as a proletarian party incapable of representing "Christian interests." While flyers to (male) occupational groups cast the SPD as a threat to wage security,[76] those to women exclusively targeted cultural issues. Like all nonsocialist parties, the Center feared the SPD would capture the female vote. Like these parties, the Center vilified SPD claims to foster gender equality. *Germania* accused the SPD of treating women like "vote cattle" (*Stimmvieh*), caring more for their votes than their virtue. The paper also accused it of violating its own rules about naming women to soviets or top spots on its ballots, while simultaneously scorning such rules as "sterile leveling" of the natural differences between the sexes.[77]

Far more vociferous were attacks on SPD "irreligion," present in all Center appeals. Lumping all of the Left under the rubric "SPD," they blamed the horrors of war and revolution on materialists "whose only kingdom is on earth." Regarding their "most important issue," the Center told Christian women that the SPD was tearing the faith from their children's hearts by ending religious instruction in schools.[78] To see the SPD's true intentions one needed only look to Russia, where wives no longer took their husbands' names and marriage was an easily dissolved contract bound only by physical attraction. To the Center, claiming that such "loss of discipline" emancipated women was an outrage—only Christianity liberated women by freeing them from slavery to male passions and abuse. Only the Center respected woman as wife and mother. The party of Bebel could never make morality and religion purely private matters, for Christian women knew that the most fundamental social question was whether or not a people embraced God.[79] The Center was careful not to discredit the SPD's welfare agenda, for it knew this was popular with both female and working-class voters. Instead, it packaged itself as the only party that united Christian ideology with a far-reaching social agenda.

Like the DDP, the Center distanced itself from its actual collaboration with the SPD, and like the DDP and DVP in this period, it wished to prevent an anticipated rush of women into the SPD. Unlike the liberals, however, the Center offered women not equal rights but protection in their true *Beruf* of wife and mother—the keystone of its message to women of all classes throughout the Weimar era. Of the twenty Center flyers for women found from the 1918–20 period, only three mentioned waged work; only two discussed it at any length. One such piece by the KFD listed demands such as job training, protection from "physical and moral hazards" in the workplace, aid to working mothers, better regulation of farm and home work, and fair wages. It argued that solutions would come not from the SPD but the Center, which represented *all* workers—female, proletarian, and *Mittelstand* (the term "class" was avoided). Significantly, in flyers for men the Center pledged to fight "giant capitalists" and promote "reasonable socialization," ideas explicitly rejected in KFD flyers that stressed socialism's "grave moral dangers" for women.[80] While the Center's constituency included female proletarians, propaganda was far more often oriented to what were seen as women's universal spiritual needs than to the material interests of working women.[81]

While all parties issued appeals claiming to support female workers, Center materials most closely resembled conservative (and later, Nazi) propaganda in their association of women's work with hard times. One KFD flyer opened, "You stand alone in the struggle for survival—far from your family, perhaps without a cozy home where you can find joy or relief after your hard work."[82] Women's work was portrayed as an unfortunate fact of life in an age of economic troubles and a scarcity of marriageable men. Because they had to, women should have the right to work, but the party and its women urged doing so in agriculture or domestic service, not professions "alien to their temperament" such as law. While the liberals also called for work to be allocated along gender lines, the Center's vision of suitable areas for women was limited solidly in the spirit of the 1891 papal encyclical *Rerum Novarum*: "Woman is by nature fitted for domestic work, . . . which is best adapted . . . to preserve her modesty, and to promote the good upbringing of children and well-being of the family."[83]

The Center did attempt to win rookie female voters, allowing more flyers for them to be issued in its name in 1919 and 1920 than in any subsequent campaign. Still, female activists' calls for more consistent and sustained agitation met with pronounced indifference. Organizationally, the party established no women's committee until May 1921, relying on the KFD, parishes, and Catholic clubs like the Windhorst League to raise money, educate, and distribute literature. While the lack of a *Frauen-ausschuss* was characteristic of the party's decentralized national structure (it had no special committees for any group until 1920), existing evidence paints a picture of a party that sat out the rush to canvass female voters or parade teams of promising female candidates. In 1920 its executive did decree that in all districts with at least five candidates on the ballot, one should be female, preferably in the second spot, but this appears to have been little heeded.[84]

This was the backdrop of the 1920 party conference at which Hedwig Dransfeld, KFD president since 1912 and longtime promoter of political education for Catholic women, articulated the mood among female activists. The KFD had distributed over 8.5 million women's flyers in 1919 yet had won little respect, as evidenced by the Center's failure to bring the group into a permanent relationship with the party. Women were responsible and serious voters—the backbone of the party, as she put it—but had yet to be recognized. Other women echoed her complaints and warned that the Center would lose female support if this did not change. In response, male delegates Hankammer and Hoffmann told women to be more active in public life, while Konen quipped that if women encountered any man resistant to their presence in the party (which he doubted), they should show him Christian patience.[85] Female activists' concerns were swiftly minimized; the women, for their part, largely avoided confrontation, as they had long been accustomed to doing, and assured the party of their loyalty in order to preserve their ability to put a "womanly" stamp on its agenda.

Some women's concerns, such as marriage law and even abortion, would find a key place in the Center's policy agenda during Weimar, but this was attributable to the party's emphasis on religion's state and public role, not the power of its female activists. In fact, these women had little clout, despite—or perhaps because of—the Center's overwhelmingly female vote, as illustrated by the case of Helene Weber's position on the Düsseldorf ballot in June 1920. Weber, a social worker and teacher with a devoted following, had been given slot four on the ticket, where prospects for election were shaky. The local assembly protested that she should have a safe position, not only because she was vital to the party, but also because losing her as a delegate could have negative repercussions among female voters. But party leaders reasoned that putting Weber in a risky spot could help the party by spurring higher turnout among women wishing to ensure their candidate's victory. The plan backfired and Weber lost. The combination of lower turnout overall and women's weak ballot positions meant that, in June 1920, the party with the strongest female vote had one of the lowest proportions of female Reichstag representation.[86]

By this point, the Center recognized that Catholic women were voting their religion with a loyalty that appeared unshakable. It seemingly did not need to offer them special inducements and could ignore the requests or grumbles of female activists without fearing retribution from Catholic women who had no political alternatives. The party treated women like *Stimmvieh*, not by flattering them, but by taking them for granted because it knew the job of mobilizing women was already being done by the Church and its all-embracing organizational networks.[87] Less than any specific strategy, it was the fact of Catholic identity and solidarity that cemented women to the Center.

The German National People's Party (DNVP) was founded in late 1918 to unite conservative and *völkisch* elements around the goal of restoring kaiser and empire. It played to women's presumed love of order, stability, and sentimentality through melodramatic bromides against the new order's threat to female concerns, defined as Christianity, marriage, and family. After a rough start in which the party finished fourth in the National Assembly race of 1919, this formula became quite successful, particularly with middle- and upper-class Protestant women. Women's support in fact became so strong, comprising just under 60 percent of the DNVP vote, that women arguably transformed this heir to the Conservatives into the people's party of its new name.[88] A major source of this support stemmed from the DNVP's ties to the Evangelical Women's League, which, while officially neutral, worked hard to mobilize women for prochurch politics. League leaders Magdalene von Tiling and Paula Müller-Otfried became party activists and candidates.[89] The DNVP solidified this base with its own women's committee, put closely to work with its propaganda department to produce more flyers for women in 1919–20 than any bourgeois party except the DDP, each with circulations of over 200,000.[90] The DNVP aggressively pursued the female vote in this period, targeting housewives, domestic workers, and rural and Protestant women. In a strategy reminiscent of Bismarck's gamble on universal male suffrage, the DNVP reckoned that enough women were unhappy with the fruits of the revolution to elect the representatives of tradition.

The revolutionary period had deeply shaken the Right, as reflected in early DNVP statements that suppressed demands with a Junker pedigree.[91] Faced with the necessity of winning women voters, the DNVP downplayed the Conservatives' fierce antifeminism by quickly endorsing suffrage and founding a women's organization.[92] A late 1918 statement welcomed women as *Mitarbeiterinnen* (coworkers): "With particular satisfaction the DNVP greets women's [entry] into political life. During the war, the German woman had to take on many of men's positions and fulfill so many duties for the state that granting her suffrage is but small thanks for her accomplishments. We fervently hope she uses these rights properly for the maximum benefit of the fatherland. The German woman is entering the often hot political arena. She must keep a cool head and always ask, how can I vote to best serve my fatherland, its future, and my family's future? She must not be led by frustration, ill temper, or daily woes, but consider that she, together with her sisters, represents the majority of German voters and, in a sense, has Germany's fate in her hands on election day."[93] Guidelines issued before the January 1919 elections continued to embrace women, acknowledging their political equality and even echoing some demands of bourgeois feminism, such as reform of married women's legal status and equal access to education. The party even condoned women's work outside the home and claimed (falsely) to have the most female candidates on its ballots.[94]

But as the revolution's power evaporated, such sentiments were eclipsed by the truly conservative, even reactionary tone that would mark the DNVP throughout the Weimar era. Never really comfortable with populist postures, the party resuscitated demands for monarchy and empire already in January 1919.[95] It also qualified its support for female suffrage in a women's committee flyer for that month's elections. The vote, its female author said, was foisted upon women by a "political spirit foreign to our own" (a variation on the Right's claim that the revolution was the work of outsiders). But as suffrage was now a done deal, women must overcome their reservations about politics to ensure that power did not fall into the hands of those who would destroy German cultural treasures. Indeed, as conservative activists raced to mobilize women for political participation—something these same circles had demonized for decades as *unweiblich*—their motto became, "The right to vote is the duty to vote [*Wahlrecht ist Wahlpflicht*]."[96]

The wait-and-see tone of early pronouncements gave way to unrelenting attacks on the republic. Like the DVP, the DNVP presented all voters with visions of a Germany mired in disgrace, materialism, and barbarism. Propagandists attributed this chaos to politics itself, a particularly salient theme in material for women, who were political outsiders identified with the private haven of the home.[97] One women's flyer vividly depicted the revolution's unwanted politicization of daily life. Politics had hijacked men's clubs, it read. Women were subjected to the bickering of Democrats, Socialists, and Spartacists, while children were roped into party struggles at school. "They" sought to rob the family of religion and left German sisters in the occupied zone prey to the lust of African troops. Gone were the days when even the poorest woman could afford a bit of chocolate for the children, when Sunday meant real coffee and cake, hearty beer, and a good cigar. Women's girlish dreams of a happy home life were poisoned as husbands grew bitter. The past had been an age of peace, order, and happiness—now one stood numb in the face of a terrible present. But women could use their power as the majority of voters to revive those golden times. By supporting the DNVP, they could strengthen the bourgeois party that united all *Volksklassen* who wanted to keep hearth and home pure.[98]

While this piece implied that the domestic sphere could be cleansed of hated politics, elsewhere materials portrayed the hearth as women's battle station. DNVP rhetoric to all groups bore an aggressive nationalism. Materials usually written by female activists told women that their special role was to defend German culture with the same resolve as the soldiers who came when called in 1914. Unlike other bourgeois parties, whose depictions of women's cultural role at this time stressed social peacemaking, the DNVP urged a vigorous war on foreign influence and stressed not equality but the differences between Germans. Asking them also to set their sights beyond the private sphere, the DNVP urged women to vote to help ward off the excesses of democracy and socialism—only "German" forms of organization were acceptable. While all parties encouraged women to see the vote as a tool to help rebuild the nation, DNVP rhetoric deployed a language of female militancy matched only in Communist and, later, Nazi campaigns.[99] Just as service in the Wars of Unification had served as justification for universal male suffrage,[100] the DNVP could justify women's political participation (it avoided the term "citizenship") through their wartime contributions and constant crusade to preserve the national cultural flame.

If female nature determined gender-specific sites and forms for this crusade, femininity rendered DNVP women activists no less nationalistic than men. They protested the "violation of the Ostmark" and the new national colors. Besides calling for Christian education or adequate welfare, their flyers and articles demanded a "Germany for Germans."[101] Meditating on the impact of female suffrage, Leonore Ripke-Kühn dismissed women's "so-called leaders" in the BDF for their internationalism and pacifism. She saw women's identification with the social not as a boon but as a potential pitfall, as their entry into politics threatened to shift attention away from foreign policy and Germany's survival as a state. Would woman, as "world mother," neglect her duty as mother of her own people, succumbing to the "black-red-gold international" of democratic socialism or "the grey international of cosmopolitanism"? Drawing on prewar antisuffrage discourses, Ripke-Kühn feared that "women's justifiable striving for freer development" might feminize male politicians. Like Paula Müller-Otfried, she envisioned activism in service of the nationalist agenda as reparations for women's "stab in the back" on the home front during the war.[102]

The DNVP's gallery of national enemies linked feminists with Democrats, Socialists, Bolsheviks, African soldiers, and Jews. Appeals to cross-gender groups like the *Mittelstand* cast the Democratic Party as a slave to "international capital"; propaganda for female voters seized upon the "party of women" slogan. The DNVP argued that the DDP only recently found its heart for women after years of opposing their franchise (a case of the pot calling the kettle black). Significantly, appeals to both sexes attacked the DDP for its ties to the *Berliner Tageblatt*, a veiled attack on the "Jewish cosmopolitanism" embodied in anti-Semitic stereotypes. They presented the DDP as a haven for bluestockings and Berlin fashion plates, not "truly German" women. There was no "party of women," the DNVP stated, only the party of the *Volk*.[103]

The Socialists were an even bigger target, as they were for all parties. DNVP materials for both female and male audiences attacked the SPD on economic grounds, arguing that it had no respect for the identity of various *Stände*, from the artists' to the housewives' estate. Like the Center, the DNVP offered the blockade and postwar economic chaos as proof of SPD incompetence. While appeals to male workers stressed insufficient wages or employment insurance, those to women stressed consumption. One flyer to rural women equated socialism and Bolshevism with food shortages. Others named ministers who had "engineered" shortages, arguing that SPD plans for nationalization would cripple industry and feed only misery. Far from bringing paradise on earth, SPD rule meant perpetuation of the "shameful" war economy and reparations, like giving away the store to Germany's enemies.[104]

Like the Center, the DNVP had a strong religious basis, which meant attacking socialism's goal to separate church and state. Flyers to both general audiences and women called attention to the financial hardship this would impose on the churches.[105] A piece for women stressed the need to preserve Christian education, arguing that socialist pedagogy taught German children to hate other classes, God, and their parents. Appeals to women also linked these issues to sexual morality, as the party was determined to head off any leftward swing of female voters. The SPD presided over a moral decline whose symptoms included equal status for unwed mothers, the "nationalization" of women, and soaring urban illegitimacy rates. Quotes from Bebel were bandied about as proof that the SPD favored "free love." To help shore up marriage against this threat, the DNVP was prepared to accept women's equal rights within the parameters of wedlock, as stated in its guidelines. By presenting marriage as women's only haven in an unsafe world, the DNVP wished to attract both the traditional wife and mother who feared change, and the single woman seeking an oasis of security where she would be honored rather than exploited.[106]

An obsession with a breakdown in the sexual order also marked DNVP discourses on defeat and the Versailles treaty, literally embodied by France's use of Senegalese and Moroccan troops in the Rhine occupation, which DNVP men and women protested throughout the early 1920s as a threat to women and youth.[107] This motif already existed in propaganda from far-right organizations such as the German Offense and Defense League.[108] By 1924 it would also crop up in campaign materials from other parties. But the DNVP bears the notoriety of being the first mainstream party to employ racist images of apelike African soldiers violating German maidens in its campaign propaganda.

Rape became a common metaphor for Germany's postwar position in materials to both men and women: "Germany is enslaved, [her] cities occupied, her men hunted and caged, her women and girls dragged off and raped."[109] A poster "commemorating" the first anniversary of the revolution linked the hated republic with a breakdown in the sexual order. Ten frames compare Germany before and after the revolution, the first two using women to signify Germany's changed position since November 1918 (see Figure 1.1). When Wilhelm II ruled the Rhine, it

Zum 9. November 1919.

Als Wilhelm II. am Rhein regierte.

Als Friedrich Ebert am Rhein regierte.

Als Tirpitz die Küste schützte.

Als man die Flotte auslieferte.

figure 1.1
"On 9 November 1919":
"When Wilhelm II Ruled
the Rhine" versus "Friedrich
Ebert's Rule" (DNVP, 1919)
(Bundesarchiv)

says, Germany was safe and happy, as depicted by a woman knitting in the shade of a garden while her apple-cheeked children play. Under Friedrich Ebert's rule, a black soldier thrusts himself upon a German woman as two other Africans leer in approval. This brazenly racist imagery links national disgrace with sexual chaos, the woman's fallen hat symbolizing the fall of the crown and her spilled parcel representing her despoiled purity at the hands of the barbaric Other. The piece argues unequivocally that revolution had emasculated Germany so badly it could not defend itself against violation by racial enemies, even on its own soil.[110]

Similar images of national and sexual violation also marked attacks on Jews. The DNVP from its founding brandished an open anti-Semitism that set it apart from the other major parties and appeared in both general literature and materials for women. These portrayed Jews as smut peddlers and warned women about "Cohn and company," who mocked marriage by advocating equal legal status for unwed mothers and their offspring. Even worse, Jews now controlled both press and state (one flyer claimed the new government was 80 percent Jewish). "Your new leaders" were a pack of slackers who would let others fight the war. They were the SPD, led by the Polish Jew "bloody Rosa" (this phrase was set in large bold type in a flyer to "female German voters") and Karl Liebknecht, "traitorous son of a Serbian Jewess." They were "the *Berliner Tageblatt* crowd" and black marketeers who insulted Christianity and the military, embraced the SPD, and allowed Germany to be overrun by Eastern Jews. It is difficult to know whether such vicious language served to attract many female votes. While race was central to the self-image of female conservative activists,[111] women voters were on average more moderate, strongly underrepresented in the vote for radical fringe parties such as the early NSDAP, whose 1920s propaganda was loaded with graphic anti-Semitic imagery. It is, at any rate, worth noting that a crude anti-Semitism was part of Weimar political discourse—not just on the fringes, but in the language of a major party—long before the rise of the Nazi Party. It is also important to note how, from the start, this was linked with issues of morality, sexuality, patriotism, and economics—a package the Nazis would later sell to great effect.[112]

Similarly dark depictions of Germany's current state stamped DNVP women's appeals with economic themes. Early pronouncements on women's work resembled the party's stance on suffrage with their initial nod to prevailing progressive winds, recognizing women's right to better wages (like the Center, they did not use the term "equal") or to choose the *Doppelberuf* of work and marriage.[113] But this quickly acceded to the demands of cultural nationalism. The early DNVP did recognize a variety of female occupations, but appeals to those workers submerged their particular interests in nationalist rhetoric. For example, an early flyer to women in commercial occupations barely addressed work issues, instead reminding women of the days when German industry reigned supreme, German culture was *Weltkultur*, and religion was secure. In contrast to appeals to male occupational groups, which even when they invoked national decline discussed the new order's impact on the material conditions of employment, appeals to women assumed that even working women were most concerned about cultural issues.[114] Their economic interests were presumed identical with their husbands'; as both men and women wrote, what German women really wanted was work for the *Hausvater*.[115]

The female workers who did have a presence in DNVP literature in this period were home workers and domestic servants. Included in the party's list of targeted occupational categories,[116] they were the subject of several flyers likely written by the women's committee, headed until 1923 by the leader of the Trade Union of Women Home Workers, Margarete Behm. Propaganda touted home work as the most suitable employment for women who could not make family ends meet through thrifty housekeeping alone—only a woman who stayed in the house could create a real home. Flyers to domestic employees (*häusliche Angestellte*) praised their decision to avoid the factory for work relevant to their future career as wife and mother. Domestic work constituted women's *Stand*—their place in society and the economy, their identity. The DNVP claimed only it respected this, unlike the Left, which would ban home work. In a weak attempt to address the exploitative conditions that were driving women out of domestic service and home work,[117] the DNVP pledged to improve their status. Yet it also stressed its advocacy of housewives' interests, demanding their representation in the Reich economic ministry. In reality, the DNVP was closely allied with conservative housewives' organizations and always sided with them in labor disputes with domestic workers. But rather than address the antagonisms between factory and home workers, between housewives and their domestic help, DNVP propaganda idealized the domestic sphere as a space where women could find an emotional satisfaction more valuable than base financial reward.[118]

DNVP propaganda by and to women laid down a strict gender separation of spheres. It also reproduced stereotypes about women's fickleness and incapacity for serious thought, warning in one flyer that women would have to overcome these to earn men's trust and prove their political maturity.[119] Women had to defend aggressively the conservative cause while rejecting everything at odds with conservative feminine ideals, including "pushy" feminism, socialism, and a women's party.[120] Radicalism, which in DNVP parlance denoted the Left, was taboo, as it was "alien" to female nature. An article in the party journal, whose author is not named, held up the SPD's Marie Juchasz as a negative role model. The first woman to address the National Assembly, she spoke not like a woman but like a "converted comrade." Her speech exhibited precisely those weaknesses feared by admitting women to Parliament—it left the "rational" field of debate for a personal, superficial tirade against the Right. Her "true German womanhood" emerged in her "warm, powerful word" on the blockade but was soon obscured behind typical SPD polemics. This depiction transformed the reformist Juchasz into a raving radical who forfeited her femininity simply by espousing socialism. Ironically, she was simultaneously too feminine—irrational and subjective—to be a good political actor.[121]

Anna von Gierke became another negative model for the political woman. A conservative feminist long active in social work and child welfare, Gierke was elected a DNVP delegate to the National Assembly. However, her local party committee in Potsdam struck her from its 1920 Reichstag ballot because she was half-Jewish (a fact moderates subsequently tried to deny as they sought to downplay the power of the party's *völkisch* wing). In response she resigned and set up a women's list in Berlin-Charlottenburg.[122] Consequently, Gierke was vilified in the DNVP press, especially by other women. One writer argued that her actions were motivated by naked ambition and confirmed the general opinion that women could not separate party affiliation from personal feelings.[123] This comment not only implied that men never let personal feelings impinge on politics but also contradicted the prevailing attitude that women's political activity was a politics of emotion, whether maternal love or sorrow at the plight of the fatherland. To criticize a woman for failing to separate her emotions from politics imposed an impossible double standard. When used for the good of the whole, women's feelings were depicted as legitimate political weapons; when used for personal gain or the good of a particular group (in this case, women), emotions signified political immaturity and selfishness. Men acting in self-interest might be criticized for their politics (as was Gierke's father, who resigned after the incident), but women who did so violated the very premise by which their political participation was tolerated.

These descriptions of two very different women reveal conservatives' basic distrust of the political woman, although to read DNVP internal correspondence in these early years is to find little evidence of gender tension.[124] Existing documents show women who consistently portrayed their relations with the party as positive, something unique in this period. After 1920 problems would emerge as the party failed to broaden its network of local women's committees or to allow women to advance outside the structures of the women's organizations. But female activists expressed no resentment at their relegation to "women's matters" and seemingly felt that their ideas had resonance within the party. The DNVP's message of vigilant femininity in defense of the fatherland appealed to these women, who saw themselves as "neither colorless women's rightists nor mere housewives [*Nur-Hausfrauen*]." Party positions on moral and cultural issues appealed to their religious convictions. Organizationally, the DNVP from the start used existing religious groups as the basis for a women's organization whose tasks and positions were well defined, unlike the Center, whose decentralized organizational apparatus contributed to its women's sense that their work went unrecognized.[125]

DNVP campaign appeals to women forcefully equated morality with Germanness, linking nationalism to the "women's issues" of religion, family, and culture, in this period and throughout the Weimar era. In the republic's earliest years when anxiety over the aims of Germany's new leaders ran high, the DNVP effectively played to the fears of its female target audience—housewives, Protestants, and workers in traditional female jobs—through melodramatic scenes invoking the good old days. Such appeals resonated with those who preferred the known quantity of the past to what Socialists and Democrats presented as the new possibilities of the present. Conservative women saw only the uncertainty of the future; their party fed that fear with images drenched in moral peril and violated national honor.

Clearly, demonizing socialism was central to the bourgeois and confessional parties' campaign rhetoric, as it had been since Bismarck's era. How did the Left respond? In this period, these parties' women's propaganda often bore a defensive character, especially in the case of the SPD. The Social Democrats, Germany's largest party from 1912 to 1932, produced the most campaign material and will be discussed extensively here. This chapter will also survey materials from the Independent Social Democrats (USPD), key players until the party collapsed in 1922 as members gravitated either toward the SPD or toward the Communist Party (KPD). The KPD boycotted the National Assembly elections and few campaign materials exist for them from this period; their campaigns will be discussed in subsequent chapters.

The SPD, true to the spirit of Bebel, was the prime mover behind the introduction of female suffrage and used that as its calling card with female voters in 1918–20. The party portrayed itself to women—mainly of the working class, though there was hope of winning progressive bourgeois women too—as the proven defender of their rights and interests, defined as political equality, legal and economic protection of motherhood, better conditions for working women, social welfare and education of youth, access to higher education, and so forth. In a message akin to that of the DDP, the SPD presented these not simply as women's issues, but as part of the larger struggle for human dignity. Both parties' early rhetoric greeted the dawn of a new Germany, signified visually by the SPD's revolution-era use of Expressionist graphics in posters promoting the new order. Women and girls, for their part, were exhorted to "emerge from the darkness" of disenfranchisement in at least twenty flyers produced for the National Assembly election alone. The SPD stood poised to reap the fruits of decades of organizing women, advocating suffrage, and welcoming more women into its leadership than any other party.[126] What other parties dreaded, the SPD desired, even expected—women were to cross class and religious lines and vote SPD because of its women's program, sentiments reflected in Socialist agitation throughout this period.

In 1918–20 the SPD devoted special, sustained attention to women in at least thirty-eight flyers specifically for them plus an additional score of pieces for general audiences that discussed women's issues at length.[127] Almost every one of these emphasized the party's role in securing female suffrage and equal rights in a constitution that women for the first time anywhere had helped frame.[128] This message also featured prominently in flyers to male groups and mixed audiences. The SPD linked gender equality with the end of dominance by "moneybags" and Junkers in a new age of cultural progress and economic justice for all. These new rights were made possible by the November Revolution, which SPD women's literature presented in a generally favorable light.[129]

While it praised the revolution, the SPD quickly distanced itself in practice and in rhetoric from its widely perceived "excesses," not surprising for a party that had come to see itself, in Karl Kautsky's words, as "revolutionary but not revolution-making."[130] General flyers from late 1918 blamed street violence on the USPD and Spartacists, who were accused of trying to accelerate the revolution to secure their own hegemony. "False revolutionaries" were instigating general strikes, which every woman must oppose. Early on, the SPD appealed to women as a moderating force who understood that polemics did not feed hungry children. A Prussian flyer to "women and comrades" contrasted screaming men with sensible women who had a responsibility to use "the rights given them on November 9" to convince men to return to work and end the chaos that threatened to ruin all.[131] While this piece undermined stereotypes of female irrationality (it was men who had clearly lost their heads), it reinforced others by masculinizing the worker. It appealed to women's desire for bread and peace but also encouraged them to take up politics and vote for the SPD, which promised class reconciliation and order.

Aiming to bring women up to speed on recent political history, the SPD told them that problems blamed on the revolution were in fact the bitter harvest of a long war and the blockade. The heartbreak of those who lost sons or husbands was caused by reactionaries who had prolonged the war.[132] German "servitude" (*Volksknechtung*, a term that would fit quite well in the conservative lexicon) was the result of the army command's rash handling of the cease-fire, the SPD argued in an attempt to dispel the growing "stab in the back" myth. As Adele Schreiber asserted at the 1920 women's conference, women must learn that it was not the revolution that was wrong, merely its timing, making it a poor measure of what socialism could bring.[133]

Despite the revolution's flaws, the SPD credited it with bringing not only legal rights but also reforms for working women. Appeals to this core constituency pointed to concrete material issues, touting women's transition from servitude to agency in terms similar to those for male workers such as civil servants. For example, women were told that, unlike the old regime's brutal denial of workers' rights, the revolution had guaranteed a voice for trade unions and the eight-hour day. (The lack of an eight-hour day for housewives was not a theme in campaign literature, although the 1920 SPD voters' handbook listed regular time off for housewives as a goal.) The revolution also terminated the Gesindeordnung, ending the semifeudal status of domestic servants. Appealing to class solidarity, the SPD urged these women, whose work relations remained highly paternalistic, to reject the parties of their bosses for the "party of domestic workers."[134] The SPD also championed equal rights for female civil servants and white-collar workers. It supported women's right to work in all fields, though, like the bourgeois and confessional parties, it presented welfare and communal politics as particularly suitable areas. No SPD materials mentioned the inequalities of the demobilization decree. Instead, propaganda stressed political rights as a precondition, but not the sole guarantor, of economic equality—only a socialist state meant true equality. Thus, women had to ensure both the preservation and expansion of their rights by supporting the only party that could bring true liberation through socialism.[135]

While flyers from the SPD (as well as the other Marxist parties) appealed to women most sustainedly through economic issues, they always circled back to the issue of suffrage. They urged women to flex their political muscles—this was no time to be silenced by fear that their rights were too new to be tested. In language that presented the vote more as a gift than a right, the SPD repeatedly expected women to show their gratitude for suffrage by voting SPD.[136] Female activists in particular expressed amazement that all women did not see the SPD as their party, as in Henni Lehmann's *Vorwärts* article criticizing prewar suffragists for flocking to the DDP.[137] Once the first election results from areas with sex-segregated ballots revealed that women preferred conservative and religious parties, the SPD reacted with a mixture of anger, disappointment, and panic that punctuated its attacks on opponents.

The SPD hammered home the incompatibility of bourgeois ideology with women's interests, defined in 1918–20 as suffrage, equality, and workplace rights. First, the SPD hit opponents on the economic front with appeals urging women to "wake up!" The bourgeois parties represented capitalism and the exploitation of workers, which hit women, whose economic dependency was inscribed in that system, especially hard. Adding insult to injury, these parties wished to raise taxes to pay for *their* war. Appealing to women's "innate" pacifism, as well as their anger over current economic conditions, the SPD blamed the "old guard" for the "hunger years" and the present slide.[138]

Second, particularly in the National Assembly campaign, the SPD attacked the bourgeois parties as unworthy of female support because all of them had originally rejected SPD motions to enfranchise women. They had slandered the suffragists and discouraged women's political education. One flyer to workers, citizens, and soldiers invoked the old Prussian three-class suffrage to discourage women from trusting the DDP. As a women's flyer put it, even though the DDP was the first to see the light, it was still a mishmash of progressives and misogynists blinded by "male pride"—only the SPD was the true "party of women." Old foes of gender equality now wooed female voters, but the SPD urged women not to fall for them, for if they won, they would revoke female suffrage as fast as they could.[139] Their history of opposing women's enfranchisement made their claims that socialism insulted women hollow.[140]

By arguing along these lines, the SPD strove to defend itself against accusations that its ideology demeaned women and the family. From the first days of female suffrage, the SPD began a fifteen-year campaign to convince female voters that its plans for women were not radical. For example, it countered horror stories of socialist excess by arguing that its commitment to social welfare proved its respect for women. It was capitalism that degraded women by exploiting their economic dependency, especially when many could not find husbands. Tacitly agreeing that marriage was women's ultimate goal, the SPD claimed to be the truly moral force because it worked to improve life for those compelled to work.[141]

figure 1.2
"Mother, Think of Me!
Vote Social Democratic!"
(SPD, 1919 and 1924)
(Hoover Institution)

SPD literature drew on women's identification with social welfare to appeal to them not only as workers but as mothers. In a well-known poster first used in 1919, a scruffy but robust child urges mother to "Think of Me! Vote Social-Democratic!" (see Figure 1.2). This piece, in which realism replaced the complex Expressionistic graphics of revolution-era posters,[142] mirrors SPD appeals' shift away from celebration of new republican ideals to the nuts and bolts of policy. Later versions of this poster, in fact, list specific SPD social welfare achievements beneath the illustration. Elsewhere the SPD portrayed itself as the party whose assistance to mothers and children would benefit the common good. A front page *Vorwärts* article on women and local politics demanded, for example, an end to tenement housing, which bred disease and immorality. The only reference to abortion or birth control in published party literature from this period, it previewed the SPD's embrace of "positive eugenics," arguing that the population would only grow through sound housing and agricultural policy, not forced childbearing.[143]

Materials presented the SPD as the most vigilant defender of motherhood, reminding women that the party had fought for *Mutterschutz*, guaranteed maternity benefits such as paid leave after childbirth, long before others latched onto the phrase. In 1919 SPD women had been key in securing continued maternity allowances at wartime levels, which contemporaries hailed as one of the first pieces of legislation achieved with the help of women representatives.[144] The SPD press contained lively discussions of motherhood that supported the rights of unwed mothers, something nonsocialist parties portrayed as antimarriage. Willy Steinkopf depicted unwed mothers as victims of seduction whose children had done nothing to deserve inferior status. Women in the SPD press were far less apologetic: Ilka Schütze argued that such children often sprang from a love free of the materialism marriage had come to symbolize, while Louise Schroeder criticized the double standard that never censured men with illegitimate children. Echoing utopian socialist ideals, Adele Schreiber demanded a new morality that made maternity everyone's concern. Lifting women's yoke of dependence would elevate motherhood and build, not erode, the family.[145]

But such views rarely made it into campaign propaganda for broad consumption, nor were they shared by everyone in the party. The SPD usually walked a more conservative line in its rhetoric and practice. For example, its 1920 voter handbook recommended film censorship, evidence of a cross-class consensus that postwar Germany had witnessed a moral decline. This line took on racist tones when the 1920 SPD conference passed a motion from Marie Ansorge and Clara Bohm-Schuch protesting the use of African troops in the Rhine occupation as an "insult to the German *Volk*" to which "thousands of defenseless women and girls would fall victim."[146] At this same meeting, Helene Grünberg characterized women as mothers and wives first, who needed help to devote more time to their families. In perhaps the most telling example of the party's attempt to present a morally conservative face, Bebel's name appeared only once in SPD literature from 1918 to 1920, in a *Vorwärts* article by radical feminist Minna Cauer praising him as a pioneer for women's rights.[147]

These moves sprang from a defensiveness conservative critics, particularly the Center, successfully imposed on the SPD. Pleading its own case, the SPD argued in four women's flyers that it had been misrepresented on moral issues and that its social welfare program made its agenda more moral than that of the self-proclaimed guardians of virtue. Yet the SPD in the early Weimar years underestimated the centrality of religion to women's voting preferences, as shown in its attacks on the Center Party, which shifted from reasoned critique to invective. For example, it accused the Center of lying about the SPD's religious stance, arguing that it was the Spartacists who aimed to eradicate religion. The SPD supported freedom of conscience and a "practical" Christianity that promoted happy families and children through peace and social welfare, while the Center silenced workers to serve capital. It also claimed to have been misrepresented regarding religion in schools. It argued that, despite the Center's constant criticism, that party had in fact helped fashion the current compromise making religious education voluntary. The SPD maintained that schools now taught class harmony and critical thinking, while Catholics preferred to terrorize students into blind faith and mental numbness (*Verdummung*).[148]

Walking onto thinner ice, SPD propaganda demanded the churches' legal and financial independence, arguing that state subsidies could be better used in programs for mothers and children—what, it asked, was un-Christian in that? If the workers' movement could survive on the contributions of poor proletarians, one women's flyer asked, why couldn't the churches? Pushing even harder, the SPD brushed aside its own actions in August 1914 to ask, "Where were the 'Christians' when it was time to protest the world war?" It presented the Center's use of religion as a political tool as the most blatant sign of hypocrisy: "Women! Protect your religion from those who use it for political slogans; from those who drag your hearts' silent glow for the higher, the majestic, the holy onto the dirt-encrusted fields of political battle! We want no one to be forced into religious profession. We want to ensure that the state does not misuse religion as a tool of power."[149] This attempt to play to female reservations about the "dirt-encrusted" field of politics (inconsistent with the SPD's broader message encouraging women to become political) likely did little to convert women with religious sensibilities to the Socialist camp.

As with the liberals and conservatives, when attacking the Center the

SPD tried to deflect attention from issues of morality or religion back to women's enfranchisement. Days after the revolution, one flyer claimed, the Bavarian Center Party rejected female suffrage because "women belonged in the kitchen." Now the Center had reversed itself, herding women to the polls and preying on their political inexperience by filling their heads with lies about Social Democracy. But, the SPD claimed, when women judged objectively, they would find that everyone—Protestant, Catholic, or "whatever"—must support the party that gave women freedom, equality, and a voice.[150]

The SPD's emphasis on equal rights did not yield the number of female votes the party had hoped for. In Weimar's first national elections, national averages showed a significant gender gap in the party vote—the female vote had, in fact, cost the SPD delegates.[151] Anger and frustration at women's "ingratitude" cropped up increasingly in discussion. While the SPD never shared liberals' fears of a woman's party (it worried more about defections to the Center), some early flyers characterized women as apathetic or too emotional. The 1920 voter handbook stated that if SPD bills were defeated in the legislature, it would be women's fault.[152] Propaganda, particularly from 1919, reflects the SPD view that it had already sewn up the female vote by virtue of its women's program. Perhaps the party's repeated insistence that equality was now reality worked against it when women perceived that this was far from true, or (to some) far from desirable.

Party writings show a variety of responses on how to attract more women voters. Men were largely silent in these debates; despite rules that the entire party should engage in mobilizing women, it was in fact left up to female activists. Clara Bohm-Schuch argued that propaganda for the June 1920 campaign should stick to economic facts, but Marie Juchasz urged more attention to the "female psyche." Helene Grünberg, noting women's rising bitterness, urged more discussion of their daily worries if the SPD was to win them away from the Center and Right. These women all agreed that the SPD had to convey to untutored women the difficulties of making politics; economic crisis, the vagaries of coalitions, and the Versailles treaty all restricted the SPD's ability to realize its program. Propaganda must make clear that setbacks were not the fault of the SPD, but the fault of parties to its right.[153]

Debate over how much women's propaganda should emphasize gender rights, material concerns, welfare, or culture had already emerged among female activists by 1920. While Juchasz's focus on social welfare and the "female psyche" would soon dominate, other women did not want their party to trumpet its dedication to equality only to relegate women's concerns to a separate, less valued female sphere. They criticized the SPD's failure to live up to its egalitarian ideals, particularly on economic issues. At the 1919 women's conference, they argued that Socialist men were still not convinced that firing a woman because of her gender was wrong, as confirmed by their support for the demobilization decrees. SPD women joined the National Assembly motion protesting that decree and criticized the double standard of the demobilization questionnaire, which forced women to justify their need to earn wages.[154] Other expressions of dissent are harder to locate, though some appeared in a DNVP Women's Committee pamphlet issued around 1921.[155] While this is a heavily biased source, it is safe to say that frustration was fermenting among female activists. Flashes of anger could be heard from women in any party, but they rang with a particularly dispirited tone when voiced by SPD women, whose party made such a show of its commitment to gender equality. This tension would continue to vex the SPD throughout the 1920s.

The SPD in 1918–20 hoped its program and past advocacy for women's issues would pay off. Appeals focused on the SPD's role in securing for women the "gifts" of equal rights and suffrage, assuming that female voters across class lines would define their primary interest as gender equality. At the same time, the party hedged its bets with a battery of women's appeals defending its stance on religion, the SPD's version of the "cultural" issues stressed by parties to its right. But this propaganda contained remarks that were often impolitic. The SPD also seemingly failed to distance itself, in the eyes of women voters in particular, from the perceived excesses of socialism at home and in Russia. The SPD would eventually narrow its gender gap, partly because of a milder tone on religion, greater emphasis on social welfare, the return of economic stability after 1924, and the rise of the far more radical KPD. But in 1918–20 the SPD could only watch as Bebel's prophecy that female suffrage would work against the party came to pass.

The Independent Social Democratic Party (USPD) survived as a force in Weimar politics only for a short time, splitting in 1922. During its lifetime it competed with the SPD and KPD for the vote of the proletariat, particularly its dispossessed elements. It worked to mobilize women through publications (*Gleichheit* and *Die Kämpferin*) as well as a stream of campaign literature admittedly thinner than that issuing from the SPD. Its propaganda addressed women as workers, mothers, housewives, home workers, domestic servants, and even white-collar workers, defining its goals as welfare for mothers and children, equal wages, nationalized industry, communal households, and, ultimately, the end of capitalism. The USPD also spotlighted unwavering support for gender equality in all of its appeals, even those to mixed-sex audiences.[156] But its vision of equality extended far beyond political rights—it demanded liberation through socialism. USPD women's literature, in fact, often reads like a primer on the basic tenets of Marxism, explaining how women's specific demands were part of the larger struggle of the working class. Appeals painted in bold, melodramatic strokes the USPD's fight for what it defined as women's true equality, alongside its fight for the liberation of the worker from bourgeois reaction and SPD betrayal.

The USPD's founding impulse came with the SPD's support of war credits in 1914; the war also became a touchstone in its campaign propaganda. Appeals stressed the USPD's pacifism, a stance assumed to be especially appealing to women, who "naturally" possessed a deeper sense for "positive forms of life." Its rejection of war stemmed from the party's commitment to socialist internationalism, which appeals linked to a critique of capitalism, the SPD, and religion—all key themes in USPD women's literature in 1918–20.[157]

USPD materials as a whole explained why capitalism was detestable; women were told that they had the most to gain from its demise because they were its most defenseless victims. Typically, flyers mixed melodrama with statistics to spin tales of disease, poverty, and misery that displayed women and children as the most tragic casualties of the class war being waged by capitalist parasites. Women had long ago been forced from the home by the "whip of hunger"[158] and subjected to boundless exploitation in the workplace. The gender-based discrimination women faced under capitalism was also addressed in women's flyers that focused on their material conditions of life. One flatly stated what no other party would admit, that women were paid less simply because they were women. Female activists' protests against workplace discrimination also inflected materials. They decried that, during the war, women earned less working the same jobs as men—jobs made even more dangerous as wartime exigencies gutted safety standards. As thanks for their service after the war, women got demobilization and low (if any) unemployment benefits. USPD women called the demobilization order a "truly reactionary" male law designed to reassert women's position as cheap, reserve labor and housewives, as dictated by the interests of capital.[159]

In the USPD lexicon, bourgeois parties represented the interests of capital—the few—versus those of the workers—the many. These parties, who were blamed for the war, promulgated a corrosive nationalism to keep the masses divided. But national solidarity was a myth, argued the USPD. A women's flyer contrasted English and American relief aid to German women and children with the Weimar state's uncanny ability to find funds for armaments, no matter how insolvent it claimed to be. Analogous to other parties' demands that women submerge particularist interests for those of greater good, the USPD instructed women to reject the selfish goals of capitalist militarism for the collective welfare, defined here as the international proletariat.[160]

Women should also detest the bourgeois parties because of their dogged opposition to female suffrage. Like the SPD, the USPD depicted these parties' heart for women as a recent discovery motivated by the desire to win their votes. A women's flyer likened such "shameless" wooing of the "wife of the working man" to the smooth crooning of a Don Juan who would drop her once the seduction was complete. This sexually charged imagery, with its implications of infidelity (the "wife of the working man" betrays her class), also invoked women's physical experience of suffering as a basis for class solidarity: "Only too well you have . . . felt with your own bodies the sins a money-hungry ruling class can commit against working people. *You have starved while they feasted!* . . . *You have feared for your husbands, your lovers, while they pranced with 'their officers'!*"[161] The piece aims to demolish any understanding with bourgeois feminism: the women of bourgeois parties might address proletarian women as "dear sisters," but in fact they were out to protect their own class interests. The USPD, in a style the KPD would later perfect, often presented such dramas of betrayal both to expose the paucity of gender solidarity and to prevent any from forming. While the party hoped to win women with its stance on gender issues, their special interests were never allowed to detract focus from those of the whole, the proletariat.

This theme of the incompatibility of gender interests across class lines also appeared in a piece in *Die Kämpferin*. Its female author, describing a DDP woman singing the national hymn, posited that nationalism violated true femininity: "When a woman's soul sings that anthem to military slaughter, 'Deutschland, Deutschland über alles,' and spurns talk of brotherhood and unity—peace—among peoples, then goodness and love of mankind no longer have a home in female hearts. The reshaping of politics, to which the 'eternal feminine' (in Goethe's words) calls women, fails."[162] Women's flyers called attention to bourgeois women in the Reichstag who vetoed USPD bills for expanded workers' maternity benefits or equal legal status for illegitimate children but approved funds for the military and reparations. For all their talk of sisterhood, the USPD argued, these women's only real interest was sustaining private property and the double moral standard underpinning it.[163]

In this enterprise, the bourgeoisie found willing collaborators in the SPD, which the USPD claimed had let down both women and the working class time after time. The USPD privately acknowledged its roots in the SPD but argued in flyers for general audiences that the course of the revolution revealed the SPD to be reformist cowards who mouthed socialist phrases to fool the proletariat. SPD hands were stained with the blood of war dead, as well as the mothers and fathers killed in Noske's brutal counterrevolution.[164] To blue- and white-collar women, the USPD argued that while the SPD had long been the only party to recognize their work issues, it had compromised them by allowing fat cats and black marketeers to take control. Women's flyers from 1920 also blasted the SPD for abandoning women by knuckling under to its coalition partners on *Mutterschutz* and civil code reform. The SPD had let women's rights be watered down in a constitution that had little impact on daily life, while the USPD remained dedicated to the fight for true liberation.[165]

The other major foes of women and workers, according to the USPD, were the political agents of religion. The USPD acknowledged that hard times drew women in particular to religion, but it hoped that exposing the hypocrisy of religious institutions would keep women away from the confessional parties. In true Marxist fashion it portrayed religion as a tool of capitalism: "They want not only the labor of you and your husbands and control of your bodies—their claws are out to grab your souls! They numb your children in their schools and churches! They preach patience and submission, the better to exploit you!"[166] Christianity appears as a faith of the haves that instilled a sense of powerlessness in the have-nots; the priests (*Pfaffen*, a derogatory term for clergy with Reformation-era roots appropriated in this period by the Left) had already shown their true colors during the war. While appeals to mixed-sex audiences attacked religion as the enemy of social progress, materials for women added a reminder about Pauline doctrines of female submission and acceptance of suffering as God's will. It argued that this dogma cultivated a ripe audience for the Center Party, which used every tool, down to the confessional, to ensnare women's souls for political purposes. Women must tear the scales from their eyes—as Luise Zietz asked, "Do you want to remain poor and unfree?"[167]

But voices within the party advised caution when criticizing religion. Frau Keinath at the November 1919 women's conference warned that it would be foolish to rob women of religion and leave them with nothing. Socialism must be offered as an alternative, a new faith that would create a free and equal society on earth.[168] Socialist discourse had always contained evangelistic elements, but now that women had to be incorporated into politics, the USPD elaborated more on women's place in the promised land. Appeals and articles for women strove to illustrate the Marxist position that work outside the home was a vital step toward emancipation because it freed women from financial dependency and enhanced their solidarity with the proletariat. While many USPD images reinforced women's common perception of work as painful, underpaid drudgery, others described how socialism would transform work into a source of satisfaction and benefit for both individual and community. Technology and communal households would alleviate the double burden of housework and wage work. Significantly, this vision reproduced the prevailing division of labor—women would run the communal kitchens and nurseries of the future. Even in the present, women were called to work in agencies dealing with youth, welfare, and education, as well as police vice units. Women would also be valuable on communal soviets because these dealt with provisions, housing, and schools. Mathilde Wurm at the 1919 women's conference went so far as to demand a "natural division of labor" that would raise the value of female labor and end women's relegation to the most undesirable jobs (in contrast, Anna Ziegler and Luise Zietz saw a danger in removing women from "men's" work and insisted on support for women's right to work without qualification).[169] These examples show how deeply embedded notions of gendered spheres of activity for the sexes were, even among some of the most progressive women of the day.[170]

Socialism would benefit not only women workers but the family as well. Like Communist and some SPD propaganda, USPD materials blamed bourgeois morality for destroying the family by subordinating it to capitalist property relations. Guided by the assumption that women were more prone to internalize bourgeois moral codes,[171] the USPD tried to convince women that socialism would end their status as property and foster the family through better living conditions. Socialist Russia was promoted as a society that "accommodates motherly impulses to the fullest."[172]

Although the party emphasized material issues in its appeals, USPD discourse to women did not neglect what all parties saw as a specifically female domain, culture. It argued that socialism meant the cultural elevation of the workers. Money now spent to fund the military or compensate dispossessed nobles could be used to promote culture for all. Women could help realize this happier world, not only by publicly joining the working masses and their representatives in the USPD, but also by ensuring that socialism penetrated the hearts and minds of the working class—a job, as Frau Keinath put it, carried out in the private sphere through the "love of mothers, wives, and sisters."[173] Even radical socialist women saw the home as site of women's unique, primary influence.

Party blandishments did not yield the strong female vote the USPD had hoped for; like the SPD, USPD observers quickly jumped on statistics indicating that the female vote had cost the party Reichstag seats.[174] This inflamed tensions within a party already racked by huge ideological divisions. An anonymous blurb in *Freiheit* bluntly stated that women's support of conservative and religious parties proved their immaturity. Mathilde Wurm defended women, condemning the double standard that women had to "demonstrate political maturity," unlike men, who were often just as uninformed. But other USPD women shared men's frustration with female political behavior. Articles in publications by and for women often painted them as easy prey for reactionaries, at sea in a flood of party choices. While these materials also portrayed assured, informed women, comments like Bertha Braunthal's predominated: "Women's damned selflessness [*verdammte Bedürfnislosigkeit*], their patient acquiescence to what they see as an unavoidable fate, makes them willing objects of exploitation in bourgeois society."[175] Such anger forced female activists to reassure their comrades that women's votes for reactionary parties were a passing phase, and that focusing on issues of particular interest to women would not dilute the power of the working class.[176]

This frustration also produced some political soul-searching at party conferences. In 1919 consensus emerged that USPD women's propaganda had to change. Female members complained about the state of the women's committee and its journal, *Die Kämpferin*, which many felt was treated as an afterthought—an extra wurst fried up for the ladies, as one woman put it.[177] This combined with criticism of men's lingering inability to treat women as equals in work and politics. All agreed that the party must do more to educate women about socialism and the soviet movement. As Zietz noted, the party had produced only three women's flyers for the National Assembly election, a figure that had to improve. This advice was seemingly heeded in 1920, as more campaign material was created for women. But at the October 1920 conference, female delegates continued to argue that deficient propaganda was failing to attract female voters. Zietz complained that local branches failed to order or distribute the flyers the women's committee designed. Braunthal, now secretary for women's propaganda, took this as a personal attack, lashing out here and elsewhere at other party women.[178] Such fighting occurred within the larger context of the USPD's heated conflict over whether to join the Third International and accept closer ties to Moscow. As members lined up on opposite sides of that issue, propaganda and women's issues became lost in this growing schism.

The USPD offered women voters a program that put their concerns about work, rights, and family at its center, albeit within a strongly Marxist framework not designed to reach beyond a working-class audience. Its press also opened some rhetorical space for expressions of female individuality.[179] Additionally, the USPD pioneered the Left's use in Weimar political discourse of suffering female bodies to represent both female and proletarian servitude, a motif the KPD would make a staple of its iconography. USPD appeals contained strands of both the SPD's emphasis on the welfare state and the KPD's vociferous rejection of capitalism and bourgeois morality. Like these parties, the USPD largely ignored culture while critiquing religion; that it won fewer female votes than the SPD in this period can likely be traced to its even more radical tone on this issue, as well as its language of class war, which arguably repelled women voters.[180]

As socialist politics fractured after the revolution, the USPD's position in the middle of the left wing grew increasingly untenable. By 1922 its women scattered, with Sender and Wurm gravitating to the SPD's left flank, while Braunthal joined the KPD; Luise Zietz died in 1922. The party that sought to be a progressive advocate for women could not hold together.

Propaganda for women issued between 1918 and 1920 reveals the gender preoccupations of Germany's major political players, the men and now the women who were reshaping the national discourse. As all parties pursued the newly enfranchised woman with scads of material, they commonly assumed that the way to win her was by stressing issues of gender equality and suffrage, especially in the 1919 National Assembly campaign. On the heels of both the revolution and the war, during which women of all classes had proven themselves worthy of citizenship through their service on the home front, all parties felt that it made political sense at least to acknowledge women's rights. They saw the need to welcome women into their ranks and promoted female candidates as proof of their dedication to women's concerns. This made 1918–20 a time when female activists had unprecedented access to the means of defining female identity and public roles. Optimism reigned particularly in the Democratic and Socialist camps.

Was this assumption that women were most interested in equal rights issues connected to German women's experiences at the time? We can infer that women embraced the new responsibilities of suffrage by looking at measures such as their voter turnout, which hit nearly 90 percent in January 1919. Further evidence lies in women's visible attraction in the early Weimar years to political gatherings and organizations—their membership in socialist parties and trade unions, for example, doubled or tripled between 1918 and 1920.[181] Even women who disliked the republic took up the rights it gave them, engaging in a flurry of organizational activity designed to inject "womanly influence" into the masculine sphere of politics. Rhetoric from all parties—and the female activists who authored most appeals—encouraged this, welcoming women and the "unique" traits they brought to public life.

Yet arguably the most pressing issues in most women's lives—their economic and material concerns—found only a hazy reflection in propaganda. Materials from 1918 to 1920 constructed woman's economic role in terms of her relationship to the workplace; her consumer role went largely unexplored. Perhaps this comes as no surprise at a time when the female worker had become more visible than ever. From USPD to DVP, propaganda treated work outside the home as a fact of many women's lives, and every party competed to show that it would represent working women's interests. Appeals acknowledged the rapidly expanding female white-collar workforce. Some parties even addressed the less visible women in domestic and agricultural labor (housewives, in contrast, had not yet become a hot topic), as the DNVP pledged to improve their plight in order to end the flight from these fields, while the SPD sought to integrate them into the working class by extending them the legal protections industrial workers enjoyed.

Yet all parties also critiqued the present state of female labor, the Center and DNVP all but rejecting it outside the home as harmful to the family. Specific issues women continued to face at this time, such as inadequate training, grossly unequal pay, and lax safety standards, were glossed over in women's propaganda, in contrast to the detailed attention to employment concerns in materials for male workers. The plight of war widows was rarely articulated. Except for the USPD, no party consistently championed women's right to work without restrictions. Nor did any party admit in campaign appeals their support for female labor's demobilization after the war, which clearly violated the gender equality parties like the SPD and DDP claimed to hold dear (as female activists noted). Perhaps this omission was smart tactically — men across class lines clearly supported demobilization, while the thousands of women who quietly left their wartime jobs offered little inducement to take a principled stance here. Propaganda reveals that all parties more or less defined women of every stripe not by their economic roles but by their domestic ones. All women were mothers or potential mothers. Hence the widespread call for *Mutterschutz*, whose presence in women's appeals reveals both a broad acceptance of the welfare state and a consensus that the state should promote reproduction.

While early Weimar propaganda bore an optimism about the republic and its possibilities for women, an equally strong discourse of defeat set in, especially after 1919. Although the Left and Right disagreed on the causes and remedies, there was general agreement that Germany was in moral decline.[182] In the context of a shocking military defeat and shake-ups in the political — and gender — order, this message seems to have resonated with female voters, as witnessed by their disproportionate support for socially conservative parties. Despite the relatively limited revolutionary outbursts in Germany, non-Marxist parties' rhetoric about "socialist excesses" and moral decay indicates the pervasive fear of Bolshevism that gripped the bourgeoisie and even many proletarians. The DNVP took this to the extreme as it constructed "fortress Germany," whose women would defend the national hearth. That party's fixation on the Rhine occupation made it a pioneer in the use in Weimar political discourse of violated female bodies to represent immorality and the "disgrace" of the Versailles treaty. These protests against what came to be called the "black shame," which would be supported by every party except the USPD and the Communists, reveal not only acute anxieties about race and female sexuality but also a full-fledged crisis of masculinity that permeated Weimar political discourse from its earliest days.

The antidote to these crises was "rebuilding," which became the most common metaphor in women's propaganda across the board. While thousands had suffered physically from the war and the blockade, common images of *Trümmerfeld Deutschland* were even more of an index of Germans' psychological damage and desire for some kind of national healing. Women became the perfect vehicle for this message. Despite criticism of their alleged immaturity, apathy, or irrationality, all parties portrayed women as essential to the project of rebuilding, bringing the uniquely female impulses of motherliness, love, and selflessness to this fight, whether defined as the fight for German culture, the survival of the republic, or the proletarian revolution. The message to women was clear from the start—their interests could best be met within existing political bodies. Accepting this became the way for women to prove themselves worthy of the gift of political rights.

2

Stabilization and Stability

:

Women and the 1924 Elections

Thinking back on the inflationary years an extravagant image of a hellish carnival appears. . . . It was a time of intense revaluation—in the economy and culture, in material as well as psychological things.

—Hans Ostwald,
Sittengeschichte der Inflation

A great deal had changed since Weimar's early days. While the republic was marked by trouble practically from the beginning, its first days at least also carried a sense of possibility and even optimism among its supporters. But since 1920 its pathologies had multiplied. No stable governing system emerged at the national level, and the SPD, midwife of the republic, shunned a national role after 1920. Rightists staged coup attempts in 1920 and 1923; while these were put down, assassinations targeting "national traitors" claimed hundreds of progressives and leftists. The Communist Party (KPD) vowed to fight in memory of its own slain leaders, but its October 1923 uprising never even got off the ground. The tense political atmosphere was only the half of it. The economy lurched from war-induced inflation into hyperinflation precipitated by the Franco-Belgian occupation of the Ruhr in January 1923. "The time when money died" saw a sweeping collapse of not only material but also spiritual values that shook the nation to its core.

President Ebert invoked emergency powers in late 1923 to restore order, temporarily banning the KPD and the Nazi Party. Emergency rule was also used to institute a new currency, the Rentenmark, along with harsh deflationary policies. Finance Minister Hans Luther tightly restricted credit and instituted taxes that fell heavily on the middle and working classes. The new currency was valued at 15 percent of the old, eliciting howls of protest from the middle classes whose savings were decimated. Over 200,000 tenured civil servants (*Beamten*) were dismissed to balance the budget under the October 1923 Personnel Retrenchment Decree (PAV), while those retained had to swallow massive pay cuts. Finally, the eight-hour day was suspended in practice as industry strove to enhance its competitiveness through large-scale rationalization and mechanization schemes, creating high unemployment among skilled workers. For many Germans, the cure for inflation seemed as bad as the disease.

In this context, the May 1924 Reichstag election, called when a parliamentary majority refused to extend the state of emergency, became less about who was responsible for inflation than about whom to blame for the harsh stabilization. Voters punished parties associated with the Weimar coalition (the DVP, DDP, Center, and SPD) and rewarded "antisystem" candidates. The use of emergency decrees to carry out stabilization meant that government parties had no power to shape it, yet they were tarred with responsibility for the process—a condition that compromised the legitimacy of the Weimar system. This particularly accelerated the decline of the liberals, who became displaced by single-issue parties that played to middle-class anger at the economy and the unpopular party system. The political fallout of the inflation was an unhealthy fracturing of bourgeois voter loyalties long before the depression and rise of Nazism.[1]

The outcome of May's election made the formation of a governing coalition all but impossible, as the two largest parties, the SPD and DNVP, refused to work together. The victorious DNVP further estranged possible partners by making its entry into government contingent upon rejection of the Dawes Plan. This plan to help Germany meet its obligations under the Treaty of Versailles set up a schedule of reparations payments funded by taxes and duties, combined with international supervision of the Reichsbank to ensure a stable currency and balanced budget. The DNVP saw this as a violation of German sovereignty, while the Weimar coalition parties supported it as the only way to stabilize both the domestic economy and foreign relations. Although nearly half of DNVP deputies eventually ratified the Dawes Plan, coalition talks failed and a new election was called for December. The Berlin press reported intense and often violent clashes during that campaign,[2] yet the sense of crisis that pervaded May had dissipated as the economy rebounded. The Weimar coalition parties managed to recoup some votes, though the DNVP and splinter parties remained popular.

Women were confronted with particular hardships during this period. The same PAV that slashed the civil service also permitted the dismissal of married female civil servants, including teachers, if their economic provision appeared secure. It was another link in a chain of laws aimed at reducing women's employment in certain fields, starting with demobilization in 1919 and continuing through the 1920s, as PAV articles on women were retained even after the rest of the decree was lifted in 1925.

Hyperinflation had also greatly affected women, as their domestic work of procuring food and clothing became a frantic race against hourly devaluation. Savings and fixed incomes lost all value, a dire situation especially for widows or others on fixed incomes. As money became worthless, many women and girls bartered sex for the butter, shoes, or other items they and their families needed to survive. Hans Ostwald wrote that every foreign man, whose dollars or pounds made him an instant millionaire, had a "currency girlfriend." His *Moral History of the Inflation* is stocked with images of asphalt cities gripped by an erotic frenzy verging on insanity. Even more prosaic accounts noted an erosion of paternal authority, exploding divorce rates, and more public and "deviant" sexuality. For better or worse, the inflation had cut away the last shreds of Victorian morality.[3]

These changes were most visible in cities like Berlin, where publicists created the images that dominate historical memory of this era. Yet while the stories were often overwrought, at their core was the truth of a very profound, universal sense of disorientation and bitterness, as once secure existences evaporated in a surreal numbers game. The fact that so many lost determined that the inflation would cast a long shadow over the 1924 elections. But was this the case for propaganda for women? Would recent events bring more detailed debate over economic issues, or would parties prefer to invoke loftier themes like culture and maternity to female voters assumed to be more emotional than calculating? Would parties continue to stress gender equality now that balloting had shown that women preferred those that stressed religion? As we explore which themes and assumptions dominated 1924 women's propaganda—first from the government parties, then the opposition—we must keep in mind that these campaigns occurred at a time when female suffrage was no longer novel, when years of relentless political and economic upheaval enhanced the longing for stability perhaps most palpably among those responsible for holding society together, women.

In the campaigns of 1924, the Democratic Party tried mightily to divert attention from its inability to protect middle-class economic interests during the inflation and stabilization. A campaign strategy memo instructed speakers to focus instead on foreign policy, labor issues, and the threat of extremism, while promoting democracy and a "healthy" nationalism. Reliance on prudence and maturity, the party argued, was the only way to nurture the recovery begun with the introduction of the Rentenmark and anchored by the Dawes Plan. In this way, the DDP aimed to portray itself as the savior of the economy and defender of the national interest. Still viewing itself as a party capable of uniting all Germans, it tried to rally voters around a message of social harmony and hard work as the keys to prosperity, political stability, and international respect.[4]

But the strategy could not halt the stampede of voters from the political middle in May 1924. The DDP was part of the regime held responsible for the inflation and hated stabilization—no amount of damage control could counteract this in the minds of voters. It was perceived as being too close to both big business and the Social Democrats. Key pillars of its constituency—civil servants, white-collar workers, the urban middle class—drifted to the right wing and single-issue splinter parties. That December a recovering economy and an aggressive fight to regain these voters helped the party rebound somewhat, especially in Berlin, but fracturing bourgeois loyalties, internal divisions, and dwindling finances began to undermine the political health of the DDP.[5]

The Democrats' propaganda for women in 1924 reflected the party's overall strategy of highlighting a foreign policy based on mending international relations to secure a revision of the Versailles treaty and a domestic policy stressing class reconciliation and a sober approach to economic recovery. Materials for women, however, tended to focus on the latter, linking economic restructuring with issues of culture. They invoked women's "cultural mission" to help lead reconstruction, which would yield peace and prosperity in the domestic sphere.

The May 1924 campaign saw the DDP noticeably defensive about the election's main issue, stabilization. By holding up party cofounder Hjalmar Schacht as the "father of the Rentenmark" in both general literature and propaganda for women, the DDP hoped to link itself in the public mind with the end, not the process, of hyperinflation. For example, a poster depicting a cheery housewife with bulging shopping bags proclaimed, "The housewife smiles again at last. Who brought freedom from the endless hunt for money and groceries? The Rentenmark from our Schacht!"[6] A flyer constructed as a letter from one woman to another extended this metaphor, stating not only that Schacht had sired the new currency ("it's not hard to become a father") but that he had taught it to walk.[7] Such direct reference to the plight of female consumers or stabilization, however, appeared less than a focus on generic economic demands, as in past campaigns. Appeals to homemakers, for example, argued that DDP positions on housing and lower taxes made it the "party of 13 million housewives"—a marked departure from its 1919 "party of women" slogan.[8]

Civil service layoffs furnished another example of how the DDP tried to shake off association with an unpopular stabilization measure. The fact that the PAV had been enacted by emergency decree gave the DDP room to argue that it had tried to mitigate its harshest aspects and was still fighting for its repeal. To women, the DDP tapped the language of female equality it had used so heavily in 1919, linking PAV article fourteen's trashing of women's right to work with the threat to women's rights as a whole. It blamed the decree on the Right (here the DVP and DNVP), for whom female equality was "a thorn in the eye." Railing against these "reactionaries," the DDP packaged itself as the only champion of women's economic rights in the bourgeois camp, arguing to the growing ranks of female teachers, for example, that women's right to work must be protected, particularly as marriage opportunities remained scarce.[9]

The DDP also launched attacks on the Right's antifeminism, reminding women, as in 1919–20, that the DDP was the party of their "leaders" in the women's movement. Appeals urged women to recall that it was the republic that brought them the vote, and they continued to claim that the Right would abolish female suffrage, calling it "no accident" that the Völkisch Bloc had no women candidates. One pamphlet quoted complaints from DNVP women that their party violated its promises of equality; it also cited DNVP men who characterized their women's co-operation with women of other parties as a covert *Frauenpartei* responsible for such "disasters" as women's admission to judicial office in 1922. This, the DDP maintained, proved that the Right happily exploited women's vote but had no respect for that right to vote (the *Stimmvieh* concept).[10]

The DDP not only attacked the Right on women's issues but also portrayed them as a threat to German recovery in all of its literature throughout 1924. Women's propaganda in May argued that a right-wing victory would jeopardize the stability begun with the Rentenmark, just as the murder of finance minister and prominent republican Walther Rathenau by rightist thugs in 1922 had triggered hyperinflation. Right revanchism would also heighten the danger of war—a central choice for women in May's election, the DDP argued, was war or peace. One flyer, signed by "a German woman," begged women to reject the fantasies of those who believed a new war could liberate Germany: "The dead speak to you! . . . The radicals want war—we want peace! We don't want to run Germany into the ground—we want no militaristic adventures, no new inflation. We want peace and order!"[11] Most striking is the way the term "radical" denotes the Right, not the Left. Unlike 1918–20, the Left was barely targeted in 1924 DDP women's campaigns. The specter of communism did appear in December materials, but in the wake of assassinations, the Hitler putsch and trial, and conservative moves to sink the Dawes Plan, it was the Right's "brutality, rawness, and lack of cultivation" that voters—particularly women—were told to fear most.[12]

The DDP maintained that the only way to beat the Right was to stand up for democracy,[13] a tall order at a time when the republic was universally blamed for the economic catastrophe that had befallen nearly every German. Commitment to the republic threw the DDP on the defensive against charges by the DNVP and Völkisch Bloc that it was ineffectual, unpatriotic, and "Jew-ridden." This defensiveness is most visible in the women's flyer on Schacht's "raising" of the Rentenmark, which denied that Schacht was a foreign Jew: "[That's a] clumsy anti-Semitic lie! If he were a Jew, his intentions and deeds would be no less German and national than they already are. But Dr. Schacht was not born in Sweden, but Germany . . . and he is not a Jew!"[14] Such a response could not placate those who saw stabilization as a Jewish plot to ruin the middle classes, nor did its tone create an image of the DDP as a strong party.

The DDP was at pains to assure voters it was sufficiently nationalist, arguing that the best way to defend the fatherland was to reconcile all classes, faiths, and sexes. But if appeals to other special-interest groups emphasized unity (particularly *class* unity) as crucial to *economic* recovery,[15] women's materials always crowned this discussion with the idea of culture. Invoking the language of moderate feminism, the DDP argued that women could be most effective in the work of fostering a healthy cultural nationalism: "Woman is called to concern herself foremost with issues of education, youth welfare, and so on. The woman of the educated middle class, whether she has a *Beruf* outside the home or not, is the true bearer of culture."[16] By 1924 all parties assumed that women voted on the basis of cultural issues—the DDP was not ready to cede this terrain to the Right and now strongly embraced *die Kulturmission der Frau* at a time when its economic record was a major liability.

The DDP's 1924 discussion of culture, however, largely avoided the themes of religion and education that were becoming standard currency in this field. Instead, they addressed culture in terms traceable back to Louise Otto, the mother of German liberal feminism. In 1843 Otto wrote that women's love of *Heimat* and fatherland necessarily produced a love of democracy and freedom.[17] Eighty-one years later, DDP women linked women's cultural mission to the preservation of democracy, urging them to use their maternal role to anchor morality and democratic culture in the home. This motif of woman as a healing and unifying force had been present in earlier campaigns, but it gained new urgency as the events of 1922–23 radicalized German political culture to an unprecedented degree.[18] Alarmed by women's apparent propensity to trust the Right, DDP literature reminded them to see the benefits they enjoyed under the current system. In light of declining rates of female electoral participation after 1919, appeals urged women not to retreat from politics but to maintain long-term vision (the opposite of what was needed to survive the inflation, when long-term saving left one only with piles of worthless notes). Pleading for *Sachlichkeit* (sobriety or rationality), the DDP exhorted women to set aside their feelings to see what was at stake—the republic to which they owed their rights and its champions, the DDP.[19]

Yet few women or men heeded the party's message that May, as the DDP scored only 1.65 million votes, a mere 29 percent of its 1919 tally, making it the election's big loser. The strong showing of extremist and antirepublican splinter parties lent DDP literature for December a new urgency. Concern over female political apathy translated into a concerted effort to win women's votes in December, as the party created more propaganda for them than in the previous election.[20]

As in May, December appeals to women argued that a basic tenet of democracy was gender equality. They spotlighted the feminist leaders in their ranks. An appeal in the *Berliner Tageblatt*, in fact, even resurrected the "party of women" slogan—its only appearance in 1924—again linking this to democracy and women's rights. The appeal was also intended to discredit the idea of a woman's party, which resurfaced in 1924 and was explicitly rejected by DDP women at their national conference that August.[21] Women must shun not only a women's party, but extremist parties as well. December's dominant campaign motif stressed women's duty to detoxify the social and political atmosphere. Still rejecting the language of class conflict purveyed by the other bourgeois parties,[22] the Democrats urged women to act as mothers and reject all forms of radicalism. Building on the prevailing idea that women were natural exponents of "the religion of peace," female activists in particular argued that to be a woman was to be a Democrat because the DDP meant reconciliation, order, freedom, and bread.[23]

As in May, "radical" largely meant rightist.[24] Gertrud Bäumer argued at the November party women's conference that the Right's version of community meant a restoration of old social conditions and privilege—such a *Volksgemeinschaft* would be none at all—while the DDP's would allow diverse opinions to coexist peacefully. Right-wing anti-Semitism was also more forcefully condemned in December. Women speakers denounced racial hatred as unworthy of a cultivated people in attacks that appeared not in flyers but the press, on which the DDP had long relied. Lenka von Körber, for example, accused *völkisch* and nationalist groups of undermining youth's respect for cautious rebuilding and serious thought. She warned mothers that youths' flirtation with the swastika was anything but harmless—women must see the danger in any display of anti-Semitism. Campaign appeals to women, as in May, also blasted the "Reaction" (a term for the Right normally used only by Marxists and, later, Nazis) as misogynist and "patriarchal." Tracking women's position within each party, one flyer dubbed the DNVP "repressive" and "thoughtless," while noting that the DVP had only one electable female candidate on its ballots—"and they expect women to work 'selflessly' for their party!"[25]

December women's propaganda also took on the Left, specifically the KPD, whose strong showing in May alarmed Democrats (even though these gains had not come from women). Vague usage of the term "Left" also conveniently created rhetorical distance from the SPD, with whom the DDP was often accused of being too friendly. One women's flyer argued that although the Left recognized female equality, it held women back through "false party discipline" (a phrase from 1919–20) and squelched female influence by blocking their women from cooperating with those in other parties. Assuming women to be "naturally" pacifist, DDP propaganda argued that the Marxist dogma of class war "contradicts woman's most basic nature and prevents her fulfilling her special tasks." In contrast, the DDP's program and actions proved that women's nature and tasks could be best put to use there, to advance both their sex and the *Volk*.[26]

This theme of anchoring women to democracy was developed in the DDP's main women's pamphlet for 1924, *Betrachtungen einer werktätigen Frau*. Its diary format chronicled one woman's education in social relations and politics. Though it criticized the "excesses" of the revolution, the piece targeted the antidemocratic Right. In a swipe at *völkisch* tribal romanticism, it claimed that the republic more closely resembled the Teutonic age when the Germanic peoples were not dominated by kings. But a mere republic was not enough for women—unlike France, Germany gave women a political voice. Answering those who claimed that the democratic system brutalized elections, the writer argued that this was only so because of the divisive acts of a few radicals (the DNVP and KPD were singled out). These groups and their cheap promises had to be rejected, not the system itself.

Continuing the DDP's plea for realism and rationality, the pamphlet also addressed the economy. While a republic was the best form of government, it read, it could not make everyone rich overnight—could a kaiser or a dictator? Echoing nineteenth-century liberal notions of harmonious cooperation between *Hausmütter und -väter*, the piece painted an idealized economy in which managers, owners, and workers labored as one for common goals (a theme that also marked appeals to businessmen and workers). In a formula that must have struck a sour note with those whose hard work had been no defense against ruin during the inflation, it declared that hard work, not utopian fantasies, would bring freedom, happiness, and prosperity.[27]

As in May, the DDP tried in December to dissociate itself from harsh stabilization policies by presenting itself as the party of economic democracy, unlike the allies of big agriculture and industry in the DNVP and DVP. Women's materials reflected this, speaking to women as consumers and workers by claiming that these parties' agricultural tariffs and cartel deals would raise prices and bring more discriminatory measures like the

PAV to the workplace. Women, the DDP argued, suffered first under these parties' policies and would have only themselves to blame if they elected these enemies of economic fairness.[28] Women's propaganda also updated earlier calls for equal pay for female workers, including equal unemployment benefits.[29] Economic democracy even made it into a pamphlet for *Beamten*, which restated the DDP principle of equality of all classes and sexes, though it avoided direct mention of the situation of female civil servants. Yet while DDP women strove to keep gender equity issues in propaganda and on the party agenda, they encountered resistance, as allies like Anton Erkelenz lost ground within the party to advocates of other economic interest groups.

The politics of democracy and social reconciliation can be described as the DDP's version of the increasingly fashionable cultural motif of "new sobriety." In the postinflation drive for stability, such politics were presented as the most rational. This formula was problematic, however, when applied to women because both men and women in the DDP (as in all parties) considered emotion the best way to appeal to female voters. Gertrud Bäumer, for example, criticized the Right for using romantic appeals to "exploit women's instincts." She did not disapprove of a political role for female instinct—it was the "perversion" of women's "healing instinct" for divisive ends that she regretted.[30]

Erkelenz's 1924 guide for campaign organizers sounded a more exasperated note. Addressing the party's lack of greater success with female voters, he remarked on the success of the Center, DVP, and DNVP: "By speaking to the woman at the hearth and nursery, they can use grand slogans. Because we Democrats appeal more to reason, our men proceed with extreme caution and prudence. With women, one must appeal strongly to their sense of duty and responsibility . . . [and invoke] national and religious tasks."[31] Other critics had also noted a certain dryness in DDP propaganda,[32] so in 1924 the party attempted to inject more emotion into the mix. A 1924 Christmas pamphlet, for example, depicted a "working woman" who could only back a party that "took the rational course" and supported gender equality, but who also favored the DDP because "as a woman, I see our particular task in building and preserving, not destroying—in other words, to bridge oppositions in love and understanding and fulfill in political life the tasks that fall to us in the family."[33] These words, placed in the mouth of an unmarried female worker, show how women were called to forget themselves and create a democratic people's community with a uniquely German essence. As in 1918–20, the

DDP, particularly its women, continued to search for an updated model of female citizenship compatible with political activity. Women's literature appealed to reason, though traditional female roles invested with emotion were the instruments for its application: women must use their hearts *and* minds to support the DDP agenda.

If campaign propaganda portrayed women's work as essential to the democratic mission, internal writings reveal the party's indifference and even hostility to women's concerns. As early as May 1919, DDP women complained of "broken promises" and "passive resistance" to equality within the organization.[34] A party man observed in 1921 that most men were not convinced that women's work in public life was needed, which he blamed on the ill effects of competition unleashed by demands for equality. He urged women to reject "gender egotism" and see that all problems, even "women's issues," could only be solved with men in a division of labor that allowed the strengths of each to shine.[35]

The idea of separate gender spheres had informed DDP materials from the start, mingled with an oft-proclaimed commitment to equality. The women who usually wrote these appeals were bourgeois feminists who believed that the sexes were equal in value but different in their natures and tasks. But they also soon realized that their party would never work to realize the implications of its stand on equal rights if not prodded. Marie-Elisabeth Lüders became the DDP's conscience on women's rights, tirelessly calling attention to the plight of female civil servants, demanding legal recognition of housework as part of marital property (which never happened), and advocating a law to guarantee women's right to be jurists, lawyers, and judges (which did pass in 1922 and 1924).[36] She started a fracas at the 1921 party conference by challenging the DDP to democratize itself: "No progress is made . . . because [reform] always stops short of women. . . . The politics of gender and *Stand* are incompatible with democracy. Democrats voted against allowing women to run girls' schools. (Hear! Hear!) Under the pretext of reducing the number of civil servants, women have been forced out of administration and men allowed in. (Hear! Hear!)"[37] Such censure could shame the party into actions such as the 1922 resolution condemning firings on the basis of gender as unconstitutional, or the April 1924 protest against the dismissal of tenured *Beamtinnen*. Yet such gestures did not translate into legislative action. The DDP highlighted them in appeals to women but quashed them in materials for mixed or male audiences. In a May 1924 Reichstag speech on the PAV, Herr Schuldt said the DDP had considered how the measure "deprived women of their rights" but ultimately felt the cuts were needed.[38] Such issues were still seen, all rhetoric to the contrary, as mere "women's issues." In addition, competition between rival party factions meant that by 1924, the DDP's most ardent advocates of gender equality (pacifists and reformists, including *Berliner Tageblatt* editor Theodor Wolff) had become outsiders, while the economic interest groups who provided much of the DDP's funding—and who represented bourgeois constituencies the party desperately wished to recoup—ascended.[39] Economic need and the crisis of liberalism combined to push women's "special interests" into the background.[40]

The DDP's staggering losses were part of a larger trend of bourgeois defection from the liberal middle and not solely attributable to any strong female exodus.[41] But certain aspects of the 1924 campaign may have played a role especially in female voters' absence from the "party of women." For instance, negative appeals to them curiously failed to take on the splinter parties, some of which attracted support from widows or women on fixed incomes. Second, contemporaries noted women's visible political weariness and sinking turnout after years of frenzied mobilization. To combat this, Erkelenz suggested more afternoon teas (though empty coffers meant the ladies would have to bake their own cakes) instead of loud, smoky assemblies that "couldn't be more unappealing" to women. Yet by its own admission, the DDP lacked arresting visuals and compelling themes, relying on nineteenth-century warhorses like Stein and the 1848 revolution in public gatherings.[42] Ultimately, however, after the tumult of hyperinflation and political mayhem, perhaps no amount of rational pleading or clever propaganda could make women forget the DDP's impotence during stabilization or erase their desire for a return from politics to stability.

In 1924 the DDP's commitment to agitation among women wavered. It produced fewer materials that year, due in part to a severe loss of funds.[43] Lack of interest also played a role, as evidenced by two major campaign strategy papers that failed even to mention women.[44] The novelty of female suffrage gone, disappointment with women's failure to respond to the "party of women" meant less desire to use scarce resources to win middle-class women who increasingly turned a cold shoulder to the liberal Democrats.

The national liberal German People's Party entered 1924 in a similarly unenviable position. It was the most obvious representative of the hated stabilization, as its chair, Gustav Stresemann, was chancellor when the emergency decrees were enacted. Facing internal divisions between a Stresemann wing, which had wished to soften inflation's impact on the masses, and industrialists around Hugo Stinnes, for whom inflation had been a boon, the DVP papered over its differences at its March conference and entered the May election under the motto "party of the *Volksgemein-schaft*." This, however, was no declaration of class harmony but a paean to the fatherland as great social healer. This "people's community" would be led by the bourgeoisie and the DVP, against the "divisive" influence of Marxists, Socialists, Democrats, and splinter parties. DVP campaigns aimed not to bridge the divisions in German political culture but to squeeze maximum electoral gain from them.[45]

Like the DDP, the DVP suffered devastating losses in May 1924.[46] During the campaign it had tried to shift voter attention to the causes of inflation, pinning blame on the Left. Indeed, its main theme throughout all of 1924 was the need for a "bourgeois bloc" against socialism and its ally, the DDP, to foster middle-class recovery. The DVP asked the bourgeoisie to view recent economic sacrifices as the price of freedom and pledged to return that faith by seeking to modify "unjust" stabilization measures. In December it modified this message by trying to make the election a referendum on Stresemann's foreign policy, subordinating domestic issues to the goal of liberating Germany from the Versailles treaty. Economic issues refused to die, however, as the recent founding of the Revaluation Party prevented the DVP from capitalizing on its diplomatic successes. Its image as the party of big business and the stabilization hobbled it throughout 1924, as its middle-class constituency splintered and swung to the right.[47]

Participants at a March 1924 meeting of regional women's committee representatives urged their party to stress the "economic, *völkisch*, and moral significance of maintaining a healthy *Mittelstand*" in the upcoming campaign.[48] DVP women's propaganda in both May and December took this cue, appealing to bourgeois women's desire for stability in both the material and the moral realms. Stability, they argued in flyers for women and civil servants, was jeopardized by Marxism and could only be guaranteed by a strong Germany under Stresemann's foreign policy. Stability also hinged on national unity, which for women meant doing their part in "their own" sphere. As the DVP railed in general against political splintering, women's literature argued that separate spheres would prevent a splintering of the *Volk* by curbing gender competition. In this way, women could show that they were selflessly working for the *Volksgemein-schaft* by supporting the "party of social realpolitik."[49]

On the economy, general materials held up the DVP as the party most capable of sustaining recovery through its foreign policy. Women's appeals stressed demands for better civil service wages and lower taxes, while claiming that the DVP's role in ending the Ruhr occupation and securing the Dawes Plan had made economic recovery possible. Now speaking more pointedly to women consumers, particularly housewives, women's flyers trumpeted Stresemann's leadership and the Rentenmark's introduction as bringing relief—"at last," one could again properly run a household.[50] Unlike the DDP, which blamed economic collapse on the Right, the DVP blamed the Left, including the "traitorous" DDP. As in flyers for occupational groups, DVP women's materials linked SPD policies of a controlled economy and an eight-hour workday with empty shops and high prices, in contrast to "today's freer market" with shops full of affordable goods. While flyers for artisans or shopkeepers criticized the SPD as bringing *economic* chaos, women's flyers linked it with *social* chaos and a "moral breakdown" during the inflation. The DVP portrayed its own role in recovery as a return to not only economic but also spiritual health, marked by thrift, order, religion, and a strong national spirit.[51]

A gendering of economic interests also permeated DVP discourses on female labor. The ideal woman did not compete with men because this splintered national unity but worked in spheres appropriate to her sex: social welfare and teaching. Women's propaganda in 1924 stressed the DVP's claim to fight for better conditions and respect for these female occupations, whose ranks were swelling at this time. Female activists led this charge, their writings arguing for a secure female influence in education by hiring women to run girls' schools at pay equal to men. The DVP also pledged to free education from "socialist experiments," including a separate curriculum for girls with lessons in housework, social work, and physical discipline that would transform them into models for a positive *Volkskultur*. Materials also endorsed the goals of the growing housewives' movement, shown, for example, by party women in Hessen who established a Home Economics Aid to match daughters of the ruined bourgeoisie with experienced housewives who would train them in household management.[52] Propaganda on women's work centered increasingly on winning more respect for domestic labor to enhance its appeal for young women, another part of the drive toward stability.[53] Anna Mayer's 1921 pamphlet urged legal recognition of housework's contribution to family assets, though she found the idea of putting a money figure on this damaging to marital harmony. Reform, she argued, should not aim to end wives' "natural" economic dependence on husbands but redress egregious imbalances to benefit the *Volk* by making marriage more attractive.[54]

Defining women's work as active love of neighbor and *Volksgemein-schaft*, the DVP in December 1924 named itself the "party of productive women of all *Stände*."[55] This play on the DDP's "party of women" slogan was also a dig at "women's rightists" who saw equal rights as the crowning achievement of women's paid labor, implying that equality was prosaic compared to nobler work in the feminine sphere.[56] Indeed, discussion of equality in the workforce was decidedly muted; as in 1918–20, women's work outside the home appeared in 1924 DVP literature more as an unpleasant fact of modern life. Gertrud Wolf's 1921 pamphlet sanctioned demobilizing women from jobs for which they were physically unsuited, but it added that because work was necessary to survival for millions of women, it was not fair to punish the few who worked for reasons besides need. A 1924 *Deutsche Allgemeine Zeitung* piece by a young working woman posited women as victims of feminism because they were now expected to work outside the home (*Berufspflicht*).[57] A women's flyer echoed this backlash by demanding lower prices so a husband's wage could support a whole family (interestingly, a flyer for male civil servants invoked the beleaguered family father).[58] Another *Deutsche Allgemeine Zeitung* story subtly conveyed right liberals' mixed feelings on women's work, depicting an angelic young widow who managed the family firm after illness and war claimed its "natural" male heirs, nurturing it until she could pass the torch to her own son. Work did not diminish her femininity—she still found time to be a mother—but it also did not define her. She was instead a mediator, making her a model of the selfless woman who worked not for personal gain but for the good of her family and, by extension, the nation.[59]

The DVP's heavy courting of the male civil service and white-collar vote now muted any commitment to female equality. Flyers to these groups were silent on the special problems of women in their ranks.[60] Only one addressed female white-collar workers, speaking of the equal importance of employees and employers but failing to offer even platitudes on gender equality.[61] Women's materials demanded more for respect for women's work and protested PAV article fourteen,[62] though discussion of the decree—the "saddest chapter in the history of the civil service"—in propaganda not directly for female audiences either ignored article fourteen or tacitly supported it. For example, one pamphlet urged protection of the rights of married *Beamtinnen*, while another saw no problem in firing unwed mothers or married women if they received adequate severance pay.[63] No materials addressed real issues affecting women, such as their higher unemployment or the material plight of widows.

Love, not money, drove women's lives, in work and in politics. DVP women's literature presented charity work as the ultimate manifestation of female politics—the politics of love. Women in politics were also characterized as the source of spiritual and ethical renewal, an antidote to the corrosive behavior of men. The DVP called women to act in spheres where they were "experts"—communal politics, home economics, social welfare, and population policy—where their undervalued aptitude for *Kleinarbeit* (literally, "small work" or details) would enhance men's talent for large-scale abstract planning.[64] In their writings, DVP women trumpeted their own work to fight prostitution, venereal disease, alcoholism, and white slavery, as well as the long-standing *Mutterhilfe Wanderkorb* project, which provided baby goods to new mothers. While DVP propaganda made the now required nod to *Mutterschutz* and expanded welfare services, DVP women saw their private charity work as an antidote to Socialist domination of state welfare agencies. Charity created heroines, they argued, with immeasurable influence among the world of women (*die Frauenwelt*). The *Wanderkorb* brought joy to women who formerly met "the stork's" visits with tears, according to a piece in the party paper; this was the extent to which the DVP addressed reproductive issues in 1924.[65]

Campaign propaganda bore a more generic mention of bourgeois women's social work, infused with a cultural mission that had nationalism at its core. Since 1919, appeals to women linked materialism, moral decline, and the trashing of *Kultur* with the Left, the revolution, and the Versailles treaty. The DVP carried this into 1924, labeling itself the "party of the German family." It reminded women of their private duty to uphold family life through Christian national ideals, as the party fought in public for Christian schools and a stronger Evangelical church. Religious renewal also appeared in non-occupation-specific appeals that embedded religious practice and "Germany's cultural heritage" in a broad program of *economic* recovery, while women's appeals presented culture as women's particular national project.[66] DVP women no doubt contributed to this nationalistic discourse. Their writings in party journals reveal that they viewed culture, nationalism, and morality as one package that could rally women across class lines to defend marriage, family, and faith.[67] As with economic recovery, the DVP women's agenda linked culture and religion to moral renewal, revival of the national spirit, freedom from Versailles and the "war guilt lie," and an end to the degeneracy represented by inflation, socialism, and class war.

Fears of degeneracy also appeared in materials invoking the "black shame on the Rhine." In 1919–20 the DNVP and Anti-Bolshevik League had initiated the use in propaganda of African soldiers as signifiers of German disgrace, portraying the occupied zone as a sexual battlefield. The DVP picked up this motif in a Prussian election flyer from February 1921 — a high point of international debate on the subject — depicting "German women on the German Rhine who must submit to the blacks."[68] In 1924 the DVP continued to harp on the "undeniable brutalities of the blacks" in its electoral handbook and in a women's pamphlet, despite the fact that the issue had largely been defused by the impending evacuation of most African troops and the implementation of the Dawes Plan.[69] Exhibiting this as yet another sign that the moral order had been turned upside down, the DVP played the champion of a return to decency, as in a 1924 women's flyer: "My dear husband and I vote DVP because it believes: 1. Children should *again* [my emphasis] respect their parents, especially their mothers. 2. Young men should respect young ladies."[70] At a time still marked by inflation-era "immoralities" such as women smoking,[71] the DVP — particularly its women — hoped that representing a return to "family values" would win middle-class women's support.

While tying women symbolically to the family, the DVP was also at pains to prove that it supported women's rights (though feminism and "women's rightists" were depicted as unbecoming),[72] an impulse that emanated from female activists, many of whom still had ties to the BDF. Yet despite frequent collaboration with women from other parties, DVP women strove to define themselves in ways that distinguished them from their rivals. They argued that their party's "practical work for Germandom" put it closer to women's concerns than the "party of women" or the "truly antiwoman" SPD. At the same time, DVP women's materials criticized *völkisch* parties that wanted female votes but had no female candidates. The imagery of a postcard portrayed the DVP as a political home for all women: among the eight figures under the DVP banner were a young, "modern" woman as well as an older *Hausfrau* in traditional dress.[73]

Yet the DVP was still vulnerable to criticism about its treatment of women. After 1919 it increasingly edged women out of safe electoral mandates, in favor of candidates representing occupational groups; a similar phenomenon occurred within powerful party committees.[74] Other parties pointed this out, hoping in 1924 to score points with female voters, to which one DVP man replied that his party simply wanted trained women. He went on to praise DVP women for working not to further their own sex but to restore national honor.[75] DVP women agreed that a gender division of political labor was the best way to exert influence and end "counterproductive" competition. As Beda Prillip put it, women's activity could inject morality into political life not to "feminize" it but to counteract fragmentation.[76]

As in 1918–20, DVP women in 1924 steadfastly affirmed their commitment to party and fatherland, not "one-sided *Frauenpolitik*." Yet this could not mask their conflicts with the party or among themselves. Men were from the start uneasy with women's ties to extraparty organizations,[77] sentiments inflamed by renewed calls in 1924 for a women's party. Anna Mayer admitted that the danger of a women's party was great because parties did not know how to utilize women's strengths.[78] Katharina von Oheimb, who soon quit the DVP to stump for a *Frauenpartei*, blamed the list system for quashing female political influence by making women beholden to party cliques. She knew of what she spoke—she lost her own mandate to a male defector from the DDP, despite being one of the DVP's much touted "personalities" and a high-ranking leader. A combination of impolitic comments about a women's party, a "scandalous" personal life that raised eyebrows among men and women alike, and a falling out with Stresemann, all served to render her influence (much of which possibly derived from her wealth) worthless by 1924.[79]

In 1924 the DVP repeatedly scolded women for their alleged political apathy, a "sin" against the *Volk* and the bourgeois antileft front.[80] DVP women took a more constructive approach, touting their organization as a friendly setting where women could test the political waters.[81] It is questionable, however, how committed the DVP really was to winning female support. Internal memoranda from this period consistently note organizational confusion at the local level about the tasks of women's groups, as well as remarking on the difficulty in retaining local female leaders.[82] DVP women tended to blame each other for their own lack of power; personal rivalries and bruised egos blocked any unified effort to fight encroachments on women's position by special-interest groups.[83] In terms of propaganda production, my search uncovered only one national pamphlet and eight flyers produced solely for women in all of 1924. Although this was due in part to lack of funds, the DVP also now had a higher priority—winning back male civil servants and white-collar workers. Not only could women's materials not jeopardize this, but when it came time to allocate resources, women's interests were increasingly shortchanged.

In summary, in 1924 DVP rhetoric to and about women admitted the continued existence of a "woman question," as revealed by its brief mention of some of the barriers women still faced in public life. Yet, as the party's main women's pamphlet stated, such questions must be put on hold at a time when "all forces must be mobilized for the great [work of the] whole."[84] Besides betraying a reluctance to view women's issues as different in quality from class or occupational issues, these words betray the persistent sense of crisis perceived by the DVP and its middle-class target audience. As in the republic's first years, this crisis was both national and moral, now exacerbated by an inflation that had subverted any sense of security the bourgeoisie might still have possessed. DVP women's appeals in 1924 kept alive this aura of crisis, which both justified women's continued political engagement and mandated that "women's issues" be subordinated to the higher national agendas of revitalizing bourgeois economic and political power, restoring moral order, and repressing socialism.

The Center Party had been a constant member of ruling coalitions since 1919, producing two chancellors, including the incumbent, Wilhelm Marx. Thus, like the SPD, DDP, and DVP, it carried into the 1924 campaigns the burden of association with the Weimar system. It tried to compensate by limiting discussion of the economy to its fight against the emergency decree's excesses and its role in the currency stabilization, deemed necessary to save "order" and "the nation." It also argued that Germany's problems could only be solved through international cooperation, which allowed it to depict the hawkish DNVP and Völkisch Bloc as the main obstacles to recovery. The strategy yielded modest results, as the party maintained its standing at 13.4 percent of all votes cast.[85]

The main theme of 1924 Catholic Center campaigns was the party's role as middle road between the extremes of left and right. Framing its appeals in religious terms, the Center spoke the language of *Volksgemeinschaft*, like the liberals, but avoided the rhetoric of class conflict. In 1924 it criticized its opponents for spreading hate and splintering the nation. At its October conference, the Center, which saw itself as a people's party, dubbed itself the "mirror of the *Volksgemeinschaft*," the only group with a harmonizing ideology and willingness to see through unpopular but necessary measures. Discontent surfaced, however, as critics from its working-class wing argued that cultural values did not a socioeconomic policy make. It also faced flagging support from local clergy who disapproved of its coalitions with the SPD and DDP. Party leaders clung to the gospel of centrism, but they knew that, at a time of political splintering, holding together a motley collection of Catholic democrats, workers, conservatives, women, and even *völkisch* sympathizers would be no easy task.[86] In December, after the extremist victories of May, the Center staked its claim to the unifying middle even more strongly, urging voters to accept sober politics, not extremist illusions. It blasted the Communists as agents of class war and criticized the Conservatives for their elitism and coziness with the Völkisch Bloc—a victory of any of these, it argued, meant anarchy at home and weakness abroad. While the Center was on the defensive, its constituency did not collapse (unlike the liberals'). Aided by steady economic recovery, it was able to retain, if not expand, its base, winning 13.6 percent of the December vote.

Center appeals had always pledged defense of the family and religion, particularly in materials for women; 1924 was no exception. That year, two issues remained constant in women's appeals: the war against political splintering and extremism and a commitment to the "women's issues" of family, motherhood, education, and social welfare. The Center had long viewed the family as the basic unit of the state and seat of female power. It pledged to win more respect for women's role in the family and block the assault on Christian values. It had at last incorporated the message of the Christian women's movement, which stressed not gender equality but protecting the women's sphere, particularly as women's "natural" sense of duty and sacrifice was closest to Catholic values.[87]

The Center treated 1924's number one topic, the economy, in either vague or melodramatic terms. Women's propaganda referred to the inflation a "scourge of need" (*Peitsche der Not*) and a "sea of tears," as women struggled to procure the "little things" the family needed.[88] The inflation itself was never directly named, only the litany of suffering that accompanied it: unemployed husbands, worthless pensions, and so on. The Center preferred to couch economic recovery in social terms in both 1924 campaigns. Like the liberals, it argued that radicalism heightened international tension, which could revive inflation.[89] Just as the Center was the party of social mediation in the public sphere, women could be agents of social peace by easing suffering and defusing political tension in private.[90] Female activists predicted this message would make an impression—as

Fräulein Gosewinkel argued at the 1922 convention, talk to women about social harmony first and they will eventually understand the economy.[91]

Social harmony was one current in the larger stream of culture. Convinced that this was the main women's issue, the Center put its mission to defend Christian culture at the heart of every women's appeal in 1924, with the ongoing fight for catechism in schools at the top of the agenda. Other recurrent cultural issues were the campaigns against smut, alcoholism, and divorce reform.[92] Abortion also received frequent mention, more so than in liberal propaganda. *Germania* warned of an "ominous" softening of legal and public opinion on this issue, predicting a pending assault on Catholic social and cultural policy views as economic recovery allowed legislators to turn to other matters.[93] Reviving turn-of-the-century images of the *Zentrumsturm*, or fortress Center, a new siege mentality marked 1924 agitation directed at the party's new pillar of strength, female voters, who had to be mobilized for this fight.

The Center described this battle as a new *Kulturkampf*, which in 1924 seemed to come from all sides. Where women's propaganda in 1919–20 portrayed the SPD as the chief enemy of culture and religion, a 1924 Berlin flyer warned of the "Liberal-Red front."[94] Materials from 1924 presented an even graver threat from the Conservative and *völkisch* side. The right wing was considered more dangerous because its appeals to past national glory played on women's emotions. Women were warned in both elections that if they backed the Right, they supported the possibility of a new war. One flyer urged them to listen to their war dead; *Germania* urged them to reject militarist adventures. Women, "the givers and preservers of life," must reject male squabbling and unite against extremism. Not only instinct but common sense told them that the middle would lead to continued economic, social, and spiritual recovery. Women must show the same maturity they had in 1919 and support the Center.[95]

Rhetoric on female labor also meshed with the party's view of culture as a women's issue. Just as women guarded culture and morality, their economic activity had to accommodate the Catholic community and its notions of domesticity. Materials invariably depicted families in which husbands earned the bread while wives managed the *Kleinarbeit* of consumption, housework, and child care. Both men and women in the party had largely come to accept women's work outside the home if need demanded, but propaganda's tone remained more in line with the fourth of *Germania*'s "ten commandments" for wives: "If you wish to be queen of your home, don't spend your days outside its walls."[96]

Certain forms of women's work such as social welfare were condoned for bringing "motherliness" to the public sphere. Marie Timpe in *Germania* depicted higher education in similar terms. Study could enhance Catholic influence in female careers, particularly medicine and public health, which needed Catholic women to stem the rising tide of neo-Malthusianism. It could also benefit marriage, which still best corresponded to female nature. In other words, women's work and education could be seen as additional tools in the battle for Christian values.[97]

But the Center's commitment to female economic equality in principle was weak in 1924. Education "for its own sake," for example, produced the "he-she" (*Mannweib*), alienated from her own sex. Materials usually portrayed women as wives of workers or part of a family enterprise, demanding equal rights for those who worked to support others. For example, the December election handbook urged the government to close the gender gap in unemployment payments to women with dependents (implying that women without dependents had no such claim to equal treatment). Propaganda was, however, practically silent on the civil service retrenchment decree. The issue only surfaced in *Germania*, where Julie Ermler described it as the unavoidable sacrifice of a few for the many. While noting that it hit women unfairly, she saw teachers as the only irreplaceable female civil servants because of their role in girls' education. The party apparently did not consider the PAV's impact on female civil servants worth mentioning in its entry on the subject in the 1924 handbook; in 1925 it voted for retention of its articles pertaining to women when the rest of the decree was scrapped.[98] The PAV's absence from women's propaganda was no cover-up—indeed, the Center made no secret of its hostility to women's work outside the home. Rather, it considered the issue relatively unimportant compared to women's cultural role and consistent with their "natural" sense of sacrifice.[99]

But the Center may have overestimated party women's capacity for sacrifice, if rising dissent among female activists is any indication. During 1921 Christine Teusch (one of the party's few female Reichstag delegates) and others critical of the party's lack of continuous recruitment among women drew up plans for a separate organization to coordinate propaganda and education and to represent women's issues to the party at large.[100] Debated at the 1922 conference, the proposal unleashed heated debate over women's role in the party. Some men questioned the need for a women's organization and argued that a separate women's conference would be unfair to men. Frau Hessberger retorted that they were being uncooperative, and she questioned those who allowed special meetings for youths (assiduously courted during the 1920s) but felt threatened by similar activities for women. Women had different interests and natures, she said, and the party must do more to win them or risk losing them to apathy; ironically, Hessberger made her plea to empty benches.[101] Hedwig Dransfeld, who as KFD president had years of experience mollifying male skeptics, reassured them that the organization would exist as a Christian (not "humanist") environment in which to educate women in ways consistent with their "psyche." It would fortify party unity, not splinter it.[102] Ultimately the resolution passed, and that year saw the formation of new Center women's groups nationwide.

Voting statistics indicated falling female turnout across the board since 1919, a trend Center women viewed with alarm, especially as their party was so dependent on the female vote. In 1924 they warned that the increasingly violent character of campaigns would offend women, hardening their "silent bravery" in the National Assembly election into "cold pessimism." "Campaign screaming" had invaded even the family dinner table.[103] While these women blamed apathy on women's "universal desire" to heal psychological and economic wounds that campaigns reopened, they also attributed it to women's frustration with their lack of political influence. This also explained, in their view, the renewed call for a *Frauenpartei*.[104] Center women stressed the need for more female candidates to counteract such feelings of impotence. Dransfeld noted that a party rule, reaffirmed in January 1924, that a woman be given a safe ballot position in districts with at least five secure mandates was ignored,[105] while various occupations and *Stände* had safe spots and even pushed for more. Women argued that this not only violated the ethos of *Volksgemein- schaft* but also would hurt the Center in the Reichstag's coming assault on Christian values. Other parties knew their women would be especially valuable in this fight—for the Center to have no female representatives would be an embarrassment.[106]

As in 1919–20, female activists were the only ones writing about how to mobilize women in 1924. They continued to seek ways to express politically their ideal of femininity. Dransfeld, for example, called on women to establish new "political customs," starting with damming the flood of propaganda at election time. Ironically, the party's output of literature for women did in fact shrink drastically in 1924. While at least eighteen flyers were produced in January 1919 alone, only two national flyers specifically for women were found for all of 1924. Furthermore, the lion's share of material for women was published by the Catholic press, casting doubt on the Center's stated intention to expand its appeal beyond the Catholic milieu, at least regarding women. The KFD, which had produced so much literature earlier, was missing in action in 1924, its function ostensibly replaced by the new women's committee. While the establishment of this body would seem to indicate a commitment to mobilizing women, we have seen how it met with skepticism and resistance. The Center's organizational journal reflects this: after regular reporting on the women's group in 1922, in 1923 its section of the paper—which doubled as its official organ—was cut and the space given over to youth issues. That the December 1924 election handbook had a chapter on winning youth but none on women confirms the Center's growing tendency to take female voters for granted.

The Center presented 1924's drive for stability as the fight to restore a cultural climate in which women's nature and special roles found respect, where Christian family values would purge society's "sick love of self" (*gekränkte Eigenliebe*).[107] Women's rights were implicitly part of this "egoism," as the Center defined women strictly in relation to God and family.[108] Its rhetoric made woman the symbol of a pragmatic, harmonizing middle in public and private, just as the party staked out the political middle. Yet any attention to winning female voters had weakened; the party at large remained firm in its belief that Catholic women would follow their confessional identity and vote Center. At a time when it had bigger fish to fry, wooing a doggedly faithful constituency seemed less urgent.

The SPD, the fourth party linked with the Weimar system, in 1924 faced opposition on all sides. At its 1921 conference it set out to fashion a new image as a reformist people's party capable of uniting all working Germans under the banner of a democratic welfare state, a strategy carried into 1924. Campaigns stressed an agenda of expanded social services and housing, restoration of the eight-hour day, and a redistribution of the tax burden away from the working and middle classes—in short, systematic legislation to advance working people's interests over those of the *Bürgerblock*. In foreign policy, like the other Weimar coalition parties it favored cooperation with the Allies to win a revision of the Versailles treaty. These goals were threatened by both the Right, whose words and deeds imperiled the republic, and the Communists, whose divisiveness the SPD contrasted with its own constructive pragmatism.

These themes also marked propaganda to women, though the SPD changed tactics in this area over the course of 1924. In May it used its press, flyers, and rallies as before to convince women that it would work to expand the welfare state as the economy recovered. It depicted the inflation as a capitalist game that had victimized all working people and demanded legal code reform and a new population policy. This, set within the SPD's overall agenda, failed to mollify voters angry at the system; many working-class men that May swung to the KPD, while women went with the Center or the Conservatives or did not vote at all.[109]

Since 1919 the SPD had fretted over its inability to attract women, especially those of the working class. As a remedy, the June 1924 women's conference approved new tactics to win the "politically indifferent woman," who had abandoned politics after the heady first days of female suffrage. Central to the strategy was a new women's magazine, *Frauenwelt*, modeled on popular bourgeois women's publications. Edited by a man, it was designed as a sugar pill to subtly impart Socialist messages in items on fashion, home, and child care. Another change was a new type of assembly that mixed entertainment with political speeches. The goal was less to proselytize than to create positive associations with the party name in women's minds — a kind of brand-name marketing designed to make women more receptive to follow-up propaganda.[110] Thus, in December the SPD campaigned with the same basic themes for women as in May. But its new tactics, increased attention to welfare and maternity issues, and a more moderate tone combined with the economic recovery to help the SPD start recouping female support.

Inflation was a prominent theme in SPD campaigns to both sexes in 1924. The party blamed the catastrophe on the Right's war economy and big capital, which engineered the inflation for its own profit. Campaign imagery juxtaposed fat profiteers with gaunt widows and housewives. While luxury did appear in the person of the bread or rent usurer (*Wucherer*, a popular term with anti-Semitic undertones),[111] the SPD more commonly depicted both poverty and luxury as a woman. A general flyer for May juxtaposed dancing couples with an emaciated woman: "Here flows champagne, there tears." Appeals for women routinely portrayed them as the martyrs of inflation, asking, "How can you vote the same as women who sleep late and dress well?" While the SPD tried to evoke unity among a broadly conceived class of the cheated by presenting the inflation as an issue of social justice, it undermined gender solidarity by encouraging women to relate to the victimized woman rather than the one who embodied the parasitical classes.[112]

The SPD also linked inflation to foreign policy in both general and female-directed flyers. Like the DDP, it equated "radicals" who opposed Stresemann's fulfillment policy (the DNVP and KPD) with war and renewed inflation. Women's flyers used female tasks and roles to convey this message. One published "official recipes for turnip dishes," cleverly associating *völkisch* saber rattling with the wartime starvation winter of 1916–17. Appealing to housewives' and mothers' desire for stability, the SPD portrayed itself as the party of international peace and reconciliation. As Clara Bohm-Schuch put it, the SPD had to appeal to women's "life feelings" to draw them into politics and defeat male war lust.[113]

SPD critiques of the Right stressed not only the risks of revanchism but also its irrationality, irresponsibility, and misogyny. Materials replayed earlier themes that charged the DNVP with still wishing to end female suffrage and lying about religion and school policy to scare women from the SPD.[114] The SPD told women that the DNVP and DVP would dismantle welfare programs and end female civil servants' right to work, while their tariffs to aid big landowners took bread from children's mouths. These parties treated women like *Stimmvieh*, herding them to the polls to "save the fatherland" then back to the hearth afterward.[115] The Völkisch Bloc was another foe of women's rights, though SPD propaganda in 1924 portrayed the "swastikas" as more ludicrous than sinister.[116] Asking women, "Have you forgotten how it used to be?," a mass of materials urged them to "prove that five years of political equality have made you free" by rejecting the Right.[117]

General propaganda branded the Communists as collaborators with the DNVP and Nazis in a destructive vendetta against social democracy.[118] This discursive warfare had a gendered dimension, as the SPD used KPD women to symbolize the Communists' alleged lack of respect for the working class. Ruth Fischer, leader of the KPD's left wing, was targeted in both 1924 campaigns. One flyer related a speech in which Fischer called the use of Rosa Luxemburg's ideas to cure party deviation akin to curing gonorrhea with a dose of syphilis. The SPD piece screamed that Fischer's remarks were an insult surpassing the vilest anti-Semitic slander, and it urged men and women to honor Luxemburg's memory by voting SPD (a tortured bit of logic in its own right). Other flyers invoked a scene in which Fischer and other KPD deputies entered the Reichstag blowing toy trumpets to express their view that the parliamentary process was a farce. One claimed that Fischer took politics as seriously as she took marriage — she was on her third husband. Another juxtaposed a cartoon of the trumpet incident with the now clichéd image of a haggard woman and child, stating, "This 'concerted' parliamentary work of KPD delegates will not ease the distress of voters."[119] Another flyer used a photograph of Russian women's leader Alexandra Kollontai dressed in silken finery to attack the hypocrisy of KPD complaints over SPD politicians' wages. The piece stated that it was not out to defame any one person (it also listed the salaries of Zinoviev and Radek), yet its use of Kollontai — a woman notorious for promoting free love — combined with the innuendo over Fischer's three marriages, can be seen as part of the SPD's attempt to associate itself with sobriety, family, and honesty, as opposed to Communist indulgence, immorality, and duplicity. Here, negative female models were used to affirm class solidarity — these women had forfeited the right to represent the working class, as did the party they represented.[120]

As in 1919–20, the SPD portrayed itself as the longest-standing champion of female equality (though the only 1924 piece to invoke Bebel made no mention of his work for women).[121] Publications spotlighted delegates' work on issues such as women's admission to the judiciary, as well as emphasizing attempts to reform marriage property law and secure equal educational opportunities for both sexes.[122] The SPD also stressed its defense of women's right to work and better working conditions. It addressed many types of working women, particularly during its October recruiting week, as part of a broad effort to convince workers of both sexes that their interests could not be represented by the parties of management and capital.[123] Besides the customary appeals to factory women, the SPD addressed female white-collar workers, whose increasingly proletarianized jobs made them no better off than industrial workers, and *Beamtinnen*, to whom it reiterated its commitment to their right to work. There were also appeals to farm women, encouraging them to see their common bond with urban women and to reject the politics of big landowners. Finally, as part of a strategy to reach more isolated women, the SPD directed material at domestic servants, home workers, and housewives. Servants, while now equal in the eyes of the law (the SPD reminded them), were still prey to economic and sexual exploitation. Home workers suffered the lowest wages and poor health, which would only worsen if women's right to work was curtailed. Housewives, too, were not outside the class struggle because their work depended on whether their husbands had jobs. Alone, these women's lives would never improve, but, the SPD declared, closing ranks with all workers in the Social Democratic movement would bring economic justice and the sunshine of freedom.[124]

While the SPD repeatedly argued that women's right to work must be protected, its portrayal of their work was uniformly negative. Articles and campaign appeals, usually written by women, depicted women "whipped" into work without consideration of their "female characteristics." Even "clean" office jobs subjected women to lecherous bosses.[125] Marriage no longer offered a respite, as the double burden of wage labor and housework made the ideal of home a myth. While Margit Freund in *Vorwärts* suggested that men help out more at home like their American counterparts,[126] the party line stressed shorter work hours as the best way to help women "fulfill all their tasks." The SPD addressed women as workers and urged them to see all the types of work they did as productive labor. Yet it was the man whom propaganda routinely depicted as the "provider," his identity rooted in his work. Woman's identity was still based on her domestic duties, as seen in the way she was the target audience for flyers on food prices or housework. Contradicting socialist theory of women's emancipation, SPD propaganda buttressed the notion that, at least in the short term, work would do anything but set women free.[127]

The "happiness of motherhood" (*Mutterglück*) was still portrayed by both male and female Socialists as women's greatest fulfillment. This dream was dashed as couples could not find apartments or afford to marry, when happy homes were undermined by high prices, long work hours, and welfare cutbacks. The SPD pledged to improve the working woman's life through a combination of equal rights, welfare for mothers, better housing, secular and equal schooling for boys and girls, and a general "uplifting of the family." This was how SPD women's literature addressed "culture" in 1924. Unlike in 1919–20, when it attacked Center "lies" about its position on religion and schools, in 1924 the SPD attacked political Christianity as part of the "bourgeois morality" that permitted capitalist exploitation and an ill-conceived population policy to ruin working families. Materials argued that true morality consisted in protecting women's right to become mothers when they wanted, in an atmosphere where their children could lead happy lives. While this stance was pronatalist and essentialist, it was also, as Cornelie Usborne argues, progressive because it placed women and their right to control reproduction at its core.[128]

This philosophy also informed SPD treatment of abortion. This period set the terms of a debate that culminated in the 1931 mass rallies for legal abortion. The SPD press was instrumental in this process, using incidents such as the trial of the chemist Heiser, who performed the procedure on over 400 poor women, to denounce a capitalist order that drove women to abort.[129] One particularly incendiary women's page article accused Christian natalists of trying to reenslave women to *Kinder, Kirche,* and *Küche.*[130] Bourgeois women were no allies either—they either sanctimoniously disapproved of abortion or hired a doctor to remove any "problem" that threatened their pleasure. This same hypocrisy obstructed recognition of equal rights for unwed mothers and their children; as Heddy Crüger put it, sex outside marriage could be more moral than within.[131]

Such defiant language was limited mainly to the women's page of the party press (in articles appearing after the elections), although campaign materials did mention legal first trimester abortion as part of a desperately needed "rational" population policy. Such policy would combat venereal disease through sex education, ease access to contraception to prevent abortion, augment *Mutterschutz*, which the SPD told women was *its* work, and end female commodification through prostitution. The SPD proclaimed its goal to be the creation of a new morality.[132] As one appeal argued, women's economic liberation went hand in hand with moral liberation.[133] Just as the Center aimed to rally women by predicting a "culture war" against its ideology, so the SPD tried to mobilize them for its own cultural crusade.

While Communists criticized SPD reproductive politics as timid, the fact that a mass party addressed them at all is remarkable.[134] Yet, with one exception, it was SPD women who raised the issue, while men were indifferent, divided, or downright hostile.[135] This was consistent with Weimar parties' larger tendency to relegate "women's issues" to female activists. In the SPD this division of labor meant, for example, that women had their own conference, but "women's issues" were largely absent from the general meeting. Friction between party men and women, already visible in 1919, rose throughout the early 1920s. SPD men repeatedly blamed women voters for thwarting an SPD majority, a line female activists internalized as well. While some blamed an earlier lack of agitation among the mass of working women, materials tended to ascribe women's "incorrect" behavior to a tendency to view politics as "men's work" and to ignore the link between politics and the home.[136]

The SPD worried particularly about the apparent effectiveness of conservative and religious attacks; in May it responded as before by chiding women for backing parties portrayed as hostile to their rights. After June, however, tacticians began to imitate these same parties, assuming, as Helene Meinig argued at the 1924 women's conference, that they won women because they targeted their feelings. Thus, the new SPD women's periodical, for example, abandoned a style of polemic that Marie Juchasz said went over most women's heads. *Frauenwelt* aimed to win back proletarian women who read mainstream fashion magazines by meeting their desire for escapism within a socialist framework — as editor Richard Lohmann said, women wanted to forget their misery, not read about it.[137] Winning women was essential to the SPD's goal of becoming a mass people's party. Thus, women's propaganda had to convince them that the SPD was their true ally and that their participation was vital to a welfare and peace agenda in which all women had an interest.

Based on its number of materials and rallies during 1924, the SPD could not be accused of neglecting women.[138] When it came to female candidates, however, female activists saw much to be desired. The SPD instituted quotas in 1924 to guarantee women a percentage of parliamentary and party positions, but these were not met in practice.[139] Bohm-Schuch protested the use of women's names on election lists merely as bait for female voters.[140] The Württemburg delegation to the 1924 women's conference moved a formal protest that women's representation in the party was not commensurate with the number of female voters. This was defeated in favor of a milder resolution, sponsored by the Juchasz wing, that expressed "regret" that women had not been taken more into consideration in candidate selection and urged women to create conditions to facilitate more women's entry into Parliament. In other words, they blamed themselves for their lack of representation and the SPD's loss of female votes. Sophie Christmann stated that women's lack of solidarity and education explained their lack of power, while Marie Juchasz urged women to exercise humor and self-criticism before blaming men for their problems.[141] Campaign appeals reflected this, warning women that if they remained passive, they would have only themselves to blame if *Mutterschutz* and suffrage were dismantled.[142]

Despite this capitulation, there was some pronounced criticism of patriarchal attitudes at the women's conference. Frau Hörrath-Menge argued that the party's silence on the PAV proved that the equal rights the SPD loved to take credit for existed only on paper. SPD women agreed that "incorrect" female voting was the fruit of centuries of exclusion from politics,[143] while Elisabeth Thümmel in 1924 demanded an end to blanket condemnations of female voting behavior, pointing out that in some regions women exhibited more loyalty to the SPD than men. These critics, who were usually from the SPD's left wing and often former USPD members, also criticized *Frauenwelt*'s lack of socialist content and questioned the emancipatory potential of women's relegation to the narrow field of social work.[144] While this group was a minority in 1924, its views would gain currency throughout the 1920s and convert even Juchasz to a tougher approach to women's relations with the party.

SPD campaign propaganda to women in 1924 reflected both a residual sense of crisis from the inflation and the desire for stability exhibited by other parties. Like the other Weimar coalition parties, it warned voters of the dangers of extremism; it invoked women's domestic roles and pacifist "predisposition" as weapons against radicalism. It went to great lengths to present itself to women as constructive and pragmatic, both by what it said (contrasting its work with KPD "shenanigans") and what it did not say (it dropped its scathing critique of political Christianity). Even its discussion of abortion and birth control was couched in terms of strengthening morality and families.[145] KPD polemics also made the SPD look comparatively tame, which likely helped elevate the Social Democrats' standing among working-class women. The combination of economic recovery and new recruiting tactics began to pay off in a slowly rising female vote and increasing female party membership that would continue into 1933.

Turning to the opposition parties that scored such impressive gains in May 1924, we will first examine the Communists (KPD), whose position as the second major party vying for the working-class vote made much of its rhetoric a debate with the SPD. By 1924 the KPD had graduated to mass party status; a brief look at its origins and past tactics will help put the party's 1924 campaigns to women in context.

The KPD was established on 30 December 1918 as a union of forces on the far left. From the start it had close ties to Moscow, with the endless doctrinal disputes such a link entailed. Despite the amount of noise and fury it unleashed in early 1919, the KPD, banned and broke, had little influence in its first years; the USPD was the political home of the radical working class at this point.

Its fundamental rejection of parliamentarism drove the KPD to boycott the 1919 National Assembly election. This, however, did not preclude the production of propaganda—in fact, the KPD became the only party to organize issue-oriented campaigns and extraparliamentary activity in the fallow periods between elections (a strategy the Nazis would later copy). For women, in 1919 it produced materials for a relatively differentiated group of female workers — factory workers, housewives, agricultural workers, and shop clerks.[146] Yet its ideological imperative to draw women into the revolutionary proletariat was in practice a low priority for a party still getting on its feet.

The year 1920 saw the first systematic discussion of how to win women for the party. The first women's conference that February established a women's secretariat (FRS) to direct agitation. This was not, however, a separate women's organization, as in the case of the SPD or bourgeois parties, but was to be tightly connected to the KPD as a whole, in line with the tenet that women's liberation could only occur within the framework of the liberation of the proletariat. There was, however, recognition that the different conditions of women's lives and their separation from the industrial settings where most KPD agitation occurred mandated a different kind of propaganda. Hertha Sturm elaborated on how this might look. Women, she argued, were cut off from political life by the triple burden of wage labor, housework, and reproduction. This made them prone to reformism and short-term thinking. Thus, KPD propaganda had to show that their lives would only improve in a fundamental, lasting way with the end of capitalism. Women had to recognize their class position and become fighters for the proletarian revolution. Raising awareness, however, was not enough — they had to be brought into strikes and demonstrations to anchor this sense of class solidarity. Agitation had to be tailored to women's "primitive" way of thinking, avoiding theory in favor of concrete issues such as high prices, poor housing, motherhood, children's education, and health. Sturm urged party comrades to see these not as women's issues but as concerns of the entire proletariat. It was only because women still bore the effects of them that they had to be treated as "women's issues" — in fact, women must be shown how a socialist society would make these communal concerns.[147]

The KPD tested this model when the now legal party participated in the June 1920 Reichstag elections. Its flyers addressed several types of working women to show how their sufferings stemmed from capitalism. This campaign also saw the advent of the "doom and gloom" motifs that would mark KPD materials throughout the Weimar era. Flyers for women tried to convince them that their lives had only gotten worse, to prove that parliamentarism and reformism offered only quick fixes.[148] This motif of suffering could create ideological confusion, as in one poster that contradicted the socialist theory that women's work outside the home was a precondition for emancipation: "What is the worker's lot? He works day in and day out, creating wealth upon wealth, while his wife and children starve. . . . He works, while do-nothings live in palaces. He toiled in the trenches while war profiteers caroused. He was at the front, while his wife was driven into the factory."[149] Such language was typical of the KPD's tendency to portray women as victims, unlike men, who were depicted as active proletarian warriors.[150] From the start there was skepticism that women would ever become revolutionary, reflected in their propaganda's scolding tone. One 1919 speaker barely disguised his hostility to women, whom he called the "dupes of priests." A 1920 flyer urged women to quit complaining and stuffing their heads with the lies of the bourgeois press. Even Hertha Sturm believed few women would become revolutionary—the best to be hoped for was benevolent neutrality.[151]

Throughout 1921–22 the thrust of KPD women's agitation remained much the same. Propaganda demanded better wages for women, with the ultimate goals of equal pay for equal work; a shorter work day; protective legislation and maternity care; higher unemployment payments; and women's right to work.[152] In 1922 the party also began a campaign against paragraph 218, which criminalized abortion.[153] Guidelines from late 1921 issued a call to draw housewives into the fight against the inflation and profiteers. This strategy, combined with the continuing campaign to win factory women, would start to pay off as a deteriorating economy sparked female interest in the KPD message. These newcomers had little knowledge of politics, but the FRS believed it could win them over, given the necessary support. The party, however, did little to nurture this nascent trend, instead devoting itself to agitation in factories. FRS memos repeatedly complained of a lack of materials for interested women and attacked the party daily, *Rote Fahne*, for not running its articles. Every party conference invoked the need for more women's propaganda, yet the items women produced were not being distributed or even published.[154] As Eric Weitz argues, the KPD "could envision the contours of a new society out of strikes, but not out of crowds of women at the marketplace forcing merchants to reduce their prices."[155]

Following an aborted national uprising in October 1923, the KPD was banned as part of emergency rule designed to stabilize the economy and subdue radical movements. Illegality precipitated a process of "Bolshevi-zation," in which the KPD restructured itself on the Moscow model. This also entailed a sharp turn to the left, a ruthless fight against reformism, and strict focus on radicalizing the industrial proletariat through factory cells (despite the fact that unemployment and state/employer strategies were ejecting radicals from the workplace). It would prove fatal as far as winning women, for by concentrating on the factory and failing to estab-lish a viable housewives' organization, the KPD squandered the potential of women politicized by the inflation.[156]

The KPD ban was lifted on 1 March 1924, in time for the party to par-ticipate in the May election. Yet illegality and the organizational shakeup had left it in disarray, as reflected in the small number of flyers pro-duced. Materials that did appear painted an apocalyptic vision in which the coming Reichstag would be the last, with the forces of revolution vying with the fascists for control. A May women's flyer told factory women, housewives, and widows that the Reichstag was merely a tool of big capital. It spun an unrelenting tale of misery, in which the "American-ization" (i.e., rationalization) of factories mandated survival of the fittest, women's health and freedom be damned. Speaking to a common experi-ence of proletarian women, propaganda depicted scenes of impoverished women reduced to seeking alms from "reactionary" bourgeois women welfare agents.[157] Similarly, a general flyer to *Beamte* argued that disregard of the rights of female civil servants had reduced them to beggars.[158] Like the SPD, the KPD claimed, with much justification, that women had suf-fered the most during inflation. Yet in stark contrast to the SPD's agenda of reformism, the KPD urged women simply to seize the provisions they needed. Its relentless rhetoric of suffering aimed to drive women to the brink so they would stop waiting for a better life to be given to them and rise up to take it themselves.

While it was acceptable to awaken women by invoking personal suf-fering, women must act for the sake of the larger proletarian crusade. The KPD push for legal abortion, for example, was not simply about a woman's right to control her own body but a fight against capital and its need for cannon fodder and cheap labor.[159] A *Rote Fahne* cartoon from May 1924 reiterates this. It depicts a group of proletarians being sentenced by a judge—the men for robbery, murder, and breach of the peace, the women for prostitution and abortion. The women's crimes are sexual and specifically female, yet placing them beside the men makes all appear victims of class justice.[160] Unfortunately, women still did not see their lot in class terms, according to KPD literature. "Proletarische Frauen!" stated, "We'd be traitors to our husbands, families, and our class if we let the slaughter of the working class continue unopposed," implying that was exactly what women were doing. *Rote Fahne*'s feature page on Women's Day negatively contrasted "obedient" German women with those of Saint Petersburg, whose 1917 demonstrations precipitated the Russian revolution. Other articles lamented the lack of solidarity among working-class women, noting, for example, a case in which an SPD woman had abortion protesters ejected from the Reichstag. Another expressed shame at housewives who attacked women with jobs and demanded their removal from factories—such behavior weakened the anticapitalist front.[161]

The KPD polled well enough in May 1924 to become the fourth largest party, though its success did not come from women voters.[162] Not only did its radical image repel most women, but its focus on factory cell agitation bypassed housewives whose experience of inflation might otherwise have made them receptive to the KPD message. The party's complete misreading of the situation becomes clear in a March 1924 *Parteiarbeiter* article on how to win women. The KPD's task was to breed revolution by mobilizing the industrial proletariat; because over one-third of all workers were female, revolution could not happen without them. Thus, the top priority of women's agitation was to win supporters in every factory— despite the fact that over half of all female labor occurred in small shops, offices, farms, or homes. "Street cells" were to replace "unsystematic propaganda" among housewives, but few details about this emerged.[163]

Tension between the sexes also undermined agitation among women. *Parteiarbeiter* noted that most men who embraced the need to win women in theory did nothing in practice. The rank and file still resisted women's right to work and equal wages. A report from Dresden noted that KPD men still possessed the "petty bourgeois" opinion that women were comrades in the home but not in the coming battle to usher in socialism.[164]

Reports from the women's section leave no doubt that women were abandoned in the KPD's push to the far left. The FRS complained of no party or press support for International Women's Day. Leader Bertha Braunthal wrote that repeated requests for materials were ignored and the party central had sent no word on how to prepare for May's elections. *Rote Fahne* even failed to run a full women's page during the campaign, despite an abundance of material submitted by the FRS.[165] The issue of women candidates was another sore spot, as few women were given safe places on ballots and candidates nominated by the FRS were overlooked. The KPD's lack of female delegates at the local level was "further proof that our comrades believe women can simply be shut out of the tasks of making revolution and . . . administration."[166] Women warned that the SPD and bourgeois parties were more consistent about both propaganda and female candidate selection, which in fact was not necessarily true, and that the KPD was not doing enough to counter them.[167]

A letter in which Braunthal asked party matriarch Clara Zetkin to intervene on behalf of the FRS reveals the organization's desperate straits in early 1924. After listing her grievances, Braunthal wrote that she and the FRS would take no responsibility for a bad election result, as they had done their best with no support. She believed the FRS was being punished for not moving quickly enough to the left.[168] Yet, perhaps in an attempt to save her job, her subsequent report on FRS activities at the April party conference painted a positive picture, calling Women's Day a major success and praising female comrades' indispensable work to keep the party afloat during the ban. The party, in turn, confessed its sins of omission and pledged to make women's agitation a general concern.[169] But the efforts at amelioration ended quickly: in an 8 May letter to the party central, Braunthal threatened to air the KPD's neglect at the International Women's Conference in Moscow. This would prove to be her last salvo; the FRS was dissolved four days later and women's agitation put directly under Politburo control under the direction of Erna Halbe. Halbe was fully behind the antireformist factory cell tactics, which Zetkin went on to criticize in vain in Moscow.[170]

The KPD press in the period between elections in 1924 reflects both the party's Bolshevization and its focus on working women. It portrayed sentiment against "double earners"—working women who could in theory be supported by their husbands—codified in the PAV, as false consciousness detrimental to class solidarity. *Rote Fahne* discussed the conditions of women's work within the complex of the hated Dawes Plan, which was blamed for lower wages, retrenchment, and high female unemployment. It urged women to see themselves as workers first, even if unemployed.[171] Russia was repeatedly invoked as the model of a better society, where women earned equal wages for equal work and two months' fully paid maternity leave.[172] Other pieces linked bourgeois morality, prostitution, and abortion.[173] The official KPD press gave no quarter to the SPD over abortion, disputing *Vorwärts*'s account of the Heiser trial, even though its own reading of the incident as an indictment of the bourgeois order differed little from the SPD's.[174]

Despite the KPD's depictions of real hardships and its constant championing of female emancipation and economic equality, women resisted the party. A revealing report from the Reich Commissar for Public Order in August 1924 stated unequivocally that the KPD had almost no influence on working-class women, attributing this to female resistance to radicalism and the KPD's lack of local networks to conduct women's agitation. Its reference to KPD successes among housewives during the inflation implied that this type of victory was a phenomenon of the past.[175]

In the December 1924 campaign, the KPD tried to sustain a sense of crisis in both general appeals and propaganda to women. It focused on Dawes Plan "slavery," restoration of the eight-hour day, and persecution of Communists.[176] Materials continued to portray women's lives as endless misery caused by capitalism and SPD betrayal of the working class. *Rote Fahne* described proletarian women as slaves to the machine and the kitchen, their children mired in the dreck of living conditions that bred venereal disease and prostitution.[177] KPD propaganda's tendency to portray women and children as the main victims of capitalist society did not disappear with economic stabilization. On the contrary, the KPD felt its audience was mobilized most effectively by misery. It harped on this, as in an anti-DDP cartoon in *Rote Fahne* that juxtaposed a haggard proletarian woman and her children with the caption, "Hunger is abolished! Schacht's Rentenmark has banned all misery! Vote Democratic!"[178]

In KPD discourse, women's bodies were sites of misery: "Your body tells you that just as the slave's fate depends on the good will of the master, your fate depends on the profit of the factory-owning class."[179] Abortion appeared in the same terms, its defining female image the pregnant Kollwitzian mother who already has more children than she can feed. The KPD blamed proletarian physical decline squarely on capitalism: "Is a man who works ten hours a day in a monotonous job for a dog's wage guilty if his desperation drives him to drink and abandon his family? . . . Is a woman guilty if she lets her housework go to ruin? No—the slave driver who forces her to work for pennies an hour until deep in the night is!"[180] In KPD rhetoric, real problems had one solution: revolution. Little wonder that women, assumed responsible for maintaining family and home, rejected this model for parties that offered the more concrete relief of welfare or the comfort of religion.[181]

If women were signifiers of suffering, they could also represent luxury. While the SPD used women in 1924 to comment on the inflation (the Kollontai flyer is an exception), the KPD used them to represent the "face of the democratic republic."[182] The SPD, in this view, was a pillar of the capitalist order, allied with the bourgeoisie to oppress the working class. Women's literature in particular depicted the SPD's prowoman stance as a ruse. An ingenious *Rote Fahne* piece reproduced a page from the SPD women's press that wrapped the text of an election appeal around an ad for soap powder. Implicitly commenting on the blurring border between political and product advertising, the KPD likened consumer society's illusions to the illusion that voting SPD would improve women's lives: just as the "freedom" to choose among brands was no true choice, the "freedom" the SPD claimed it gave women was none at all. As the KPD argued, proletarian women wanted not simply the same piddling rights as men but real emancipation in an equal society.[183]

Women voters continued to resist the KPD in December, a trend only reinforced by economic recovery.[184] Internal postmortems once again criticized the lack of resources and attention to women's propaganda, while a women's section memo blamed organizational reshuffling, claiming party members did not know that women's agitation was now everyone's job.[185] Erna Halbe's report reveals some debate over whether or not the factory cell strategy worked with women, as several activists criticized the neglect of housewives and urged more linkage of women in factories with those outside. But Martha Arendsee dismissed fears of losing housewives as exaggerated, while Frau Lux argued that what the KPD lost elsewhere, it gained hundredfold with each committed factory woman. These women agreed that economic recovery had bred "illusions" among women, which the SPD capitalized on with its emotional appeals.[186] But the KPD also banked on women's emotions and tried to stir them up just like every other party; the outrage came when women did not respond "correctly."

KPD images of women mixed uneasily with the language of struggle: women were the bowed victims of the capitalist order who made do instead of fighting. When working-class women rejected the order to end their suffering through *Kampf* with the proletariat, the KPD contemptuously cited their "petty bourgeois" illusions, timidity, and religiosity. It failed to see that women's positions as mothers, wives, and consumers fed their desire for stability and safety for their families—goals threatened by the civil war the KPD preached. Just as the party's overheated rhetoric backfired with many male workers alienated by its refusal to countenance limited goals,[187] women who longed for some kind of normalcy could not be mobilized by a melodramatic language of crisis in 1924.

The extreme right of the political spectrum was staked out by the National Socialists. A fringe party with little national standing, the NSDAP was outlawed after Hitler's failed November 1923 coup. It participated in its first national election in May 1924, under the name National Socialist Freedom Party (NSFP; in Bavaria, the Völkisch Bloc). Despite the ban, the National Socialists were in fact riding high in early 1924. Hitler had used his treason trial that winter to mount a vigorous personal defense that transformed antirepublicanism into patriotic virtue. The trial was a publicity bonanza for the Nazis, the national press providing a solid month of free publicity. Now a known commodity, the NSFP capitalized on voter disgust with the republic to win a surprising 6.5 percent—just under 2 million votes—in May 1924, outscoring the DDP's 5.7 percent return. Yet these gains proved ephemeral, as internal disarray would combine with the return of relative stability to defang the party's antisystem invective, pruning its vote back to 3 percent in December.

National Socialist campaigns in 1924 dished up the crude stew of anti-Marxist, anti-Semitic, and anticapitalist rhetoric found in the NSDAP program, the Twenty-Five Points. Not limiting their address or recruiting to one class or religion, the Nazis hoped to profit from widespread discontent. They sold themselves as the purest incarnation of the antisystem force needed to end the dominance of "Jewish" capital, which allegedly controlled the liberal parties and cooked up the inflation for its own gain, and Marxist parties that sought to enslave the German worker to Soviet Russia. Not class struggle but a strong national *Volksgemeinschaft* would free Germany from such foreign and internal enemies.

Viewing politics as a purely male province, the National Socialists initially saw no urgency in winning women voters, nor did they ever allow a woman to represent them in the Reichstag. While the Twenty-Five Points demanded protection of mothers in the interest of the nation's health (*Volksgesundheit*), neither it nor the 1924 campaign guidelines said anything about propaganda for women. The party had no official women's organization; the few women who joined did so without special efforts to recruit them.[188] Yet while women were not a central focus of Nazi agitation and recruitment until 1931, there was some effort to speak to them even in 1924.

The National Socialists never wavered in their conviction that the sexes belonged in separate spheres. Not unlike conservatives and liberals, they saw domestic and reproductive tasks as women's true work, to be valued as such. They also admitted that necessity forced some women to join the labor force. One 1924 flyer even addressed itself to male and female civil servants, though the body of the text said nothing about women. Espousing a strict gender division of labor, the movement's goal was not to integrate women into the state as competitors of men but to foster their work in ways that were supplementary. For example, a 1920 article in the party organ, *Völkischer Beobachter*, said that while there was no reason to bar women from advanced study, it was foolish to create a strata of "half-educated" women when there was a shortage of domestic servants.[189]

The 1924 Nazi pocket calendar listed ten commandments for women, which delineated their roles in a "catechism of common sense." The ideal woman was faithful and pleasing to her mate without being coquettish. She loved her man for who he was, as nature demanded. She was honest, selfless, and unambitious, coveting only man's *Bildung*, wisdom, and honor. These commandments reflected a world in which women passively admired men's deeds without trying to imitate them. They rejected artifice in favor of a transparency of motive and action. A recruitment flyer for the Völkisch Defense and Offense League, a group in the NSDAP orbit in the early 1920s, similarly attacked modern art, novels, cinema, and theater for prostituting the female body and reducing love to a game. The breakdown of clearly defined roles signaled cultural degeneration, making the woman who sought power or money a demonic symbol of the dreaded egotism infecting German society.[190]

From the beginning, the NSDAP demanded a "return to spirituality and morality in sexual life," linking rampant capitalism with declining public morals. It used the language of "sexual Bolshevism" that was common currency on the far right, as seen in 1918–20's discourses on the nationalization of women and the "Black shame." One Völkisch Defense and Offense League flyer portrayed "our daughters" selling themselves to Jews (though the girls' white dresses and aloof expressions signify their still unsullied inner purity). Another league flyer from 1921 juxtaposed gluttonous Jews (two men and an obese woman) with a poor but noble "German" couple. The German woman covers her face in shame as a drunken Jew grabs her, while her husband can only look on helplessly. This use of women as emblems of both luxury and poverty is not unlike that of the KPD and SPD, though the message is radically different.[191]

Other radical right materials implicitly and explicitly blamed Jews for urban modernity and the "reigning machinery of art and culture" that debased women to unnatural "creatures of fashion." Jews preached free love but only with Christian girls. The modern world gave women equality, the League argued, but banished their dignity by reducing them to objects of lust. Women had to end this disgrace and save the *Volk* by summoning their "motherly spirit," a force more powerful than the strongest man.[192] Campaign materials from 1924 show the continuity of this language. A Völkisch Bloc flyer addressed women as the "protectors of the moral purity of our *Volk*": "You know how horribly deep morality has sunk in the November Republic under the influence of profiteer Jews who buy the pleasures of German girls with lucre squeezed from your men and brothers." Germans could not marry because their paltry wages were not enough to set up a household, even if they could find an apartment. An early Nazi poster summed up the notion that the Jews were engineering Germany's problems, depicting a sinister hook-nosed figure lurking behind the blonde visage of Germania, both poised above a coffin.[193]

The National Socialists, like all other parties, heeded voting figures suggesting that women responded to parties with a religious message. Their 1924 propaganda, while not directly addressed to women, noted charges that the movement opposed religion. A flyer from Bavaria, stronghold of political Catholicism, blasted religious parties' "misuse" of spirituality, especially the Center, which had sold out the Christian worldview for cooperation with the very Marxists who wished to abolish religion. It quoted Catholic clergy who accused Center politicians of being interested only in political power. The Center had helped parliamentarism into the saddle and endorsed a constitution more dangerous to Christianity than *völkisch* ideology had ever been. The Völkisch Bloc claimed its desire to keep religion out of politics was no call for a new *Kulturkampf* but the desire to preserve Christianity.[194]

While the National Socialist parties registered a surprising degree of success in the May 1924 elections, this did not come from female voters. Women were largely unresponsive to radical parties, including the Nazis. The few materials they produced for or about women in this period are more important as a point of comparison with those of other parties. The Nazis said nothing about women not already heard in conservative or even liberal circles, though their discourses on Jews and sexuality took a conservative message to its ugliest extremes. Like the SPD in 1919–20, the Nazi movement tried to convince women it had been misrepresented on religion, though by 1924 the SPD had replaced this with a message stressing a constructive social agenda, something the *völkisch* right had not done. Seen from the vantage point of later years, 1924 Nazi propaganda for women contained both seeds of future tactics—defaming the Center and Socialist parties, draping itself in the mantle of Christianity, rejecting female "emancipation"—and a crude style based on a rabid anti-Semitism the NSDAP would muffle in its quest to become a mass party.

The DNVP's dogmatic anti-Weimar stance and nonparticipation in government enabled it to garner the lion's share of the protest vote in 1924. As the largest *Sammelpartei* on the right, with 950,000 members in 1923, the DNVP from the start had been torn between its radical *völkisch* and more mainstream conservative wings. While it unequivocally favored extreme nationalism and anti-Semitism, its growing reputation as a haven for putschists and terrorists compelled it to draw a line against radical tactics at its 1922 conference. It entered the crisis year 1923 unified against reparations, the Rhine occupation, and what it saw as an illegitimate regime. It was able to capitalize on its position outside government in May 1924, becoming the second largest party.

In 1924 the DNVP hammered away at a central issue—the Dawes Plan, portrayed as a "second Versailles" designed to enslave Germany to foreign powers. The party, however, was rocked that August when nearly half its Reichstag delegates voted to ratify the plan, choosing economic realpolitik over ideological purity. The DNVP nearly split but managed to collect itself again to campaign that autumn for a Christian social monarchy free of Jewish and French dominance, socialist instigation, "parliamentary humbug," and international capitalism.[195] It did well in December, though gains by other parties diluted its strength.

The wealthy party produced a plethora of propaganda for a wide range of social and economic groups, from students to veterinarians. Women were also heavily targeted by the DNVP National Women's Committee, which furnished materials in both 1924 elections that assiduously cultivated female discontent with the regime that had presided over the financial ruin of the bourgeoisie. Yet economic issues were not the focus of women's appeals. Instead, they used a blend of xenophobic nationalism and Christian family values to convince female voters that the DNVP alone could restore German order and a well-defined, respected sphere for women.

Unlike appeals to craftsmen or artists,[196] only one women's flyer directly mentioned the inflation, making the ludicrous claim that the Rentenmark was the creation of DNVP finance expert Helfferich, not Schacht or Stresemann. Others mentioned taxes, tariffs (telling housewives that agricultural tariffs would stimulate the rural economy, benefiting the whole country), and the need for a "just" currency revaluation. Yet overall, the DNVP was relatively inattentive to these issues, betraying its belief that any deeper discussion of economics simply did not interest women.[197] The same was true of women's labor issues. Despite a range of flyers addressed to both white-collar and blue-collar female workers, specifics on concrete matters rarely appeared. For example, a flyer addressed to working-class women was actually about the threat to youth from smut-peddling capitalists (in an attempt to use the Left's language against itself) and socialist attacks on Christianity.[198] The DNVP was compromised by its close association with civil service elites and the German National Shop Clerks Association (*Deutschnationaler Handlungsgehilfen-Verband*, or DHV), which for years had adamantly opposed female white-collar work. Thus, general appeals to these occupational groups ignored women's specific problems.[199] Flyers for working women—written by women who themselves supported a gender division of labor—glossed over topics such as the PAV in favor of broad attacks on the Weimar system. This regime, they argued, promoted corruption over honest work and would permit the scandalous retention of unwed mothers in the civil service. Arguing that women's rights existed only on paper, the DNVP pledged to create an order that would protect their "well-earned rights," whose shape emerged in materials that promised to "justly" compensate women who quit their jobs upon marriage, and to "fairly value" women's nature and work.[200]

This attitude placed women in the domestic or social work spheres where their tasks could be invested with higher meaning. Nurses, for example, were called to heal a *Volk* sick from the quackery of socialism and pacifism. (In contrast, a flyer for doctors also invoked "moral and social diseases" afflicting the *Volkskörper*, but stressed occupational interests first.) Speaking to women in domestic settings, the DNVP vilified the SPD, complaining that since it had ruined the economy, only nouveaux riches and Jewish profiteers could afford servants. Echoing arguments of conservative housewives' associations, who were themselves battling proposed regulations on domestic labor,[201] DNVP propaganda condemned SPD attempts to impose an eight-hour day in this sphere as foreign to the "nature" of housework. To home workers the DNVP blasted the Left's ongoing effort to outlaw their work as a socialist plan to drive women away from their families and into factories. As chair of the *Heimarbeit-erinnen* organization Margarete Behm claimed, women wanted freedom in work (including freedom from having to work), not the dictatorship of international capital.[202]

Such comments fit in with the party's discourse on nationalism, which depicted a Germany besieged by foreign enemies, Jews, Socialists, and Democrats. This vision of a nation plagued by internal and external enemies also lay at the heart of materials for women. In them, the DNVP demanded an economic recovery plan under German leadership, not the internationally sponsored Dawes Plan that robbed the future of the nation's children. Just as socialism was trying to dethrone the German *Hausfrau*, international forces had debased the Germans until they were no longer lords of their own manor (*Herren im Hause*).[203]

According to this logic, the Versailles treaty, which permitted the Rhine occupation, was tantamount to national rape. The DNVP also continued to invoke the literal rapes reportedly perpetrated by French African troops on German women, even as these troops were being removed. Female activists were particularly obsessed with this theme, seeing themselves as guardians of the nation's moral strength, perceived in racial terms.[204] Only women's flyers mention Africans openly, castigating the "reds" for preaching international brotherhood even with the French and the "black devils." They argued that this "shame on the Rhine" was the shame of all German women and, unlike the Weimar parties that appealed to women as pacifists, urged women to "listen to their blood" and demand revenge.[205]

If this discourse about African soldiers was sexualized, the DNVP's persistent anti-Semitism generally was not. Jews appeared in flyers to every target group as an economic threat, a motif also employed in women's literature. Just as the April party conference pledged to fight Jewish influence at all levels of society, a flyer for rural women demanded a state without Jewish civil servants, politicians, and teachers. Russian Jewish immigrants, it argued, stole bread and housing from Germans. Another flyer implied that Jews had been comfortably making war profits at home while German men died at the front.[206]

The sexual component of DNVP anti-Semitism was veiled, for example, in its repeated linkage of Jews with internationalism of both the Marxist and capitalist variety. Surrender to international forces had emasculated Germany; what was needed was a national force that would preserve male honor in politics, as Karl Paumgarten put it in one particularly vicious anti-Semitic tract for workers.[207] Women were warned that the SPD and DDP, because they were saturated with Jewish influence, carried sterility and death. Another flyer linked democracy, Jews, and "soulless" female emancipation. In it, three "cheaters" hold cards that read "freedom," "equality," and "brotherhood"; a caricatured Jewish woman holds the "equality" card. Clearly, the DNVP posited that Jews were part of a plot to upset the organic unity of Germany's social, economic, and sexual order, leaving it prostrate before foreign enemies.[208]

The DNVP also played the anti-Semitic card in a half-hearted attempt to woo working-class audiences by discrediting their parties. It argued that all socialists were Jews who recognized no fatherland, illustrated by an image in which an SPD "hack" spits on a Germany depicted as an old woman in rags. Flyers for women also attacked the Left by reinforcing prevailing associations of Marxism with civil war and chaos. They mined women's predisposition to religion, arguing that the revolution had delivered the state to atheists.[209]

Tackling favorite themes of SPD literature, DNVP women's flyers tried to argue that the "corrupt" SPD had rejected every Conservative proposal to help workers. It built apartments for party bigwigs (*Bonzen*), but it claimed there was no money for the kind of single homes that would free youth from the poisonous environment of urban housing. The DNVP also argued that the SPD was not as prowoman as it claimed, having all but ignored them in its 1921 program. The DNVP touted its own program, in which the clauses on women were drafted by Evangelical women's leader Paula Müller-Otfried, as corresponding to the needs of true German womanhood.[210]

The DNVP also tried to discredit the liberal and Center parties for cooperating with the SPD. This unholy alliance, it told women, was responsible not only for German servitude to foreigners but also for godless schools that mocked Germany's glorious past and forced children into such unwholesome activities as naked gymnastics and singing the "Marseillaise." *Völkisch* parties were no alternative because they lacked clear goals and a firm religious commitment, rendering them useless in the assault against Christianity.[211]

The DNVP argued that only it was powerful enough to fight for German culture and religion. While this line also surfaced in appeals to teachers and "cultural" workers,[212] it was the heart of appeals to women, who embodied culture. These flyers underscored DNVP dedication to restoring religion in schools. To arrest moral decline, the party promised to defend marriage—the "summit of culture"—by thwarting any liberalization of divorce laws or recognition of the rights of illegitimate children. It denounced legal abortion as the first step to "nationalizing women" (that old specter from 1919). It blamed falling birth rates, urban blight, and economic chaos for the "degeneration" of the German "race" and pledged to protect the family from revolution and indiscipline. Finally, it would guard true femininity within the family, *Volk*, church, state, and political life, against soulless leveling (*Gleichmacherei*).[213]

As in 1918–20, discussion of DNVP women's relations with their party did not surface. The party's pronounced antifeminism, its near lack of female candidates,[214] and its tendency to confine female activists within the women's organization might lead one to expect some discontent, as in other parties. Yet if dissatisfaction existed, it did not emerge in surviving documents.[215] DNVP women rarely broke party discipline, despite the fact that after 1919, as Scheck argues, the DNVP treated women like workers— a social group they wanted to represent without having to make genuine concessions to it.[216] Unlike workers, however, many bourgeois women, especially Protestants, could see their demands and identity writ large in the party platform. Women activists, who tended to be particularly nationalistic, religious, and often racist, generally agreed with the party's sexual division of labor and their role as representatives of culture, religion, and morality.[217]

This same division of roles marked propaganda to female voters, which relied on emotion-laden appeals to religion and culture. Yet these themes pervaded not only women's flyers but also general appeals, suggesting an attempt to portray them as part of a holistic ideology, not unlike efforts by the Catholic Center. This gave women both a place within the larger party and a clearly defined role, rhetorically uniting them with peasants, workers, youths, and intellectuals in a national *Volksgemeinschaft*. In this way, the DNVP successfully appealed to the tradition-minded woman, who preferred this vision to the uncertain equality embodied by the New Woman.[218]

In 1924 the DNVP saturated voters with images of revolution, moral decay, and invading hordes (red and black) to evoke an aura of crisis in which the fatherland was imperiled as never before. It presented its economic and political struggles as a battle for home and farm, child and faith. Women particularly were beckoned with visions of a rejuvenated culture, free of corruption and foreign dominance, where children could grow as part of a free *Volk*. Aggressive nationalism and blatant racism did not blunt the party's appeal, although on their own they were not enough to attract female voters, as their aversion to the NSDAP implies. Rather, it was the language of religion and morality delivered by a viable major party that could not be blamed for past policies that continued to draw strong female voter support to the DNVP in 1924.

Appeals to women wrapped 1924's central issue, the inflation and stabilization, in the cloak of culture. The government parties, who wanted most to dodge their association with Germany's economic problems, spent the most time defending themselves on it, depicting themselves as the agents of both economic and social recovery. They presented international cooperation and a politics of sobriety as the path to a security threatened by extremism, especially on the right. The antisystem parties, free of the burden of power, rejected these arguments as so much hot air, as symbolic of a larger political pathology, whether they defined it as capitalism, Marxism, or the "Jewish conspiracy" lurking behind both.

As in 1918–20, propaganda often presented women as key to a party's mission in 1924. The Weimar coalition parties appealed to their "innate" female pacifism, urging women to act as agents of peace both in public and in private to save the republic. The KPD and DNVP, in contrast, bucked such notions of femininity to a certain degree, as they preached a more combative stance. The Communists wanted women cadres for the revolution, while the DNVP sought German women to help fight a cultural war for the soul of the nation. The cultural front was indeed women's special battle station in the majority of propaganda from 1924. The lingering atmosphere of crisis from previous years can even be said to have brought women to the forefront by making them indispensable to each party's vision of the new order.

In another sense, however, this discourse of crisis drove specific women's issues into the background, as their "special interests" had to be set aside until larger battles were won (an argument rarely applied to other interest groups). Propaganda glossed over most of the pressing questions women faced in the material world, such as the fact that they were more likely than men to be unemployed through 1924 or more prone to be shoved into a domestic service job compatible with their "nature." Parties that promised women to defend their rights as workers backpedaled in practice, as was seen with the passing of the PAV. The SPD, for example, tried to win women with promises of fair treatment, while in fact caving to male-dominated unions by curbing its position on work for equal wages after 1920. Some attention to the growing numbers of female professionals did crop up in propaganda, though their concerns as workers were overshadowed by their potential for maternity. One female job that did receive new, sustained attention was that of consumer. Because her concerns did not threaten prevailing notions about the division of labor, they could be more easily represented in propaganda than the material concerns of women in less "feminine" occupations, whose right to work was still under attack at this time.

Unlike in 1918–20, when newly granted rights and suffrage were central themes in all parties' appeals to women, only the DDP and SPD still farmed this terrain in 1924. Every party still claimed to be the truest women's advocate, but practically no one defended women's rights without hitching them to some greater justification or set of interests. The KPD was most militant in calling for gender equality, but they submerged those calls in a language of revolution and class conflict to the disregard of real problems. The SPD's discourse of equal rights was more in touch with many women's reality, but rhetoric often failed to match practice. Parties to the right of the DDP continued to define women's interests as religion, culture, and morality—themes that resonated with many female voters, though not when uttered by paganistic National Socialists. As before, all parties in 1924 discussed women's interests in terms of the welfare of the whole, whether defined as the nation, the German race, Christian ideology, democracy, or the proletariat. Woman's primary identity was still rooted in her nature and domestic roles, not work, though the need to assert the importance of class over gender solidarity did allow her to be used as symbol of both exploiter and exploited.

In the end, however, propaganda from 1924 did reflect one aspect of the lived experiences of both women and men: it was part of an attempt to make sense of the recent crisis that touched everyone. After a hair-raising time of political assassinations, coups, foreign occupation, and hyperinflation, Germans universally agreed that the social order had been turned upside down. The parties translated that consensus into appeals stressing the need for a return to order—moral and sexual as much as economic. They differed, however, on what constituted morality, ranging from the Left's calls for a socialist order that would free women from sexual commodification and endless childbearing to Center and Right demands for a renewed Christian morality with clearly delineated gender roles. Interestingly, the Weimar system parties tried to bring an air of sobriety to this debate, while extremists hoped to sustain a mood of crisis, seeing misery as their best recruiting tool. Women's own political behavior in 1924—their falling participation and rejection of the most radical parties—reveals their overriding desire for stability after the nightmare of inflation and political violence.

3

Culture versus Butter

:

Women in the Campaigns of the Golden Twenties, 1925–1928

The formation in January 1925 of the Bürgerblock coalition, led by the DNVP, DVP,
and Center, ushered in a period of relative
stability and prosperity known in Weimar
lore as the Golden Twenties. Foreign Minister Stresemann's efforts to readmit Ger-
many to the club of leading European powers were crowned by the 1925
Locarno treaty and Germany's admission to the League of Nations in
1926. Domestically, the Reichstag elected in December 1924 was able to
serve nearly a full term. Even President Ebert's sudden death in 1925 produced no seismic jolts, and war hero Paul von Hindenburg was elected
his successor. The economic recovery that had already taken the wind
out of radical sails by late 1924 endured, pushing the Nazis in particular
back into the shadows of national politics. A further sign of stability was

the relative lack of political passion exhibited by both parties and voters: turnout for the 1928 Reichstag election was Weimar's lowest (75.6 percent) in a contest that produced little heat, making it the republic's last (if not only) national race conducted in a benign fashion.

Yet stability was fragile and superficial. While no new elections were forced until February 1928, when the Bürgerblock split over religious education, no stable governing coalition that corresponded to the majority emerged between late 1924 and 1928; the largest party, the SPD, preferred opposition to compromise with the hostile DNVP. Enemies of the republic were everywhere; even the new president was hardly a democrat.

Economic recovery, too, was built on the sand of American loans. Tight credit resulting from 1923–24's stabilization measures spurred a rash of bankruptcies; many small businesses succumbed and larger firms gobbled up more of the economic pie. Farmers, facing rising costs and sharper competition, marched on markets in Schleswig-Holstein in January 1928 to demand higher import tariffs, lower taxes, cheaper credit, and less state spending on welfare. Even the middle classes, whose economic fortunes improved during this period, never shook off the memory of the inflation, nor did they forgive parties who reneged on promises for a full currency revaluation. As a result, broad sections of the bourgeoisie continued to abandon their traditional representatives in the DDP, DVP, and DNVP for special-interest parties. While these voters were not yet radicalized, this destabilization of traditional loyalties had disturbing implications for Weimar democracy; without it, the later rise of the Nazis is inconceivable.[1]

The period between 1925 and 1928 also saw an intense drive toward industrial rationalization to enhance German competitiveness, complete with assembly lines and efficiency studies. The eight-hour day vanished, while mechanization brought unemployment for large numbers of older, high-paid men let go in favor of unskilled workers, which increasingly meant girls and women.[2] Rationalization, in fact, reinserted women into fields they had been forced out of after the war, such as chemicals and metallurgy. The growing consumer goods economy served to create yet another "feminized" sector of the changing industrial labor force.

Streamlining also hit the tertiary sector: 25 percent of white-collar employees lost their jobs, while those retained swallowed pay cuts of up to 75 percent. This branch also experienced a continuing influx of female labor. The 1925 census gave statistical weight to what many had already intuited: now nearly 1.5 million women held white-collar jobs—three times the number in 1907. The number of female professionals also continued to grow, particularly in social services and health care. Most white-collar women, however, were found in clerical or retail jobs. They became the prototype of the New Woman, whose image dominated the popular culture of this period. Contemporaries such as Alice Rühle-Gerstel and Theodor Adorno were skeptical that this visibility signaled emancipation. Youth and beauty became job qualifications, especially in retail. Newer "female" types of work tended to reproduce the traditional sexual division of labor in which women performed tasks men increasingly found undignified. They were paid correspondingly less and rarely made it into managerial positions.[3]

Still, the image of emancipation was powerful enough to become an inseparable component of historical and popular thinking about Weimar's "golden age." In many ways, the burgeoning mass culture of the period was responsive to women's demands for a greater share in public life.[4] Women's rising purchasing power made them a target audience for movies in a country that had more cinemas than anywhere else in Europe by the late 1920s. Not only did the flourishing illustrated press employ more female writers and cover more women's issues, but women got their own magazines such as the highly popular *Die Dame*. Observers such as Hans Ostwald saw a new age of female self-assertion, especially in sexual and physical matters, as ancient taboos loosened under the influence of new attitudes.[5] Many participated in new leisure patterns, preferring mixed-sex sporting or cultural activities to the organizational life of an older generation of feminists. Young women were less likely to join a political party or even vote (contributing to steadily falling turnout among women as a whole), which earned them a reputation for frivolity.[6] They savored the "weekend," which became a middle- and even working-class institution, as Germans claimed their inalienable right to spend Sunday at play.[7]

The most profound change was the widespread acceptance of a young woman's right to a period between girlhood and marriage in which to earn for herself and even experiment with different "lifestyles." There was a recognition that the war, by obliterating a generation of men, had engendered a new "female type," the independent, single woman. Historians have admonished that this New Woman was a surface phenomenon and that gender stereotypes remained relatively constant in the postwar era. More than half of all women, for example, still worked in agriculture or family businesses, and the percentage of married women in the population had actually risen since 1910.[8] Yet there was a widespread *perception* that roles were changing, fueling sustained debate among observers of both sexes about where it would all lead (in this regard Germany was no different from France or Britain). Seemingly innocuous displays of independence such as "masculinized" fashions or the *Bubikopf* hairdo occasioned anguished hand-wringing over the state of the nation's women. While many, particularly the young, greeted modernity and incorporated it into their lives, others damned it as the end of *Kultur*.

The mid-1920s also saw the rising popularity of the sex reform movement, which sought to help women combine a healthy sex life with a more "rationalized" lifestyle. Prussia and Saxony set up marriage counseling centers to educate couples about issues like birth control. Paid maternity leave, which the state had begun to address during the war, was integrated into workers' health insurance in 1927 (though benefits covered only full-time employees). The Left—particularly the SPD, which spearheaded these reforms—maintained that adequate social welfare combined with frank advice on sexual matters would transform working-class marriage and family life into a positive experience for all.[9]

Despite a certain acceptance of female independence, motherhood was still universally seen as the highest fulfillment of women's existence. Falling birth rates, coupled with rising divorce and abortion rates, galvanized concern over women's diminishing desire to bear many children. Census figures reporting a jump of nearly 50 percent since 1907 in the number of women in industry—with the biggest increases among married women and those aged 20–50—aroused fears about the nation's ability to reproduce itself. Opponents of women's work used the numbers to argue that work was bad for women, an opinion even voiced in Socialist quarters.

Concern over high abortion rates, as well as rising mortality from botched attempts, came to a head in the debate over paragraph 218 of the legal code, under which abortion was punishable by up to five years in jail with possible hard labor for both the woman and the abortionist. In 1926 the SPD, spurred on by its female delegates, with support from liberals, brokered a compromise that reduced abortion to a misdemeanor carrying three to six months in prison (KPD bills for full legalization were shot down). Reformers were motivated by a combination of humanitarian, feminist, and eugenic concerns about the social and medical condition of the next generation of mothers and children.[10]

Desire to make marriage and motherhood more attractive options for women also instigated such growing phenomena as Mother's Day. Prussia began to award china cups or 100 marks in cash to mothers of twelve or more children, symbolic gestures meant to distract attention from family allowance schemes that had not materialized.[11] In the home, the principles of streamlining, exemplified by Bauhaus design, were touted as keys to reducing the drudgery of housework, though their more exacting standards of cleanliness ultimately drew women closer to the home and reaffirmed their identity as household managers.

Contemporaries noted that the 1928 election lacked burning issues and inspired little voter interest.[12] Yet at a time when the New Woman and women's bodies were at center stage in public discourse, can the same be said when we consider the interests of female voters? Did campaign appeals to women tackle reproductive issues? Did hotly disputed pop phenomena like the *Bubikopf* penetrate political discourse? Examining the themes that marked party propaganda from Weimar's Golden Twenties will illuminate how Germans tried to make sense of the increasingly visible independent woman and reveal whether changing attitudes about sexuality and leisure shook debates about politics, the economy, and the welfare state.

The tenth anniversary of the republic in 1928 offered a chance for reflection on the new order, including its implications for the women it had enfranchised. The party most closely identified with the republic, the SPD, celebrated in upbeat propaganda that championed its benefits. A placard announcing a speech on the anniversary by spokeswoman Toni Sender praised the revolution for rewarding women's economic activity with political equality. Propaganda for both women and general audiences maintained this theme and projected it in 1928 through an anti-Bürgerblock lens, hoping to win women away from the DVP, DNVP, and Center by reminding them that these parties had long opposed women's equality. Local and national appeals during the Golden Twenties highlighted the SPD's work for suffrage and its status as the party with the most female Reichstag deputies.[13] Its 1925 program demanded the end of all discriminatory laws, while presidential campaign appeals told women that no enemy of female suffrage should lead the republic—a reference to Hindenburg, the "marshal with antiquated attitudes about women."[14] Even a gender-neutral pitch to civil servants in 1928 invoked gender equality, linking economic and political justice in a broad language of republican citizenship.[15] SPD women's materials linked the republic with woman's status as an equal "people's comrade." Appeals, such as a *Vör-*

warts piece on International Women's Day, portrayed democracy as a basis from which workers' representatives could generate a truly social republic. Their focus on women's rights was informed by both a desire to appeal to women across class lines and the SPD's identity as the party that represented the interests of working-class women (and men) in ways the bourgeois parties never could.[16]

One of Weimar's most striking political posters, "Volksgenossen wählt Sozialdemokraten," depicts the social republic at the heart of the SPD's vision (see Figure 3.1). The 1928 piece shows five figures—a civil servant, a worker, a white-collar worker, a woman, and a craftsman—solemnly participating in that most basic democratic rite, voting. Their workaday appearance aims to evoke viewer identification with these "people's comrades," each of whom has a place in the republic. The female figure is young and modern, sporting the popular *Bubikopf* hairstyle; her delicate hands indicate that she works a white-collar job, though her roots are probably working class. In other words, she is a typical New Woman. This poster may be the only major Weimar propaganda piece not only to depict this controversial "female type"—she was ubiquitous in popular culture but strangely absent from electoral discourse—but to do so positively. Here she becomes a model female citizen, possessed of intelligence and a social conscience, not to mention reassuring maternal warmth.[17]

The Democrats also used the anniversary of 1918, as well as that of the 1848 revolution, to display their own commitment to republican ideals, rooted in Germany's liberal past. Its flyer depicting this republican consensus used young Germans, male and female, in both modern dress and the rustic garb of the youth movement: "Let the black-red-gold flags wave—never again the black-white-red of the kaiser throne, of reaction!"[18] A women's leaflet quoted Louise Otto-Peters's 1848 call for "female citizens for the kingdom of freedom" as a summons to national unity and a reminder that women's "leaders" supported the DDP.[19] While the DDP no longer called itself the "party of women" (1928's slogan was "the party of *Ausgleich*," or balance), women's propaganda still listed gender equality as intrinsic to the liberty of all citizens. As the DDP's general campaign privileged national over particularist interests, materials for women called them to complete the unfinished liberal project of uniting the nation in a republic of fairness and *Freiheit*. Appeals used women to symbolize the national community that male egoism and politicking had botched.[20]

Not everyone saw Weimar's tenth birthday as cause for celebration.

figure 3.1
"People's Comrades
Vote Social
Democratic": The
New Woman as
Citizen (SPD, 1928)
(Hoover Institution)

The National Socialists, back in the ring with a new centralized propaganda apparatus designed to help the party attain power through legal means, railed against ten years of national humiliation under the "Weimar system" and SPD "rule."[21] In a similar fashion, the conservative DNVP latched onto the anniversary as a chance to survey a decade of moral decline and national disgrace. A 1928 flyer, "Defend Yourself against Germany's True Rulers!," summarizes the DNVP's general message. It trotted out old demons—the SPD, KPD, France, the Jews—who were allegedly holding hardworking Germans hostage to special interests. Addressing various occupational groups, it argued that taxes, "party dominance," corruption, and mob rule were sinking the *Mittelstand*. A panel addressed to women depicted a smoking teenager perusing a book on "free love" before a placard that shrieked, "There is no God, only Bebel and Lenin!" It asked, "Shall your children become brats like this 'enlightened' product of secular education?"[22] This appeal to women through religion made strategic sense at a time when their loyalty, especially in Protestant areas, contrasted with men's increasing defections from the party.[23] To women the DNVP stressed the same "Christian, national, social" message as before, making the protection of religious instruction in schools its primary cultural—and hence, women's—issue in 1928.

Ultimately, the 1928 campaign boiled down to a contest between Left and Right, a discursive struggle between "economic justice" and culture. While culture remained a fixture of women's propaganda across the board, at a time of relative stability and prosperity, the SPD worked aggressively to focus female voters' attention on fundamental issues like welfare, which the party argued had never looked so promising.

Invoking the republic's tenth anniversary was a way for its supporters to discuss the fate of material issues under Bürgerblock rule. The DDP, for example, in appeals to peasants, white-collar workers, and the *Mittelstand*, depicted the Bürgerblock as a club for big industry and inflation profiteers. A flyer for both sexes contrasted this with the work of a female politician, veteran feminist Marie-Elisabeth Lüders, for small pensioners. Another entitled "Women, think about it!" depicts a despairing young mother besieged by rising prices, rents, unemployment, and taxes, under the caption "never again *Rechtsregierung*" (government by the Right). But the DDP tended to submerge its discussion of material concerns in tepid appeals to what it viewed as safer, broad ideological themes—a strategy that failed to reverse its declining fortunes at the polls.[24]

The SPD, on the other hand, hit pay dirt in 1928 with a clear, consistent emphasis on bread-and-butter politics. Although it had regained its position as the largest party in December 1924, it stayed out of national government, reluctant to repeat the experience of May 1924, when it paid at the polls for its association with economic policies over which it had no control. The Social Democrats used opposition constructively to support Stresemann's foreign policy and lead the charge for domestic reform, crowned by the 1927 unemployment insurance and welfare laws that made Germany an international model. They also enacted an ambitious program of social programs and new housing at the state and local levels where the party was strong. Hoping to profit from its support of welfare programs,[25] the SPD campaigned aggressively in 1928, spending over 2.5 million marks and dispensing over 2 million items, from flyers to soap bars carved with the party logo.[26] Its efforts were rewarded with a clear victory of 29.8 percent of the national vote (up from 26 percent in December 1924), a result widely read as a positive sign for the republic. The party benefited from economic prosperity and its image as a productive force for social policy. It was also helped by solid turnout from organized labor and defections from the Center and bourgeois parties, as more Catholic male workers, white-collar workers, and public employees went SPD that year.[27] It also attracted more women: in areas where votes were counted by sex, 31.5 percent of all women voted SPD, just behind 32.9 percent of men.[28]

In 1928 the SPD targeted the ruling Bürgerblock coalition. It promised measures for the common person: more protective legislation in the workplace, revival of the eight-hour workday, bigger pensions, and redistribution of the tax burden. Like the general propaganda, women's materials stressed economic issues such as the cost of living, unemployment, and housing. They reflected the prevailing assumption that social policy was women's prime public concern, a view endorsed strongly by Marie Juchasz, who headed both the SPD women's and workers' welfare organizations. Addressing female voters in their multiple roles as women, mothers, and *Menschen*, appeals linked a social policy emphasis with reproductive questions and gender equity.

SPD propaganda focused on economic issues throughout 1925–28, attacking center-right policies for the unacceptable state of labor (2 million out of work, 2 million working only part-time). Appeals in 1928 to occupational groups such as civil servants focused on Bürgerblock policies' negative effects on status and wages.[29] Those to women often stressed consumption, linking protectionism, for example, with empty cooking pots and physical degeneration (illustrated by the ubiquitous Kollwitzian image of proletarian mother and child).[30] A 1928 piece that asked "How do you live?" depicted a mother and child outside the gates of a regal manor flying the imperial colors, arguing that the Bürgerblock defended the wealthy, leaving widows, the unemployed, and victims of war and inflation in the cold. Another women's flyer argued that DNVP-backed "inflation profiteers and Junkers" robbed small savers and peasants, while "Christian" industrialists bankrupted small craftsmen. *These* forces routinely violated the rights of the "little people," not the Socialists, who allegedly had no respect for property.[31] It was the social welfare state, which aimed to create materially secure and active citizens out of all members of the *Volk*, that represented true morality in SPD discourse.[32]

The KPD expressed many similar demands in its propaganda for women, despite its intensified hatred of the SPD, whom it declared in 1927 to be "social fascists" and communism's greatest political enemy. These issues were summarized in a 1928 flyer, "Frauen, das sind eure Feinde!"[33] In it, the KPD demanded lower taxes and tariffs, a living wage for proletarian families, an eight-hour workday, better maternal welfare services, and legal abortion. It insisted on cheap, sanitary housing and secular schools with free lunches. Women's "enemies"—capitalists, Junkers, and the SPD—wanted lower wages and longer hours to perpetuate working women's slavery (these "enemies" are depicted arm in arm beside a voting urn, signifying the Communist view that suffrage was the mere illusion of equality); the KPD would eradicate capitalism, class justice, fascism, and the threat to Soviet Russia. Like the SPD, the KPD was aware that many women voters were heavily swayed by "culture," but they insisted that "bread issues" would most effectively draw female masses.[34] Unlike their rivals, however, the KPD depicted the kind of compromises to win immediate reforms made by the "social fascists" as treachery to the ultimate goal of revolution.

Both Marxist parties deployed a language of a just social order (*gerechtes Gesellschaftswesen*), carried over from 1924, with women's bodies—wan or plump, ruined or robust—at its center. This continued through the 1926 Communist-led campaign for a referendum on the expropriation of former imperial princes, which the SPD joined after initial trepidation. Though this drive fell 5.6 million short of the 20 million signatures needed to make it binding, it did garner much popular support. The propaganda it generated to both sexes contrasted royal wealth with proletarian suffering. Appeals to women used images of suffering children to argue that resources gained from the expropriation of princely families could be used for housing, medicine, food, and recreation.[35]

This idiom of class struggle, often linked with antimilitarism, lingered into the SPD's 1928 campaign. While committing itself to democracy and appealing to a wide range of occupational and social groups, the SPD still relied on this discourse to mobilize its core working-class constituency for the goal of socialism. A 1928 poster, "Wer rettet Deutschland?," links economic and military policies, contrasting the Bürgerblock's drive for more battleships with SPD social achievements. Bürgerblock politics are illustrated by a soldier in a gas mask and a dead child, while a worker and smiling baby represent the SPD. It is worth noting that in this poster, a man holds the baby—the use of images of children to mobilize support was not limited to materials aimed solely at women, indicating social policy's privileged position in both SPD propaganda and legislative activity.[36] The relationship between military and social spending also permeated materials to women, which depicted capitalists and clerics (the Center Party came under special attack) approving new battleships while vetoing money to feed needy children. Flyers for mothers published in 1928 linked the SPD's "war against war" with housing and other social policies that would foster healthier proletarian children, aid pensioners (represented by a poor woman), and improve conditions for working women.[37]

The KPD's 1928 battle against capital, the Bürgerblock, and all "anti-worker" parties (from DNVP to SPD) mirrored the SPD's message. Both general and women's appeals blasted the economic policies of the "capitalist republic" and continued to expose vast social differences in wealth, as in the campaign for princely expropriation. This fight against the Bürgerblock also bore a vivid streak of antimilitarism, used to foment resistance to noble power and Hindenburg's presidency. During the 1925 presidential race, the KPD reminded women that, as field marshal, Hindenburg had used their men as cannon fodder on the so-called field of honor—hoodwinked by nationalism, they died so capital could thrive. The same forces of militarism had run Germany before the war, propping up a system that stonewalled on women's rights and set troops on proletarian women and children. "Guns versus butter" was a cornerstone of the expropriation campaign, carried through celebrations of Hindenburg's eightieth birthday. Women's presence in arms industries also induced the KPD to link their dismal working conditions with war and the lie of patriotism. Finally, KPD antimilitarism was fueled by its growing attachment since 1924 to Moscow, as propaganda harped on militarism as capital's mobilization to crush proletarian revolts in Russia, China, and at home.[38]

While the Catholic Center Party produced little propaganda for women during 1925–28, it too weighed in on the guns versus butter debate. Women's flyers produced for Wilhelm Marx's 1925 presidential bid, while reluctant to attack Hindenburg aggressively, reminded women that the aged marshal represented war—as "comrades of fate" in 1914–18, women surely wanted no new militarism. Besides, women's citizenly and motherly tasks demanded that respect for military achievement not blind them to the need for a candidate who represented political experience, social justice, freedom, and *Volksgemeinschaft*.[39] Other flyers to this effect, one of which was issued jointly by women of the SPD, Center, and DDP, stressed these parties' commonalities and cooperation on issues such as welfare. Similarly, a 1928 Prussian appeal presented the Center as part of a team committed to democracy, social policy, and economic justice, unlike the shrill special-interest parties.[40] Clearly, the Center hoped especially to retain working Germans by linking itself with the popular welfare agenda—a strategy that seems to have been less successful with male voters than with women, who stuck by the party in 1928.

A radically different use of the language of fairness came from the DNVP, whose call for a "spirit of balance" depicted the German nation as victims of SPD "party dominance." DNVP literature not only affirmed bourgeois antisocialism by invoking the recent Barmat scandal,[41] but also tried to drum up working-class antisystem sentiment with caricatures of SPD hacks (*Bonzen*, a term also beloved by the Nazis) who drank champagne and chased skirts.[42] Women's flyers picked up this line. A pro-Hindenburg leaflet idolized him as a clean liver who represented "purity in public life," unlike the dirty politicians of the SPD and Center. It also invoked fairness to protest the expropriation of princes, arguing that this would violate nobles' equal rights to property (using the Left's own language against it). Significantly, the female activists who wrote DNVP women's propaganda used the term "equality" to denote not women's rights but conservative Christians' "equal right" to state-funded religious education and "freedom" from Socialist influence.[43] Their anger was fueled by a decade of SPD dominance in municipal government, which shrunk the influence of conservative, bourgeois women like themselves.[44]

The DNVP's unrelenting war on the Left also pivoted around nationalism. While nationalist rhetoric had always been the DNVP's stock-in-trade, in this period it reacted to SPD and KPD campaigns against militarism. DNVP women still promoted strong nationalism and rejected an "innate" female pacifism. For example, a Hindenburg flyer assured women that age had not diminished his "manly vigor" (*Manneskraft*, which also denotes virility), he would restore German honor emasculated by leftist pacifism. Antileftism also extended to economic issues, though women's materials limited discussion to the housing shortage and Socialist dominance of welfare, to deflect attention from the DNVP's failed promise of a full currency revaluation. Even SPD control of municipal welfare was presented less as a career or a material issue than as a cultural one. The women who wrote this propaganda told female voters that the DNVP social agenda was rooted in private, confessional charity, where welfare work truly belonged.[45] Presenting its "national, Christian" crusade as above ideology, the DNVP disingenuously demanded that party interests be removed from welfare to better fight need and "moral damage" among German mothers and children.[46]

DVP women's materials maintained a similarly strong nationalistic thrust. In the wake of Stresemann's foreign policy successes in the republic's middle period, the party offered the middle classes nationalism to compensate for their material losses while pledging in its 1927 manifesto to work with others in a liberal spirit to reconstitute the fatherland.[47] Foreign policy dominated the DVP's 1928 general campaign as well as propaganda for women from this period. A 1925 flyer expressed female gratitude to Hindenburg, "the great one," whose loyalty to the national past and the Christian faith made him the ideal candidate.[48] Party journal writings by female activists praised the Queen Luise Bund, declared that the Rhine must remain forever German, and asserted the need to strengthen the "white race and German culture." They demanded laws to ensure that women who married foreigners could retain their citizenship so as not to sever their bond with the fatherland. In musings on New Year's Day 1928, Clara Mende, chair of the German Women's Anti-War Guilt Lie Committee, hoped for greater national awareness to spring Germany's fetters and heal its moral malaise. Military spending did not seem to trouble DVP women, who saw foreign policy as a place to assert a nationalistic influence to counter female pacifism on the left. Yet unlike the bellicose DNVP, the DVP and its women saw reconciliation and participation in international summits as a better way to win leverage over reparations, border areas, even colonies. A prescient article from 1925 predicted that the next European war would be an all-out affair that women would fight with the weapon of work. Women's future strategic importance, it argued, mandated that female equality become real to make them full participants in the nation's defense.[49]

The DVP's linkage of nationalism and female labor brings us to the next set of themes from 1928, women's work. Reflecting current debates over rationalization in both the workplace and the home, as well as the shifting shape of the female workforce revealed by the 1925 census, propaganda imagined appropriate forms of women's work. These discourses were informed by such things as the 1922 Personnel Retrenchment Decree (PAV). The PAV, which allowed married female civil servants to be fired as double earners, was lifted in August 1925. Yet in a blatant disregard of women's constitutional equality, the DNVP, DVP, and Center (with support from their female delegates) assured the retention of clauses that still allowed married *Beamtinnen* to be fired as a cost-cutting measure—a largely symbolic gesture, as only a tiny number of women actually fit this category. Clearly, the issue of whether women even had a right to work remained a live one.

The SPD, which set the general tone of the 1928 campaign, spoke at length about women's work. Its 1925 Heidelberg program restated the party's commitment to women's right to work, as did its women's propaganda. In 1926 it blasted the PAV and other cases of discrimination as the naked opposition of capitalists and their political representatives to gender equality.[50] A major pamphlet addressed to several groups, "Who Must Vote Socialist?," used women's specific burdens, such as inadequate maternity leave, to illustrate their common bond with all oppressed. Another poster, whose prose could have flowed from a KPD pen, proclaimed, "Women to the front, to battle for victory!"—the victory of the working class, within whose ranks women's personal suffering could be alleviated.[51] While calls for women to join proletarian ranks had always been found in SPD materials, they became more insistent after the release of the 1925 census. Figures showing a steady rise in the percentage of women working buttressed the argument that women must seek paid work outside the home to create solidarity with the working class—a precondition for the transition to socialism. As several female activists argued, it was crucial to awaken female "job satisfaction" (*Berufsfreudigkeit*) and end the notion that woman belongs in the home.[52]

The KPD argued along these same Marxist lines. Appeals demanded an end to exploitative home work (most of which was done by women) by placing all production in factories, while mandating checks on rationalization to prevent a machine-driven pace from breaking women physically. Like the SPD, the KPD called for continued expansion of women's work outside the home. It also demanded gender equity in pay and conditions for all types of work, including agriculture, white-collar jobs, and the civil service (it protested the PAV in this spirit). It called for eight weeks' maternity leave before and after delivery at full pay (going beyond the six weeks at partial pay provided in the 1927 law), as well as a ban on female work around hazardous materials. Yet, unlike the SPD, which viewed legislation as the best way to attain these goals, the KPD insistently pointed to factory cell agitation—industrial strikes today, revolution tomorrow.[53] Representing the most downtrodden elements of the working class, the KPD saw the SPD's willingness to compromise with other parties to win reforms as detestable treachery to the proletariat and the revolution,[54] of which women should be a vital part.

Yet ambivalence over whether work constituted women's primary identity lingered even in the Marxist camp. At the 1927 SPD women's conference, Emma Sydow, for example, remarked to shouts of agreement that when unemployment was high, married women had a duty to make room for men in the workplace.[55] While a 1928 campaign flyer to male civil servants (urged "man for man" to support the SPD) invoked their "betrayal" by the Bürgerblock,[56] propaganda for women failed to name the injustice done to women by the PAV. SPD campaign appeals tended toward a generic invocation of "justice" and "equality" rather than specific issues that could cloud the simple language that propagandists deemed more effective.

SPD depictions of female work often undermined the theoretical imperative that women seek wage labor to attain solidarity with men. While they dismissed the old saw that "a woman's place is in the home," they also noted that rising female workplace participation drove down wages and doubly burdened women with housework. A 1928 flyer echoed past pronouncements about capitalism's impact on the family: "Over one-third of working women are married. Factory, office, warehouse, and manor have torn her from the family circle and forced her to earn her bread, destroying the family of old. Social Democracy merely takes the logical conclusion from this development and demands for woman the same rights as for man."[57] Such statements were penned to convince women that because working outside the home was now inevitable, the best way to improve their lot was to support socialism. Yet negative visions of female work played into the hands of the Center and Right, tending to drive women to embrace those parties' pledge to end women's need to work rather than put their faith in long-term Socialist promises.

The KPD too purveyed negative images of female labor. Demands that theoretically stemmed from an interest in working women's welfare, such as protective legislation, tended to surface as an afterthought to the larger goal of proletarian solidarity. For example, the KPD's explanation of why home work had to be abolished focused on its negative effect on factory wages—its effects on the masses of female home workers came second.[58] Similarly, its opposition to rationalization focused less on its impact on women's health than on the way it replaced skilled male with cheap female labor. Male unemployment, one piece noted, was 37.4 percent in December 1927, while women's was only 24.4 percent. In KPD discourse, women depressed wages, while their passivity and pliability made them ideal strike breakers, signified by their falling union membership.[59]

Most striking is the way the party whose basic philosophy demanded that women view themselves as members of the *working* class often failed to present work as women's primary identity. For example, a general flyer from KPD chairman Ernst Thälmann's 1925 presidential bid associated the stabilization winter of 1923–24 not only with longer work hours and economic austerity but also with female labor. Another declared that Thälmann represented "workers and their wives," as though a "worker" was by definition male.[60] Women could be the revolutionary vanguard, as in a 1925 poem that portrayed proletarian mothers heroically challenging soldiers: "Brothers, before your guns stands a new world . . . / Wade in our blood 'til you can take no more / Go on and shoot—our victory is secure!"[61] A page from the 1926 calendar shows a young woman with a red flag leading the masses over the slashed corpse of a bloated capitalist, coins spilling from his belly.[62] Just as often, however, women routinely appeared as a pillar of capitalism, laming the class struggle through their ideological backwardness, religiosity, and embrace of SPD reformism or bourgeois women's organizations. By harping on their willingness to take abuse, the KPD hoped to rouse women's anger to induce them to join the red front, yet this message ultimately blamed women for their own—and by extension, their class's—exploitation.

On the right, the DNVP found itself responding to the Left's agenda regarding female labor. It restated its support of equal pay with equal training and achievement (qualifiers that allowed inequities to persist) and mouthed phrases about easing the double burden. Yet its favorite topic in this area continued to be home work, consistent with the views of conservative women activists. Materials argued that women who worked outside the home could not protect their children from omnipresent moral dangers, a "fact" the SPD ignored in its battle against home-based production. In this way, the DNVP hoped to subvert the SPD's image as friend of the woman worker—a hypocritical gesture from a party whose support for working women extended only to those in the domestic sphere. The DNVP stance on maternity leave, for example, was to facilitate marriage for female civil servants by supporting severance pay for those who left their jobs after the wedding. The DNVP continued to bank on the notion that women saw work outside the home as drudgery and would rather stay at home. Its appeals to working women always returned to family and culture, which the DNVP still saw as the primary concern of even those in full-time careers. Uncoupling women from class, it invoked an "innate" female desire to improve life for children, possible only through a rejection of class struggle and embrace of the national, social, Christian DNVP.[63]

Like conservative natalists, the National Socialists, in the scant women's materials they produced in this period, allowed women space to be clever, but only in a "practical" sense. Science, the *Völkischer Beobachter* reported, "proved" that man's larger brain made his sphere the intellect, while the design of woman's brain predisposed her to culture and sensibility. Nazis decried a "perverse" society where healthy women resisted having children because of egoism or the need to work. Yet they acknowledged that many women were forced to work in articles delineating "appropriate" female occupations such as the needle trades, housekeeping, domestic service, and the "healing love" of social work. As in 1924, Nazi ideals differed little from conservative, Catholic, and even much liberal writing on the subject.[64]

The Catholic Center Party had always maintained a strict adherence to separate gender spheres. A 1928 *Germania* appeal referred to the home as women's "ministate" (*Kleinstaat*). It urged women to bring to politics their impulse toward domestic compromise in order to balance the ranks of male complainers and shirkers who were poisoning public life.[65] Again, the Center's vision of female activity and labor entailed bringing motherliness into public areas such as social work, education, and local politics. A 1928 list of possible female careers included academics, sales, police work, and dentistry—fields that could be imbued with "feminine" content with few ideological contortions.[66] This surprisingly broad conception of women's work in the women's page of the party paper reveals some diversity of opinion about female roles within the Center camp. Differences also surfaced over renewal of the PAV in 1925. Helene Weber reported in the party yearbook that female activists had originally demanded repeal of articles that singled out women civil servants and teachers for dismissal, only to be rebuffed. The party eventually agreed on a compromise in which a *Beamtin* could be fired if she could be supported by someone else, though she could fight this if her dismissal would impair the functioning of her department. Weber presented this compromise as an improvement over the article's original form.[67] This incident reveals both women's lack of clout within the party most dependent on their votes and the strength of the view that women in "male" occupations constituted a threat.

Liberal discourses reveal similar ambiguities about paid work and female nature. The DDP showed glimpses of 1919–20's strong gender equality stance, remaining the only bourgeois party to address specific groups of working women with more than just cultural platitudes. A flyer for female postal workers, for example, discussed hours, wages, and rationalization, arguing that only the DDP's vision could bring genuine help and equity. Women's materials noted the party's fight against "the Damocles sword of cold retrenchment" looming over female civil servants and blasted the DNVP for rejecting Lüders's motion to rescind the entire PAV. Propaganda written by women cataloged DDP struggles to win extended maternity leave, improvements for professions such as midwife, and promotions for white-collar women. DDP women pushed for expanded career opportunities, such as female police, in order to realize the democratic goal of utilizing all *Volkskraft*.[68]

Yet this rhetoric of equality was noticeably scaled back from earlier campaigns, not least due to special-interest groups, particularly employers' organizations, whose contributions the Democrats needed more than ever as their membership and vote dwindled during the mid-1920s.[69] Publicly, the DDP downplayed special interests' role in national life and aspired to elevate public discourse by stressing broad national themes over narrow economic issues in 1928 (though it did maintain the convenient tactic of issuing appeals to occupational groups that invoked their material interests). To women this meant more emphasis than ever on their ameliorative social and cultural role. A 1928 flyer showcased Marie-Elisabeth Lüders as a women's advocate who combined a cool head with a warm heart. A 1928 pamphlet for general audiences presented the work of female politicians in this way: "Many of you believe that political women are no 'women.' They have no time for the household, they are 'masculinized.' This is wrong, honorable reader! If masculine means possessing energy, clear goals, and a sense of community, then these women are!" Candidate Illa Uth, in addition to being a suffragist and champion of the oppressed, was described as "a wife, a housewife, indeed a good housewife!" Homemaking as a *Beruf*, a theme once exclusive to the DVP and DNVP, now emerged in DDP materials, at least some of which were authored by women. An appeal to female postal workers demanded regulated compensation for women leaving the profession, so that "you too can marry and create a home," reinforcing prevailing notions that work was a less desirable life option for women than marriage and family.[70]

Similar views marked DVP propaganda's take on women's economic role. It depicted the female element as indispensable in economic life, necessary to foster cooperation and combat social splintering.[71] A 1928 flyer to white-collar women used language not unlike that addressed to other groups, urging them to vote because all *Stände* were needed in the DVP's work for *Volk* and state.[72] The DVP preached gender equity in wages and promotion (on condition of equal training) to enable women to contribute more fully to the greater good. While this could even be interpreted as a call to end gender stereotyping, as implied in an article in the women's pages of the Berlin party paper,[73] DVP women's propaganda preferred to discuss work in gendered terms. It called for female work where its motherly "essence" could blossom, such as nursing. It also restated demands for more female teachers, who would help foster national rejuvenation through a special curriculum for girls that cultivated womanhood through basic academics, gymnastics, and home economics.[74] Like most bourgeois feminists, DVP women saw an expanded field for women's "innate" skills as the best defense of their right to work. They extended this to politics, which allowed women to combine the roles of mother, educator, protector of life, and citizen. A 1928 women's flyer urged women to embrace careers and politics so their "warm understanding" of Germany's misery could rescue the nation. The model woman served *Volk* and fatherland by bringing the values she personified in the home—silent devotion and selfless love—to the public.[75]

While the DVP's 1928 handbook criticized the DNVP as hostile to female equality in politics and the economy, the DVP itself had a shaky history in that area, as can be seen when its support for the PAV is examined. Rather than denounce the unconstitutional extension of its clauses regarding women, the DVP in 1928 urged campaign speakers to stress its new guarantee of severance pay and women's expanded right to contest their dismissal. While these reforms were "not completely satisfactory," they were presented as an improvement; if DVP women opposed this position on the issue, their protests never appeared in party publications.[76]

There was one area in which DVP women's materials set the tone on a major theme in the 1928 campaign: the emphasis on the "occupation" of housewife. Housewives, Else Frobenius argued, were not only the majority of female voters but also upheld the bourgeois order rooted in home and family. Appeals echoed language first used by bourgeois feminists in the 1890s, who described housework as a "cultural occupation" (*Kulturberuf*), whose key role in reproducing the social order had emancipatory potential for women.[77] For example, one piece referred to women's "trade" as the nation's material, spiritual, and cultural "maintenance estate" (*Erhaltungsstand*), their unique contribution to an economically and socially balanced society. Like any other branch of industry, housework demanded research and rationalization, which the DVP proudly claimed to promote through Charlotte Mühsam-Werther's position as housewives' representative on the Reich Economic Council. Technical innovation could help women better meet the challenges of this *Beruf*, while consumer education would also benefit the community. Materials urged women to buy German, comparison shop, and revive the ethos of saving, which had been weakened by inflation and the lust for luxuries.[78] Appeals to other *Berufsgruppen* stressed wages and status in the public sphere, assuring each group that it was an integral part of the *Volksgemeinschaft*. Women's appeals, in contrast, showcased the private, stressing the links between the economy of the home and that of the nation. The DVP promoted homemaking as a *Beruf* to enhance its importance as unifier of women's economic and motherly contribution to the *Volk*.

Opponents to the DVP's left also addressed this domestic labor in their propaganda as never before. The DDP flyer, "Women Think about It," implied that women must shake off their irrational support of the Right before their material lives could improve. Other women's flyers urged presumably ignorant housewives to see the relationship between state policies and the price of bread. One even stated that unless women realized that consumption and tariffs fit together, they could never be good citizens or good housewives.[79]

SPD materials displayed an even more sustained interest in housework as a women's issue. Propaganda from this period painted a world where the crushing double burden of housework and wage labor left women no time to contemplate the relationships between their work, home life, and politics. While concerned about rationalization's effects on conditions in factories, the SPD placed hope in household technology to ease housework and end the home work still performed by many women and children. Lamenting the contradiction that low wages prevented women familiar with technology at their jobs from reaping its benefits in the home, *Vorwärts* urged women to organize for better wages so that worker households could afford modern appliances. Caught up in the uncritical fascination with technology that gripped many in this period, SPD propaganda was blind to its negative aspects, such as the way it bound women more firmly to the home by imposing higher standards of cleanliness. It greeted the day when affordable household technology would make a woman technical director in her own factory—only capitalism stood in the way.[80]

In addition, the SPD, like the KPD, embraced the long-term goal of the communal household. *Vorwärts* posited a new family based on comradeship to replace the bourgeois family built on the slave labor of women's housework. Socialism offered women an end to servitude by communalizing domestic tasks, granting them the ability to develop as equal, cultured individuals in a society that offered their children a better future. A socialist society would not quash motherliness but put it in the service of a wider circle.[81] Like the KPD, the SPD's vision of the communal household was marred by a failure to rethink the sexual division of labor—reproductive work was still women's domain. Its discussion of housework and technology was also limited to the SPD press, while campaign materials preferred to paint women's work in the broad strokes of economic justice, social welfare, and class unity.

While *Germania* commented that the 1928 election lacked "great issues,"[82] the Center Party, along with the DNVP, tried to make a "great issue" out of religious instruction in schools. After 1918 a strong movement to secularize primary schools took off in several northern and eastern states. Ambiguities in the law and the constitution induced advocates of maintaining religious instruction to respond with a campaign for a school law (Schulgesetz), which would allow parents, not the state, to determine the religious character of local schools.[83] The Center and DNVP, which designated culture and religion as women's primary domain, made the Schulgesetz the centerpiece of their women's propaganda in 1928. The bill's failure to pass was made an emblem of the continued cultural decline perceived in these quarters, though the broader discourse of moral emergency appeared to have lost steam as a campaign theme in 1928.

The Center made the Schulgesetz central to its 1928 campaign as a way to rally Catholics, who saw religious education as a bulwark against an anti-Christian society. Interestingly, propaganda that addressed this and other "cultural" themes was not addressed solely to women (though the party did define schools, moral protection of youth, and marriage law as particularly vital to women's interests). As in 1924, the Center highlighted them, less as a way to attract new constituents than as a way to confirm the party's rootedness in the Catholic milieu at a time when this cross-class constituency split over the economic issues that dominated the 1928 election.[84] The centrist party showcased its commitment to religion, while continuing to preach the message of social justice, class reconciliation, and peaceful nationalism that made it a bridge between opposing factions in society and politics. But while it advocated cooperation, it blasted specific parties who failed to support the Schulgesetz. The liberals, in flyers to parents, were accused of waging a new *Kulturkampf*. In 1919–20 the Center had used this term to attack socialism, and in 1924, the Right. Now, in 1928, it was the liberals' turn to be pilloried as the supposed ringleaders of a front to destroy community, deliver youth to rootless secularism, and undermine family life—a characterization that ironically appeared just as liberal power was evaporating at an astonishing rate. While the Center had long decried the DDP as godless freethinkers, in 1928 it reserved particular anger for the DVP, which rescinded its support for the Schulgesetz bill because of differences over how much say parents should have in the operation of schools. The Center even lashed out at the Protestant-identified DNVP, whose failure to back the bill unanimously was derided as "two-faced" politicking. Propaganda went on to "unmask" the "red-liberal front" on other cultural and moral issues such as censorship, venereal disease, and divorce. As the Center told its male and female constituents, it was the only party true to Christian education and culture.[85]

The DNVP also focused on religious education. Propaganda from the mid-1920s for local elections (in Berlin, for example) presented schools as a major concern of both mothers and fathers. The DNVP promised to mandate a curriculum that would teach respect for Germany's glorious past, Christianity, and *Heimat*. Only a strong national party, not feeble splinter parties, could stop taxes from going to socialist utopians and "sex reformers."[86] Both local appeals and national materials used religious education to address both sexes, as part of the conservative narrative of moral decline and "persecution" of Christian national interests since the socialist revolution. It blamed the SPD for the corruption of youth through smut and class struggle at school. In the guise of religious tolerance, socialist pedagogues undermined respect for God and authority. The SPD's true attitude toward spirituality, the DNVP argued, lay in Bebel's declaration that religion and socialism were like fire and water. These charges had been staples of the DNVP repertoire since 1918; despite the calmer political climate in 1928, the DNVP trotted them out again, using the tenth anniversary of the "crime" of the revolution to present a neat tale of a decade of decline.[87]

The DNVP's 1928 pamphlet on schools, written by Evangelical Women's Association head Magdalene von Tiling, was directly addressed to female readers. Elsewhere, the party plainly stated, "Here especially we rely on the tireless and true help of women in the fight . . . for everything that makes life worth living—the eternal, the power of religion and Christianity, morality, and the power of ideas in society and state." It echoed Bismarck's comment that female influence would strengthen the nation in this way—"If women hold fast to politics, I consider it secure."[88] The DNVP's continuing equation of women with the moral and cultural realm could not have been made more explicit than in a 1928 poster that used an 1889 painting of a peasant and her granddaughter reading the Bible: "We hold firm to the word of God! Vote German-National."[89]

Unlike the Center and DNVP, the DVP could not make Christian education an issue in women's appeals because it voted against the Schulgesetz. This made it far more defensive on the issue, arguing that it had opposed the bill not to eradicate religious instruction but to retain the Christian character of schools without sacrificing academic freedom to clerical dominance.[90] The DVP took aim at an easier target, the Left, denouncing to women "socialist education experiments" such as naked gymnastics and mandatory kindergarten as representative of local SPD dominance and the *Unkultur* of the capital.[91] It conjured up the complex of moral decline it had used since Weimar's early days, repackaged in the mid-1920s as a crisis of youth. All women, it argued, could ease this crisis by being motherly friends to girls. Politics was another tool. Several appeals highlighted female DVP parliamentarians' work on issues of housing, aid to large families, and campaigns against alcoholism, tuberculosis, and venereal disease—the "front line battle" to protect the Christian family.[92] Their materials showed DVP women as the vanguard of the moral protection of youth, resulting in the 1926 law censoring "smut and filth." They also demanded a "service year" for teenage girls and for young men to funnel them into respectable adult society. The implication was that protecting youth strengthened the fatherland.

DVP propaganda tried to shift the terms of culture away from religion toward protection of the nation and liberal freedoms. Women's materials from this period bore a pronounced national-liberal focus, as summarized in a May 1928 flyer. "We women," it said, "vote DVP because as citizens we feel a responsibility to the whole," not just one social or economic group. They supported the DVP because it enacted its program with the courage of national convictions, meeting the challenge of power at a time when mismanagement by the Left threatened to sink the economy. It also fostered a responsible cultural agenda by preventing clerical dominance in schools and supporting better housing and tax breaks for big families. Its role in social policy muffled Socialist influence and brought real aid such as occupational health insurance.[93] Trying to counter its image as an instrument of big capital (an image reinforced by its alliance with the DNVP against princely expropriation), the DVP invoked the language of *Volksgemeinschaft* in appeals to peasants, small business owners, civil servants, students, and pensioners to paint itself as the party capable of unifying the nation above base economic interests. And while the DVP still claimed to promote equality in public, political, and economic life, its version of an orderly people's community bolstered cherished notions of separate gender spheres, trotting out the bogeymen of poverty and strikes, which women's preservation instinct naturally rejected.

In 1928 the DDP also seemed adrift on cultural issues. Unlike the Center or DNVP, it lacked a salable cultural agenda. After years of running on a cosmopolitan platform that found little resonance among the masses of middle-class women (and men) voters, it now embraced a less controversial generic commitment to freedom and focused more on domesticity and youth in appeals to women. Propaganda placed women in the family context more than ever. This reflected the growing chorus of commentators who proclaimed female emancipation a disappointment, such as Gaston Rageota, who wrote in the *Berliner Tageblatt* that most women would forsake it to possess the allure of the disenfranchised Frenchwoman.[94] A poster from 1928 dramatically illustrates the DDP's continuing turn away from the "party of women" message. It depicts a female figure in classical republican dress standing behind her son; the text reads, "Women care for home, prosperity, and knowledge." By using an idealized maternal icon in French Revolution–era garb, the piece posits republicanism as the best vehicle for women to fulfill their maternal and cultural tasks.[95]

Such tendencies also emerged in appeals addressing culture. Agnes von Zahn-Harnack wrote in a piece distributed during 1928's recruiting week that youth education was women's most important *Kulturarbeit*. Woman's innate antimaterialism and ethicism made her the people's conscience, a natural democrat able to bridge differences within the nation as within the home.[96] This call to end splintering dominated the few DDP appeals that invoked culture in this period, which maintained a commitment to progress and culture without specifying the nature of these terms. The most burning cultural issue of the day, the Schulgesetz, appeared only once, in a 1928 anti-SPD pamphlet for general audiences. "Three Questions for Women" reminded female voters that the Center's goal of "clerical dominance" was anathema to a democratic people's culture, but it avoided mentioning the school bill by name.[97]

From the start, the DDP had been divided between left liberals such as publicist Theodor Wolff, who categorically rejected any form of religious instruction or state censorship, and cultural moderates like Anton Erkelenz, who dismissed Wolff's fury over antismut legislation as much ado about nothing.[98] Some key DDP women who bucked the party line in 1926 to vote for the "smut and filth" law, particularly Gertrud Bäumer, tended toward cultural romanticism, declaring the "eternal mother instinct" the antidote to a soulless mass society.[99] By invoking cherished progressive ideals of tolerance and egalitarianism while simultaneously paying homage to less radical notions of women's social and cultural role, the DDP hoped to regain more culturally conservative female voters. Its plummeting support indicates that this strategy converted no one, as a steadily rising vote for single-issue parties combined with apathy and demoralization in traditional DDP strongholds to reduce the party to a measly twenty-five Reichstag seats in 1928.[100]

The liberal DDP and DVP were not the only parties to lose votes in 1928—the Center and DNVP also slid. These two parties' attempt to focus voter attention away from material to moral issues failed to pack much of a punch that year beyond core followers—a core that was more female than ever. The urgency surrounding moral and religious questions had receded as Germans enjoyed a spell of political tranquillity and economic recovery. The fate of the Nazis in 1928 is a case in point.

If the DNVP lost support in 1928 because it could not keep its economic promises, the National Socialists' base wilted from its national peak in May 1924 as stability deflated its antisystem tirade. In 1928 the Nazis managed to attract some of the disaffected, particularly among the peasantry and petty bourgeoisie, with rants about "tax Bolshevism," "international finance capital," creeping inflation, an ailing rural economy, and "fulfillment parties" who complied with the Versailles treaty.[101] NSDAP propaganda also continued to use a lurid discourse of perversion and disease. Most relevant sources found from this period come from the party press, which presented Nazi ideology in a less filtered form than flyers. As always, it furnished mountains of "evidence" that Jews were the primary sexual threat to the German race. The Jew saw women as slaves and sexual objects; the "hidden designs of his Asiatic blood," unsatiated by mere conquest of the blonde, drove him to perversities the "normal Aryan brain" could not fathom. Articles also pointed to "Soviet-Judea," a dystopia of godlessness, crime, broken families, hunger, and unemployment that the Left wished to import to German soil. The Nazi press blasted socialist and bourgeois women's movements for remaining silent about such defilements of womankind because they, like the parties, were beholden to Jews. True Germans, it argued, revered marriage and valued women equally, even ascribing to them certain male traits.[102]

The few relevant Nazi flyers from this period also used overheated language. A 1926 flyer on "Bolshevik bloodlust" listed mass slaughterhouses, torture, and the "socialization of women by common criminals" as hallmarks of the Marxist state. Vienna, where Marxism allegedly ruled unchecked, was a haven of free love and illegitimacy. Nazi materials also blasted the crass materialism exhibited by America or German couples too hedonistic to have children. As always, Nazi critiques of capitalism returned to the issue of race and mandated rejection of Judeo-Bolshevism as destructive to German survival and the honor of its women.[103]

As in 1924, NSDAP materials in this period also blasted aspects of Catholicism. One Catholic Nazi wrote that he did not want the church using his money for "nigger missions" to promote a race of lawless, immoral spawn. The *Völkischer Beobachter* repeatedly demanded priests' removal from government because they blocked the *völkisch* agenda and tolerated "Marxists" (code for the SPD). As in 1924, the NSDAP claimed it was not attacking Christianity but merely wished to purify religion by detaching it from the "chamber of lies." Yet the tone of its rhetoric, which elsewhere proposed the sterilization of "inferiors," did nothing to neutralize its pagan image and reveals a disinterest in systematically cultivating a female constituency at this point.[104]

Strong anti-Semitism or radicalism had little mass appeal in 1928, as even the NSDAP realized.[105] The DNVP understood this as well. The tone of its propaganda (unlike its 1926 party conference, where race war was alive and well)[106] was less vicious and largely free of the racist bile of 1924, reflecting the moderate political climate of the mid-1920s. While campaign propaganda continued to confront women with images of moral decay and a leftist threat, it was not painted in the lurid colors of earlier years. Highly sexualized images had been replaced with a language of religious morality. The DNVP did not totally relinquish its former combativeness, however, reminding women that life was *Kampf*, a struggle for Christianity and family that made the hearth women's battle station.

The SPD's stress on economic and welfare issues strongly marked 1928. But to reach women, the party could not sidestep culture or religion—instead, it linked them to social welfare. Appeals to women argued that Germany's self-appointed guardians of morality were the same forces that supported child labor and military spending. The SPD was still at pains to convince women that it was not against religion but coerced religious practice and undue clerical influence, which it used to justify its opposition to the Schulgesetz bill.[107] As before, SPD attempts to criticize political Christianity often fell into anticlerical rhetoric, owing to persistent anti-Catholic strains within the party. For example, a piece called "The Sins of the Center" used images designed to make priests look silly, such as mummies whose nether regions were covered on order of clerics who forbade nudity in the classroom. A cartoon in *Die Wählerin* asked why more churches were being built when there were such dire housing shortages—"So we can pray for more housing to be built." Such statements, designed to appeal to the SPD's sizable "freethinker" constituency, were sure to offend religious voters, of which women were the majority.[108] Yet these lapses occurred less often than in earlier years and never approached Communist ferocity. For example, KPD women's materials slammed religion as a manifestation of false consciousness to which women were particularly susceptible. They railed against the Schulgesetz as "mental stultification and slavery" (*Verdummung and Versklavung*). As one pamphlet argued, enlightened women had a duty to explain to their religious sisters why disparities of wealth existed. It was time to end submissiveness and fight for a better world on earth.[109] For both the KPD and SPD, statements on religion and culture aimed, as in 1924, to attack as hypocritical those parties that supported capitalism while using the pulpit to portray the Left as hostile to family values.

SPD materials on other aspects of culture stressed tolerance and free speech. For example, the 1926 law against smut and filth, promoted by bourgeois feminists and religious women, was portrayed as a gag on free expression (the SPD viewed its own use of censorship against the KPD in Prussia as politically justified). Elsewhere, a 1928 flyer by women of the Reichstag fraction attacked anti-Semitism as the vilest insult to Jewish mothers who lost sons in the war; rightist reactionaries, who let Germany bleed dry during the war, were the people's enemies, not Jews, who were no better or worse than anyone else.[110] The SPD presented its position on culture as the struggle for a higher morality based on a true appraisal of social conditions and clarity about individual responsibility to the community.

The Left used the same language of striving toward a new morality to discuss reproductive issues, the last major theme of 1928 women's propaganda. Motivated by their female delegates, the SPD, KPD, and DDP had for several years called for a population policy to address rising numbers of abortions and maternal deaths, inadequate maternity leave, and the need for marital law reform. In this period, an alliance even formed between the moderate Left, bourgeois feminists, and some Center politicians to end police control of prostitution. This stemmed from the case of suspected prostitute Lisbeth Kolomak, a seventeen-year-old who died in 1926 at the hands of a Bremen police physician after being forcibly treated with the harsh antisyphilis drug Salvarsan. The case, which became a national media sensation, helped prompt passage of the Law to Combat Venereal Diseases in February 1927, which decriminalized prostitution and shifted supervision from the police to medical authorities.[111]

Reproductive issues weighed heavily in the SPD agenda going into the 1928 election, although truly frank discussion was limited largely to the SPD press and its women's pages.[112] However, a 1928 election pamphlet, "Die Frau in der Politik und im Beruf" (Woman in politics and work), spotlighted SPD women's legislative work on reforming divorce and marriage property law, women's parental rights, abortion, prostitution, work issues, and welfare policy. Its scope reveals a range of activity, which, though limited by the need to compromise with more conservative parties, constituted the most productive period for these issues in Weimar—a productivity heavily attributable to party women, who saw work on population and welfare issues as the best way to show their party how indispensable they were.[113]

SPD speakers' materials for Prussia also listed the abolition of abortion paragraph 218 as a topic for assemblies, though most campaign flyers from 1928 did not mention abortion or birth control directly but used terms such as *Mutterschutz* to place reproduction in the context of a more marketable social policy. A Hamburg flyer, for example, praised local SPD leadership for instituting better midwife training and maternity homes for poor and unwed mothers. Another linked economics, gender equality, and reproductive issues to promises that SPD policies would produce healthy offspring, in contrast to the current degenerated state of millions of proletarian children caused by years of bourgeois politics and moral hypocrisy. This juxtaposition of healthy and deformed children illustrates the concept of "positive eugenics": social medicine to heighten welfare's efficiency by reducing the ranks of the physically and mentally disabled. This view, which had gained popularity within the SPD throughout the 1920s, stemmed from what policy spokesman Julius Moses called the state's need to preserve and strengthen its greatest capital, human beings.[114]

Economic analysis of abortion was central to leftist discourse, as was the use of reproductive issues to translate popular discontent into support for working-class parties. Writing in *Vorwärts*, Toni Breitscheid stressed abortion's class character, warning that bourgeois women, as much representatives of capitalism as men, would be no allies in the fight for progressive policy.[115] Herr Knack's comments at the 1925 conference show how the SPD saw reproductive issues as central to the quality of working-class life. Germany, he said, needed to make the physical and spiritual health of all the basis of a comprehensive policy of public health that addressed alcoholism, venereal disease, tuberculosis, housing, prenatal care, and even homosexuality.[116] If this aimed ultimately to reinforce class solidarity for socialism, there was also, as Cornelie Usborne argues, a genuine impulse to improve the quality of life for women. *Vorwärts*, for example, argued that while capitalism was to blame for family suffering, this did not give men license to vent their frustration on their wives.[117] Knack's call for a comprehensive population policy demanded that any measures in this area be part of a larger social policy rooted in the equality of the sexes.

Egalitarian as these sentiments may have been, campaign appeals still portrayed marriage and motherhood as women's ultimate fulfillment. The 2 million postwar "surplus" women with little chance for marriage appeared as a "problem" group plagued by heartsickness. An appeal by Marie Juchasz cited the "tragedy" of women deprived of marriage and motherhood who had to find other activities to fill their lives.[118] Her words were intended to encourage women to become politically engaged, yet, as in the SPD's discussion of women's work, they also reinforced prevailing notions that marriage was women's top priority. SPD discourses continued to display tensions between the recognition of increasing female independence and the pull of the family.

Similar tensions marked KPD discourses. While denying the existence of a "woman question," the KPD knew that the conditions of female proletarians' existence differed from men's and must be addressed if they were to be won. Thus, women's propaganda spotlighted both work and reproductive issues, arguing that together they formed the crux of proletarian women's interests—interests only the KPD made a priority.[119]

Abortion, which first appeared in KPD literature in the early 1920s, became dominant in women's propaganda in this period. Total abolition of paragraph 218 topped the list of demands in a 1925 campaign flyer to women workers and housewives, illustrated by a woman being choked by the paragraph symbol (§); another poster from this period fashioned that same symbol into a snake coiled around a defenseless woman.[120] Communist appeals, like those by the SPD, placed abortion and reproductive issues in an anticapitalist framework. Kurt Hiller found it grotesque that a society that gladly sacrificed millions in war should show such concern for an embryo. Bourgeois feminists who refused to sanction legal abortion or KPD *Mutterschutz* bills proved they were more interested in protecting capital than women. As with economic issues, demands for legal abortion regularly appeared in flyers for general audiences because the KPD saw it not simply as a women's issue but a case of class justice.[121]

At one level, the KPD demanded changes to end the crushing physical and psychological burden of endless childbearing (*Gebärzwang*) on top of wage work and housework. Yet overwhelmingly, KPD appeals presented abortion and reproduction as economic issues. It blamed the growing "flight from children" on a system that left women "exploited in factory, office, and farm; cheated in the marketplace; robbed of their youth, health, spiritual growth, even the joy of motherhood—this is how woman lives under the capitalist yoke." In contrast, Russia's birth rate was said to be rising because women there enjoyed generous maternity aid, the kind German women could have if not for opposition to KPD ventures. The KPD argued that its reproductive policies would elevate Germany to the level of Soviet Russia, while the SPD sold out women's interests to compromise with Bürgerblock interests.[122]

KPD language was informed by the assumption that every woman desired the "joy of motherhood" but was kept from it by economic conditions. Another dimension emerges when we consider that support for abortion ran counter to the principle that the revolution needed masses.

Abortion's centrality to the KPD's agenda stemmed from pressure by party women.[123] Yet despite their use of the feminist, individualist-sounding slogan "Your body belongs to you," KPD appeals never justified legal abortion on the basis of individual choice.[124] Similarly, they were slower to address contraception and sexual counseling than the SPD.[125] While 1928 campaign appeals linked poor housing and economic need to such crimes against women as incest and police-run prostitution, abortion remained the focus of the KPD's treatment of sexual and reproductive issues. It provided a better example of "class justice" and gave writers more room for melodramatic embellishment, consistent with the strategy of mobilization through misery. The KPD used abortion as an instance of personal suffering to mobilize female support, then quickly delegitimized that suffering as a prime motivator by melding it into a class argument. Its focus on a very real problem faced by millions was no doubt partly responsible for a slight increase in its female vote in 1928.[126] Yet its rigid class framework and *Kampf* mentality continued to repel the majority of working-class women, who backed the SPD.

In the non-Marxist camp, only the Center's propaganda tackled abortion head-on in this period. As with the schools issue, the Center portrayed itself as a besieged fortress on abortion, its 1924 prediction that public and administrative opinion would soften having come to pass with the 1926 reforms. A 1926 fact sheet for speakers laid out the party's objections to the new milder penalties under paragraph 218. It presented the issue first and foremost in moral terms—abortion was murder. Second, abortion, along with rising use of contraception, harmed "national political and economic" interests by speeding German population decline. Finally, it endangered mothers' health not only physically but also spiritually.[127] Whereas the Left's moral critique of the "class justice" of paragraph 218 had an economic core, the Center's began with Christian morality and worked to embrace natalist concerns that were partially economic.

Although Center materials in this period that discussed abortion or divorce were not pitched just to women, the party's position was rooted in its view of their role. Viewing motherhood and marriage as women's ultimate roles, it sought to protect their right to have children raised in the faith by pushing measures promoting big families and Catholic schools. It argued that easing divorce would trample women's rights by leaving them vulnerable to abandonment. Abortion also debased woman, in the

Catholic view, because it degraded motherhood. The Center depicted defense of the family—the seat of women's power—as a better defense of women's rights than feminism, which offered only barren independence, as posters depicting the Center as the family's guardian made clear (see Figure 3.2).[128]

The DNVP too had long depicted family, community, and church as women's sphere. Just as the party painted the Left as a threat to Christianity, women's appeals lumped quotes from August Bebel with Soviet Russian decrees to "prove" the Left's antifamily intentions. They portrayed proposals to reform divorce law as a "Bolshevization" of morality. Abortion, surprisingly, figured little in DNVP campaigns in this period, appearing only once, in an anti-SPD pamphlet. Its author, Hannah Brandt, claimed that the recent reform of paragraph 218 would increase venereal disease and "wild" morality, but she stopped there, as though naming abortion would be stooping to the enemy's level. Instead, the women who wrote these materials felt their audience was best maintained by an unswerving focus on the "unified leftist front against marriage and the family," portraying the unpopular republic as the embodiment of both moral and economic turpitude.[129]

The liberal parties were similarly evasive in their discussions of abortion and reproduction, despite the fact that many liberal female delegates had participated in the drive to reduce abortion to a misdemeanor. No DDP literature for women or mixed-sex audiences contained a word on abortion.[130] DVP materials in this period noted female deputies' work on abortion and marriage law reform, but they obscured the exact scope of their efforts behind observations that "solutions had been difficult to find." Campaign appeals did not mention reproductive issues in any precise fashion, though internal writings stated that certain reforms of divorce and abortion were not objectionable.[131] The DVP dodged the reproductive issues that featured prominently on the agenda of opponents to its left and right. If its muted discussion of the Schulgesetz was designed not to antagonize Christian women, its noncommittal stance on abortion and divorce reveals an ambiguous posture toward bourgeois feminism. Caught between two fronts, it tried to present itself as protector of both liberal principles of universal rights and nationalist principles that made the family key to regenerating society and fatherland. As before, the weight tipped to the national side, illustrated by a poster depicting a woman and child before the old imperial flag proclaiming, "Vote DVP for our sake!"[132]

figure 3.2
"Provide for Our Future—Vote Center" (Center, 1928) (Hoover Institution)

If many parties found it hard to confront the issue of abortion, they were even less inclined to represent the figure of the New Woman whose image loomed so large in the popular culture of the Golden Twenties. The sexual and economic independence she embodied were seemingly too controversial to be represented in Weimar political discourse, which favored the maternal female. The New Woman remained a charged absence, though she could surface in propaganda if transformed into a potential mother (as in the SPD's "Volksgenossen wählt Sozialdemokraten") or an object of ridicule.

For example, KPD materials did not depict the New Woman herself in this period but made bourgeois women who strove to attain that "look" favorite targets in propaganda for female audiences. A 1927 pamphlet contrasted the proletarian woman's care-filled existence with the "lady" whose biggest worry was her weight. A *Rote Fahne* piece showed a slimming treatment using hot paraffin wax on the skin: "The proletarian woman is spared such worries. . . . A shrinking wage packet or her husband's dole money [keeps her thin]." Another *Rote Fahne* outburst, "Why They Are Rationalizing," ran photos of opulently dressed women with the caption, "The good lady's toilet needs can be met without the aid of year-end sales." Images that used men to symbolize bourgeois decadence featured the bloated capitalist, while his wife chased the elusive thinness of the gamine New Woman. Unlike the *Arbeiter-Illustrierte-Zeitung*, whose proletarian women often resembled the New Woman,[133] the official KPD press and propaganda from this period still relied on the stock female figure of the prematurely aged wretch. They routinely juxtaposed the haggard female proletarian driven to the sleazy abortionist with the "lady" who could pay for a private doctor—as a 1928 flyer put it, "The bourgeois *Weibchen* goes to the sanatorium, you go to prison." They also drove home the lack of common interest between women of different classes.[134]

This relentless division by class spilled into a preoccupation with fashion, a site of intense popular debate during this less heated phase of the republic. The heavy presence of fashion, particularly in the KPD press, shows a willingness to use tools such as advertising to critique mass-produced fantasies. One *Parteiarbeiter* piece even praised party cells that used flyers disguised as fashion ads to capture female (and even male) interest. There was an admission that proletarian women were interested in fashion: "It's the heart's desire of countless girls to wear pretty clothes and be admired; many seek to become models as a way to escape their class."[135] Of course, the contradictions of capitalism made such escape impossible, we are told. Images of fashionable women in this period were used to critique the Bürgerblock, as in a 1926 advertisement for the *Rote Fahne* that depicted the class enemy as a "grande dame" dripping with jewels shaped like swastikas and iron crosses. If the Nazi press lambasted fashion as a "Jewish-dominated" field whose masculinizing styles repelled "right-thinking" men,[136] the KPD used what was seen as a distinctly female vice to signify the depravity of a society in which bourgeois women gleefully danced to the "whip of fashion" while proletarian women scrimped to buy necessities.[137] For the Left, the fashionable New Woman was detestable because she was idle and parasitic; for the Right, she was dangerous because she was unmotherly.[138]

As our survey of the themes in women's propaganda during this quiet election period reveals, issues that impacted women's daily lives—social welfare and reproduction—had a relatively high profile. Was this attributable to an improvement in female activists' position within their respective parties? To a certain degree, yes, particularly within the SPD, which set much of the agenda on women's issues in the 1928 campaign. But even there, as across the political spectrum, women still had to fight to make a dent in wider party circles.

A mix of positives and negatives marked the SPD. Several positive signs for women were noted in this period. The 1925 party conference lowered the number of female members needed for a female seat on the party committee, while the 1926 yearbook reported an increase in education groups and activities for rank-and-file women. The 1927 yearbook reported that women now constituted nearly 25 percent of all members, as a support base that had withered in the early 1920s continued to rebuild.[139] Similar optimism crept into discussion of female voting behavior. Since 1919, both SPD men and women had blamed female voters for the strength of conservative parties, doing so again after Hindenburg's victory in 1925. But women refused to be scapegoats for decades of "false politics" that barred them from political life. Max Schneider wrote in the SPD social science journal that, statistically, women were quicker to support the SPD than men had been; given time and education, he argued, there would soon be gender parity. Likewise, Anna Siemsen's 1928 analysis said that in Catholic areas, women voted Center, but in industrial regions their vote for the SPD was as strong as if not stronger than men's. Even *Vorwärts*, usually critical of women voters, noted the narrowing of the Austrian Social Democrat gender gap and predicted similar results in the next German election.[140] This came to pass as more concerted, centralized campaigning finally appeared to bear fruit.[141]

But other tensions surfaced in internal debates over women's relationship to the SPD and strategies to win female support. One group of women criticized their relegation by the party and its women's organization to welfare as merely replicating the sexual division of labor in the home, which would not aid emancipation. In 1926–27 Dora Fabian and Toni Pfülf urged a revival of socialist emancipation theory, arguing that women should not remain content to be "welfare aunts."[142] SPD women's leader and "welfare aunt" par excellence, Marie Juchasz, dismissed such criticism, beginning her report at the 1927 party conference with an update on the Workers' Welfare Association. Responding to both male and female critics, she defended the tactics adopted in 1924 to attract apolitical women described in chapter 2. The cheery *Frauenwelt* and entertainment gatherings, she argued, gained the ear of indifferent women who could then be introduced to socialist ideas, while women more intensely interested in the party and socialism could read *Die Genossin*.[143] This did not placate the growing opposition of SPD women that crystallized around *Frauenwelt*. They blasted its lack of socialist content and refused to promote it in their local groups. Even those who agreed that a nonconfrontational style was more effective with the female masses noted the magazine's poor quality. The critics ultimately were able to force the replacement of Richard Lohmann with Toni Sender as editor in November 1927.

Another bone of contention in this period was the timing of the women's conference. It was traditionally held the day after the party meeting, which meant that women's resolutions had to wait a year for a hearing before the full assembly, by which time they were easily tabled or forgotten. In a clear display of indifference, the party executive rejected female activists' request for a new meeting time, saying it had no desire to brood the eggs hatched by women.[144] Women on the SPD left reacted angrily but were outnumbered by those around Juchasz who saw no need for change. In fact Juchasz, herself a member of the party executive, successfully lobbied for a resolution that women's conferences be held "only when necessary," ending this regular national forum for SPD women to air their views.

As before, SPD women continued to demand more female candidates at all state levels. They complained at the 1925 party conference that the pool of women candidates had not been expanded and in 1927 blasted the fact that only 1.5 percent of SPD deputies in local government were female.[145] While the SPD did have the highest percentage of women of any Reichstag delegation (13.2 percent in 1928), party women still perceived a double standard. Elise Scheibenhuber remarked that party men still believed that a woman's family took precedence over her public life; no woman was spared inquiry into her family's attitude toward her public activity, something never asked of a man.[146] Likewise, Frieda Fröbisch at the 1927 women's conference noted that women were often excluded from office on the grounds that they lacked experience, yet men were never asked to prove their qualifications.

Despite tensions, the party and its women had reasons to be optimistic. The SPD's 1928 women's campaign placed the social and reproductive themes widely seen as "women's issues" at the heart of the party's overall agenda. In one sense, the party grew more conservative as it toned down antichurch rhetoric and compromised on issues such as abortion. But in another sense, it could point to progressive, practical work in areas that directly benefited many women. The SPD—particularly its female delegates, cooperating with those from the KPD and liberal parties—made Germany a world model in areas such as maternity benefits.[147] The roots of its increased success among women may have lain in both its more conservative pragmatism, which was attractive to women voters more likely to be religious and politically moderate, and its clearer definition of women's interests: bread-and-butter economic issues, reproduction, mother and child welfare, and legal rights. These were basically the same issues the party had always presented to women, but now in the context of constructive opposition, economic conditions that allowed some implementation of the welfare state, and better outreach to potential supporters, they coalesced into a formula increasingly successful with female voters.

The KPD, in contrast, still struggled to win female support. As in 1922–23, police reports noted lively female interest in Berlin, particularly at rallies on war or high prices. There was also strong female support for the 1926 expropriation referendum.[148] The KPD even gained slightly with women in the 1928 election, benefiting from rising unemployment, which radicalized some proletarian districts. Finally, the Red Women and Girls League (RFMB) attracted significant numbers of working-class women from outside the party ranks. Though this stagnated by 1928, interest in the RFMB indicates a desire among women for proletarian social forms and programs.[149]

Unfortunately for the KPD, women seemed to want to remain outside the rigid confines of the party. In 1927 they made up only 13 percent of party members (16,200 women total), and the KPD continued to draw the lowest percentage of female votes of any major Weimar party.[150] Mobilizing strategies in place at the time did little to improve this record and, indeed, may have exacerbated the problem. With the rise of an ultraleftist leadership around Ernst Thälmann in 1925, the KPD continued to bring itself into line with Moscow. Its priority became formation of a proletarian *Kampffront* based in factory cells, with perpetual campaigning both for the larger goal of revolution and for specific issues of working-class interest.[151] The KPD did not lie dormant between elections but repeatedly intoned the need for mass unity, education, and revolutionary will like a mantra. Lenin's ghost was invoked to remind skeptical comrades of the importance of winning women, who were becoming an ever greater part of the industrial proletariat. Organizationally, working women were to be grouped into factory cells (or unemployed cells when appropriate); the majority of women whose work was still performed in the home, small shop, family business, or farm were to be mobilized in street or village-based cells. These cells, in turn, sent representatives to delegate assemblies to voice demands that could then be used to further mobilize the female masses. In addition, the RFMB was set up in 1925 as one of several "front organizations" designed to rally the indifferent and keep them away from groups lacking a radical class perspective.[152]

While this may have made sense on paper, mobilization was complicated by the KPD's contention that female division along class lines obviated the "woman question." Just as strategy after 1924 demanded that agitation among women be the task of the party as a whole, so it saw women's needs (at least in theory) within the larger framework of working-class problems. Concerns specific to women were more frequently integrated into general lists of demands than in other parties; materials delineating "women's issues" were rare. Images and languages of struggle intensified in KPD propaganda as a whole during this period—a discourse that, as both Kontos and Weitz have noted, was aggressively male. The central image in materials for the 1926 referendum, for example, was a muscled proletarian man smashing symbols of noble power. KPD guidelines exhorted functionaries to rail against union reformism—what was needed were shock troops. Revealingly, one women's pamphlet referred to Mother Russia as the "fatherland of the Revolution."[153]

Women's materials—whose authorship is impossible to determine with certainty—expressed this *Kampf* mentality as a total rejection of reformist palliatives. The KPD saw welfare as a right to be seized, not a concession to be bestowed or compromised by a paternalist state. To root out charity and "SPD traitorism," the KPD instructed its women to infiltrate welfare organizations (despite official rejection of separate spheres, welfare was still women's arena).[154] The communist movement founded the RFMB, International Workers' Aid (IAH), and the Social Policy Task Force as alternative sites for welfare work. Yet the issue of welfare embodies the

KPD's quandary in its attempt to win women. On the one hand, it needed themes that would interest them, such as work, reproduction, and welfare. On the other hand, ideology demanded that women transcend immediate solutions and set their sights on the long-term goal of revolution. The KPD tried to steer around this by pointing to Russia's achievements for women, hoping to lend the revolutionary model credibility, concrete expression, and immanency. Yet women's continued imperviousness to the party reveals their rejection of the *Kampf* model in favor of relief in the here and now.

Responsibility for their resistance also lay in both the flawed cell strategy and continuing male indifference to female mobilization. Despite evidence to contrary,[155] the party maintained the fiction that cells were effectively mobilizing women, highlighting particularly industrious *Genossinnen* or groups. These cells, along with the RFMB, offered sociability as well as empowering potential, encouraging women to take to pen and podium to conquer feelings of inferiority.[156] But to what end? Collecting *Kampf* funds, linking women to the revolutionary *Kampf* front, and fighting imperialist war to protect Russia were abstract goals unlikely to excite women interested in equity issues or seeking help with their burdens.

Internal memos unmask entrenched indifference and hostility to women behind the facade of support for their demands. Directives in 1925 continued to argue that women suffered from "backwardness" and constituted the strongest support of capital. Bourgeois parties and women's groups courted working-class women more than men because they knew their class awareness was weak.[157] The KPD proclaimed the cell structure more egalitarian because it made women equal members of the struggle. Yet inequality still reigned. Though cells were not to be gender-based, street cells were treated as "women's work," auxiliaries to factory cells. A 1926 Reich commissar report even made the disturbing allegation that the KPD used women as bait at demonstrations—cadres were instructed to shove women who had been placed at the front of the ranks to provoke a police response, which could later lead to accusations of police brutality against women.[158]

Comments from KPD women activists testify to party rigidity and indifference. Women's work, they wrote, was "abandoned" to female functionaries. Internal memos conveyed common gripes about the lack of propaganda material and clerical help. Erna Halbe complained that the central committee made decisions on women's propaganda without consulting the women's section first, sowing a mistrust that even led her to threaten the entire section's resignation if problems were not aired in an open forum; the party failed to respond.[159] Most damning was a 1928 women's section memo plainly stating that the KPD did not know how to use methods, issues, and slogans tailored to women's interests. As if in response, *Parteiarbeiter* subsequently reported on an assembly using music and comic skits that became a rousing success because its themes and format struck a chord with women.[160] It is unclear whether this was imitated elsewhere.

Ultimately, even if a few activists recognized these deficiencies or encouraged creative solutions, the party overall was deluded about how to win women and continued to press for more factory agitation, ignoring the ways this form of mobilization bypassed most working-class women. As always, KPD assessments of its failure to attract female support put the blame not on tactics or the party's message but on women's illusions about politics, religion, popular culture, and class.[161]

If the KPD erred tactically in its efforts to mobilize women, at least it made a concerted effort. Throughout this period, it and the SPD made a full court press to win female support with a barrage of propaganda, articles, publications, and forums aimed at women. Parties to their right, in contrast, noticeably scaled back their efforts out of indifference, arrogance, or insolvency.

Indifference characterized the NSDAP. After 1925 the party devised an extensive, centralized propaganda apparatus modeled on the Communist cell structure. Yet if it was concerned enough about female voters to state that one-third of cell members should be women, this was not reflected in propaganda materials produced in 1925–28. A checklist from April 1927 included materials for workers, the unemployed, and peasants, but none for women.[162] Even the *Völkischer Beobachter* devoted practically no space during the 1928 Reichstag campaign to women or women's issues. One 1927 article in that paper outlined women's role in the movement, delineating a female sphere of activity completely outside detested party politics. It mocked party women's organizations as gossip mills for wealthy show-offs and ridiculed the political woman, not surprising for a party that rejected female candidates out of hand. Women's true mission, "corresponding to the female element," was to support and expand *völkisch* spiritual-cultural ideals, complementing the economic-political struggles of SA and SS men. Women did their political duty by teaching their daughters about the dangers of "Jewish lechery" and raising sons to choose mates of their own "race."[163] The party's lack of attention to women at this point did give female Nazis some ideological and organizational lee-way.[164] Yet if party ideology was not completely monolithic, there was never any doubt over the need to define and separate gender attributes and activities. This perception informed, for example, denunciations of feminism for both "masculinizing" women and feminizing men through pacifism. The 1926 National Socialist pocket calendar reproduced the "ten commandments for women," which stressed female honesty and passive admiration for the heroic male. Among 1927's "ten commandments for the SA Man" was "be a German man to women, helpful and obliging, full of reverence for manly excellence [voll Ehrerbietung männlicher Güte]." As Joseph Goebbels put it, man was warrior, woman mother.[165]

A 1928 poster, however, presaged the propaganda shift the NSDAP would undergo before the next national election (see Figure 3.3). With a text that reads, "Mothers, Working Women—We Vote National Social-ist," it depicts a nurse, a mother and child, and a young woman at a desk. It targets women likely to vote conservative or liberal by invoking maternity and "womanly" work, but it also acknowledges the reality of women's expanding white-collar work and steers clear of radical con-tent.[166] Such comparatively moderate, broad-based appeals would come to mark NSDAP attempts to recruit women after 1929, as the party sought to leave the fringes of political life by reaping the depression's whirlwind of despair.

The Center Party likewise produced little in the way of propaganda for women in 1928. While the Center did not suffer as badly as the liberals, it lost over 400,000 votes in 1928, 15.2 percent, down from 17.3 percent in December 1924. Significantly, this estrangement of over one-fourth of Catholic voters was largely a male phenomenon. Catholic women were overrepresented among those who implicitly backed their party by ab-staining from the 1926 referendum; in 1928 their share of the Center vote rose as men's declined.[167] This is even more notable when one considers that, unlike its competitors, the Center did not address one flyer or pam-phlet in either campaign exclusively to women, nor did Germania run a women's page on election day. While the party handbook urged more at-tention to organization and mobilization in general as the party's Catholic base cracked,[168] propagandists relied on mixed-sex appeals stressing cul-tural themes to mobilize women, while women activists' writings were relegated to the party press.

Conference protocols and other extant internal materials likewise re-veal no discussion of women's party role. Helene Weber's brief remarks in the party yearbook about gender-based disagreements over the composition of the PAV are among the few instances where friction between female activists and the party came to expression in this period.[169] As the KPD example shows, the amount of ink spilled is not necessarily a positive measure of women's power in a party. Yet the Center's total absence of debate, combined with the fact that it ran only three viable female candidates in the 1928 Reichstag election, indicates a lack of concern about expanding its female constituency. Although the church and the 250,000-strong Catholic Women's League continued to serve as constituency builders, sinking female turnout nationwide was a potential time bomb for the party that owed its strength to women voters. A combination of rising female apathy and male defections meant that, in 1928, the Center returned its lowest number of Reichstag delegates (sixty-two) since 1871. Its lack of systematic propaganda among women and the paltry amount of materials produced in this period indicate a reliance on formulas and institutions that had worked in the past, though the numbers suggest the Center may have had less reason than before to be confident of maintaining, much less expanding, its female vote.

The DNVP shared many of the same dynamics as the Center. It too had a seemingly sturdy base of religiously oriented female voters mobilized by Evangelical women's groups. An anonymous piece in the party journal noted in 1927 that while successful with female voters in the past, the DNVP should not rest on its laurels.[170] Yet in 1925–28 it produced far less propaganda than in previous periods. Deteriorating finances surely played a role in this, as the party remained wracked by tensions following its near split over the Dawes Plan in 1924. It was divided between a moderate faction that favored a government role to serve agricultural, industrial, and civil service interests and a radical right that believed entering a coalition would torpedo the party's antirepublican credibility. Moderates ultimately ascended, and the DNVP joined national coalitions in 1925 and 1927. Yet despite this period's more conservative climate (marked by Hindenburg's victory in 1925), the DNVP's government role brought falling voter support and declining membership, as the party was unable to redeem its wild promises for a full currency revaluation. Pensioners, peasants, and small investors felt the DNVP had sacrificed their interests to those of wealthy landowners, aristocrats, and industrialists, a mood reinforced by dogged DNVP opposition to the 1926 referendum on princely expropriation. These voters, who had seen the DNVP as the best alternative in 1924, gave their protest votes to single-issue splinter parties in 1928,

figure 3.3
"Mothers, Working Women—We Vote National Socialist. List 10" (NSDAP, 1928) (Hoover Institution)

reducing the DNVP to only 14.2 percent of the vote, down from over 20 percent in 1924.

Not only did the party's ailing finances result in less propaganda for women, but priorities were a key factor as well. No soul searching about women's role within the party surfaced in surviving evidence; in stark contrast to KPD efforts, the DNVP activists' journal had only one article on mobilizing women in this period. Campaign claims to support women's political work had no effect on candidate selection. Only 5 of 103 elected DNVP Reichstag delegates were women in December 1924; in 1928, only

2 of 73.[171] As before, the larger party seems to have been utterly un-concerned about how to win women, fobbing off their mobilization to housewives' organizations and Protestant groups while its official women's organization still lacked viable local chapters in some places.[172] Female activists kept largely silent on this issue, loyally serving the party that reflected their own nationalistic, Christian worldview. Yet while the national, Christian aims of this struggle still corresponded to the desires of many female voters, some quietly joined men frustrated with the DNVP's failure to fulfill its economic promises — after all, they had material interests too, something the nonsocialist parties tended to forget.

The two liberal parties, the DVP and DDP, should have benefited from the relative economic stability of Weimar's middle period. Yet both were decimated as splinter parties tore into liberal support by rallying significant sectors of the bourgeoisie passed over by recovery. The trauma of inflation and a sense of betrayal over revalorization ran deep in the middle masses the liberals had always relied on for support. The liberals' continuing insistence that they represented the nation as a whole (though in fact they were tightly linked with special-interest groups) did nothing to win back these voters. Unwillingness to play to middle-class material concerns left liberals vulnerable to attack by single-issue parties, whose vote peaked in 1928.[173]

DVP writings on female voting behavior expressed confidence that women would support the party for its moral, national message. Yet unlike the Center and DNVP, whose church ties availed them of large women's organizations, the DVP had to work harder for its share of the female vote. It is not surprising that the DVP, whose electorate was slightly more than half female, produced more materials solely for women in 1928 than either the Center or DNVP, even in an election year with few flash point issues.[174]

DVP publications also reported a flurry of activity by the women's organization — meetings, charity drives, Christmas bazaars, and so on. DVP women were praised for their hard work and loyalty to Stresemann.[175] Internal documents, however, tell another story of anger and dysfunction. On the one hand, DVP women had well-defined, separate spheres of work centered around areas they themselves defined as naturally female — social welfare and culture. On the other hand, DVP women were increasingly left to tend their own field while key decisions were made without them — and they knew it. Unlike Center or DNVP women who gladly subordinated their demands to their parties' cultural crusade because they saw their demands inextricably tied to that agenda, DVP women, with their ties to bourgeois feminism, clearly wanted more than relegation to one side. Internal memoranda in 1925–28 reveal a familiar process of women being offered hopeless slots on local ballots while occupational representatives got plum positions (one male leader disingenuously claimed this had nothing to do with the gender of the candidate — it was not the party's fault that most *Handwerker* happened to be male!). Women's organization leaders knew that more and more party men believed that women had no interest in local politics, so there was no point "wasting" a mandate on one of their representatives. DVP women repeatedly protested this view in internal circles, to little avail. Women lost seats on key party committees, such as the executive, less than ten years after their inclusion had been deemed "absolutely necessary."[176] Stresemann in 1927 could still address the party central committee as "meine Herren," despite the fact that women held 10 percent of its seats; the dismal state of the women's organization was similarly invisible in the protocols of all-party meetings. DVP women still had an active role in writing women's propaganda, but the cultural themes they stressed were largely relegated to women's appeals. The party was more than happy to exploit the loyalty and political work of women who shared its national liberal ideology, having long adapted to the pressure to acknowledge women as activists and voters without significantly altering its basic principles. Clearly the DVP wanted to do well with bourgeois women but not at the expense of what it saw as its core constituency of white-collar men. When these male voters left the party or failed to vote, winning them back became a top priority; when women exhibited the same behavior, they were branded an unreliable group to whom only limited resources should be devoted.[177]

In the period leading up to the 1928 election, DVP materials lacked the sense of acute moral and social crisis of earlier campaigns. Women's literature did invoke a "crisis of youth" both to justify party women's own work and to urge women to shake off their apathy to prevent socialist policies from further weakening the family. Yet these appeals were noticeably lackluster, avoiding hot issues directly related to women's welfare — divorce and abortion. The DVP and its women limited their discourse to a bland vision of female equality as defense of the right to motherhood and family, complemented by an expanded public role that made women equally important in the struggle for the fatherland. A tepid rehash of earlier themes, this message failed to ignite female voter interest or stem the party's hemorrhage of support.

The DDP was in an even more critical condition. Internally it was disintegrating as its vote splintered so badly that the 1928 election reduced it to just twenty-five Reichstag seats. Division did not bode well for women's work within the party that had once embraced them so openly. Dire financial straits prevented the party from staging the multimedia campaign it had envisioned for 1928. A strategy memo by Hans Ehlerman for the May election noted women's rising dissatisfaction with their lack of influence within parties, which contemporaries identified as the cause of their falling turnout and apparent disinterest in political events.[178] Within the DDP, published and unpublished sources from the period reveal loud and persistent complaints from women over party neglect of women's propaganda, organization, and even women's issues in the legislature. While DDP propaganda attacked the Right as hostile to women's rights,[179] women claimed that the DDP itself sacrificed those rights in party deal making, as in its failure to support equality for Prussian female civil servants in 1927.[180] Internally, the women's organization was left to wither between elections. Women who strove to keep the organization alive worked to exhaustion, often without even reimbursement for expenses. As Gertrud Geisenheyner argued at the 1928 women's conference, men still viewed women as incapable of handling big tasks. Marie-Elisabeth Lüders's postelection critique was even more damning of the party's "patronizing tolerance of women and their work," which "blatantly demonstrated their [view of them as] inferior" and annoyed women to a degree that should not be overlooked.[181]

Lüders had reason to be furious. In late 1927, the women's group in Berlin, the most vital DDP bastion in the country, had to wage a battle to secure a safe mandate in the upcoming election for her, the DDP's most prominent woman after Gertrud Bäumer. After much wrangling, not least because of hostility from party women in Potsdam, Lüders was compensated for her shaky position on the Reich list with the number two slot in Potsdam II; she and Bäumer were the only DDP women elected to the Reichstag in 1928.[182] The DDP's shrinking number of Reichstag seats meant fiercer competition for the few safe ones remaining. The growing dominance of special-interest politics meant that women were being squeezed out to make room for economic groups' candidates. Interestingly, a breakdown by occupation of candidates who made it into the Reich ballot listed Bäumer, Lüders, and women's organization chair Martha Dönhoff, respectively as "political civil servant" and "freelancers" (*freie Berufe*), while the remaining women on the ballot were classified as housewives.[183] Seemingly, an elite group of female notables could transcend the category of "women" at times, though as Lüders's predicament shows, in the fight for power, gender prevailed over other identities, to women's disadvantage. This did not go unnoticed by DDP women, angered that the party, which had once given women special consideration to help them gain a foothold in politics and once sold itself as the "party of women" in the hope of reaping the female vote, now reduced them to competing with occupational groups. Paula Ollendorf protested this in 1928, invoking a key theme in propaganda that women were qualitatively different because they served the whole, not one narrow interest.[184]

Widespread concern over female voter apathy, a constant theme in this period's flyers and internal writings, did not bolster women's case for more resources. One set of women around Bäumer and Helene Lange blamed this lack of interest not on the party but on the legacy of women's exclusion from politics. Bäumer and BDF activist Else Ulich-Beil saw women's lists, for example, as a symptom of a larger crisis of party politics, not a feminist issue.[185] Just as the Left pointed to a socialist future to remedy women's particular hardships, these DDP female notables looked to the future reconciliation of all Germans in a *Volksgemeinschaft* to end gender inequalities. Lüders, supported by many local activists at the 1928 women's conference who, like her, were more involved in the thick of pragmatic political work, swam against this current of romanticism, even though they too rejected a women's party and agreed that the party needed to "humanize" its image. Sadly, Lüders would find herself on the outside after the DDP's restructuring in 1930.

The DDP clung to a language of citizenship in its drive to cultivate a new republican spirit.[186] In 1928 its vision of female citizenship attempted to reconcile both heart and mind, public and private, worker and mother. While appeals played to both reason and emotion, visual images of women, more likely to be seen by the broader public, bucked the trend toward New Objectivity and increasingly employed more sentimental images of femininity. While general appeals called for an end to political and social splintering, it was women who symbolized unity, the only ones capable of forging the national community that men, through egoism and deal making, had botched.[187] Yet the DDP could not even unify itself. In its quest for a formula to halt the erosion of the political middle, it would soon embrace a nationalistic ideal of the strong state that would tear Democrats apart.

Unlike the 1924 elections, in which inflation and stabilization dominated, the campaigns of 1925–28 had no single galvanizing issue. The SPD, KPD, and to some extent the DDP used opposition to the Bürgerblock to organize their appeals to all groups, including women. The SPD's persistent emphasis on its sweeping welfare agenda appears to have been successful here. The SPD and DDP used a language of social fairness to posit female equality as a necessary component of political and economic justice in a social republic, while the KPD dismissed everyone to its right for tolerating systemic inequalities that could only be rectified by revolution. Bürgerblock rhetoric, in contrast, defined protecting women as defending their interests as mothers, wives, and housewives in a *Volksgemeinschaft* no longer riven by class. Thus, all parties continued to employ the various discourses on gender equality each had devised during Weimar's early days. But unlike in 1918–19, these no longer held center stage, as their ability to rally female voters was now seen as limited at best.

While the Left made a strong case for welfare as the ultimate women's issue, culture persisted as a focus in women's propaganda, with the Center and DNVP exploiting the hottest cultural issue of the period, the Schulgesetz. This topic was so central to the Center's 1928 campaign—indeed its very identity—that it seemingly felt no need even to address appeals on the subject directly to women, banking on the strength of Catholic women's religiosity to guarantee votes. Both the Center and DNVP used religion in schools to present an image of Christian morality under siege in a godless republic. The liberal parties, which knew the issue was bound to hurt them with more conservative female voters, tried half-heartedly to defend their objections to aspects of the school bill but preferred to ignore the issue. Even the SPD, which like the liberals attacked "clerical dominance," muted any virulent anti-Christian utterances, leaving that to the KPD.

The Left preferred to stress abortion and reproduction in appeals to women, depicting the creation of conditions where every child was wanted and provided for as the true definition of morality, a message the SPD highlighted in appeals showcasing its social welfare activity. The KPD, for its part, made abortion central to its attempts to mobilize women, painting the issue in stark colors designed to rally female masses made ragged by endless childbearing (even as that reality was receding among the proletariat). Only the Center returned the Left's salvo, denouncing abortion on religious, as well as natalist and eugenic, grounds; the other major parties largely kept silent. Yet there was one thing on which all could agree: motherhood still constituted women's main source of fulfillment and the wellspring of their identity. The maternal female body was the dominant visual signifier of woman, as even the KPD relegated its androgynous female figures to Münzenberg's publications, such as the *Arbeiter-Illustrierte-Zeitung*.

It is surprising that at a time when the New Woman was a central figure in the popular imagination, she was more a charged absence than a literal presence in propaganda imagery. The KPD, which attempted to incorporate other popular culture phenomena such as fashion, held her up for derision but confined her to the party press. The SPD's 1928 poster depicting "people's comrades" came closest to rendering a version of the New Woman as a welcome member of the *Volksgemeinschaft*. In contrast, the DDP by 1928 all but abandoned its high-profile equal rights feminism, as reflected in its increasing reliance on comfortingly maternal young women in its posters. Instead of embracing the New Woman, Weimar parties were more likely to embrace the New Objectivity of the rationalized household, giving woman's role in the home new luster at a time when many feared she would abandon it for single independence.

While women remained central to each party's vision of Germany's future, the very existence of the nation was less at risk in this period than at any time since the republic's inception. The DDP's call that it was up to women to realize the liberal dream of a truly united Germany aroused little interest. Women's growing preference for popular entertainment over feminist organization, particularly among the younger generation, manifested itself politically in falling voter turnout. While this apathy caused a marked degree of distress among the established parties, if they had foreseen the unsparing radicalization the depression would soon bring, perhaps they would have counted their blessings.

4

Saviors or Traitors?

:

Women in the Campaigns of the Early Depression Years

The decline of the mechanized female dance troops so popular in the "golden" days before the crash of 1929 also stands as a farewell to the New Woman who loomed so large in the debates over the changing face of femininity in the 1920s. The depression forced the New Woman—whose currency as a party political recruiting symbol was already quite limited—to don a more somber expression as she faced an all-out attack on her right to work and a climate in which her experimentation with gender identities was increasingly reviled as a treacherous distraction from the serious business of solving the country's dire malaise.

On the surface, the 1928 elections had seemed to signal renewed strength for republican forces: the SPD won a decisive victory, and right-wing extremists went home empty-handed. The SPD emerged from opposition to head a coalition under Hermann Müller, but this alliance did not survive Germany's slump triggered by the Wall Street crash of October 1929. Müller's cabinet fell in March 1930 over the issue of unemployment relief, as spiraling joblessness put unprecedented strains on the available funds; the SPD chose to bow out of government rather than watch industrial interests dismantle this pillar of its welfare program. Hindenburg subsequently named the Center's Heinrich Brüning chancellor and, invoking constitutional article 48, granted him emergency powers aimed at robbing the Reichstag of any real power and excluding the SPD from national politics for good. Brüning henceforth governed without Reichstag consent as Germany began its slide from parliamentary democracy into authoritarian presidential rule.

Brüning's top priority was to end the reparations decreed by the Versailles treaty (and renegotiated in 1929 under the Young Plan) by demonstrating that Germany could not meet its payments because its economy was too weak. Thus, he deliberately inflamed the economic crisis by slashing state spending on social programs, raising taxes, and allowing employers to break contracts and roll back wages. When the Reichstag challenged his economic plan, Brüning obtained its dissolution in the summer of 1930; new elections were called for September. The timing of this decision increased the likelihood of a victory by the National Socialists, who had recently racked up a string of strong showings in state elections.

The depression that had set in by mid-1930 was the latest economic disaster to batter Germany since the war. At least one-third of the labor force would be unemployed by 1932. The crisis also magnified anxieties felt by the middle classes, whose economic position had long been precarious, and heightened the universal desire for an end to political squabbling. For women, this age of anxiety brought certain unique burdens. Appearances suggested that women were not as hard hit economically as men, due in part to the fact that the depression struck first at heavy industry, not the consumer industries where women dominated the labor force. Women were also underrepresented in unemployment statistics as they were more likely to work part-time. In many respects, however, the depression hit women harder than men. Women were more likely to have unemployment benefits denied or terminated early. As the primary users of social services such as health insurance or rent control, their ability to keep the household functioning was stretched to the limit by government cutbacks.[1]

Working women also suffered discrimination that men did not. While they continued to find jobs more easily, their wages were markedly lower and employers used fear of dismissal to extract extra underpaid work. The depression hit the tertiary sector, of which women comprised one-third of employees, extremely hard, causing a 171 percent surge in unemployment between January and September 1930.[2] Many white-collar women, especially those over age twenty-five, took pay cuts or demotions just to keep their jobs.[3] Yet these hardships remained all but invisible in public discourse. The period witnessed a renewed campaign against "double earners," which was reminiscent of postwar demobilization decrees and the PAV. Initially led by conservative white-collar organizations like the DHV, the battle against women's right to work gained increasing support at a time when more and more fathers lacked jobs.

Attacks on working women demonstrated continued concern over women's ability to fulfill what was seen as their highest function, motherhood. These fears only intensified as women driven by economic desperation underwent illegal abortions in numbers that topped 1 million in 1930. While debate over abortion would peak in 1931, the issue, already a theme in socialist and Catholic propaganda since the mid-1920s, won new urgency as agitators for further reform of paragraph 218 linked abortion to unemployment and social welfare cuts, as in a 1930 rally in Berlin's Sportpalast.[4] Simultaneously, pronatalist groups established Mother's Day as an unofficial, but widely observed, holiday. This celebration acquired special importance as the desire to return women to an exclusively domestic role ran strong, but the state could not afford expanded support for working mothers or large families. Mother's Day was a painless way to glorify motherhood without providing real material benefits or opening messy debates about the changing contours of maternity and femininity.[5]

Although the depression was setting in, the popular press in 1930 still showed piquant interest in such topics as skirt lengths, female driving, and smoking. Fashion articles from the period betray a growing backlash against the New Woman, with her short hair and androgynous physique. While some critics expressed reservations about the so-called return to femininity, busts and hips were back. As the *8-Uhr Abendblatt* declared, men no longer liked boyish women.[6] Lest such topics be dismissed as nonpolitical, Erich Fromm's surveys reveal the strong emotions invested in seemingly trivial matters such as the use of cosmetics, which respondents overwhelmingly saw as pernicious and "unworthy of a woman or mother."[7]

In addition to this return to femininity, the early depression years saw a crisis among men "emasculated" by an ineffectual democracy, stalemated party politics, and an economy in which their wives were more likely to have a job than they. Writers like Leonore Kühn and Agnes von Zahn-Harnack dismissed men as "worthless," while Katharina von Kardorff revived calls for a women's party to clean up the mess men had made.[8] The flip side of this was a public discourse marked by virulent misogyny, as many increasingly blamed the "sickness" of German society on female emancipation. The battle of the sexes, which seemed to subside during Weimar's stable interlude, found fresh recruits as the economic crisis deepened.

This resurgent mood of crisis spurred high voter turnout, particularly among women, for the 1930 Reichstag election—the highest since 1919.[9] The 1930 election's greatest significance, according to the dominant narratives of German history, lay in the national breakthrough of the Nazi Party, which rocketed to second place (the Communists took third), all but extinguishing the liberals and setting every party on the defensive. Building on the respectability accorded by its recent alliance with the DNVP in the drive against the Young Plan and aided by the snowballing catastrophe of the depression, the NSDAP convinced many voters that it was the only force powerful enough to restore the nation's health and unity by freeing it from the Weimar system. How did the meteoric rise of this openly misogynist party affect political discourse on women? Could parties afford to express support for gender equality at a time of rising extremism and mounting economic disaster? How did the rhetorical struggle to control the female body through debates over reproduction, social services, and female labor look at a time when the welfare state threatened to collapse and abortion reached epidemic proportions? Examining the parties and their propaganda in 1929–30 illuminates how political actors' visions of women's roles were filtered through fears fueled by yet another dizzying economic crisis and mounting political radicalism.

While the National Socialists did not surpass the SPD as Weimar's largest party in September 1930, their rise from a paltry 2.6 percent of the vote in 1928 to 18.3 percent made them 1930's clear victors. This overnight victory was foreshadowed by gains in regional elections in 1929, indicating that the NSDAP was positioning itself as the most viable party of protest even before the depression's full impact was felt. Now possessed of a better funded, more professional propaganda apparatus led since April 1930 by Joseph Goebbels, the NSDAP took its propaganda circus across Germany, staging over 34,000 rallies in the month prior to the Reichstag election. Its method was to attack the Young Plan and the disintegration of national politics into a "heap of special interests." It hammered away both at the traditional bourgeois parties, which it claimed had delivered the middle classes into the clutches of "Jewish finance capital," and the Left, which aimed to reduce Germany to a satellite of Moscow. The NSDAP's youthful dynamism starkly contrasted with the dazed, weary visage of the bourgeois parties, allowing it to appear to rising numbers of Germans from all segments of the populace as the force best able to revive the nation.[10]

Women were most notable in the Nazis' 1930 campaign for their continued absence as a propaganda target. The NSDAP's goal of expanding its support base particularly among the middle classes would not have a specifically female aspect until 1931. Yet the lack of a concerted pitch to women did not preclude their support, particularly in Protestant cities such as Magdeburg and Leipzig.[11] From the party's inception, a core female group had been attracted to various aspects of its platform, from anti-Semitism to anti-Marxism. Often introduced to the movement by a male relative, these women were united by the comradery of persecution and the idea of a female crusade to purify national culture with the holy flame of motherhood. From well-heeled conservative defectors to struggling *petites bourgeoises*, all shared deep anxieties about modern life and women's future. Such fears also underpinned less committed women's rising tendency to vote NSDAP as the depression stoked anger at the "system." While few actually joined the party, more women granted it their vote after 1929.[12]

This trend was not the result of any systematic effort to cultivate female voters. No flyers or posters specifically for women appear to have been devised for the 1929 or 1930 campaigns.[13] Nor was agitation among women a subject of propaganda directives. The 1929 pocket calendar was thick with musings on the roles of youth and soldiers but thin on women's place in the movement. No women's appeals ran in the *Völkischer Beobachter* for the 1930 election, with the exception of a rather odd address to "working women in the KPD." Tellingly, the *Völkischer Beobachter*'s election day edition ran appeals to youth, peasants, workers, and *Mittelständler* but not to women, indicating the scant regard in which the party held them.[14]

The few extant Nazi materials in 1929–30 that spoke to or about women in some fashion come from the party daily and miscellaneous fly-ers, which were still anchored in the languages of anti-Semitism, *Kampf*, and racialism deployed since the early 1920s. The *Völkischer Beobachter*, for example, continued to "unmask" white slavery rings run by rapacious Jews. A *Jugendbund* pamphlet trotted out the Walkyries to delineate the "duties and work of our sisters." It called the home women's battlefield against "junk that bears the stamp of foreign lands or the Jewish pro-ducer. . . . Back to plainness and simplicity. . . . When our girls especially have achieved purity and joy of heart, we will say to the *Heimat*: beloved homeland, when you wish, I will present you with the new race you need to attain freedom!"[15] Similar hyperbole appeared in a 1930 *Völkischer Beo-bachter* piece on Mother's Day: "No other word in our glorious and rich tongue has a sweeter and, at the same time, more mysterious tone than this blessed word 'mother.'" Maternity was clearly the embodiment of a female virtue capable of unifying the *Volk*, a common motif on which the Nazis put a marked racial spin. This was coupled in the Nazi press with polemics on the nation's loss of morality, abortion, contraception, urban culture, and the "dematernalization" of women exemplified by the New Woman.[16]

Claudia Koonz has shown that before the NSDAP began paying much attention to its female supporters in 1931, they had a degree of orga-nizational and even doctrinal flexibility. But official utterances clearly cast women in supporting roles: "German women must help us! Today's male sensibility [*Mannessinn*] is cluttered with knowledge and job worries, when not sodden with alcohol or tobacco. . . . No one takes charge to end mismanagement and restore order to the state. . . . Thinking women, with their fresher, invigorated senses, must intervene—even if it's only get-ting men to read and informing them about today's problems."[17] While rhetorical space was granted the politically aware woman, her room to act was clearly limited. She herself should not take the lead in public af-fairs but use her "senses" (contrasted with the "knowledge" that "clut-ters" men's sensibility) to inspire men. In Nazism's "antirational" politics, women could hold a key position—a passive, symbolic one.

Nazi writers saw women's "natural" role as mothers as the culmination of female activity. They advocated a compulsory service year to prepare girls for motherhood, with an eye ultimately to limiting female employ-ment outside the home. Just as in the mid-1920s, Nazis added their voices to the chorus of conservative and liberal pronatalists, decrying a society where healthy women shunned childbearing out of "egotism" or economic need. While the party still acknowledged need as a justification for female work outside the home, the depression fed prejudices that many women were "stealing" jobs from family fathers merely to satisfy their desire for frocks and sweets. An anonymous letter in the February 1930 *Völkischer Beobachter* blamed a "female system," in which firms allegedly hired fifty women for every five men, for the loss of male white-collar jobs. The author painted this as a gender war: "The women have a very good organization and pursue the same goals as men—they even fight us from their position as the majority."[18] This "voice from the *Volk*" articulated a view that only gained popularity as the depression dragged on.

The letter's characterization of expanding female white-collar labor as a *Weibersystem* can be seen as part of the NSDAP's overarching antisystem discourse, which sharpened in 1930. While its gendered aspect was still mainly relegated to lurid sexual exposés in the party press, attacks on parties identified with the Weimar system unwittingly betrayed Nazi attitudes toward women. To attack the SPD, for example, the *Völkischer Beobachter* reprinted a 1919 USPD flyer, adding a caption demanding that the Left be held accountable for the 1918 revolution (the fact that the SPD and USPD were not identical did not daunt Nazi watchdogs). Interestingly, the flyer chosen was addressed to "female and male voters" (note the order of address) and listed women's enfranchisement as the revolution's second great achievement after ending the war.[19] Though the NSDAP caption made no reference to the vote, the use of this particular flyer constituted a veiled denunciation of female suffrage, which was closely tied not only to the USPD's image but also to the republic itself. In the context of the NSDAP's continuing refusal to allow female delegates and violently antiwoman comments by Nazi bigwigs, such moves reinforced the party's misogynist image—a *Frauenfeindlichkeit* the Left would exploit in its own campaigns.

Another negative appeal tacitly linked the republic with the political woman. A *Völkischer Beobachter* cartoon mocking the recent merger of the DDP and the Young German Order depicted order leader Artur Mahraun on the lap of an obese, bejeweled woman labeled "the black-red-gold plutocracy"; her features are stereotypically Jewish and she is unnaturally large, while Mahraun is reduced to the size of a boy.[20] The image aimed to discredit Mahraun for backpedaling on his anti-Semitism by allying with the liberal DDP, long depicted by the Nazis as *the* party of "Jewish capital." But it is also consistent with *völkisch* discourse, which since the early 1920s linked democracy, Jews, and "soulless" female emancipation to posit a Jewish plot against the organic unity of Germany's social, political, and sexual order. Here this fear of the Other is linked to fears unleashed by women's simultaneous political and sexual emancipation. The image argues that this can only produce the disastrous masculinization of women and the feminization of men.[21]

While the NSDAP had not shed its crude anti-Semitism by the 1930 campaign, it was plainly making a bid for respectability to become a mass party. This involved refuting charges of being anti-Christian, as in a 1930 communique (also carried in the party press) crediting the Nazi culture minister in Braunschweig for saving prayer in public schools. Rather than lash out at the Center Party as in the past, this document contrasted Nazi "positive Christianity" with SPD "red culture action" (*rote Kulturtat*), playing to entrenched bourgeois antisocialism.[22] This can also be read as an overture to women, regarded as more likely to vote according to religious issues. Yet if unwavering female support for the Center in 1930 is any indication, such rhetoric did little to erase the Nazis' pagan image among Catholic women, who at any rate were unlikely to have even seen a lone item in the Nazi press. The NSDAP did, however, expand its female base in Protestant areas. Its stress on a *Kinder, Küche,* and *Kirche* role for women and its war on "cultural Bolshevism"—themes long articulated by mainstream bourgeois parties—began to resonate among women who increasingly felt that their traditional representatives were no longer able to stem Germany's moral decline.[23]

The NSDAP's drive for respectability also included attempts to shake off charges that Nazis were Bolsheviks in brown shirts. This surfaced in the only national appeal explicitly for women found in 1930. The piece, which ran on the front page of the *Völkischer Beobachter*, quoted a Romanian Communist on Russian child labor abuses to demolish the KPD myth of a Soviet paradise. Asking if they wanted to bring such misery upon themselves and their children, it urged proletarian women to spurn working-class "traitors" by voting National Socialist.[24] By using images of suffering children, which were absent from appeals to men, the NSDAP hoped an appeal to women's "motherly" nature would puncture class solidarity, while demonstrating sufficient anticommunism to bourgeois voters.

Those rare instances in 1930 where Nazi propaganda invoked women in some fashion remained consistent with rhetoric from earlier campaigns, leaving little doubt that the NSDAP had not yet begun seriously to court this constituency. The NSDAP envisioned a maternal sphere of female activity away from party politics to complement men's struggle against republican weakness, Jewish dominance, Marxist treachery, and the confusion of social and sexual order personified by the emancipated woman. Yet while its misogyny surely alienated many women voters, promises of security and clarity increasingly appealed to others anxious about how to keep the home fires burning, whether or not they were forced to get a job. Economic catastrophe would combine with the NSDAP's assiduous cultivation of a female constituency after 1930, as well as the glaring inability of the parties women had supported in the past to solve the nation's crisis, to help the NSDAP close the gender gap in its voter profile in 1932.

Moving from the radical to the mainstream Right, we find the DNVP, whose 6 percent drop in the 1928 election precipitated the ouster of leader Count Westarp for Alfred Hugenberg, media mogul and head of the party's far right wing. Hugenberg set out to purge the DNVP of the economic interest groups that had split it over the Dawes Plan in 1924 and seduced it into government in 1925 and 1927. He wished to transform the party from an amalgam of Christian, nationalist, and conservative elements into a monolithic bloc fused by the "iron hammer of Weltanschauung."[25] In 1929 he gathered the DNVP, Stahlhelm (the rightist veterans' organization), and the NSDAP into a "national opposition" to the Young Plan in particular and the republic in general. Such coziness with the Nazis, however, alienated moderate conservatives and precipitated a spate of dramatic resignations by Westarp and others who feared that extremism would isolate the party and leave conservative interests without political muscle. On the eve of the 1930 election, the DNVP was in disarray.

Hugenberg's drive to retool the DNVP to compete with the NSDAP for the anti-Weimar vote stalled in 1930; the party polled only 7 percent, losing almost 2 million votes and nearly half its Reichstag seats, as bourgeois voters increasingly expressed their anger at the system with a vote for the NSDAP. The DNVP did manage to retain its rural Protestant base.[26] Its female support, while slipping numerically, also remained proportionally strong—where votes were tabulated by sex, 9.1 percent of all women voted DNVP, as opposed to 6.5 percent of all men. In fact, women proved more loyal, constituting a rising proportion of DNVP voters as men fled to the NSDAP.[27]

The DNVP's disarray most likely explains its sudden dearth of materials for women. The few found from the 1929–30 period indicate that the basic themes addressed to women had not changed drastically. Like general appeals, those to women cheered the demise of the "Young [Plan] Reichstag." Economic need induced by the staggering burden of reparations caused millions of women and mothers to wonder how they would clothe and feed their own. Antireligious, antinational elements still held sway; material misery combined with a resurgent cultural Bolshevism to prepare the ground for a second German revolution. Against this stood only one defense—a union of all nationally minded men and women behind a new program. Instead of raising taxes, the state should foster growth with high import tariffs and strict needs tests for unemployment aid. Church and family must be protected. Toadying to foreign powers must accede to a revived national spirit—goals, women were told, promoted only by the DNVP and Hugenberg.[28]

Such themes were nothing new in DNVP propaganda, although its tone in this period shows a level of anticommunist hectoring not heard since 1919 and a growing shrillness in Weimar political discourse. Appeals depicted a situation in which Germany's cultural decline coupled with economic collapse to erode the nation from within, making it ripe for a Marxist coup. This was presaged in 1929 electoral appeals from Saxony, where such rhetoric was hitched to the memory of the KPD-SPD government of 1923. For example, one flyer for general audiences entitled "A Second Soviet Saxony Imminent?" combined images of inflation money, poor women and children, and urban guerrillas proclaiming, "All power comes from the street!" The revamped DNVP had lost none of its flair for playing to the class prejudices of bourgeois Germans.[29]

Materials also underscored the DNVP's belief in a fundamental antagonism between Christianity and Marxism, as in a 1929 pamphlet by Evangelical women's leader Magdalene von Tiling.[30] Interestingly, this piece from one of the DNVP's most prominent women did not address women at all. Similarly, women were not the sole audience of a 1929 flyer to "all Christians."[31] As in previous campaigns, the "threat" to religion and religious education figured prominently on the list of the nation's ills in both local and national general appeals. Yet women were still the primary, if unaddressed, audience for appeals stressing religion, materials written increasingly by Tiling, who had climbed the party ladder from city to state to Reichstag delegate by 1930. She and Paula Müller-Otfried wrote slogans for the 1930 contest that reflected their belief that Christianity should be a central campaign theme.[32] This tactic also constituted a response to the NSDAP's grab for the bourgeois protest vote. Hoping to undercut it by stressing Nazism's pagan roots, the DNVP presented itself in 1930 as the surest force for Christianity.

A 1930 pamphlet from the DNVP women's group (authored by Tiling) traced another source of national weakness to liberalism, echoing past denunciations of the ideals of 1789 from both DNVP men and women. Tiling argued that while liberals stressed equality and individual freedom, conservatives emphasized difference and a divinely ordered *Ständegesellschaft* based on hierarchy, obedience, and honor to combat social splintering and foreign "servitude." While she did not explicitly outline women's position in this order, her call for "social understanding" can be decoded as a call for women to abandon liberal ideals and rediscover their "natural" domestic role. Tiling elsewhere described *Frausein* as woman's *Stand*: domestic chores constituted precisely the work God demanded of her, not striving for equality, which exacerbated the postwar dislocation that had delivered Germany to godlessness.[33] This rejection of female activity that "competed" with men's or impinged upon women's primary duty to God and family had been central to DNVP women's propaganda from day one. A 1930 campaign illustration on page one of the Berlin party newspaper expresses this continuity (see Figure 4.1). Addressed to German women and mothers, it depicts a fair-haired beauty (whose long tresses signify her distance from the New Woman) cradling her contented children, all bathed in a heavenly glow. This vision of maternity spares no sentimentality to equate womanhood with motherhood and protection of mother and child with the DNVP.[34]

This vision of femininity also continued to inform DNVP pronouncements on women's economic role, focused almost exclusively on the occupation of housewife. The only 1930 campaign pamphlet specifically addressed to women detailed laws affecting housewives. It restated the DNVP's commitment to housewives' presence in the Reich Economic Ministry, something the Center, DDP, and SPD allegedly opposed. The DNVP also stressed its fight for new regulations on domestic servants based on the "relationship of trust" between employer and employee—laws informed by an understanding of this economic arrangement as a domestic partnership into which Socialists and others with no understanding of the "nature" of home work tried to inject unwarranted class antagonism.[35]

Likewise, party journal descriptions of female activists, likely written by women themselves, reflect an organic social model in which female public activity stemmed from a loving domesticity. The late Margarete

Behm, head of both the Women Home Workers' Union and the DNVP women's committee until 1923, was praised for the godliness and "single-mindedness intrinsic to female nature" with which she had pursued her tasks. Paula Müller-Otfried was feted on her birthday for her social welfare work. Käthe Schirmacher's obituary noted that she had spent her youth *im Kampf für die Frau* (she had once been a radical feminist) but shifted her focus to the "fate of the fatherland" during the war, making her a "truly German woman." This description powerfully reinforced the notion that feminism was at odds with "true" femininity, Germanness, and the good of the *Volk*.[36]

Women in the DNVP found themselves in a potentially difficult position in this period. Hugenberg was bent on supporting policies that would sharpen political and economic crisis with the ultimate goal of destroying the republic. DNVP women, even if they were as ideologically hard-line as party men, were also more likely to be engaged in the ameliorative work of charity or welfare, which dealt with the human fallout of such radical policies. Furthermore, the DNVP's poor record in such areas as female candidates—something Hugenberg, who now dominated the executive, showed no interest in addressing—could have made it vulnerable to a female exodus. Westarp's breakaway Conservative Party, in fact, tried to lure women by proclaiming its commitment to women candidates such as former DNVP member Anna von Gierke.[37] Yet no hemorrhage of support occurred among female activists. Nor do internal documents reveal any dispute over women's relationship to the party, as in previous years. But if activists remained committed, there were signs that the loyalty of female voters was softening, as Protestant women increasingly embraced the NSDAP's antimodernism. Furthermore, collaboration with Hitler made it difficult for the DNVP to repudiate convincingly the NSDAP and its "paganism" in 1930. Women were still less likely than men to defect to the Nazi camp, but the DNVP's lack of a concerted effort to reach them in 1930 was a dangerous oversight. As the NSDAP capitalized on a deepening national crisis to present itself as the best alternative, the DNVP could no longer assume that its traditional sources of female support would yield the votes they had in elections past.

In 1928 the Center Party suffered its worst ever result in a Reichstag election, dropping from 17.4 to 15.2 percent of the vote.[38] Like the DNVP, the Center subsequently veered right, choosing for its leader Ludwig Kaas, a conservative monsignor with Vatican ties. But he quickly proved to

figure 4.1
"German Women! German Mothers! Think of Your Children! Vote German National! List 2" (*Unsere Partei* [DNVP], 1 September 1930)

be unpopular and incompetent, and the function of maintaining member loyalty devolved to Chancellor Heinrich Brüning, behind whom the party threw its support.[39] This new era in Center politics saw more anti-Weimar language, a waning commitment to republicanism, and a rising desire for a strong leader (though the party disdained the rabble-rousing of certain aspiring dictators). The Center's 1930 campaign stressed the need for a *Volksgemeinschaft* and stronger state authority within the framework of a healthy democracy. This was wed to the other main issue, the economy. As one general appeal stated, this election was about work and bread for the German people, which could be secured only by overcoming the "party mentality" and the "heaps of special interests." Promoting pragmatism and competence, materials used buzzwords like "responsibility" and "determination." At stake, they declared, were not isolated issues but the very health of the people's state. Center propaganda in 1930 portrayed a party unified by a "will to order" capable of tackling this challenge.[40]

Women's propaganda couched these concerns in terms of the election's cultural importance. The *Volk* was battling not only for its economic survival, but marriage, family, and Christian culture were also at stake. As 1930's "battle slogan" read, "Woman stands behind the Center because it protects her moral value under the law; it is determined to preserve the moral foundation of the *Volk*—the Christian family—from the powers of social radicalism" and the "cynical, destructive rage of cultural Bolshevism."[41] Catholic women pledged out of love for their *Volk* and their children to support leaders "guided by the Christian spirit" in the "struggle to rebuild." A new mobilization strategy inaugurated at the 1928 Catholic Conference argued, among other things, that the power of motherliness called women to surmount the "worst damage of our time."[42] While Center campaign propaganda had used this motif for years, literature from 1930 conveys a heightened sense of crisis in which women, because of their "special gifts" of compromise and caring, embodied what could save the *Volksstaat* from ruin.

As before, the family dominated Center discourse. In this period, the Center, like the DNVP, saw the family locked in a two-front war against economic crisis and a continued assault on Christian politics. Its December 1928 conference—its last during Weimar—passed a women's committee motion urging the Reichstag to ease material burdens on large families. It firmly opposed divorce reform and equality for illegitimate children, despite the strains this put on relations with coalition partners. While these "family issues" affected women most directly and were usually promoted by female politicians, Center literature presented these not as women's issues alone but as part of the larger Catholic worldview.[43]

Women did, however, have a newly urgent role to play—the "great art of mothers to make the father once again head [*Hauptperson*] of the family."[44] Performing this could spell the salvation of the nation from moral decline and civil war. As the male chair of the Catholic Mothers' and Maidens' Union proclaimed at the Catholic Conference: "All is tottering. New foundations must be laid—not only by the strong arms and chivalrous courage of men, but by women with their firm will, rich hearts, and noble sensibility who will give their all to rebuild our *Volk* when a *Volksgemeinschaft* is most needed." Other appeals played to Catholic women's loyalty to church and *Volk*, a *Treue* indelibly wedded to the nature of womanhood. Conversely, the Catholic press and Center appeals often blamed women for moral degeneration. Bishop Johannes von Münster (whose call for "core troops" [*Kerntruppen*] to combat this decay reflects the rising tone of violence in early 1930s public discourse) stated, "A people rises and falls with its women. Christianity has done a great deal for woman, and it always comes home to roost when she is indifferent to the faith. The main duty of Catholic mothers remains the Christian education of children. It is this concern for the sanctity of family life that will determine whether our nation's sick stock can be restored to health." The message was clear—woman could be savior of the nation and culture, but if she failed out of indifference or disloyalty, she brought down everything around her.[45]

Center propaganda in 1930 repeatedly condemned radicals who "reject everything, who know no other means than violence, slander, and destruction."[46] While this included Nazis,[47] materials for both women and mixed audiences continued to locate the biggest threat in the leftist and liberal camps. *Das Zentrum*'s election issue condemned liberalism's "sins" and attempts from "the Marxist side" to legalize common-law marriage and "free love." This left-liberal "cultural alliance," not Nazism, promoted blasphemy and hedonism. Abortion, too, remained another area where the Center marshaled moral and even eugenic arguments against this liberal-Marxist war on Christianity. It argued that the 1926 softening of paragraph 218 paved the way for full legalization, endangering not only marriage and family but also the nation's future stock. It blamed booming abortion rates not on the economy but on the "free . . . advertisement of abortifacients," a "pestilence . . . our cultural liberal opponents" condone. The Center held the Catholic position, which rejected abortion even to save the life of the mother, in the belief that "the child in utero is a unique, immortal soul that needs our protection even more because it is the most innocent and helpless of creatures."[48]

Women in Center discourse constituted a force to protect the weak and the young from other dangers such as "sexual slavery," smut, and alcohol. They could do this as politicians: a *Germania* piece highlighted female party leaders, who combined competence in social legislation with an ability to bring love and spirituality to public life. These comments reflect a preoccupation in the 1930 campaign with women's presumed ability to restore ethics to politics. While appeals to all audiences portrayed the election as a choice between responsible deeds and demagogic agitation, women's materials promoted femininity as a civilizing political force. Helene Weber asked, "What are you, state—solely masculine or abstract, as you have been portrayed? . . . Women also belong to the people's state, . . . which grows much more out of family and school life than we realize." This argument was originally offered in the nineteenth century to justify a greater public role for women. In 1930, with the dramatic growth of extremism, the Weimar coalition parties emphasized it in appeals that urged female cooperation to restore hope and humanity to public, political life.[49]

Women could also protect the weak through welfare work. As social work pedagogue Helene Weber argued at a campaign rally, the welfare state was particularly invaluable at a time when public order was under siege—remarks that served to critique Brüning's gutting of social services, as well as to justify certain forms of women's work. Elsewhere, 1930 appeals did not question woman's right to employment outside the home, though work still did not define her, as implied in *Germania*'s claim that "whether mother or worker," women knew that only the Center held "Catholic *Frauen- und Mutterrecht*" sacred.[50]

Indeed, the Center defined woman's chief political task, regardless of her station, as using her vote to strengthen the representatives of Catholicism. In 1930 this became a chorus of blame aimed at women who failed to vote. Women were not the only ones scolded—an "army of 11 million nonvoters" had undercut the Catholic crusade against Bolshevism and smut in the last Reichstag.[51] But appeals to them implied that women's apathy stemmed from a poor understanding of the demands of citizenship. No matter how ingrained loyalty, responsibility, and love of fatherland might be in female nature, after twelve years of suffrage women still had to prove themselves worthy of the vote.[52]

Did the latent mistrust of women expressed by both Center men and women extend to gender relations within the party? Evidence from this period suggests that the party continued to pay no particular attention to its female audience. For instance, only four of the sixty-eight Center Reichstag delegates elected in 1930 were female. Yet a postmortem in *Germania*'s women's page blamed this on female voter apathy, which statistics show actually decreased in 1930, and unwillingness to do party service for this result, not the list system that increasingly favored occupational representatives.[53] Despite the spiritual power Catholic ideology assigned women, they were unwelcome in the corridors of Catholic political power.[54] The potential of female power to transform politics was central symbolically to 1930 Center women's literature, yet any attempt to instrumentalize it was preempted by a worsening depression, growing class schisms within both the party and the nation, and Center women's reluctance to challenge their own party.

Mobilization of female voters continued to be done more by the church than by the party, which produced many general flyers in 1930 but no flyers and only two pamphlets specifically for women.[55] *Germania* explicitly equated party and church when it called Catholic women's vote an "expression of loyalty" to church and *Volk*. On election day, its women's page quoted Pope Pius IX, who said the faith demanded that all be the best citizens they could be.[56] Center disinterest in women's propaganda is thrown into relief when compared with its effort to attract youth, deemed the most necessary group to cultivate after the party's poor showing in 1928. The party press and conference discussed strategies for mobilizing youth at length, while women were absent from the list of target groups.[57] Reasons for this were implied in a *Germania* appeal to young women, which urged a more visible movement of young Catholics, warning that the KPD and SPD had long understood how to mobilize its youth.[58] At a time when the face of radicalism was getting younger, the Center felt pressure to bind Catholic youth to the party. The loyalty of women, in contrast, who statistics had "proven" were more immune to extremism, was questioned in 1930 but without the urgency aimed at malleable youth.

Ultimately, the results of the September 1930 election once again vindicated Center reliance on female loyalty. While its overall vote slipped from 15.2 to 14.8 percent (losses minimal compared to those of the other major nonconfessional parties), women continued to comprise about 60 percent of Center voters.[59] Unlike Protestant women, who were increasingly torn between the DNVP and NSDAP, Catholic women gave the lie to Center accusations of disloyalty. Women's propaganda continued to focus on family, faith, and morality, but the urgent tones long used to paint these issues gained real power from the fears stoked by the depression. A discourse of order, responsibility, and ethics combined with the idea of woman as a font of healing love to reinforce female support for the party that remained more than a vote but a personal and collective identity.

Like the DNVP and Center, the DDP faced mounting internal strife after its weak showing in 1928. A rightward drift prevailed at the 1929 congress, where delegates assailed the dominance of cosmopolitan Berlin and political horse trading; they repudiated past attempts to enhance workers' management role and committed the party to an unabashed focus on middle-class material interests abandoned earlier. To seal this new orientation, in July 1930 DDP chair Erich Koch-Weser announced an alliance with the Young German Order to form the new German State Party (DSP). The hope was that it would grow into a bourgeois unity party attractive to left liberals and moderate conservatives alike. The new party also distanced itself from the very republicanism the DDP had long struggled to create. Those on the DDP's left were dismayed by the DSP's shift toward a language emphasizing the primacy of the state, a change heralded by the new name. Some, like Anton Erkelenz, resigned in disgust at this shotgun marriage to the openly anti-Weimar Young German Order. The order, led by Artur Mahraun, assailed "partyism" as an agent of national fragmentation and envisioned the republic's evolution into a higher form of democracy based on a *Volksgemeinschaft* ideal that subordinated individual welfare to that of the nation. Its willingness to pursue these goals within the existing system set the order apart from other youth groups. But its antagonism to the DDP's left and its anti-Semitic past unsettled Jewish liberals and adherents of the DDP's tolerant ethos, who found themselves abandoned in their party's attempt to beat the radical Right at its own game.[60]

The DSP's 1930 general campaign took its cue from an idea promoted by both Mahraun and Gertrud Bäumer: the way to win mass support was to stress values rooted in an "organic" people's democracy and a new idealism.[61] On a more pragmatic level, appeals also promised fiscal reform to aid middle-class taxpayers and denounced splinter parties, the DVP, and DNVP for preaching social unity while playing interest politics (a case of the pot calling the kettle black). The DSP also rejected radicalism and "socialist experiments" but did not limit this to the Left, blasting the NSDAP for dividing the nation and masking its "socialism" with fraudulent claims to defend middle-class interests. In fact, within the bourgeois camp, the DSP was most determined to expose and condemn Nazism in the 1930 campaign.[62]

Just like literature for occupational groups and youth, DSP women's materials focused on social splintering. In an attempt to co-opt Nazi rhetoric, they decried pervasive "self-interest [*Eigennutz*] and contempt among *Volksgenossen*." The DSP set "rebuilding against destruction! Peace against civil war! Unity against splintering! The needs of state versus interest politics! *Volksgemeinschaft* against class war! We demand respect for every people's comrade; citizenly responsibility; security against unemployment; protection of the family; fit housing; honesty in public life; streamlined state organization that does not trample local character; fiscal thrift and order; a strong foreign policy in the spirit of peace and freedom!" This election, women were told, was about the *Volksstaat*— "the land of their children"—and the economy. Reminding them of their rights as citizens and duty as the majority of voters, the DSP argued in Bäumerian language that the state needed both male creativity (*Männerschaffen*) and female influence (*Frauenwirken*).[63]

To combat splintering and radicalism, the DSP set itself up as the party of the *Mitte*, symbolized in images depicting united supporters of different occupations, ages, and genders.[64] This message was central in appeals to both sexes that called for a balance between *Beruf* demands and the needs of the fatherland. Yet if all segments of the *Volk* must rally to save the state, women were portrayed more than ever as doing so because of their family role, while men appeared motivated by a mix of material and loftier political considerations. The family was absent from DSP appeals to male groups or youth, but it took center stage in women's appeals in 1930, crowning the DDP's shift since 1919 from an equal rights focus to a stress on motherhood as women's prime political motivator.[65] As a 1930 appeal put it, while the future of Germany's children concerned all, "*gerade die Frauen* want reassurance that our political situation [will foster] healthy children and better times."[66]

A creeping transition to mother as the main visual representation of woman that began in the mid-1920s also continued, exemplified by one of six posters created for the 1930 campaign (see Figure 4.2). The piece, which simply reads "Vote List 6," depicts a child painting the number six with the help of his young mother. This female figure is boyishly slim but with a trace of rounded hips endowed perhaps by pregnancy. Her hairstyle is a marker of distance from New Womanhood, as what initially looks like a softened *Bubikopf* proves to be long hair tied up. While the DDP had never sold itself by using the image of the New Woman, its rhetoric of gender equality had implied a degree of sympathy for women in her position. Now, in the context of the party's evolving visual and verbal vocabulary, this striking piece from 1930 (credited only to a Berlin graphics firm) appears as an attempt to recast the sexualized body of the New Woman as a maturing maternal body whose main desire is to help children by promoting the DSP—a message directed at the young voters so ardently courted in this period.[67]

The same shift to maternal imagery occurred in campaign literature as well. Women's appeals for the 1929 Saxon election made an argument long used by both the DDP and bourgeois feminists: women were needed in government because "they know where the shoe pinches housewives and mothers." Highlighting female candidates' social policy expertise, materials stressed housing, welfare, school reform, utilities, and cultural institutions—local issues important to both mothers and working women.[68] These appeals balanced this with a nod to equal rights issues. In contrast, propaganda from the new State Party spoke almost solely to women's maternal "nature." For example, an appeal to "women of all *Stände*" discussed only themes of interest to mothers. Another urged women to attend rallies to "become aware of your responsibility as a woman," a formula inconceivable in an appeal to men.[69]

The DDP's warnings about radicalism's threat to state and family became even more insistent in 1930, denouncing Nazi and Communist "rowdiness" whose way was paved by the SPD. While propaganda condemned extremism from both the Left and Right, the DSP agitated more against the NSDAP than the other bourgeois parties. Curiously, women's appeals were more strongly anti-Nazi than those to occupational groups, which were just as likely to blast socialist economic policies or "class warfare." Women's appeals stressed the Nazi threat to civility. A June 1930 flyer for Else Ulich-Beil described a train ride during which a Nazi ranter told a *Dame* who asked him to lower his voice to shut up: "If this is the culture the Nazis will bring, we know who our enemy is." Else Fisch wrote in another appeal that economic crisis elevated those who preached the need for a strong hand. Rising brutality could be seen in campaign rallies punctuated by fistfights, a threat to order that also jeopardized peace in the home. Women and men must unite to restore sanity to public life.[70]

The DSP made other pleas for *Sachlichkeit* directly to women. One flyer stated that women did not want to "cook party soup." They would tolerate no curbs on freedom and their finer sensibility shunned political crudeness. Understanding that politics was the art of realism, women rejected empty promises and valued DSP conscientiousness.[71] Appeals im-

figure 4.2
"Vote List 6—State Party": The New Woman as Mother (DSP, 1930) (Hoover Institution)

plied that women in particular could defuse destructive passions and restore rationality to politics, a message parallel to the Center's theme that women could restore love to politics.

Yet the ideal woman also heeded emotion and natural forces. Gertrud Bäumer's "open letter" of 1930 discussed woman's political role in these terms. Women who correctly perceived the "sickness" of current political life could find a home in the DSP, which merged experience with youth. It united many—she listed democrats, Christian socialists, young liberals, unionists, employers, clergy, farmers, artisans, and city dwellers (note the absence of Jews, long a mainstay of left liberalism)—in a party that valued spirituality and culture over materialism.[72] Bäumer's key position as one of the driving forces behind the new DSP itself symbolized the triumph of a romantic motif combining woman, nature, and culture over the DDP's former "party of women" stance.

It should be noted that these two strands had been present in DDP discourse from the beginning and still coexisted, as seen in a 1929 joint declaration by DDP and DVP women calling for gender solidarity to enhance female cultural influence and "motherly presence" in public life, end double standards, and equalize economic opportunities. This mix of what Karen Offen terms "relational" and "individualist" feminisms had long informed bourgeois feminists' insistence that equal rights were not mere special-interest pleading but would aid both state and *Volk*.[73] This marked 1929 women's appeals in Saxony, which focused on BDF activist Else Ulich-Beil as a female voice for the *Mitte*.[74] One flyer invoked the DDP's fight for gender equality by asserting that the Saxon election was about "woman's self-assertion" and female solidarity's potential to win better housing and equality for working women. A November 1929 Berlin appeal picked up this thread, asserting that the DDP represented justice, progress, culture, female equality, and protection of all, regardless of *Stand*, property, or religion.[75]

By the 1930 election, however, this message, salable at the local level because it could be hitched to the concrete issues around which communal elections revolved, gave way to nebulous romanticism in the national campaign. Marie-Elisabeth Lüders, the most tireless fighter for gender equality in the bourgeois camp, disappeared from DSP appeals. The tone of women's propaganda instead favored that of a party journal tribute to the recently deceased Helene Lange. This women's page piece championed Lange's work for girls' education, women's legal rights, and *Gleichwertung* or "equal valuation"—a term that conveys her and Bäumer's "separate spheres" view of gender.[76] By 1930, the equal rights feminism that distinguished the DDP's first Weimar campaigns gave way to *Gleichwertung*, which stressed women's "unique attributes" as a way to end social discord.

The one place where vestiges of the DDP's commitment to equal rights could still be seen was in DSP discourses on female labor. Materials lamented that female work in all spheres still lacked due recognition and compensation.[77] A 1930 flyer to working women even obliquely acknowledged rising sentiment against double earners: "You want *above all, work* and, through your own achievements, to care for yourself and yours by exercising *your right to work.*" The party restated its pledge to protect working women's interests.[78] Also, as before, it was unique in addressing specific female job categories, as in 1929's flyers to kindergarten teachers and social workers. Yet the address in a 1930 flyer to "businesspeople, women, entrepreneurs, and employees" betrays the entrenched view that "women" constituted a category apart from occupation.[79]

Another 1930 flyer to the "working woman" shows an interesting mix of the DDP's stress on equality and the DSP's new focus on *Volksgemeinschaft*, with its anticapitalist undertones. Women, it said, wanted the right to work but not to be its slave.[80] The piece—the only one in the DSP's national campaign addressed to working women—implied that women should not be *forced* to work, a tension between femininity and paid labor consistent with the Young German Order's corporative state model, which would place female representatives in a "women's chamber" apart from the main body where representation would be based on *Stand*, or occupation.[81] On the other hand, this formula was ambiguous enough to allow space for the working woman in a vision of the *Volksgemeinschaft* different from conservative or Nazi models that rested on restoring women to their "proper" workplace, the home. Appeals to women point up tensions within the new DSP rhetoric, uncovering places where the DDP ethos could not be completely eradicated, no matter how weak or compromised.

This tension is an index of a larger identity crisis in liberal ranks, evident in the DSP's refusal to touch the issues of abortion and sexuality, unlike the Catholic or Marxist parties, whose well-defined constituencies allowed them to take strong positions. One 1929 article in the party press stated the DDP position on abortion, rejecting full legalization because "most women were forced by men to abort" but favoring milder penalties to spare the poor.[82] Yet no campaign propaganda in 1929 or 1930 mentioned abortion, sticking to established feminist demands such as ending the "bordello economy." One served up a lukewarm critique of NSDAP "lies" about white slavery, but this was the only 1930 DSP women's propaganda to address Nazi racial pornography or anti-Semitism.[83] Attacks on the NSDAP in women's appeals relied less on critique of specific issues than on Nazism's broad threat to civility.

Similar fuzziness marked the DSP's approach to culture and religion. State and local appeals in 1929 continued to invoke cultural and moral issues DDP women had long embraced by rejecting "indiscipline" and supporting religious education "unfettered" by dogma. In 1930, however, only one women's flyer invoked the cherished liberal goal of religious tolerance. When invoked, culture was always linked to the antisplintering, public reconciliation cry.[84]

Past calls for women to shake off apathy and "irrational" support of the Right intensified in 1930 as the DSP—and the republic itself—fought for political survival. While lectures about nonvoting were not limited to women, women continued to be portrayed as particularly disinterested, timid, fickle, and ignorant of their political duty, while men's sin lay in voting incorrectly for splinter parties. Bäumer's open letter, while sympathetic to women's desire to avoid a poisonous political culture, argued that the fate of the fatherland and its children was in female hands more than ever.[85]

Concern over female apathy, a recurring issue in internal circles after the 1928 election, dampened party interest in women's recruitment, which in turn further weakened female activists' power. That did not keep them from continuing to protest their lack of influence. Paula Ollendorf at the September 1928 women's meeting summarized party attitudes toward female candidates: when newly enfranchised, women were courted, but with the rising dominance of special interests, "male party leaders . . . sacrificed women first."[86] As if in response, 1929 Saxon flyers spotlighted Else Ulich-Beil's number two list position and appealed to female solidarity to prove that a district with a woman in a leading spot could win.[87] While votes were not tabulated by sex in this election, the fact that the DDP won only four seats may explain its subsequent failure to nominate a woman in local elections that November in Berlin, a city where it had always polled well.[88]

In August 1930 party business manager Werner Stephan assured a concerned BDF that local branches had been instructed to give female candidates promising candidacies.[89] Stephan's words ring hollow, however, in light of the DSP's treatment of Marie-Elisabeth Lüders in 1930. During the party's reorganization, her spot on the Potsdam ballot was given to a conservative, *Arbeitssekretär* Willi Dietrich. In exchange she was given slot ten on the Reich list—in 1928 only nine Democrats from that list won a mandate. This was likely payback for Lüders's increasingly sharp criticism of the party's treatment of both female activists and voters,[90] as well as her open skepticism about the marriage with the Young German Order, whose notions of a "women's chamber" contradicted her lifelong crusade for women's right to enter Parliament on equal terms. The response of Bäumer, a prime mover behind the alliance and now the party's unrivaled female luminary, is telling. Securely ensconced in spot three, she claimed that the DSP had done all it could for Lüders and dismissed "sinecures" for female candidates. Stephan, in a fit of wishful thinking, said that Lüders's spot was in fact "very good." Richard Frankfurter and women's committee chair Gertrude Wittstock were among those who protested but to no avail. When the votes were counted, the party's foremost women's advocate lost her Reichstag seat in 1930.[91]

This incident typifies the scrapping of female interests in the transition to the DSP. In the republic's first days, the DDP linked women's rights to democracy; as its focus on democracy severely weakened with the founding of the DSP, so too did this discourse on women's rights. Even with the pervasive equation of femininity and culture in the 1930 campaign, women were not even named in the DSP's cultural manifesto or program.[92] Declining female influence within the party partly stemmed from the fact that its shrinking vote meant fewer female mandates. But other forces also hastened this decline. Bäumer's stress on *Volksgemeinschaft* sought a secure role for women within an essentialist gender framework, a "separate spheres" focus that party men—most of whom were long disinterested in promoting or funding a proequality agenda—could live with. Ultimately, women as an interest group were pushed aside as the DSP joined the stampede to win both an increasingly reactionary bourgeoisie and youth, deemed by all to be 1930's great untapped constituency.[93]

The 1930 election proved a complete debacle for the DSP, its ambitious campaign plans thwarted by a chronic lack of funds and organizational chaos.[94] The party hit a nadir, losing 20 percent of the DDP's 1928 total and garnering just fourteen Reichstag seats. Its emphasis on the needs of the state over individuals won no new supporters and alienated old ones. Women for their part failed to respond to the DSP's stress on their role in preserving family and culture. Materials from 1930, in which a dominant image was the young mother as symbol of unity,[95] did little to win bourgeois female voters who could find the same equation of woman with culture and maternity executed more convincingly elsewhere. Woman as equal citizen, once the centerpiece of DDP appeals, faded, as symbolized by the ebbing political clout of Marie-Elisabeth Lüders. Just as parliamentary democracy now lacked bourgeois defenders, so too did female equality.[96]

A flyer for the 1930 Reichstag election depicted the DVP as a solid block draped in imperial black, white, and red, in contrast to a split DNVP and crumbling DDP.[97] In reality, the DVP was itself eroding. Its inability to reconcile the divergent interests of its supporters was exacerbated by the depression. Stresemann's sudden death in September 1929 cleared the way for the ascendance of the party's proindustrial right wing (though industry's financial contributions dried up). His death also scuttled talks with the DDP to forge a liberal unity party. In fact, DVP leaders decided that closer ties to the conservative DNVP would best stop the deterioration of the political middle, putting the DVP in line with other bourgeois and Catholic parties' rightward drift after 1928.[98]

Both special-interest parties and now the NSDAP gnawed at the DVP's base. Yet in 1930, despite warnings from people like women's committee leader Elsa Matz, the party was slow to recognize the gravity of the Nazi threat.[99] As in earlier years, it hoped in 1930 to convince voters that the enemy was on the left; when it did attack the NSDAP, it played up Nazism's "socialist" aspects. The DVP posited that the election was about broad national issues, particularly the economic crisis and international relations (long a pet theme of Stresemann's). It attacked its main rival, the DDP, for sabotaging bourgeois solidarity, while presenting itself as the true party of unity in a 1930 cartoon depicting a doctor, woman, peasant, and worker locking hands.[100] Yet while the DVP tried to tap the same desire for unity as other bourgeois parties, it still preached class division, typified by its criticism of the DSP's pledge to cooperate with the SPD.

In 1930, campaign materials for women, which also bore tones of class division, stressed the issues of ethics and morality that female activists hoped all party propaganda would promote.[101] A general flyer summed up the message to female voters that year: "German women! You want a healthy state where German essence and Christian sensibility—the foundations of a truly German family life—rule."[102] It told women that the DVP was the best hope to guide Germany through the current crisis, as it was the only bourgeois party that had not changed its stripes. Finally, like the DDP and Center, it hoped to reverse falling female voter turnout, inventing to that end the slogan "You too are the state!" Materials urged women to use their political rights to defend religion and family—a mix of "modern" and "traditional" notions of femininity mirrored in Anna Mayer's formula, "The old Germany we love, the new Germany for which we live."[103]

Nationalism, which dominated DVP women's materials in 1928, was modified in the 1930 campaign to "defense of German-Christian culture" from the corrosive, antifamily materialism of Americanization and communism. Such "soullessness" flourished because of rampant special-interest politics and party "dictatorship." In this fateful election, appeals to women stressed moral responsibility in politics as the glue that would repair the nation; in their own lives, women's "unique influence" could make the nation whole again.[104]

This message of unity had a religious cast, particularly in women's literature, as the DVP openly vied with the DNVP for the sizable Protestant female vote by spotlighting its ties to the Evangelical church. The lone women's pamphlet for 1930 delineated how the DVP had long been a watchdog for church interests, supporting antiblasphemy laws, observance of religious holidays in Prussia, and the fight against freethinker propaganda. It rejected a concordat with the Vatican as special privileging of Catholicism. Religious instruction in schools was also a recurring demand, though the DVP, stung by the Center's 1928 criticism of its failure to support the Schulgesetz bill, couched this in vague terms, claiming to support a bill that would "educate children in the spirit of Christianity" within a streamlined school system that transmitted German heritage. In its drift to the right, the DVP abandoned classical liberalism's defense of religious toleration in an aggressive attempt to win Protestant women whose loyalties were increasingly up for grabs with the resurgence of the NSDAP.[105]

As before, DVP women's materials placed religion within a national cultural crusade, a cultural crisis invoked in propaganda for general audiences as well. The assault came from Hollywood, whose power threatened not only the German film industry but also the moral health of youth.[106] It also came from Soviet Russia. While one flyer weakly denounced all forms of radicalism by urging voters away from "Marxists or anti-Semites," DVP literature openly depicted the Left as the greatest danger to "Bismarck's Reich, *Kultur*, family, home and state, the civil service, property, and the currency." A campaign magazine lambasted "Reds" who allowed dance halls to open on All Souls' Day, with an image linking Marxist atheism and American permissiveness by depicting half-naked women whirling to the strains of a black jazz band, adding excessive female sexuality to the list of threats to German culture and religion.[107]

Threats to the family dominated DVP women's appeals, such as "marriage Bolshevism" (*Ehebolshewismus*), listed in the 1930 glossary of campaign themes as a key issue. Campaign appeals promised tax breaks and more single homes to foster the nation's "most precious asset"; the party press obsessed about the effects on matrimony of "mass society," à la Russia and America with their "comrade marriage." The DVP told women, the target audience for this message, that it supported the impulse to secure female equality within marriage but rejected easy divorce and unwed cohabitation as deleterious to a child-rich German future.[108] Campaign materials were much more moderate than the party press, where strong pronatalist language was likely to surface. For example, a *Berliner Stimmen* piece on women's political role said the state must ensure procreation and keep population policy out of the hands of the Left, which would distribute abortifacients to youths. Campaign propaganda, in contrast, made but one reference to abortion, stating the position shared with the DDP and many bourgeois feminists that, while abortion was objectionable on health and ethical grounds, the law's harshest provisions needed reform. The liberals again dodged this issue at campaign time. For the DVP, any strong expression of support for abortion reform could only distract from its focus on religion and family.[109]

Similarly, welfare was peripheral in 1930 DVP materials for women and men. The KPD's 1929 bill to "protect mother and child," however, did prompt a response. The DVP, fixated on declining fertility, told women that some form of *Mutterschutz* was needed to stem population decline but the KPD bill was utopian and too expensive. Notions that the Left was irresponsible also informed claims expressed in one general appeal that the health insurance system was corrupt. The wealthy Katharina von Kardorff went so far as to assert that unemployment aid was a mere popularity tool of the SPD. Linking her argument to the idea of the Left as anti-*Kultur*, she said it was absurd for the state to support able-bodied workers when war widows and pensioners—the nation's culture bearers (*Kulturträger*)—got only a pittance. The 1930 women's pamphlet argued the welfare state should be protected, especially in this time of need (not to mention the fact that it was a major source of female jobs), but that responsible self-reliance must return as well.[110]

While appeals invoking pronatalism and culture addressed prevailing assumptions about female nature, DVP women also continued to promote female interest in the "masculine" sphere of foreign policy as integral to national power and cultural vitality. In 1929 they demanded new colonies and a resettlement policy for East Prussia. A 1930 women's flyer cheered the Rhineland's liberation from occupation. Yet while DVP women were squarely nationalistic, their writings remained upbeat and avoided the ugly tones of the far Right. Some DVP women, in fact, quit the Queen Luise Bund because of its growing dominance by the Stahlhelm.[111]

A recurring "national" concern of female DVP activists and bourgeois women's groups in the BDF was the status of German women married to foreigners. As they had before, 1930 women's materials demanded their citizenship be upheld to bolster Germandom abroad, as well as to support female equality. Similarly, a flyer urged "reasonable change" in married women's legal rights to reflect their "worth and position in the family."[112] Gender equality was discussed in the 1930 campaign solely in terms of women's family role. In contrast, female writers for the party journal profiled distinguished women politicians, academics, and pilots (reflecting the period's fascination with aviation and aviatrixes). Their internal writings explored an expanded range of permissible "female" activities, while materials for public consumption at election time flattened this horizon, tying woman squarely to *Kirche* and *Kinder*.[113]

Similarly, election materials tied the working woman to the *Küche*. A women's flyer pledged to support her "struggle for existence" and equal promotion but also called for women's work "wherever she can do something that suits the best of female nature."[114] This meant the "occupation" of housewife, central to DVP women's literature since the mid-1920s. The 1930 women's pamphlet put housewifery at the head of its section on female work, noting that over 75 percent of the national wealth passed through housewives' hands. Household rationalization as a key aspect of the national economy was heavily touted by DVP women in the party press and the DVP Reichsklub. Like the DNVP, with whom it vied for the title of housewives' advocate, the DVP's discussion of all types of women's work stressed its larger cultural import over concrete economic demands, language that separated this female *Beruf* from the implicitly male "worker" wooed with economic themes. Like their discussion of equality, campaign materials flattened debate about women's work, while the women's page of the party press presented a more complex view.[115] For example, *Berliner Stimmen* demanded a more open civil service and an end to the PAV, while the 1930 women's pamphlet waffled on whether the decree should be revoked. A lexicon of "women's issues in the campaign" praised female clerks' demand for early closing hours on Christmas Eve as evidence of "Christian devotion" to the family. Would the same demands by men be read this way?[116]

Falling voter turnout in the previous national election was less of a theme for the DVP than for its DSP and Center rivals, though it shared these parties' concern over the indifference of many citizens, particularly women. One appeal, under the motto "I too am the state," used upbeat tones to urge women to show determination, faith in the *Volk*, and unity. In contrast, Gabriele Langheld in the *Deutsche Allgemeine Zeitung* criticized women's indolence, false assumptions about femininity's incompatibility with politics, and cluelessness produced by a flawed political system.[117] Several cartoons that ran close to election day in newspapers affiliated with the DVP are worth examining as evidence of a general preoccupation with the issue of voter apathy in 1930 (see Figure 4.3). One in the *Deutsche Allgemeine Zeitung*[118] juxtaposed the "Woman of Yesterday and Today." The woman of yesterday lounged with a cigarette and a magazine on election day, while the woman of today joined her sisters at the polls. Another, in the independent *8-Uhr Abendblatt*, asked the "unfortunately still urgent" question, Is the "Cooking Pot More Important than the Ballot Urn?" Its text is less compelling than the accompanying cartoons, one of which jokes that appearances by film stars and fashion shows at the polls would draw women, while another shows a *Dame* at her dressing table asking, "Which color shall I wear—black-red-gold or black-white-red?" These images convey the assumption that women treated their political choices as casually as they chose their wardrobe. It was perhaps excusable that the "cooking pot" would keep them from voting, but the women in these images spent election day loafing or daydreaming. Besides providing negative role models, these cartoons also strove to portray voting as stylish and totally feminine. The *8-Uhr Abendblatt*, a proponent of female equality popular with middle-class Berliners, urged women to defend their "cleverness and independence" by voting: "One doesn't become man's comrade simply by playing tennis with him."[119]

In terms of women's status within the party, literature for general audiences used female politicians and candidates to paint a picture of party comradery. But DVP discourse as a whole exceptionalized women and constructed citizenship as male. For example, unlike DDP, SPD, or KPD materials, which routinely placed female faces in crowd shots, DVP flyers portrayed all male faces. This carried over to women's role in the party: all women who spoke at the DVP Reichsklub in 1928–29 did so at ladies' teas, not common lecture evenings. The DVP *Archiv* had not one mention of women in all of 1930. After September's election, the party retained the dubious distinction of having the lowest percentage of female Reichstag delegates (other than the NSDAP, which had none). In an August 1930 letter to the BDF, the DVP argued that steep losses made it impossible

Die Frau von gestern und die von heute

Kochtopf wichtiger als Wahlurne?

Weshalb so viele Frauen der Wahl fernbleiben.

figure 4.3
"The Woman of Yesterday and Today" (*Deutsche Allgemeine Zeitung*, 7 September 1930 [above]) and "Cooking Pot More Important than the Ballot Urn? Why So Many Women Stay Away from the Polls" (*8-Uhr Abendblatt*, 12 September 1930 [below])

to put women at the top of its ballots, though slots two or three were being reserved for them.[120] This was true insofar as the party reserved spot two for women's committee head Elsa Matz. But the next woman on the Reich list was in slot sixteen (twelve seats were considered "safe"), and no female candidate on a regional ballot had a safe mandate. Key spots had been doled out to representatives of various occupations and regions and, increasingly, to youth.[121]

DVP women did express dissatisfaction with their status both in the party and in politics broadly, as seen in the voices raised against women's poor prospects for election in September 1930.[122] Such protests had no visible impact, and women as a bloc rarely attracted the larger party's attention. They were so inconsequential that the party executive wasted little time in 1929 debating who its new token female member should be.[123] Female activists routinely blamed women themselves for this lack of clout. Martha Schwarz, head of women's propaganda, called women their own worst enemies because of their harsh self-criticism and insistence on promoting a "women's front" instead of a shared ideology with men.[124] She was referring to the revamped women's party idea now promoted by none other than Katharina von Oheimb-Kardorff, the flamboyant *Dame* scorned in polite DVP circles, who argued that a women's party with twenty delegates could enable "female instinct" to elevate politics and do more for the "stronger sex" than one hundred women scattered among disparate parties.[125] Other DVP women who supported the goal of increasing female political influence disagreed. Lotte Garnich, who perceptively traced how women's alignment with established parties had led them to take women for granted, rejected a *Frauenpartei* because women showed no common awareness. Ideology, she argued, would only be debased in a battle of the sexes — in political work only talent mattered, not gender.[126] Others saw a women's party as a conspiratorial women's chamber (*Frauenkammer*) that would hurt equality. For DVP women, the issue was not "special rights" but empowering the female citizen whose sights were on the commonweal.[127] They agreed with the male functionary who wrote to the BDF that the only way to increase female representation was to reduce splinter parties, a formula that both fit DVP women's determination not to appear divisive and assuaged male fears of an independent women's faction.

Little was new in the DVP's message to women in 1930. The party continued to pursue an essentialist vision in which the domestic concerns of motherhood, German-Christian values, and homemaking dominated. DVP women, who maintained links to the bourgeois women's movement, also saw feminism as an invitation to bring female nature to bear on foreign policy and trade. Unlike the DDP, which trumpeted then muted a pro–equal rights message, the DVP had always stressed separate spheres, viewing women's political role through the prisms of culture, nation, and family. Yet for reasons far beyond any message to women the party could dish up, the DVP was losing its audience, both male and female, at a prodigious rate. It was the biggest loser of the 1930 election, dropping 1 million of the 2.7 million votes it had won in 1928. By 1932 it would be little more than a splinter party, as the NSDAP and DNVP carved up the votes of women and men who had once called the liberal middle home.

Having quit the government in March 1930, the SPD entered the Reichstag race in its preferred mode of opposition. From this position it ran heavily against Brüning's "revived Bürgerblock." Appeals blasted tariff and price hikes that favored big agriculture and industry, the new "bachelor tax," and cuts in unemployment aid and health insurance as harmful to the interests of all working people. The SPD's chief concern in 1930 was the loss of workers' social gains—gains it saw threatened more by Brüning and the bourgeois parties' rightward shift than by the rise of the NSDAP.[128] It criticized fascism in general terms but tended in 1930 to caricature the Nazis either as mere bully boys of big capital or rowdies like the Communists. Though the SPD assembled scores of materials and rallies for the campaign, contemporaries called its methods dry, lacking a theme that could galvanize groups beyond the core constituency it needed to do well. Furthermore, the taint of corruption and the hated Weimar "system" helped Nazi and KPD attacks on *Bonzen* salaries and the Sklarek scandal stick.[129] In 1930 the SPD failed both to expand its base and to convince working-class voters that it was still "one of them," resulting in a drop from 30 percent of the vote in 1928 to 24 percent in 1930.[130]

Women's appeals also bore an anti-Bürgerblock thrust and strove to present a unified front against the marshaling forces of reaction. Within a discourse of social justice, the SPD hoped to win women by addressing concrete economic and reproductive issues they faced daily. SPD materials at this time presented the most varied picture of female activities and concerns of any Weimar party. They not only rendered woman in her traditional role as mother and protector but also showed her as free and strong, wearing the hats of worker, mother, and comrade equally well.[131] Their propaganda betrayed the view that her political choices stemmed from her economic situation now more than ever. This emphasis on material concerns seems to have resonated: the SPD's gender gap in voting narrowed to just 3 percent, while the number of female members grew from 148,000 in 1924 (16 percent of all members) to 230,000 in 1931 (23 percent).[132]

The SPD's main concern regarding women in 1930 was to anchor them in the proletarian front against both economic injustice and the rising brutality personified by the NSDAP and KPD. It did this in appeals that meshed with liberal and Center depictions of woman as symbol of a reconciling *Mitte* by addressing women as peacemakers. It also hoped to cement solidarity by linking women's sufferings to those of the working class. A flyer authored by "the women of the SPD" urged all "women of the productive *Volk*" to defend the "broad masses," who always bore most heavily the ravages of war, inflation, and unemployment, by rejecting the Bürgerblock, Nazis, and Communists. Farm women were told to reject the Right because it would strip away benefits the workers' movement had won for them. Women's materials and general appeals both reinforced solidarity visually, depicting women with red flags or showing them shoulder to shoulder with men in a party that triumphed over persecution to represent the worker (see Figure 4.4).[133]

Yet if woman could symbolize class unity, her body also threatened that solidarity. In an International Women's Day leaflet, pictures of women working in factories, farms, and homes were juxtaposed with text that asked, "Do you think it's right . . . that millions are unemployed or enslaved into their old age so the few can revel?" While the piece used a gluttonous man to represent "the few," it also showed images of female decadence: women dancing, lounging, and displaying their legs, a visual reference to Americanized beauty pageant "girls" and dance troupes.[134] The SPD could embrace a *sachlich* New Woman in its 1928 poster "Volksgenossen wählt Sozialdemokratie" but, like all other parties, drew the line at the overtly sexual woman. Woman's loyalty could be placed above suspicion by defining her in relation to those around her: "As a good wife to your husband, good mother to your children, good sister to your fellow sisters, as good battle comrade and work colleague, you must become a member of the SPD, which has and will represent your interests!"[135]

As the largest representative of working-class interests, the SPD continued to address women as workers more than any party other than the KPD. Appeals pledged to protect their individual interests, which helped the workers' cause by attracting women comrades. The SPD promised to protect them from Bürgerblock cuts in wages and the dole. It also claimed a readiness to ease their double burden (though still assuming that housework was woman's job) and addressed conditions for farm women and domestic servants. It blasted KPD fantasies of a Soviet paradise, arguing that Russian wages were in fact sinking. The SPD trumpeted its reformism to women, presenting its fight for women workers' rights in a strong welfare state as the path to peaceful socialism and true *Volksgemeinschaft*.[136]

Unlike the DVP, DNVP, and Center, the SPD confronted the growing tension around double earners, albeit weakly and not in 1930 campaign

propaganda. Female delegates to the 1929 party conference demanded that married women's right to work be defended unequivocally because their expulsion was unjust and illogical as a solution to unemployment, views reiterated in an eighty-page volume issued by the party executive in 1929, "Woman in Politics and Work."[137] But campaign materials, which portrayed women's work as a fact of modern life, never openly declared their right to work, a measure of the SPD's reluctance to offend the male rank and file that would culminate in its support for a 1932 law limiting married women's employment. Passages in SPD literature reveal the continued lack of a primary identification of woman and labor. Internally, Marie Juchasz and other SPD women lamented the view that a woman "who has marriage before her" often failed to see work as the basis of her existence. Yet Juchasz also stated that female work en masse could be regulated through social measures—it could be manipulated at will because it did not define women's lives the way it did men's.[138] Campaign materials also often portrayed women as the managers, not earners, of household income.[139] While the SPD should not be singled out for following the prevailing trend, its rhetoric shows the gap between practice and the attempt, promoted mainly by female activists, to actualize socialist theory by treating women's work as life-defining.

The SPD's economic focus in this period produced more attention than ever to housewives.[140] Appeals linking home and politics attempted to transform women's "family egotism" into social consciousness. The price of food, they argued, was a political price. The ideal where the wife served roast on Sunday was a fiction; the reality was foul apartments, screaming children, and husbands who fled to the corner pub. Yet unlike some who blamed this state of affairs on housewives, the SPD squarely faulted Brüning and all who exploited the *Volk* in the name of profit. Only the SPD, it argued, understood their need to stretch every penny and felt a moral duty to relieve capitalist inequities through social welfare, not social robbery. This message could be read as a triumph of female activists' attempt to create rhetorical space in which the particularity of female experience and "special character" (*Eigenart*) was respected rather than dismissed as "backward"; at any rate, this pitch to housewives dovetailed with the SPD's desire to loosen conservative and religious parties' monopoly on speaking for—and winning the votes of—this group.[141]

Women's domestic role as mothers was also frequently invoked. Appeals in 1930 spotlighted SPD achievements to enhance *Mutter- und Kindschutz* and to halt dismantling of the welfare state. Recalling a 1919 poster, a child in a 1930 piece urged, "Mother! Your vote decides our future!" A Saxon flyer ripped Mother's Day as helping no one but business. Touting performance over rhetoric, the SPD hoped to steer working-class women away from the KPD and particularly the Center by presenting itself as the source of all advances for mothers and children.[142]

Sexuality, generally ignored in liberal and conservative appeals, was another central theme in SPD propaganda to both women and general audiences. Campaign materials heralded sex education and contraception as tools to improve the lot of women, youth, and working families. Two 1929 flyers touted marriage counseling centers as weapons against the "great sexual and marital need of our times"; contraceptives were weapons against the abortion "plague" that claimed thousands of female lives annually. One piece for Berlin women blasted states that cut *Muttergeld* (maternity benefits) but criminalized abortion, noting that the Nazis would mandate the death penalty for abortion. A housewives' flyer painted a grim scene: "Women, think of what awaits you if you try to prevent giving birth again, even if you do it to protect your other children from more misery. No doctor will help you; he doesn't want to break the law. No private clinic is open to you—only the quack and a jail cell. You put your life and health on the line and still end up in jail! Paragraph 218 remains in force! The bourgeois parties want it that way!" In 1930 campaign materials did not present abortion in terms of sexual freedom, eugenics, or even moral hypocrisy, as in previous years. Instead, they treated it as an economic survival strategy, a pragmatic emphasis that resonated among a growing number of female supporters as the depression tightened its grip.[143]

While criticizing other parties for viewing women as "baby machines," SPD rhetoric, as in earlier years, portrayed motherhood as women's highest fulfillment. Critiquing the bachelor tax, a women's flyer said it was not single women's fault that the war had destroyed their "life's happiness" (*Lebensglück*) by robbing them of marriage partners. It called on women and girls who, "by nature, bear the future of the *Volk* and humanity." Women at the 1929 party conference described falling birth rates as a "problem" and asserted that propaganda must make the fate of Germany's children come alive to women denied *Mutterglück*. A piece for general audiences celebrating the SPD's fiftieth anniversary counted among the party's achievements laws to help woman fulfill her "motherly duties," while a 1929 Berlin flyer noted that women's role as "above all" bearers of new life mandated their special protection from night work and dangerous substances. Male SPD activists valued women's reproductive work over their productive work. Most female SPD politicians also espoused a revived ideology of motherhood seemingly akin to the Right's biological determinism, yet theirs differed in its insistence on reproductive freedom and voluntary motherhood. Juchasz at the 1929 conference called motherhood service to the state but added that all reproductive policy must square with women's equal rights—social progress, not coercion, must be the goal.[144]

Viewing all subjects through an economic lens meant that SPD women's propaganda often disregarded "culture," including religion. While activists admonished that agitation in the "freethinker" vein would estrange women,[145] the SPD still took a few shots at Catholics in 1930. One piece told Center men and women that in nearly two years of coalition with the SPD their party had never complained of anti-Catholic bias and that campaign claims to the contrary were mere grandstanding. It was not their religion that was threatened but their jobs and their children. A housewives' flyer invoked a Bavarian priest who said women would "burn in hell" for the decrepit state of their homes, countering that the economic crisis caused by the state and capitalism was to blame. The SPD wanted humane living conditions for everyone, asking, "Is that 'un-Christian'?"[146]

Culture as such did appear, however, in attacks on Nazism. "Five Dead" enumerated those killed in street brawls, using images of a woman mourning her slain husband and the weapons favored by Nazi gangs to illustrate a "coarsening" of civility. A Saxon poster depicted "Nazi culture" with illustrations of male workers being beaten and a "Bolshevik" woman being whipped "until there was no white spot left on her back."[147] This imagery of violated bodies would only intensify in subsequent campaigns.

The SPD also hoped to win women with evidence of NSDAP contempt for their rights, though this message was only in its infancy in 1930, as both men and women in the SPD still refused to believe that women could support a party that saw them as inferior.[148] Thus, 1930 materials stressed the Bürgerblock threat to equality. Single women who wanted freedom to create their own lives must reject the parties of their bosses and vote as independent members of the community of workers, one flyer stated. In the fight between capital and labor, women must use the political rights the SPD had won for them (something the party never tired of mentioning) to protect themselves from the "few who would again reduce you to slaves."[149]

Unlike the liberals, whose support had been dwindling throughout the 1920s, the SPD did not harp on female political apathy as a grave threat in 1930. Propaganda urged women to be politically engaged but exuded confidence that the coming election would show that they had learned to draw the "correct" conclusions from their desperate situation.[150] Similar attitudes marked internal communications between party men and women. Running up to the 1930 election, their tenor was upbeat in light of the SPD's 1928 win and statistics that showed rising female support, especially among urban workers. It also seems that suggestions for less fluff and more linkage of socialist theory to daily life in women's propaganda had more impact in 1930 than earlier. While female "voter fatigue" and support for the Center and Right still vexed strategists, party writers portrayed these as solvable problems. One even challenged the orthodoxy that female suffrage had hurt the party, arguing that with continued education, women's votes for the SPD could surpass men's.[151]

For their part, SPD women appeared more confident. Even Marie Juchasz caught this wave at the 1929 conference, criticizing attacks on double earners as anti-Socialist. Yet inequities in women's position within the party persisted. Women were still seen by men and some women as less rational. It was still possible in 1930 to omit any mention of women in speakers' materials and a special report on the NSDAP.[152]

Women's position was further destabilized by the 1927 women's conference decision to discontinue separate meetings in favor of a session on women's issues at the all-party gathering. Women at the 1929 conference were divided over the wisdom of this. Marie Arning saw the granting of a women's session at the general forum as a sign that there were no longer *Frauenfrage*, only "women's issues that interest the entire public," but her subsequent statement that equality within the party was incomplete met with a hearty round of "Hear! Hear!" Frau Dr. Torhorst, urging the party to better foster comradery, argued that male party members' "chivalry" soured when women expressed independent opinions. Nanni Kurfürst complained, like others before her, that men showed indifference to women's issues and agitation, even blocking their own wives from doing party work. Anna Siemsen and others rejected myths of women's "emotional nature," arguing that *all* must work to make women equal members of the *Kampffront* in both theory and practice.[153]

Nazi gains among women galvanized some female activists to demand more attention to women's propaganda. Even before the NSDAP breakthrough in 1930, Edith Hommes-Knack traced female support for the antifeminist fascist movement to its use of traditional female imagery. The SPD had not eradicated the "medieval view slumbering in working-class hearts" that women were not men's equals; every male worker who did not support his female comrades created a woman Nazi voter lured by promises of an employed husband and her "freedom" to stay at home.[154] Yet it was only after the NSDAP's September 1930 victory that Nazi antifeminism would take center stage in SPD women's agitation, as activists of both sexes fretted about women's assumed susceptibility to Nazism's "irrational" appeal.

While the SPD in 1930 could not prevent significant numbers of male supporters from backing opponents untainted by the Weimar "system"— especially the KPD—it retained and even attracted more female support. While voter motivations are impossible to reconstruct, working-class women, particularly those from areas with strong socialist traditions,[155] were likely to be attracted to the SPD's propagandistic and legislative focus on the economic, social, and sexual problems they faced daily and repulsed by radical violence. As in 1928, the SPD's 1930 campaign placed women's issues such as reproduction and the right to work in the larger context of economic crisis, and it pitched these topics more aggressively in appeals solely for women. At least in its campaign rhetoric, the SPD acknowledged working-class women's multiple identities and played to both their interest in equal rights and their domestic duties. Yet if the party's "problem" with female voters appeared to be subsiding, the threat to its overall health posed by the polarization of national politics would force the SPD in the early 1930s to struggle to reconcile equality and difference, optimism and fear, theory and practice—with implications not only for women but for the nation itself.

Besides the NSDAP, the Communist Party was the only nonconfessional faction to score gains in 1930—gains mainly from younger, unskilled proletarians radicalized by economic collapse. The KPD had long been the party of the unemployed, and in the context of the depression, this identity brought its biggest vote ever, from 3.2 million in 1928 to 4.5 million. The voice of the disenfranchised working class, it waged all-out ideological warfare against its estranged kin, the SPD, formally adopting the "social fascism" thesis in 1929. This line, which marked Comintern strategy into the mid-1930s, declared Social Democracy—not Nazism—the vanguard of fascism because its goal to protect the gains of the labor aristocracy made it ripe for co-opting by a capitalist bourgeoisie bent on installing a fascist regime. While this directive did not shut down a certain degree of street-level cooperation, it served to fatally fracture the Left and downplay the genuine threat from the NSDAP—a bias that also pervaded campaign propaganda.[156]

More than ever, KPD rhetoric ratcheted up the level of crisis to make capitalism's collapse seem imminent. Women's materials combined this intensity with concerns about social fascism to stress the misery caused by capitalism and the "Reaction," whose promises ensnared women in particular. Directives instructed agitators to use "populist" and "alarming" tones to portray the KPD as the party that put everything on the line in the fight over wages, jobs, bread, abortion, *Mutterschutz*, and equality.[157] Materials also had to enlighten women in factories, shops, farms, and tenements about Soviet Russia, an earthly paradise German women could also enjoy if they tore the scales from their eyes and joined the revolutionary workers' movement.

But women remained highly immune to such blandishments. Female party membership in 1930 numbered 26,400, which, while up since 1929, was still below 1923 levels and stalled at 15 percent.[158] Strategists intoned the utter necessity of securing support from working women and house-wives, especially in light of the KPD's renewed emphasis on strikes as a battering ram of revolution. The relative success of the RFMB, as well as women's involvement in strikes since 1927, constituted a trend the KPD hoped to spin into higher female membership in the party's fighting front. Women, it seemed, could be fired up by a sliding economy, and fanning this flame dominated depression-era KPD strategy toward female voters.[159]

To build class solidarity, the KPD waged a relentless propaganda *Kampf* against the SPD and capitalism, in materials for both men and women in 1930. Women, for their part, must show readiness to fight and move for-ward in *Sturmtempo*, like the Russian women militarized to defend their socialist homeland.[160] This discourse of battle was lent new urgency by some SPD ministers' 1928 support for construction of two new battle-ships.[161] A 1930 women's poster accused the SPD of treason against the people, awarding millions for cruisers while cutting aid to mothers and children. A 1929 Saxon women's flyer portrayed the SPD as a capitalist cra-dling a battleship while a mother cried because her children had no bread. The KPD also used this issue to claim that an "imperialist" war against the Soviet Union was imminent. A 1930 Women's Day flyer warned against capitalist collusion to wage war on Russia, "your proletarian fatherland." Women's conferences were called to discuss the "war danger," and the party journal in this period was packed with calls to mobilize all proletari-ans for the coming conflict.[162] The gender of the audience for materials on this subject had no significant impact on the language used, with the exception of the melodramatic device of a crying mother in the women's flyer.

KPD propaganda also accused the SPD of other forms of class betrayal. A 1930 election flyer urged women to remember how the SPD set police on strikers, a reference to both Noske's brutal suppression of the 1919 Sparta-cist uprising and the May Day blood bath of 1929. As it accused its rival of brutality and militarism, the KPD simultaneously assailed the SPD for its "pacifism" in rejecting revolution. Noting that this had helped the SPD win women's votes, the KPD portrayed its foe as duplicitous—it would wage war to protect the interests of capital but not those of the prole-tariat, including women. Clearly, the KPD could not shake its addiction to an ethos of violence, despite internal admissions that it was costing female support.[163]

Intransigence also marked KPD attacks on SPD reformism, which distracted the proletariat from the revolution. Women's propaganda equated reformism with welfare. At the 1929 party conference, Helene Overlach belittled the welfare focus of her SPD counterpart, Marie Juchasz, as a diversion from the "reality" of daily life. Maria Reese, an SPD defector, argued in a scathing 1930 pamphlet that the "bourgeois" SPD had reduced women's issues to welfare and "women's rightism." A 1930 women's flyer painted welfare as a pillar of capitalism that reduced women to begging for handouts from mocking civil servants, many of whom were middle-class females. Concerned that reformism had helped the SPD win 20,000 new women members since 1927, female KPD tacticians hoped that negative depictions of the experience of getting welfare would halt that trend.[164]

SPD politicians, male and female, were also reviled for compromising with bourgeois parties and bourgeois feminists—a cabal blamed for raising tariffs, dismantling unemployment aid, upholding paragraph 218, and paving the way for fascism. *Welt am Abend* wrote that these groups swayed women with talk of *Kultur* and equality, but their bourgeois republic had done nothing for them. KPD and RFMB recruiters were to inform women of the SPD-bourgeois conspiracy to strangle the revolution that would bring true equality.[165]

The issue of women's rights was also central to attacks on the NSDAP in 1930 women's materials. The Nazis, portrayed as part of the reactionary bourgeois front, wished to keep women mindless, praising their lack of rights as "female virtue." A 1930 poster stated that Nazis saw women as second-class citizens, contesting their right to equal wages and even their right to work. They blamed women for all of Germany's problems and considered the political woman the most deplorable creature.[166]

Similar points marked KPD attacks on the Center. One 1930 flyer addressed to both male and female workers urged all to quit the church and "join the revolutionary freethinker movement." It reviled political Catholicism for scaring women with red-baiting and posited an alliance between priests and the bourgeoisie designed to keep women in the dark. The Catholic establishment saw female proletarians as *Stimmvieh* and a "reservoir of sin" fit only to toil mutely in factories. Another women's flyer even likened the KPD to Christ, arguing that its fight for the oppressed brought it only persecution, while the Center, DNVP, and Nazi "Wotan worshipers" invoked God's name to justify capitalist inequities. This formula, strikingly similar to arguments about religion in SPD women's propaganda, was informed by a party journal admonition that women could not be won with insulting caricatures of priests or Christian politicians. Yet the stridency of KPD rhetoric reveals a party unwilling to shed its militance, even to woo female voters. Its 1928 declaration of a "*Kulturkampf* on all ideologies that enslaved women" was in fact a declaration of war on its own chances for winning the masses of women who did not see religion as their enemy.[167]

As always, the KPD stressed its defense of the rights of the woman worker—the female figure it promoted and courted the most. It trumpeted its new fight for the seven-hour day, protective legislation, and four months' paid maternity leave. It also "exposed" SPD support of wage cuts, layoffs, and rent hikes that worsened the double burden and drove women to prostitution. Another flyer told women that corrupt, strike-breaking unions had never fought for equal pay or helped the female clerk who was fired for simply getting older. Alone among the major parties, the KPD came out strongly in 1930 in opposition to the campaign against double earners as an issue of class solidarity. Maria Reese accused an SPD-union *Bonzokratie* of scapegoating married working women for unemployment and playing to men's basest instincts. The SPD office in Hannover, she reported, even dismissed its own secretary for getting married. The anti-double earner cry of the NSDAP (which only a *Dummkopf* believed was a workers' party, as one women's flyer put it)[168] reflected its love of both capital and female slavery. In line with Marxist theory of female emancipation, the KPD denounced all moves to curb women's employment and relegate them to the household as undermining proletarian solidarity.[169]

While rejecting the orthodoxy that woman's true occupation was housewife, the KPD finally joined parties across the political spectrum in vying for housewives' attention in this period. It realized the necessity to win this most "backward" element at a time when its emphasis on protests at factories and unemployment offices made housewives' support of striking husbands critical.[170] Appeals addressed their presumed interest in such issues as rent control and children's playgrounds by highlighting Russian communal kitchens and free day care. Their litanies of misery evoked a state of war by linking bread and sugar price hikes to the supposedly imminent reintroduction of *Kriegsbrot* (war bread).[171] Yet, as with other female groups, the KPD's address to housewives was chiefly instrumental. Wilhelm Pieck's paean to housewives' loyalty at the 1929 conference aside, suspicion remained: was it not housewives, the party journal asked, who most often blocked husbands and children from joining our organizations?[172] The KPD aimed to rectify past oversight of housewives not for their sake but to prevent them from stabbing the movement in the back.

Accompanying this new attention to housewives in the campaign was renewed attention to mothers, a message transposed into a Soviet key. The KPD promised them the kinds of protection and services their Russian sisters enjoyed. It noted that current welfare measures offered no maternity benefits for farm women or servants. While its vision of womanhood was not blinkered by an exclusive focus on maternity, the KPD, like other parties, embraced the period's revived attention to motherhood, demanding, for example, that family law recognize it as a social service. The KPD too wanted to promote large families, but the SPD and bourgeois parties would not deign to debate its plans. KPD pronatalism emphasized the role of the state, which sanctified motherhood by guaranteeing maternal and infant welfare — in such a state, women would want to be mothers, as Russia's rising population proved.[173]

As it had throughout the 1920s, the KPD linked concern for mothers to impassioned calls for legal abortion in the 1930 campaign. Besides viewing abortion as key to female liberation, the party continued to treat it as an issue of both working-class economic survival and antifascism, instructing speakers to link abortion to wages, hours, and the threat of war. A 1929 poster trotted out the obligatory images of class justice, depicted here as a judge poised to beat a helpless woman with the "218" stick. A 1930 flyer compared Soviet Russia, where women happily chose motherhood, to Germany, where "reactionary dictators" enlisted the "female [politicians] they despised" to reduce women to baby machines. These "reactionaries" included the SPD and Center, as well as the NSDAP, which the KPD attacked most vigorously on this issue, strèssing a 1930 Nazi bill demanding the death penalty for abortion (a proposal also pilloried in SPD women's propaganda).[174] In these early depression years, which saw successful runs of two social dramas about the current law (*Cyankali* and *§218*), the KPD stressed abortion over contraception because the penalties mandated by paragraph 218 better allowed melodramatic depictions of capitalist injustice. While the KPD was the only party to make reproductive rights central to its propaganda and legislative agenda (many in the SPD also advocated this, but it was never official policy), it was ultimately guided by the desire to draw the votes of the growing ranks of abortion advocates. As with other topics of concern to women workers and mothers, abortion was used to awaken an awareness of gender oppression that then had to be channeled into the larger goal of class solidarity.[175]

This relentless discourse of *Kampf* aimed to awaken women to the war of the "sated versus the starving" in every facet of life. This language stemmed from a heavily masculine ethos that limited the KPD to the status of a *Männerpartei*—a term also used by both contemporaries and historians to describe the NSDAP, which sought its own "militarization" of women through such schemes as a mandatory service year for girls.[176] While both parties privileged the masculine politics of brute force, their messages to women differed sharply: the NSDAP's drew on traditional images of femininity, while the KPD espoused emancipation through socialism. Unlike the NSDAP, the KPD insisted that "women's issues" were central to the entire party agenda and displayed women as essential to the fighting front. This did not mask the manly tenor of the May Day slogan "Alle Mann auf die Straße!" or women's exclusion from battle at the primary sites of engagement—the street and the dole office. The KPD was aware that most women resisted its cry for civil war yet felt it was not the message that needed revamping but female consciousness—an intransigence bred by the gendered nature of the party.[177]

This attitude surfaced repeatedly in both internal writings and public appeals written by men and women. For example, the 1930 Women's Day flyer used boldface type to urge women to stop being "weak, defenseless, and dumb"; praise of female strength appeared in small print. The KPD journal routinely portrayed female proletarians as naive, easy prey for "reformist," bourgeois, or fascist women's organizations.[178] An anti-Nazi poster from the 1930 Saxon election expressed nagging suspicions about female loyalty in stark visual terms (see Figure 4.5). Depicting the kind of "freedom" Nazis had in mind for women, it showed two bloated industrialists leering at a naked, champagne-swilling woman sitting on the lap of an SA man. On one level, the piece condemns both capitalism and Nazism for reducing women to sex objects, but the woman's obvious glee also implies female treachery to the antifascist cause at a time when the NSDAP's female vote was growing. The fact that the cavorting couple rests on the back of a worker—on his hands and knees, no less—hammers home this treachery, leaving one to wonder whether women viewing this poster could have found any positive inducement to support the KPD.[179]

Despite the KPD's dim view of them, women did in fact support industrial actions in this period. They constituted 60 percent of the members of the International Workers' Aid (IAH), whose communal kitchens and relief drives sustained strikers. Yet published KPD accounts routinely subsumed such female activities to men's or overlooked women who instigated strikes. Directives instructed writers to change this, while *Parteiarbeiter* regularly ran conversion narratives relating how men reluctant to accept female comrades had seen the light. The delegate-congress movement was also initiated in 1929 to encourage self-expression and rid proletarian women of petit bourgeois ideology. While the party journal printed numerous testimonies to this movement's success, accounts always stressed women's affirmation of the Soviet Union, even if this did not mirror what actually transpired.[180] Accounts highlighting women's strike actions glossed over their specific grievances to stress the need for integration into the *Kampffront*. Ultimately, the party failed to investigate why women workers—even those radicalized by strikes and the depression—were more inclined to join the pragmatic IAH than to join the KPD.[181] Strategy and propaganda seemed to be less about helping women find their voice or grappling with issues than about presenting a unified front.

Serious self-criticism of tactics toward women was by now unlikely to emanate from female activists, as the purge in the mid-1920s greatly muted dissent. In marked contrast to the early 1920s, no serious complaints about women's position in the party surface in internal documents. The KPD journal repeatedly admonished male comrades to end their shabby treatment of women, integrate them into all activities, and nominate more female candidates,[182] but such accounts always ended on the upbeat note that the problem was on its way to resolution. One woman's criticism of the party's ignorance of spontaneous female strikes made it into the party activist journal,[183] yet such complaints were now rare. No substantive discussion of women's organizations' role took place, as the latest generation of women's leaders understood that their groups existed to channel women into the party, not to promote "feminist deviation" from the class struggle.

While the KPD made gains in the 1930 campaign, these did not come from a surge in female votes. Women's votes and party membership did rise, but they remained proportional to figures for earlier years.[184] Even the depression could not create the "transition to the political" the KPD desperately desired. Working-class women radicalized by crisis tended instead to support the SPD and its message of parliamentary work to expand

Freiheit die sie meinen!

Wehrt Euch Wählt Liste 4!

Liebmann, Frau Schilling, Neu, Mucker (Wurzen) Müller (Mittweida) Vogel (Döbeln) Schuberth (Groitzsch)

figure 4.5
"The Freedom They Mean! Protect Yourselves—Vote List 4!" (KPD, 1930) (Hoover Institution)

welfare. In contrast, KPD rhetoric—to both men and women—ridiculed such reformism and banged the drum of revolution in the streets even louder. It blasted religion and welfare as "distracting" women from the exploitation of the real world, even as its own revolutionary slogans were just as estranged from the reality of women's lives. Women's problems, which had never gotten a hearing in their own right, vanished under the KPD's exclusive focus on struggle, strikes, and social fascism. While many men could see their interests reflected in this militancy, few women— desperate for relief in their daily struggle to sustain themselves and their families—embraced the KPD, which offered them little more than pro-nouncements on the superiority of Soviet Russia and horrific visions of class warfare.

Unlike the 1928 campaign, in which no one issue prevailed, the 1930 campaign was dominated by the economy and its tone became increasingly shrill, menacing, and negative. Yet while appeals to men and implicitly male occupational groups tended to focus almost exclusively on specific economic policy issues, those to women nestled material concerns into the framework of domesticity. The theme of economic crisis emerged in women's materials, particularly in discussions of rising prices and welfare policy. It also appeared in the guise of the revived anti–double earner debate. Only the KPD addressed this issue directly, while the DSP and SPD hedged their defense of married women's right to work. The silence of parties right of the DSP indicates their tacit approval of the drive to get these women out of the workforce. Indeed, the working woman faded from appeals by the major bourgeois and confessional parties. In contrast, parties across the spectrum lavished attention on housewives—including the KPD, though its courting had a different aim. Behind the rising recognition of housewives' key economic function lies the resurgent view that homemaking constituted women's "true" occupation, a line that played to male fears of further loss of status during a deepening depression.

The rising stridency of party propaganda in this period came largely from a masculine discourse of *Kampf*, which also penetrated women's materials, particularly from the extreme Left and Right but also from the Center, which tried to marshal forces in the escalating war on Christianity. A corollary focus in appeals across the board was the need for unity, whether expressed as liberal fears of political splintering, Center and Conservative calls for firmness against cultural Bolshevism, or the Communist plea for class solidarity in the imminent war against capitalism. Unlike appeals to male or general audiences, those to women articulated this in moral terms. The Weimar coalition parties—the SPD, DDP/DSP, DVP, and Center—desperately urged women to repair a tattered *Volksgemeinschaft* with their "innate pragmatism" and "healing love." As they preached the evils of radicalism, however, their opponents on the fringes looked increasingly strong and resolute. As the NSDAP, for example, blasted the Weimar system, it also articulated a desire among Germans of both sexes to return to a mythical past of stability—including stable gender roles—that won rising support as the nation slid into chaos.

If woman personified harmony and stability, she also came under increasing suspicion of disloyalty, frivolity, and apathy. All parties presented the 1930 election to women as a gravely serious affair in which responsible behavior was the order of the day and the butterfly antics of sexual emancipation had to end. Even the New Woman became a mother. The focus of female citizenship shifted away from individual rights (though these still had a place on the Left's agenda) as the individual family continued to be subordinated to the larger family of the nation.[185] As growing social tensions raised the stakes of the Reichstag election, female apathy (which, when measured through voter turnout, peaked in 1928) nagged at the parties of the middle and the KPD, all of whom presented women's resistance to political involvement as a female "stab in the back."

While women were roundly admonished for failing to be more politically active, the parties themselves devoted fewer and fewer resources to their organization and propaganda. Parties whose female vote remained strong (the Center and DNVP) continued to take women's support for granted. But women political participants were no longer novel and female suffrage no longer much of a threat. The new focus was youth, the group deemed by every party to be the most unaffiliated, most volatile, and hence most necessary to cultivate.[186] Women's influence within both their respective parties and national politics further waned with the rise of the NSDAP. While the Nazi menace did spur some new attention to the threat to women's rights and "civility" as a whole, which women embodied, this message was not well developed in 1930, as many parties and politicians of both sexes refused to believe that women would support a movement so openly hostile to their political and economic freedom. In the corridors of national power, the NSDAP's victory reduced women's presence, a trend reinforced by the losses sustained by the parties that put forth the most female delegates (particularly the SPD and DDP), as well as the liberal parties' reluctance to "waste" its few safe mandates on female candidates.

One place where women did take center stage in political discourse was the abortion issue, which forced its way onto the national agenda as the number of illegal terminations skyrocketed in the early depression years. The KPD and SPD prominently displayed their support for legal abortion as a matter of both reproductive choice and economic survival, while the Center remained strongly opposed on moral and eugenic grounds; the DVP, DSP, and DNVP dared not touch the issue in their campaigns. However, all parties, regardless of their differences, expressed concern for the nation's "stock" and the "problem" of falling birth rates. Each took a stance they believed would help women enjoy the blessings of motherhood, assuming that motherhood was the culmination of a woman's existence, though the Left's maternalism emphasized voluntary maternity. Economic and political crisis magnified the rhetorical struggle to control the female body as that body's ability to ease the nation's pathologies was touted more and more loudly.

With a future that looked increasingly bleak in September 1930, debates over abortion, women's work, housework, and other themes took on tones even more urgent than in Weimar's first elections. While early Weimar appeals to women bore an optimism that women could bring positive change, those of 1930 shrank female horizons considerably. Whether or not the advocates of women's right to shape their own lives could make themselves heard above the rising din remained to be seen.

There has been a noticeable
rise in belief in witches.
When people or cattle fall ill,
a wizard or woman from the
countryside is consulted. . . . Near
Hamburg, a group of peasants
murdered a woman because
they believed she was a witch.

— 1932 report of the Evangelical
Lutheran Church,
quoted in Gabriele Tergit,
Etwas Seltenes Überhaupt

5

Baby Machine or
Herrin im Hause?

:

Women in the 1932 Campaigns

Often the war of flags spills

into the absurd. From one

apartment house in the West

End fly no less than five

different party emblems.

— "Vor den Wahlen,"
Berliner Tageblatt,
30 July 1932

The Weimar Republic disintegrated in 1932. That year saw the most brutal season of the depression envelop the country in a millenarian gloom. Political choices became starker as voters fled to the extremes and the NSDAP's electoral juggernaut flattened all moderate challengers. Voters confronted the choice between fascism, communism, republicanism, and authoritarianism in a punishing schedule of national elections that year: the presidential vote of 15 March and the 10 April runoff, the 31 July Reichstag contest, and Weimar's last free election on 6 November mandated when the freshly sworn-in Parliament (presided over by Hermann Göring) was dissolved in its very first session. The national and numerous state elections that year were marked by a total war of political symbols, gestures, and rhetoric the likes of which

Germany, even in the endlessly contested Weimar Republic, had never seen. Groups across the political spectrum deemed 1932 the "year of decision."[1]

This staging of identities through a war of political symbolism took the place of real debate.[2] The 1932 campaigns, fought with ferocious intensity, ironically came at a time when parliamentary power hit its nadir. The Reichstag had became little more than a rubber stamp body as rule by emergency decree became the norm. It was first sidelined in the summer of 1930, when Chancellor Brüning was given article 48 powers to bypass SPD-led opposition to his economic austerity program. Under the imperative of dismantling what employers called the "trade union state," the government aimed to break the power of social democracy once and for all, a policy continued by Brüning's successor, Franz von Papen. The government played up Germany's fiscal insolvency to the international community so that reparations payments could finally be discontinued. Enfeebled by Brüning's maneuvers over the budget, the Reichstag was paralyzed after the September 1930 elections. With the NSDAP now the second and the KPD the third strongest party, any hope for a feasible coalition was scuttled. The SPD tolerated Brüning to prevent the formation of an even more extreme right-wing government, acting out of a stubborn sense of national responsibility and tactical expediency, as doing so secured the Center Party's continued support of SPD rule in Prussia (rule that ended in July 1932 with Papen's "Prussian coup"). To many voters, however, such deals smacked of detestable political horse trading and passivity in the face of economic disaster. In their eyes it increasingly appeared that the only solution to the crisis was to scrap what they saw as the ineffectual Weimar system.[3]

All parties vied in 1932 for the protest vote, but it was Hitler and the NSDAP who successfully presented themselves as the nation's "liberators" from the republic. The party honed this attack in the presidential elections, in which Hitler put his still-growing popularity on the line by challenging the venerated incumbent, Hindenburg (the DNVP-backed Theo Düsterberg and KPD head Ernst Thälmann also ran). While Hitler was able to force a runoff, voters—particularly women—chose the symbolic stability of Hindenburg's authoritarianism to the gamble of fascist revolution. But Hitler's showing of over 30 percent bolstered his boast that he and his movement could no longer be ignored. Party slogans and imagery cultivated a sense that the NSDAP's ascension to power was inevitable.

All of these political maneuvers were staged before the backdrop of continued economic collapse. Brüning pursued ruthless deflationary measures that earned him the nickname "the hunger chancellor." Cuts in unemployment aid and social services combined with higher taxes to make sheer survival a full-time task for average Germans, especially housewives. Wage cuts, bankruptcies, bank failures, and rent strikes came to a head in 1932. Early that year, unemployment peaked at over 6 million—roughly one in three workers—which did not even include those reduced to part-time work or those who had simply stopped looking for a job. Millions of desperate men searching for direction found one in the fighting front organizations of both Left and Right, which filled their days with campaigning, demonstrations, and street battles. The Red Front, Reichsbanner, and million-strong SA offered members comradeship and the certainty of physical action at a time when chaos yet again ruled and a weak republic seemed to be emasculating its breadwinners.

The report on a rising belief in witches reflects how easily women could be scapegoated for Germany's turmoil. Proposed remedies to the economic crisis aimed to push women out of the workforce in the belief that recovery began in the home. It was not lost on many observers that official statistics recorded fewer unemployed women than men. Few bothered to interrogate such numbers, reflecting as they did high joblessness among higher paid, skilled union men in heavy industry, the tendency to undercount women as they were less likely to be considered permanent members of the labor force, and the slump's weaker impact on the consumer goods industries in which women were more prone to be employed. Instead debate quickly resuscitated long-standing resentments against the working woman, now embodied by the double earner. The campaign against married working women culminated in a May 1932 law—ratified by every major party but the KPD—that mandated the firing of married female civil servants whose economic provision appeared secure. The law affected few, but its symbolic power was undeniable: a woman's work would be tolerated only if she had no male breadwinner. The BDF offered faint protest, not least because it feared the law would encourage divorce and "concubinage," but its inability to reopen the debate stands as a mark of bourgeois feminism's feebleness by this point.[4] Like the postwar demobilization decrees and the PAV, the 1932 law shows that in periods of crisis, women's constitutional equality was sacrificed on the altar of political expediency, even by parties like the

SPD and DDP, which had long promised women to protect their right to work.

Another weapon in the battle to restore national order by repairing order in the domestic sphere came in the form of a papal encyclical issued on New Year's Eve 1930, *On Christian Marriage*. It bolstered the pervasive assumption that women had the power to save society by rescuing "the spiritual" from men's "calculating rationality," which was brutalizing modern life.[5] The pope reaffirmed the Catholic position that abortion equaled murder and contraception was considered interference in God's plan. But many women ignored such prohibitions. Up to 1 million illegal abortions were performed annually in this period; anywhere from 4,000 to 25,000 women died from them. The arrest and trial of doctors Friedrich Wolf and Else Kienle in February 1931 made abortion front-page news, as thousands of women, in a rare instance of cross-class gender solidarity, hit the streets nationwide to protest paragraph 218. As a front-page editorial in the Catholic daily *Germania* lamented, the debate had "spilled out of radical circles into the serious bourgeois milieu."[6] Such comments reveal not only the extent to which religious and conservative circles feared the public nature of these protests but also the anxieties sparked by the presence of "serious bourgeois" ladies in a female mob that evoked the threats of unfettered modernity and sex divorced from maternity, not to mention "cultural Bolshevism." By June, however, critics were calmed by the movement's disintegration in waves of class recrimination and the failure of sympathetic parties like the KPD to let women control the debate that affected them most.[7]

The dominant narratives of the 1932 campaigns stress the death of the Weimar Republic in an atmosphere of virtual civil war, but the gender dynamics of the year's electoral discourses have received scant attention, which is surprising since contemporaries commonly described them in terms we would recognize as gendered. SPD strategist Sergei Tschachotin summed up the mood of 1932 as the receding of "the logical, the explanatory . . . in favor of the emotional,"[8] terms routinely invoked by friend and foe alike to describe women's impact on national politics. The political wars of 1932 were gendered in ways that cut across neat categories of masculine and feminine, as a brawling masculinity retaliated against a state emasculated by republican politics, a hysterical, "feminized" electorate embraced extremist movements, and female politicians called vainly for cool heads and maternal love to counteract male violence.

The NSDAP's explosion on the national scene upset more categories than it stabilized by whipping up anxieties revived by Germany's second major economic crisis since the war. Its new and successful drive after 1930 to target female voters—one of the last constituencies the party had systematically failed to crack—forced others to redouble their efforts to win a group routinely seen as politically fickle. At a time when women's numerical preponderance still meant that their votes could seal the country's fate, the parties courted them in 1932 with an ardor not seen since the first days of female suffrage. The Nazi challenge dictated the issues featured in all propaganda aimed at women. Some parties' message to female voters acknowledged the power of the fascist call for a *Volksgemeinschaft* and embraced seemingly benign forms of it. Conservative and confessional party images implied that the best way to defuse political violence was to remove the most glaring sign of male powerlessness by returning women workers to the home. Still others preached open resistance to Nazi misogyny, even urging women to fight against it in the streets. Most ominously, some long-standing advocates of women's equality quietly surrendered to fatalism, aware that the republic that ushered in those rights faced grim odds for survival.

Groups across the political spectrum had long projected their hopes and fears onto women. The illustrated press, too, habitually used them as symbols of resilience in the face of crisis or to signify economic inequality, not only in the leftist *Arbeiter-Illustrierte-Zeitung* but also in the liberal *Welt Spiegel*, whose August 1932 piece on "Janus-faced Berlin" juxtaposed a woman lugging a sack of kohlrabi with a lady walking her Pekingese along the Ku'damm.[9] In an atmosphere in which women were such loaded political signifiers, could party imagery depict them as active subjects? Did the polarization of Germany's political atmosphere allow any room for subtleties in propagandistic depictions of women, or did extreme times favor cardboard cutouts signifying the healing mother, the treacherous double earner, the madonna of misery? The breakdown of Weimar's political party field demands a shift in our approach to how propaganda constructed the feminine in 1932. After a brief update on the state of each major party, this chapter will trace recurring motifs registered in campaign materials across the board. With the electorate's political choices practically reduced to a referendum on Nazism, a clearly discernable set of questions regarding women came into view: What would be the fate of women's political, economic, and reproductive rights? Was femininity compatible with a politics of violence and the street? How could women best help restore national order, prosperity, and direction—by embracing the Nazi program or by rejecting its promises as lies?

Any discussion of 1932 must begin with the party that set the year's political agenda, the NSDAP. The details of its mushrooming popularity have been chronicled elsewhere, but suffice it to say that the NSDAP continued to climb throughout the early 1930s as a combination of innovative and perpetual campaigning, aggressive fund-raising, and the respectability lent by its renewed alliance with mainstream conservatives in the Harzburg Front enabled it to harvest the protest vote as the economy continued its tailspin.[10] Hitler's presidential campaign, which plastered the country with over 4 million posters, laid down the themes the NSDAP hammered away at all year under the slogan "Enough!" (*Schluss jetzt!*). It was time, the party argued, for the "November criminals" to pay up, time for voters to put the NSDAP over the top so it could take power and restore national greatness. The NSDAP perfected the art of negative campaigning against a regime blamed for the economic crisis, government corruption, and a decadent culture bent on national suicide. Its propaganda promoted the image of an unstoppable movement determined to erase the Weimar system and restore to the *Volk* its honor, its livelihood, and its soul. This was communicated not only through words but also through the spectacle of amassed brown shirts, the ubiquitous swastika, surging crowds, and a spring airplane tour that lent Hitler the aura of a savior come down from heaven. Both male and, now, female voters responded nationwide to Nazi promises of order backed by the politics of anger and protest. On 31 July, they granted the NSDAP its highest vote ever in a free national election (37.3 percent). While we now know that the party's broad but shallow popularity would soon slide and that Hitler was only ushered into power in January 1933 by the camarilla around a dottering Hindenburg,[11] throughout 1932 the NSDAP's ascent to rule seemed inevitable to most other parties, which responded with varying degrees of protest, accommodation, and resignation.

As part of his drive to conquer power by legal means, Hitler deemed it necessary to break through to women, who had hitherto proved largely resistant to Nazism's appeal.[12] Consequently, the 1932 campaigns saw the NSDAP's most sustained effort to win female support, starting with the forced merger of all pro-Nazi women's groups into the NS-Frauenschaft (NSF) in October 1931. While the NSF often lacked funding and support from rank-and-file men, the party bestowed a high profile on the organization and women in general. Coverage of a 5 April 1932 Berlin rally is a case in point, as front-page headlines in the *Völkischer Beobachter* shouted in response to charges that the party was antiwoman, "Hitler says of the German woman, 'We would be fools to even think about removing her from our common work!'"[13] The party set out to "enlighten" the public on its positions regarding women, courting female voters with entertaining assemblies, personal recruiting, flyers, posters, and their own publication.[14] This new strategy, the party's newfound respectability, and its image as a force capable of effecting change were combined with a message to women stressing family, culture, and religion. Female activists such as Hildegard Passow and Gulda Diehl urged the NSDAP to appeal to the "motherly instinct that resides in almost every woman" with simple propaganda stressing women's role as mothers of the *Volk*, as well as touching on the broader issues of national freedom, bread, and jobs for the next generation.[15] This intensified courting was surely not the sole reason the NSDAP's gender gap disappeared by July 1932—many women were seeking alternatives to the republic, just like men.[16] But this visible attention to "women's issues," couched in the familiar terms of "traditional" values, favorably disposed especially Protestant female voters whose loyalty to the mainstream parties had been severely shaken to the new model NSDAP.

The Nazis' message to women was in most respects a carbon copy of the rhetoric of the DNVP. Yet the DNVP, which had once amassed Germany's conservative and *völkisch* elements, found its fortunes waning as the NSDAP's waxed. After its disastrous showing in 1930, boss Alfred Hugenberg strove to mold his party into an activist movement along fascist lines, enlisting his media empire to enhance his image as a strong "Führer" and ordering the formation of a militant auxiliary to attract youth. In October 1931 he was the driving force behind the Harzburg Front, hoping to infuse his party with a little fascist glamour. Yet Hugenberg, a homely man whose appearance owed more to the Victorian era than the rationalized 1920s, saw his brand of authoritarianism eclipsed by the new dynamics of reaction embodied by Hitler. In July 1932 the DNVP won only thirty-eight Reichstag seats with a poor 6.2 percent showing, although in November it regained almost a million votes as many bourgeois voters who had backed the NSDAP in protest abandoned it in disgust.[17]

Despite the DNVP's rivalry with the Nazis, its 1932 campaigns stuck with the old chestnut of painting the Left as the archenemy of German-dom. The same held for women's appeals, which rehashed familiar conservative themes: women, who "naturally" rejected Marxist materialism for its destructive impact on the soul, were to restore to the *Volk* and its youth the national will to freedom. In the three pamphlets and scant assortment of leaflets produced for women that year,[18] the DNVP renewed its call for Christian nationalism. Unlike more recent campaigns, however, it inflamed 1932's radical spirit by loudly reviving demands for monarchy, empire, and a state devoid of Jewish influence, in terms often identical to those favored by the Nazis. While the two parties shared many goals, DNVP women's propaganda increasingly attacked the NSDAP as the year wore on, contrasting Nazi recklessness and brutality with Conservative wisdom and steadfastness.

Not unlike the DNVP, the Catholic Center Party in this period desired a government of national concentration able to reassert authority and discipline in public life, though it rejected outright dictatorship. This led it as far as coalition talks with the NSDAP after the July election, negotiations that ran aground on the rocks of mutual suspicion. The fact that the Center would even consider such an alliance illustrates how far it had strayed from its original allegiance to the republic — by 1932 it openly disdained the very system it helped build.[19] While it shared with the NSDAP an antisystem rhetoric and rejected "partyism," the Center blasted radicals of all shades who propagated the "politics of illusion and catastrophe." In 1932 it denounced Nazism more aggressively than ever while remaining vigilant against the Left, especially the KPD. It presented each election of 1932 as a portentous struggle between centralized dictatorship and the "people's state" (*Volksstaat*). It rallied behind Brüning (but not his successor Papen) to plead for a return to stability rooted in Christian morality, international peace, a humane capitalism, and the rule of law.

In 1932's great war of political symbols, the Center was a conscientious objector, crying in vain against the militarization of parties. To fortify its core constituency, it relied on clichés, restricted most of its campaign advertising to *Germania*, and largely steered clear of mass rallies. To reach women, the party relied on the Catholic press and house visits, focusing less on "special women's slogans" or individual issues than on "securing women's place in family and community."[20] The year's only flyer addressed solely to women called on them to defend truth, freedom, and law against terror, religious persecution, economic injustice, and dictatorship. Helene Weber in *Germania* urged a female defense of the Christian state, Christian culture, and social justice, "treasures not so gravely imperiled since 1918." Just as women had rallied to the Center then to prevent national chaos, she wrote, so they must now cast off indifference.[21] A general-audience flyer from July that did speak the language of mass regimentation is instructive for its delineation of women's role in a "people's front." Alongside factories, a church, farmers, and men with flags and tools, two women do household chores; female domesticity was constructed as a moderating force at a time when political passions were boiling over.[22] This strong emphasis on women's stabilizing influence and "instinctual" sense of justice often stood uneasily beside the party's overall goal of fostering a "truly authoritarian government," yet this apparent contradiction had little measurable impact on the Center's support from Catholic women, which remained remarkably stable.[23]

At the other extreme of the spectrum, the Communists nourished and profited from the same sociopolitical polarization that boosted the NSDAP. The KPD had won enough votes in September 1930 to become the third largest party; its popularity, drawn almost entirely from the unemployed working class, snowballed as the depression worsened. It still espoused the need for mass struggle and the social fascism thesis, which posited the SPD—not Nazism—as the proletariat's main enemy. Propaganda continued to find the SPD lurking behind every social ill, from the poor state of workers' nutrition to Japan's annexation of Manchuria. Unlike 1930 agitation, however, 1932 agitation more aggressively targeted the self-proclaimed fascists in the NSDAP. A key motif was the image of a proletarian giant who would destroy both fascism and capitalism once and for all, as if in response to the Nazi slogan "Enough!"[24] The KPD also augmented its emphasis on factory cells with attempts to mobilize the unemployed and those outside factories through rent strikes and demonstrations at dole offices, staging a revolution through rhetoric that offered proletarian supporters consoling visions of power and retribution.[25] As before, the intent was to build a crescendo of agitation to precipitate revolution in the streets—a goal lent urgency by the seemingly imminent collapse of capitalism and the ineluctable march of Nazism.

KPD women's materials also emphasized equality, wages, bread, and abortion, all shoehorned into a class war model. Campaign materials dovetailed with efforts to organize unemployed women around demands for equal benefits, bonuses for pregnant women, free foodstuffs, and child care. The KPD also used its sweeping 1931 bill for broader social services and reproductive rights to promote itself as women's lone defender. But

1932 materials for women—as for other target groups—sounded their shrillest alarm over an issue quite removed from Germans' daily experience, the imperialist wars allegedly being planned by "the Reaction." Proletarian suffering was now depicted with graphic images of violence against women and children in both German cities and Asian villages. Propaganda also touted more than ever Soviet achievements in improving women's lives. Citing Lenin, the KPD still proclaimed women essential to victory, as signified in a 1932 general poster appeal that placed a woman at the forefront of a unified proletarian mass.[26] Female membership did rise to 45,000 by early 1933, even if women en masse still resisted the KPD message. Yet women radicalized by the depression or the abortion protests of 1931 were still more likely to gravitate toward the IAH, as demonstrated by the runaway success of Willi Münzenberg's new women's magazine, *Weg der Frau*, whose first run of 150,000 sold out in three days. Clearly, there was a female audience for the radical Left's message, though the KPD was rarely willing officially to embrace the kind of practical, even entertaining, style that made Münzenberg's enterprises so popular.[27]

While the KPD was slow to acknowledge the Nazi danger, the SPD had made Nazism the prime target of its agitation since 1930.[28] The SPD tried to answer the mass regimentation epitomized by Nazi and Communist street organizations by forging the Iron Front to defend democratic values, complete with its own logo of three arrows striking downward. But this symbol failed to capture the popular imagination; the NSDAP witheringly referred to it as a "dung fork," and it fell out of use by the July election.[29] While it attempted to beat the radicals at their own game, the SPD ultimately put its faith in the constitutional courts and the public to save Weimar. It hoped to win back voters by arguing that demagoguery sabotaged a just social state. But the party was clearly on the defensive, as its identification with the system had produced steady losses since 1928 and even opened Nazi inroads on working-class voter loyalties. The famous image from a 1932 anti-Nazi poster of a worker crucified on the swastika betrayed a fatalism bred by emergency rule, economic collapse, rising authoritarianism, and the assault on the SPD's Prussian power base.[30]

Women were a target audience for SPD antifascist initiatives launched after the NSDAP's stunning 1930 victory. Whereas 1930 appeals stressed women's role as peacemakers, those from 1932 often used images of tough young women, fists raised, to urge female solidarity with the Iron Front "against war and Nazi terror, for socialism and freedom!" The SPD argued that the NSDAP, aided by Conservatives and Communists, would dismantle the welfare state, revoke women's constitutional rights, and bar them from politics. The SPD repeatedly reminded the female majority that it alone represented the equality of each citizen, international peace, and economic justice. Women's appeals in the presidential race described the horrors of a Hitler victory: breeding schemes and slavery for pennies, if women were allowed to work at all. Like the KPD, the SPD argued throughout the year in both general and women's appeals that the Nazis were counterfeit socialists funded by industrialists and landowners to sow division among workers and peasants. It also denounced the KPD, calling its fight against the SPD a fight against the worker. To deflect attention from its own association with the system, the SPD charged that Papen's policies were only possible because of NSDAP tolerance: it told housewives that it was in fact Hitler's government that cut their husbands' wages and taxed even the salt on their dry bread. Women and mothers would decide whether imperial barons and their Nazi stooges would rule the people's state. The choice at hand was dictatorship or democracy—what would become of the children if Germany embraced the former?[31]

To a much greater extent than the SPD, the DVP suffered for its association with the Weimar system, no matter how much the party saw itself in opposition to it. Desperate in the face of massive voter indifference to national liberalism, the DVP in 1931 sought to keep pace with the militarization of politics by issuing "fighting goals" of constitutional reform to strengthen the presidency and curb parliamentary "excesses," coupled with a more assiduous cultivation of Christian, national values. Elsa Matz even posited a kinship with the NSDAP, in that both protested the influence of "cultural Bolshevism and a certain asphalt press."[32] The DVP's 1931 program echoed rightist calls for greater *Lebensraum* but denounced the "prophets of the masses" and "the herd mentality" as detrimental to the rights of "the free individual grounded in religion and morality."[33] As in 1930, it attacked the Left but also warned middle-class voters against Nazi "socialism." Fighting for its political life, the DVP hoped to absorb some of the protest vote by allying with the DNVP on national electoral lists. This unequal arrangement only hastened the DVP's demise, reducing it to seven Reichstag seats after July and eleven in November (by comparison, the NSDAP won 230 and 196, respectively). Its attempt to speak the language of antisystem politics failed, and bourgeois voters continued to abandon it like rats fleeing a sinking ship.[34]

Women's materials strove to reverse the DVP's fortunes by focusing on the threat to female honor: "It's about the soul of woman, her influence in the life of the *Volk*, her role as man's companion and comrade."[35] This phrase, from one of the few national pamphlets the party produced in 1932,[36] invokes the same combination of liberal feminism and nationalism that had always informed DVP discourse. But at a time when the DVP raced to shed its liberal republicanism in favor of an authoritarian national front, its women's materials strongly condemned Nazism for its attack on women's rights. The concentration on women's rights is even more notable in light of the fact that both male and female party activists in this period saw women as moving aggressively in a conservative, nationalist direction.[37] That said, pledges to protect women's rights were phrased in terms that upheld notions of female nature as rooted in self-sacrifice and conciliation. The same materials also warned against socialism and cultural Bolshevism. In literature for male or general audiences, these spelled the doom of the nation; to women, they were said to imperil the nation's basic cell, the Christian family—the "basis of women's lives." The DVP told women that it alone was committed to constructive compromise analogous to the *Kleinarbeit* at which women excelled. Women needed a party national enough to defend state and family but liberal enough to guarantee their passionate participation in it.

As the DVP hedged its stance on female equality, the DSP, in materials written by none other than Marie-Elisabeth Lüders, stated in no uncertain terms that women must stop Nazism or their rights would be lost. But by now few were listening. The DSP's failure to break its fall in the 1930 election sent the party reeling, unable to play the politics of mass spectacle; as Theodor Heuss put it in 1931, "We lack men who can duke it out with the other parties."[38] The DSP, like the SPD, openly called the Nazi Party the biggest threat to individual freedom and civility, not to mention the state. But the most outspoken critic of Nazism in the bourgeois camp was without allies and vulnerable to attack for its support of Brüning. Furthermore, its coffers were as dry as its leaders' speeches. The organization was in tatters after so many defeats; the party barely weathered calls from within its own ranks to disband. In July it won just four Reichstag seats; when this fell to two in November, the party could no longer even pretend to be relevant.[39]

The DSP was the last to stake the democratic middle as left liberal propaganda had intoned since the early 1920s. Yet if the party was still looking to women to save the nation, it did very little to court them. In the presidential race, the DSP piggybacked on materials produced by supraparty groups touting Hindenburg to women as the only candidate who could secure a stable future for Germany's children.[40] It created only two new women's flyers in July and none in November. Nor could it rely on the liberal press when former allies like the *Berliner Tageblatt* now steered voters toward the more viable SPD or Center. The few items the party squeezed out doggedly attacked Nazi misogyny, quoting Nazi chieftains to show that the movement would revert women to the status of maids. Simultaneously, the DSP espoused a theme similar to that of its former Weimar coalition partners, stressing radicalism's threat to culture and the family as part of the attack on women's rights. Alarmed by recent results challenging the notion that women resisted extremist parties,[41] the DSP set out to educate women, pleading for a marriage of humanism and rationality to end Germany's crisis. Its meager effort yielded little from female or male voters.

Turning to individual campaign issues, because of the exploding popularity of the Nazi *Männerpartei*, every major party's propaganda for female audiences put the spotlight on what a Nazi victory would mean for women's rights. At a time when the NSDAP had all other parties on the defensive, these parties in turn hoped to rattle the NSDAP by seizing on themes on which the Nazis looked vulnerable. For female audiences, this meant constitutional equality and religion. In fact, the Nazi challenge revived women's rights as a campaign theme to a degree not seen since the National Assembly election of January 1919. The socialist and liberal parties in particular desperately hoped to block the NSDAP's breakthrough with female voters by conjuring up dark visions of women's second-class status in a Third Reich.

The NSDAP had anticipated such attacks: a central aim of its 1932 women's appeals was to bury its misogynist image by refuting "lies" that it would dismantle women's rights. It did so by turning the debate on its head. The much vaunted equality set down in the Weimar constitution, it argued, had only exposed women to the same hardships as men. Weimar meant not emancipation but economic misery, cultural degeneracy, and national disgrace. Egoistic, liberal-democratic "leveling" debased women by clouding the essence of the female soul, sapping its strength through useless gender competition.[42] Alfred Rosenberg wrote in the party daily that political rights, which only existed in theory anyway, were no compensation for the loss of natural rights. Nazism would revive the honor of every German woman and man secure in their place in a *Volksgemeinschaft*. Women's job, Hitler told a Nazi women's conference, was to lead the sexes back to their respective spheres to restore happiness to a *Volk* mired in need and pain. To claims that it would bar women from public life, the party replied that it needed everyone—heroic men and motherly women—to erect the Third Reich. In short, the NSDAP drew on the established language of separate spheres to convince women that Nazism alone could launch a national renewal in which female forces would play a central role. It would be women's emancipator from emancipation.[43]

Central to Nazi notions of women's rights was their right to motherhood, which appeals presented as one area where the party had been miscast. An April flyer asked why women should resist a party that only wished to create the conditions for a happy family life.[44] Far from seeing woman as inferior, the Nazis proved their faith by entrusting her with the nation's young. As before, appeals in 1932 praised motherhood as the sacred site of woman's *Lebensraum*, where her personality could reach full bloom. They pledged to make her an equal comrade in the family to fortify her role as guardian of the nation's biological headwaters. Appeals did not discuss details or specific proposals to aid, say, housewives.[45] Rather they used grand language to articulate one basic theme: women could again command their maternal domain if they embraced the nation's savior, Hitler.[46]

The NSDAP pinned the loss of ordered circumstances on the liberals, but even more so on the Marxists (a term that collapsed all distinctions between the KPD and SPD) at a time when bourgeois rivals were harping on the "socialism" in national socialism. Marxists contemptibly swindled women with promises of equality and a golden future—their "thirteen-year rule" had robbed women's right to health, happiness, and maternity. Marxists had given women the equal right to stand in dole lines and preached the right to abortion because young proletarians could no longer hope to feed the children they bore. Marxists betrayed Germany in 1918 and shackled the next generation to the Young Plan. Marxists yammered that the Nazis would make women beasts of burden; the NSDAP countered that women were already there. Hitler understood that women's "true" rights were those to family, freedom, and bread.[47]

Nazi women's propaganda also painted the Left as a lackey of the Soviet Union. An April flyer argued that the true face of Marxist emancipation could be seen in Russia, which reduced women and girls to drones in a grey proletarian army. In a Nazi state, man's fist would defend the *Heimat* and exalt the German woman to her rightful position as *Herrin im Hause*, or mistress of the home, a phrase that evokes the gender division of labor in feudal society.[48] Like appeals to peasants, propaganda for women drew from the party's antimodernist wellsprings, juxtaposing images of a joyless mass society with scenes of a happy *Volksgemeinschaft* spliced together from an imaginary golden age. While the NSDAP did not seriously entertain a return to feudalism, it offered those bitter with despair over the present situation tantalizing visions of a society in which individuals gladly embraced the right to immerse themselves in an idealized national community.

A similar, albeit tacit, equation of rights with sacrifice for the nation marked DNVP women's materials. The Conservatives continued to define female nationalism in terms of culture. Women writing in the DNVP press in 1931 used florid prose to claim that women, "natural" conservatives, would always intuitively back the party that promoted female cultural influence. Appeals pledged to defend German "cultural riches," including the family and education, from the poison of "class dogma." Women's propaganda from 1932's apocalyptic campaigns also rehashed ultranationalist demands in terms more strident than those in Nazi women's agitation (not surprising at a time when the NSDAP was trying to present a kinder, gentler image to female voters). The DNVP announced to German women the end of kowtowing to foreign powers. Materials for both women and general audiences demanded a military buildup, including a new navy, as stated in the 1931 program.[49] An appeal in the DNVP journal posited woman's indispensability to the project of national "rebuilding and liberation" through her willingness to sacrifice even the lives of her children. It was her holy duty to imbue her children with the awareness that a man's highest honor consisted in military service to the fatherland. In this worldview, women's individual rights were utterly irrelevant — what mattered was vigilance in the "Christian, national" fight against weakness and decay.[50]

This rot plagued not only culture but also the state, argued the DNVP in a relentless antisystem discourse parallel to the Nazis' and rooted in a history of women's materials that attacked liberalism and the SPD. It decried the "party mentality" that severed the individual's bond with the state. A women's pamphlet linked Weimar with national disgrace, economic ruin, spiritual poverty, and barren feminism. Its female author wrote that the "terrible crime" of the revolution gave women the "gift" of the vote and rule by "the parties of Versailles." The great days of the Hohenzollerns had vanished in a welter of unemployment, leaving *Mittelstand* and *Arbeiterschaft* destitute (note the deliberate avoidance of the term "class" to describe workers). Women's love of fatherland must lead them to choose a strong Führer, Hugenberg — a man of action, not talk (a swipe at Hitler) — who would restore the Prussian spirit of honor and freedom.[51]

While Nazi and Conservative propaganda all but erased the individual from the definition of women's rights, other parties appealed to the individual, even when they subsequently redeployed women's rights for the good of the collective. Among these was the onetime *Partei der Frauen*, the DSP, whose negative ads for women aimed straight at the NSDAP, which Gertrud Bäumer characterized in late 1930 as a *Kampftruppe* against female citizenship.[52] Like all parties to the DNVP's left, it showcased the wild schemes that littered Nazi writings. One leaflet prefaced Gottfried Feder's remark that woman is "maid and servant" with his claim that "Jews have stolen our women with their sexual democracy," a sweeping indictment of both Nazi misogyny and its larger hostility to civilized society.[53] A July 1932 flyer credited to Marie-Elisabeth Lüders combined mock Nietzschean solemnity with cartoons of pigtailed damsels and macho brownshirts to belittle the Nazis (see Figure 5.1). It quoted Goebbels's novel, *Michael*, that the female's task was to be pretty and bear children while males provided food and protection, just like birds in the wild. To provoke outrage over *Mein Kampf*'s claim that girls in a Third Reich would attain rights only upon marriage, Lüders told women that this constituted denial of "your citizenship, your Germanness" — a linkage of national identity and democratic citizenship long central to DDP attempts to create a new republican language.[54] With its image of Hitler pushing aside a young woman, whose modernity is signified by her knee-length skirt and contemporary hairdo, the piece constitutes an oblique defense of the modern woman. To be sure, the DSP/DDP never embraced the New Woman outright — even the *Bubikopf* sported by the cartoon's female figure is softened — but was sufficiently alarmed to warn of Nazi hatred toward female independence, which the New Woman, for all her presumed excesses, embodied. Lüders argued that the "brown hero's" claim to be women's savior was a lie — women themselves would have to fight for their rights and their honor.

A July flyer jointly issued by "the parties of the republic" summoned women to "remain the backbone of the state you've helped build" and reject the enemies of their political participation.[55] The threat to female suffrage constituted another motif in 1932 women's materials. The SPD in particular trumpeted its role in securing the vote, as it had in every campaign since 1918, and warned that this right was on the verge of extinc-

Deutsche Frauen, Staatsbürgerinnen!

hört — urteilt — entscheidet!

Denn also sprach Hitler:

„Es gibt Staatsbürger, Staatsange=
hörige und Ausländer. Wer nicht
Staatsbürger ist, soll nur als Gast
in Deutschland leben und muß
unter fremden Gesetz stehen. Das
deutsche Mädchen ist nur Staats=
angehörige und wird mit ihrer
Derheiratung erst Bürgerin."

So seid ihr, deutsche Frauen und Mäd=
chen, Eures Staatsbürgertums, Eures
Deutschtums, von **Hitler** beraubt. So
seid ihr **im Dritten Reich** den „Aus=
ländern" und dem „blutfremden
Rassengesindel" gleichgestellt.

In dieser Unfreiheit dürft ihr deutschen
Mädchen **auf den Erlöser warten,**

denn also sprach Feder:

„Wir Jungen müssen ausziehen und
den Lindwurm töten, damit wir
wieder zum Heiligsten kommen,
was es auf dieser Welt gibt: Zur
Frau, die Magd und Dienerin ist.
Weg, Wille und Ziel dazu heißt
Nationalsozialismus".

In Eurer Rolle als Dienerin und Magd
des Herrn dürft ihr, deutsche Mädchen
und Frauen, Euer Frauentum erleben.

Denn also sprach Goebbels:

„Die Frau hat die Aufgabe, schön
zu sein und Kinder zur Welt zu
bringen. Die Vogelfrau putzt sich
für den Mann und brütet für ihn
die Eier aus. Dafür sorgt der Mann
für Nahrung. Sonst steht er auf der
Wacht und wehrt den Feind ab."

Auch in Eurem Nest gebietet der feind=
abwehrende Herr,

figure 5.1
"German Women,
Female Citizens!
Listen, Judge,
Decide! Thus
Spoke Hitler:
'There are citizens,
nationals, and
foreigners. Whom-
ever is not a
citizen shall only
live in Germany
as a guest and be
subject to special
laws. The German
girl is a national
and only becomes
a full citizen upon
marriage.' Thus
Hitler robs you,
German women
and girls, of your
citizenship, your
Germanness"
(DSP, July 1932)
(Bundesarchiv)

tion. The SPD began stressing Nazi misogyny in a 1930 flyer bearing images of a woman forced to tie an SA man's boots, another being whipped, and a female judge being spat upon. This message became the cornerstone of 1932 SPD women's propaganda. One flyer updated an old theme by argu-ing that the NSDAP courted women's votes but in power would disen-franchise them. The NSDAP lied that the vote was a meaningless right and feared its power once women discovered their true views. July women's flyers reminded readers that there was not one female Nazi politician at any level, though they did not mention right-wing attacks on SPD delegate Toni Sender. Women had to fight those who would reenslave them by electing those who gave them suffrage.[56]

To explode Nazi claims that they were the true defenders of "women's right" to motherhood, summer materials by the SPD—and, to a lesser extent, the KPD, DSP, and Center—focused on an incident in a June session of the Prussian Landtag at which Nazi delegates insulted female Socialists. The women were protesting rising militarism and the slander that Socialists had not "done their bit" in the Great War, noting that their sons had fallen too; a Nazi reportedly responded, "You stupid goats! That's what they were made for!" The phrase "stupid goats" was given maximum exposure in leftist materials as proof that the Nazis' paeans to motherhood were a fraud—they were merely interested in the production of cannon fodder. The incident was considered such powerful, unvarnished proof of Nazism's true face that it even transcended propaganda designed for women, the *Arbeiter-Illustrierte-Zeitung* splashing it across the front page of its July election day issue.[57]

Like the SPD and DSP, the KPD in its women's appeals broadcast misogynist statements the NSDAP worked feverishly to suppress, exposing Nazi promises to restore family and safe home (*trautes Heim*) as camouflage for a rollback of women's rights or noting Nazi antagonism to female politicians and workers. Yet it was not enough to point out Nazi misogyny. The KPD told women that the Nazis were no alternative to capitalism but its "stormtroopers," who profited from "class justice" while workers rotted in jail. The NSDAP tolerated the Papen government, which cut welfare and tyrannized the proletariat with taxes and high prices. The Third Reich would begin with ration cards and forced labor. Finally, materials warned of Nazi militarism, urging women to join the antifascist fight so they would not lose their sons to war. For the KPD, the Nazi threat to women's rights was not a separate women's issue but part of the class struggle.[58]

Even the increasingly rightist DVP and the socially conservative Center were moved by the Nazi threat to use equal rights issues to draw female support. The DVP, whose defense of equality had cooled since 1919, warned women to stop taking their rights for granted. Materials quoted Nazis to assert that fascism would reduce women to sexual vessels and political vassals. Drawing on the tropes of bourgeois feminism, the women who wrote these materials laid particular stress on the NSDAP's lack of female delegates and Hitler's statement that single, childless women would have no civil rights in a Third Reich.[59] Likewise, Center appeals, particularly those in *Germania*'s women's page, criticized the NSDAP's refusal to put forth female candidates and Nazi breeding schemes that would rob women of their right to independent action and personal responsibility.[60]

Both parties were prepared to defend women's rights because they viewed women as agents of morality. The Center in particular clung to a notion of women's rights primarily as the right to marriage and mother-hood. The law had to uphold society's basic cell, the family, by not under-mining the authority of fathers or the centrality of mothers. The party also urged protection of women's motherly power in the public sphere so that they could continue to help craft policies promoting Christian edu-cation and economic justice for families, pensioners, and widows. Above all, Center appeals throughout 1932 urged women to use their political rights to defeat a destructive radicalism of an unabashedly masculine hue. It reminded them of the "fateful days" of 1918 when they were called as equal citizens to help build a new Germany and urged them once more to bring their soothing influence to save the fatherland's children from civil war. Women must defend their rights because the nation needed "motherliness" to defeat the politics of hate and division.[61]

Similarly, the DVP's Elsa Matz wrote that all civic-minded women who supported the women's movement must unite to preserve female political influence not just for themselves but also for the *Volk*.[62] Propaganda for broad consumption watered down any strong defense of feminism for its own sake that cropped up in the DVP journal women's page. The journal, for example, often defended bourgeois feminism, crediting its pioneers for freedoms now taken for granted.[63] A pamphlet for women, in con-trast, criticized women's propensity to make political choices "based on [their] emotional nature." The feminism of DVP writings remained tied to the separate spheres model, rejecting Marxist or democratic emancipa-tion as "leveling" and employing the term *Frauenrechtlerei* as a slur. A July flyer bore traces of this, defending both woman's position as man's equal in marriage, work, and the state and the influence of "women's souls" on public life.[64] Female authors trusted women to recognize instinctively the nihilism of a fascist *Männerstaat*. The political expression of female nature had to be secured because it nurtured the *Mitte* and neutralized primi-tive masculinity, which, when shorn of men's innate rationality, brought chaos and ruin. Finally, women had to snap out of their own starry-eyed admiration for Hitler and ask, Where were the deeds behind his great words?[65]

The DSP, whose campaigns once came closest to a vigorous defense of equal rights feminism, also tied women's rights to *Kultur*, as moderate feminists had done for decades. Lüders begged women to see that the culture of Hitler and Goebbels was killing the culture of Goethe and Beethoven.[66] In line with the DSP's goal to raise awareness of the larger needs of the state, female activists wrote that women required peace in freedom to rebuild Germany in home and family, state and workplace. Just as during Weimar's early tumultuous years, they counseled rationality to counteract male particularism, political witch-hunts, and "swirling passions." This argument aimed to deflate one set of gender prejudices (women are insular, apathetic, unable to see the big picture; men are dispassionately rational) while invoking others about women's healing power and equanimity. DSP materials as a whole stressed the costs of mob rule to both the state and humankind. In propaganda for female voters, women's work for disarmament, "social capitalism," and civil peace represented the politics of healing over the politics of hate.[67]

The parties traded accusations not only over the fate of women's constitutional and legal rights but also over their right to paid labor outside the home. At a time when married women in particular were being chased from the workforce by renewed measures against double earners, expressions of support for women's economic rights could potentially draw female votes. But these efforts could cost male support. Furthermore, with the majority of women firmly supporting parties of a traditional cast, many clearly did not see their primary identity as that of worker. Could they be won in large numbers with pledges to protect equality in the workplace?

The NSDAP's 1932 strategy to appear more female-friendly resulted in appeals denying that the party would end women's right to work. The party courted working women as never before with flyers that provocatively declared in bold type, "Hitler will chase women out of work," to then pooh-pooh allegations that women would be fired to solve unemployment. It pledged to protect working women's interests, based on the assumption that most of them worked only out of need, not "aversion to housework."[68]

But the Socialists did not let such claims go unchallenged. The SPD charged that the Nazis would dismantle women's rights as workers, relegating them to menial domestic or agricultural labor. Noting that what reactionaries considered suitable jobs for women were those men rejected, the SPD linked women's "double slavery" with the subjugation of the working class. Appealing to both class and gender identities, it urged women to protect their rights to independence and career choice by choosing the party of their fathers, the SPD.[69] The 1931 party conference even issued a statement opposing the "witch-hunt" against the working woman, whether single or married. Not she, it read, but capitalism was to blame for massive unemployment; arguments to the contrary only undermined class unity.[70]

The KPD too linked women's lack of economic rights to capitalism, as part of its ongoing mission to convince women to identify as workers first. Nazism, as a capitalist ideology, betrayed all workers, the KPD argued. The SPD, it added, was "no better" than the NSDAP, as both were in league with capital to usher in a Third Reich.[71] KPD materials from 1932 vigorously defended women's right to work, damning measures against married women as proof that capitalism aimed to keep women mute and homebound. They exposed workplace conditions harmful to potential mothers and continued to argue that unions had done little to end working women's singular exploitation. The KPD also blasted the Center and bourgeois parties for uncoupling women from the working class through *Frauenarbeit* that kept their sights limited to the home. The positive model was the USSR, touted in a flood of materials celebrating the fifteenth anniversary of the Bolshevik revolution. Maria Reese wrote effusively about Soviet moves to end women's double burden with communal services, claiming, for example, that factory kitchen food was better than hotel cuisine. She summed up communism's benefits by writing that in the land untouched by economic depression (the catastrophe of collectivization being hidden from outsiders), women enjoyed full equality, equal wages, and the satisfaction that they were helping build a beautiful new society.[72]

But the Communist message still had limited appeal for women who increasingly appeared to be seeking freedom *from* work.[73] Hitler's program tapped this sentiment by openly promising to eliminate women's need to work. Melodramatic appeals intoned the economic misery caused by the system and the revolution, which gave women the "right" to toil in factories or department stores only to have their wages siphoned off by taxes to finance the Young Plan. Was it barbaric to wish to free women from such slavery? "Hundreds of thousands have lost their footing in the whirlwind of the big city . . . and opened the gas to end their pain."[74] Now those who had had thirteen years to fix things hoped to save face by slandering the NSDAP. Nazi propaganda did list problems plaguing working women, such as low wages, layoffs, the brutal pace of rationalization, and even the double burden. But the intent was to package the NSDAP as a friend of working women while simultaneously promising jobs for men at a family wage so that no wife would be forced to abandon her natural tasks in the home. The complex reality of how and why women worked was flattened by negative campaigns designed to mollify male insecurities and erode both sexes' confidence in the republic (see Figure 5.2).[75]

Such appeals placed the NSDAP solidly in the mainstream, especially in their use of children to sell Nazism to women and mothers. A July flyer asked, "*German women*, don't you pity the *millions of hungry, miserable children*, who have been robbed of a happy, carefree childhood by the *Young Plan* signed by the ruling parties? Who stare, old before their time, with dull, weary eyes at a *hopeless future*? . . . The misery of children and youth is above all your concern."[76] The Nazi movement promised work to youth and bread to the aged. It would revive propriety and train youth to respect moral values. This was the message of a pamphlet from Coburg, in which a proletarian mother praised a Nazi *Arbeitsdienst* program for rescuing her insolent, chain smoking son from a future without prospects (something her "idiotic" Socialist husband did not understand).[77] Like its opponents, the NSDAP sold itself to women as the last hope for the family. Unlike them, it appeared able to make its plans reality, trading on the dynamic image its propaganda promoted.

Other parties agreed that more women could be mobilized with pledges to free them from work than with promises to keep the labor market open. A DNVP flyer to housewives and mothers argued that Germany needed jobs for men and youths to keep them on the straight and narrow. It inflamed anxiety with images of a present in which the aged and infirm starved, while reassuring women that peaceful homes where children were "properly nourished" would return with the DNVP in power. Furthermore, the party that had never embraced working women told housewives it would end "horrible" unemployment so that husbands could again earn the family crust. Women's pamphlets reinforced the association of middle- and working-class financial ruin with women's need to bring in wages. One piece countenanced jobs for women compatible with their "nature" but flatly stated that married women should only work in extreme cases because work and domestic duties each "demanded a whole person to be done well." Unlike appeals from 1928 or 1930 that laid out a specific role for housewives, the DNVP's eco-

figure 5.2
"Women! Millions of Men without Jobs, Millions of Children with No Future. Save the German Family. Vote Adolf Hitler!" (NSDAP, July 1932) (Hoover Institution)

nomic message to women in 1932 was more generic. Surprisingly, at a time when the depression was a central concern of voters, the economy was secondary in DNVP women's appeals, serving more as a mere addition to the list of wrong turns since 1918. The party played to bourgeois desires for a return to order, signified by men with jobs and women able to devote themselves wholly to the family.[78]

The return to bourgeois order had been a staple of Center appeals to both sexes throughout the Weimar era. But they also recognized women's work as vital to the economy, acknowledging the realities working-class

Catholics faced. Center women's propaganda spoke out for protective legislation and even claimed to guarantee women occupational development. Yet *Germania* reiterated the even more salient belief that work was not women's proper station, echoing the recent papal encyclical by arguing that the cultural meaning of women's work must be considered, not just its financial value. Appeals in its women's page openly called for housewives and mothers to be relieved of work outside the home, as it detracted from the fulfillment of their "most important duties." The Center was also a key sponsor of the 1932 law against married female civil servants, a stance it neither hid nor mentioned in appeals.[79] Likewise its press demanded education for girls that would prepare them for their future in the family, *Volk*, and church, not cloud their minds with abstract *Wissensstoff* (literally, the "stuff" of knowledge). Reverting to the view that economic issues were of secondary importance to women, it floated vague promises to remedy women's need to work with more state aid to families and a more "organic" but still capitalist order with everyone working in his or her proper place, which for women meant the domestic realm.[80]

The alleged incompatibility of work and motherhood did not disqualify unmarried women from paid employment in campaign discourse. NSDAP materials to female audiences affirmed this, as the party sought—ultimately in vain—to win single working women. Because the "surplus woman problem" would linger for generations, an April flyer magnanimously supported working women's "well-earned" rights and promised that those who could or would not take up a "real woman's occupation" could pursue another career. All Hitler wished, a July appeal claimed, was a Germany where each contributed to the whole—the "spinster" had a role too. Clearly, the NSDAP was trying to cover all its bases with women voters; besides, it was no longer controversial to concede the right to work to single women. But such rhetoric was strictly expedient. A handful of appeals to women pales in comparison to the bulk of Nazi materials to both sexes that promised to restore the male breadwinner, denounced double earners, and used female labor to signify national disgrace.[81] Hitler's 1932 program openly declared that "work ennobles woman as well as man, but the child truly ennobles the mother." Speakers were to point out that woman's equal participation in the Soviet workforce had "destroyed" the family. While Elsbeth Unverricht could write in a November *Völkischer Beobachter* appeal that any woman who desired work would have it, elsewhere the NSDAP stressed jobs for fathers to "save the German family," as in a 1932 poster to women. While there was some ideological diversity within the party that could allow such contradictory messages to surface,[82] from the vantage point of the party's campaigning prior to coming to power, these represent the opportunism at heart of Nazism's success. The NSDAP wished both to assure moderate voters that it had no radical plans for women and to milk the gains that could be generated by promises to end women's need to work, an alluring message to both unemployed men and many women for whom work meant poor pay and low status.[83]

Assumptions that marriage and maternity, not work, defined female identity were by no means limited to the NSDAP, DNVP, or Center. In 1932 the SPD played as it had before to this sentiment, to which it attributed the NSDAP's rising success with female voters, by damning capitalism's impact on the family. A July women's pamphlet lamented the war's legacy of 2 million women "condemned" to celibacy, struggling for survival without male protection. Capitalism made Nazi promises of lifelong support from employed husbands impossible, the SPD told women, as it forced workers to choose between financial survival and the "joy" of raising a family, an especially painful dilemma for married people and for women. The SPD recognized that women were often captivated by the domestic fantasies spun by bourgeois magazines, but its propaganda was less likely to interrogate the fantasy than to fall back on generic indictments of capitalism. SPD appeals urged women to fight for their dignity as workers—one even acknowledged that women worked not just for survival but also for spiritual growth—but their tone reinforced associations of women's work with hard times.[84]

DVP materials for women produced by female activists also reflect conflict over whether femininity and work were compatible. They often strongly defended women's right to work, discarding their former emphasis on the occupation of housewife. A 1932 flyer demanded women's "equal valuation" in the workplace, while Anny von Kulesza's 1931 pamphlet addressed the double earner debate at length, questioning why the term was applied almost solely to married women but not, say, male workers who also earned interest income. But the women who wrote these appeals themselves assumed that those most interested in labor issues were single. Informing women that the NSDAP was especially keen to eject them from elite fields such as law and academe, they asked, should their talents wither because the Nazis saw single women as inferior? The DVP blasted the NSDAP not for claiming that women's supreme duty was motherhood but for living in "a fantasy world" by promising that women would never have to work. It urged working women, who understood both the necessity and the pleasure work could bring, to reject Nazism and its illusions.[85]

At a time when all parties saw the effectiveness of Nazi promises to "free" women from the labor market and restore their "natural right" to domesticity, no issue in campaign propaganda spoke more to whether women could reconcile marriage and work than the May 1932 law mandating the dismissal of married female civil servants (*Beamtinnen*). The Center, seemingly assured that its constituents backed the law, did not hide its support for it; the DNVP failed to mention it for similar reasons. In contrast, other parties strove to sell themselves to female audiences as pro–working woman while hiding their support for the law. For its part, the NSDAP strove to appear both prowoman and pro–civil servant. While elsewhere hostile to double earners, one April flyer addressed to civil servants stated that the "woman surplus" necessitated protection of the "well-earned" rights of *Beamtinnen*. (It also constructed work and marriage as mutually exclusive, stating that in the Third Reich "the working woman will enjoy the same civil rights accorded the married woman.") Yet Nazi appeals to civil servants—a group courted heavily—were geared less toward winning women than toward solidifying the male protest vote. As one piece told them, "Of course we reject double earners at a time when millions of you suffer because of the present system's fulfillment policies."[86]

The *Beamtinnen* question generated rhetorical contortions by the DVP, which had also voted for the measure. DVP women argued in the party press that each woman should be allowed to decide whether or not she could mesh marriage and career, but they could not convincingly assert this as a basic universal right because they demanded that the social impact of women's work be considered in any attempt to regulate it. They argued, for example, that women's greater aptitude for certain fields would make their expulsion from the workforce injurious to the *Volk*, as in the case of female teachers. Firings could ruin families, cause divorce, and expose young couples forced to postpone marriage to moral temptation. In the only pamphlet to address the issue (from 1931, no less), Anny von Kulesza used statistics to show that firing married women would only aggravate unemployment, as women who lost their jobs fired their domestic help. She regretted that the few cases of childless two-income couples put all married working women on the defensive. DVP women's materials from 1932 reflect this defensiveness, criticizing Nazi misogyny while recognizing their call to restore "healthy" families as "justifiable." If DVP women exhibited mixed feelings, the party at large showed its priorities by publishing no campaign materials during 1932 on *Beamtinnen*. Male civil servants were of far greater concern, and they could not be won with promises to defend jobs for hated female competitors.[87]

Similar vexations confronted the DSP. A May 1931 memo called threats to women's right to work a top priority for DSP women, while a party meeting later that year urged members to fight any attempt to curtail women's work or pay through emergency decrees.[88] Yet it is difficult to find a defense of women's work in 1932 campaign literature. In a July women's flyer, Lüders, who waged a personal crusade to convince her party not to back the law and felt personally betrayed when it did, quoted Gregor Strasser that a Third Reich would teach wives to make ends meet on a husband's salary alone, but she offered no direct comment on this attack on female employment. Instead, she linked Nazism with economic privation (symbolized by "good old pea soup"), mocking the spartan diet the NSDAP would impose in the name of culinary nationalism. No DSP appeals to any group mentioned party support for the law against married *Beamtinnen*, not even to male occupational groups, whom the vote was designed to please. Like its rivals, the DSP's stated defense of women's equal right to work was trumped by the sacrifice of a few female civil servants to angry male voters.[89]

The SPD's failure to support the rights of married *Beamtinnen* was perhaps most glaring in light of its progressive self-image and its 1931 denunciation of the "witch-hunt" against working women. Not surprisingly, campaign appeals omitted the party's vote for the firings. A November 1932 flyer to civil servants' wives claimed that the SPD had secured "proper treatment of the *Beamtentum*," though the use of this gender-neutral term rendered the plight of female civil servants invisible. Even though women now comprised an almost equal share of party voters, the SPD was less willing to incur the wrath of male supporters than to keep its promises to women.[90]

This did not go unnoticed by the KPD, which held the moral high ground as the only major party that voted against the law. In addition to familiar arguments that the Socialists were bourgeois lackeys who distracted female proletarians from the class struggle with a women's publication more oriented toward cooking than politics, KPD women's materials pounced upon cases where the SPD's parliamentary record matched the NSDAP's: both rejected full legalization of abortion and supported the law on married *Beamtinnen*. The KPD could claim to be the lone defender of women's right to work, its propaganda hammering away at the need for women to join the proletarian front. But even in its imagery, women were frequently identified not with productive labor but with house-work or children. Among Communists surveyed by Erich Fromm in the early 1930s, only 36 percent believed that married women should work.[91]

Women's work, while a prominent issue in the 1932 campaigns, was too perilous for any party to defend too strongly, especially outside the con-fines of women's propaganda. Those that defended it did so selectively, focusing on the kind of anti-Nazi attacks that seem to have kept most working women from voting NSDAP.[92] But the majority of women voted for parties that promised to liberate them from the workforce altogether. While work or even careers for single women had ceased to arouse much controversy by this time, the right to work still did not define femi-ninity for most men and women. Women voters embraced the Center and warmed up to the NSDAP, who preached freedom from work or work "consistent with their nature" for women without men to support them. This was their expression of antisystem sentiment.

Besides legal and economic rights, the other major issue on which the NSDAP appeared vulnerable with female voters was religion. All parties accepted statistical evidence that religious considerations strongly deter-mined female voting behavior. The NSDAP deemed in the early 1930s that to win female votes—as well as those of Catholics, another group it had not yet converted—it would have to reverse its "pagan" image. Thus, 1932 propaganda promoted Nazism's alleged opposition to both the "forces of atheism" and all who "misuse religion for political purposes."[93] Oppo-nents aimed to undercut this strategy not so much with positive claims of their own piety but with negative appeals that reminded the public of past Nazi statements hostile to religion or the churches. They sought to link Nazism with a nihilism antithetical to familiar forms of spiritu-ality and the humanism that the Weimar coalition parties presented as Germans' shared cultural heritage.

The Center had been the first to mount a serious attack on the pagan ethos of Nazism in propaganda to both women and men, beginning in 1924. Since 1930 the party had kept on the heat, its press continually dissecting statements particularly by Alfred Rosenberg, whose wild pro-nouncements on race and religion the NSDAP was itself squelching during this period. The Center then broadened its charge that Nazism was at heart anti-Christian by focusing in 1932 on racialism, which it argued subordinated the laws of God to the law of blood. The Center characterized this as the key threat to family and culture in propaganda across the board but particularly in *Germania*'s women's page. Center materials had long criticized the materialism of the Left as antireligious, and while this argument was recycled in 1932 against the KPD in particular, the Center, whose hold on the Catholic vote was seriously challenged by the NSDAP, exposed what it saw as the Nazi brand of materialism, which subordinated all things spiritual to racial imperatives. This critique was most aggressively deployed in materials discussing reproductive questions, as we shall see below.

The DVP used similar terms to question the NSDAP's Christianity. Retreating from 1930's single-minded defense of Protestantism, it issued a sweeping critique of radicalism's corrosive effects on German culture that transcended specific religions. Women's materials argued that the NSDAP would usher in a new cult of Hitler worship and the "myth of blood"— the difference between Christianity and Nazi "materialist racism" could not be greater. Propaganda placed this difference in the context of Nazism's undermining of authority (both governmental and parental) and the cultural damage its removal of women from public life would bring. Women were told to reject all forms of materialism and fight the "massification" of culture with refinement, cooperation, and religious faith.[94]

The SPD took a strictly secular view, presenting Nazism not as a threat to Christianity in particular but as the agent of a wider brutalization of culture. As in 1930, the SPD discussed culture and religion in these terms, declaring radicalism and violence the gravest threats to civilization. Largely resisting the common practice among bourgeois parties of addressing women primarily through cultural themes, the SPD did not use Nazi threats against organized religion to sway women voters. Instead, it continued to link political Christianity and capitalism, as in a general October leaflet that updated socialist anti-Catholicism to portray Hitler as beholden to bloated clergymen and Papen's "gentlemen's club." It also embraced the de rigueur coupling of femininity with a heightened moral sensitivity by urging women to reject fascism to protect morality, public civility, and, by extension, their children.[95]

But the Right countered with its own definition of morality, one that capitalized on the pervasive notion that it was the republic that had caused Germany's presumed decline in morality and Christian culture. DNVP appeals depicted a "great battle" between nationalist Christianity and "international" godlessness—code for Judaism, secularism, and Marxism in all its forms.[96] They attacked the Center for its Prussian coalition with the "atheistic" SPD, in a bid to attract nationalistic Catholics.[97] While nationalism and Christianity marked DNVP propaganda for all groups in 1932, appeals to women stressed as always their singular inability to live without God. One stated, for example, "God did not put us on German soil for naught, but to put His plans for Germany into action. We stand amid the dissolution of rank and the collapse of spiritual and economic life under a calculated assault on the people's soul." Women's task was to rescue German customs and German hearts "cracking under the influence of . . . godless propaganda."[98]

To appear pro-Christian, the NSDAP also presented itself as a warrior against "godless Marxism" and a hated modernity. This created an opening through which to attack the Center—something the Center had feared—but spare the Catholic faith by roasting Center politicians for fourteen years of cooperation with the "archenemies" of church and *Kultur*, the SPD.[99] The NSDAP intensified earlier attempts to argue that the true danger to religion came from its defilement for political purposes. It also accused the Center of neglecting "national feeling" and failing to stem the tide of promiscuity, jazz, Freemasonry, and freethinking. Appeals demanded a "Christianity of deed" to roll back the culture of Judeo-Bolshevism. One portrayed women thanking Hitler for reviving faith, family, and fatherland as the bases of Germandom. This linkage of religion and nationalism, long a staple of DNVP and even Center appeals, seems to have finally dispelled the Nazis' pagan image among Protestant women voters, especially in the provinces. Catholic women, in contrast, remained aloof; few would join the millions who now believed in Adolf Hitler.[100]

Like the Nazis, the Communists held that exposés of the Center Party could win female votes,[101] but their aims were radically different. The KPD was not presenting itself as the savior of traditional morality—its target was church misogyny, an old argument buttressed in 1932 by the recent encyclical. The KPD called papal condemnation of abortion callous, asking whether it was moral to force an eleven-year-old girl raped by her father to endure the resulting pregnancy. It also tried to disarm Christian women's anticommunism by refuting charges of religious persecution in Russia. As always, the KPD defined morality in material terms, comparing its devotion to workers' concerns with the Center's, whose chancellors were blamed for the depression. It contrasted images of children who had only potato skins to eat with the annual income of Brüning and prominent bishops, calling their claim that communism destroyed the family hypocritical at a time when child labor was back on the rise. In the KPD's view, the Center broadcast its indifference to capitalist injustice through its hostility to women workers' needs (symbolized by an image of a bishop tripping a female demonstrator with his staff) and to female labor itself. Allied with the SPD, the Center propped up the economic and gender status quo, smoothing Hitler's way to power. The KPD, in contrast, argued that Christian women had the right to a decent life not in heaven but on earth. Convinced that the church subjected women to a "refined torture" to erode their capacity for independent thought, the KPD could only see religion as women's enemy. Religious women responded in kind by rejecting the party to the end.[102]

If women supported parties that claimed to protect Christian morality, did the brutalized political climate of 1932 create a space in which the parties felt women could be won with anti-Semitic appeals? Apparently only the DNVP felt so. Its hymns to Prussian values were tinted with a bald anti-Semitism largely absent from its appeals since the early 1920s. A 1931 party journal attacked "anti–paragraph 218 demagogue" Else Kienle, "whose name is actually Jakobowitz-Kienle."[103] Appeals in 1932 urged women to support the DNVP to "free us from materialism, Jewish morality, and the flagrant Jewification of the German spirit in art and literature. Pride in a pure race must become commonplace among our *Volk*."[104] In contrast to the crude racism and anti-Semitism employed in the early 1920s, the 1932 model had no leering sexual aspect, and, unlike the Nazis, the DNVP in appeals did not link Jews directly to abortion or sex reform. Rather they were associated more generically with the triumph of secularism (the Schulgesetz remained prominent in women's appeals) and republicanism, presented to women as poisonous to German custom.[105]

Such discourse also served as the vehicle for NSDAP anti-Semitism this year. Like appeals to farmers or civil servants, those to women blamed Jews for the excesses of modernity—in this case, the *Unkultur* of sex reform, since sexuality was a "women's issue."[106] But the NSDAP in 1932 cloaked its anti-Semitism in respectable garb, suspending the vulgarity of *völkisch* propaganda from the early 1920s and relegating Rosenberg's rants about "Jewish-Marxist soul poisoning" to the party press.[107] It now invoked the type of socioeconomic anti-Semitism long churned up in German politics during tough times, such as the argument in a flyer to

Catholics that the Center had allied with the SPD to sell the *Volk* to "international Judaism."[108] The NSDAP did not deny its bigotry but conveyed it more subtly. For example, a flyer denying that a Nazi state would reduce single women to the same legal status as Jews reassured readers that women would be full citizens; the Jews' inferiority was not refuted. Indeed, the piece closed with women's "thanks" to Hitler for guarding their purity against "Jews and their comrades."[109] With this repackaged anti-Semitism, easily swallowed with a strong shot of antisystem hyperbole, the NSDAP's transition to respectability was complete.

The parties' contest to appear most moral was staged particularly for female voters' benefit. Competing definitions of morality inevitably begged discussion of reproduction, seen universally as a topic uniquely relevant to women. The 1931 marches that mobilized thousands of women across the country to protest abortion paragraph 218 put a women's issue on the national agenda to an unprecedented degree, making it a potentially volatile campaign theme the following year. The KPD and, to a lesser degree, the SPD hoped that their support for legal abortion would win them female votes, and their campaigns showcased this. The NSDAP, in contrast, was an avowed critic of abortion and in 1930 even proposed a bill demanding hard labor for offenders, a move that could peg it as unsympathetic to women. In the 1932 elections, which came hard on the heels of a broad-ranging mobilization against an unpopular reproductive law, how were issues of abortion and sexuality handled in propaganda for women?

The DNVP evaded abortion, pausing only in 1931 to slander Kienle by calling attention to her husband's Jewish surname.[110] Elsewhere the Conservatives mentioned the sexual issues of the day only once in women's materials, in a 1932 pamphlet that briefly restated Christian objections to divorce reform and abortion.[111] Campaign propaganda bore little trace of the eugenic, racist concerns about foreigners' rising fertility that party women—many of whom now embraced the profascist National Opposition movement—expressed at their 1931 meeting.[112] Instead, materials expressed nebulous anxiety over physical degeneration as a danger to the spirit, with which women were "by nature" most in tune. Racial vigilance also seasoned the recurrent formula that women—through their bodies—were the preservers of German culture and custom.

If the NSDAP set the agenda in this period on most other issues, it let others drive the debate on abortion. The *Völkischer Beobachter* did not cover the 1931 rallies, except for one August piece that blasted a speech by Else Kienle against paragraph 218 as a "cultural disgrace." Party publications for true believers did take up abortion, echoing Goebbels's argument that the Left's demand for legalization exploited women for base propaganda purposes.[113] Articles described the "horror" of legal abortion in Soviet Russia. *Deutschland Erwache!* used "testimony" from a former Communist to expose women's right to control their own bodies as soulless and defeminizing. The author, unable to raise a child because "everything in Russia is so expensive," got an abortion at what she describes as a filthy, prisonlike state hospital; when it was over, she cried and longed for Germany.[114] In contrast, abortion was present but muted in campaign propaganda, perhaps because the NSDAP's position was well known or, more likely, because its call for hard labor for offenders could not be reconciled with its new push to appear prowoman. When abortion did surface in 1932 appeals, it was not openly named but merely implied in mantras on women's duty to guard racial purity. The NSDAP preferred to slip abortion — and liberated sexuality in general — into the larger complex of "cultural Bolshevism" that enslaved the honor of both women and Germany itself.[115]

Other parties were not about to let the Nazis pass off their views on sexual issues as run-of-the-mill conservatism. The Center had vilified the Left as an agent of easy divorce, "free love," and legal abortion.[116] But in 1932 it warned even more loudly against national socialism. Appeals to Catholics argued that Nazism violated God's plan by sanctioning the murder of the sick and handicapped. The Center played to female supporters' desire to defend beleaguered territory by stressing that the Nazis would dismantle the institution of marriage to foster procreation by the "fit." While Center propaganda did not tackle anti-Semitism per se, this appeal blasted a Nazi statement that a healthy, even illegitimate, Nordic child was worth more than a legitimate Jewish one.[117] Appeals also quoted Rosenberg that childless women were socially inferior and that sanctions against adultery should be relaxed to allow the husbands of barren wives to "rectify" the situation elsewhere. A piece for general audiences cited the "stupid goats" incident, while others averred that Nazi plans would reduce women to "baby machines," a phrase normally used by the Left against opponents of legal abortion. The Center's opposition to contraception and abortion in all but life-threatening cases was bolstered by the 1930 encyclical,[118] but it argued that "crass racial materialism" would destroy the bonds between family members, "mechanizing" individuals to serve racial imperatives. This would be a particularly brutal fate for women, whose very fulfillment lay in motherhood. Nazi breeding schemes would dash their hopes for peaceful domesticity by animalizing motherhood and leaving them vulnerable to abandonment.[119]

The DVP, which assumed most women would choose motherhood if they could, had always targeted bourgeois women with the pledge to preserve marriage and family. While its 1930 campaign located the main threat to these in Soviet and American mass culture, 1932 women's materials focused on Nazism. The DVP, like the Center and socialist parties, tried to roast the Nazis in their own juices, quoting Hitler, Gregor Strasser, and others to show that a Third Reich would reduce German women to baby machines. Materials argued that Rosenberg's plans to legalize polygamy and elevate unwed mothers of racially pure children had Hitler's blessing. They also accused the NSDAP of poisoning children against their parents, an argument once made against the Left. As always, the DVP stated its blandly expressed commitment to monogamy and large families, urging mothers, "the guardians of life and domestic peace," to reject all incursions on the sanctity of the family in the name of freedom, individual responsibility, and child welfare. But the DVP kept conspicuously silent about abortion, a stance it shared with the DSP as well as the BDF, to which many female liberals still professed allegiance.[120]

The SPD's use of reproductive issues to discredit the NSDAP bears a different complexion than that of the Center or DVP. The SPD hoped to win female votes by affirming the movement against paragraph 218. Whereas in previous years it used the lack of reproductive rights to indict capitalism, its 1932 women's appeals employed this as ammunition in the assault on fascism. Retreating from earlier campaigns' proeugenic messages, they stressed past Nazi pronouncements that women would only attain full civil rights upon giving birth and reminded women of the NSDAP bill to stiffen penalties for procuring not only abortion but also contraceptives. Nazi policy would not restore women's "most beautiful right" to motherhood but would force proletarian women to produce surplus population to keep down wages. SPD appeals called for legal abortion in the first trimester under a doctor's supervision, though one that claimed the party was working to abolish paragraph 218 glossed over the SPD's rejection of a recent KPD bill proposing just that. Unlike the KPD, the SPD limited abortion to women's appeals, despite the warm reception given Grete Zabe's suggestion at the 1931 party conference that reproductive issues be placed before both sexes.[121] But the SPD was less likely to wedge these into a rigid class framework or display women as martyrs, instead treating abortion and contraception as real problems needing concrete remedies.[122]

SPD claims to support reform stemmed not from an embrace of sexual liberation but from its long-standing view that the state had a responsibility to foster healthy, voluntary maternity. The New Woman appeared nowhere in 1932 campaign material, perhaps because the SPD was chastened by readers' negative reaction to *Vorwärts*'s serialization of Irmgard Keun's novel about a sexually liberated young woman, *Gilgi—eine von uns*.[123] In fact, the SPD distanced itself from "unorthodox" sexual behavior by using it to discredit the Nazi movement. It echoed other parties' claims that the Nazis would legalize polygamy to encourage procreation by the racially fit.[124] A November appeal asked mothers if they could entrust their sons to SA leader Ernst Röhm, a "proven" homosexual.[125] This discourse on deviant sexuality was part of the SPD's own attempt to cultivate respectability by uncoupling socialism from "free love" with showy indignity over Nazism's debasement of women and children. It played to widespread homophobia by allying itself with "healthy popular feeling" and reaffirming the nuclear family ideal.[126] Even its support of some criminalization of abortion matched mainstream sentiments that the state should promote higher birth rates and police sexual morality at a time when the nation's morals seemed to be collapsing.[127] Youthful androgyny in the service of the Iron Front was permissible, but sexual behavior was generally delimited in SPD appeals by the monogamous heterosexual relationship and healthy maternity.[128]

More so than any other party in the early 1930s, the KPD invoked abortion in nearly every women's appeal, reflecting a broader emphasis on sexuality and youth in the wake of the anti–paragraph 218 movement's collapse. A plethora of posters from 1931 and 1932 used familiar images of haggard women to depict them as victims of the law and maternalist ideology, defended only by the KPD. The SPD, which seemed an ally, revealed its treachery by voting against a total lifting of paragraph 218 and the KPD's sweeping 1931 *Mutterschutz* welfare bill.[129] While one flyer implied that abortion constituted a uniquely female "political crime," the KPD still doused the issue's feminist potential in class rhetoric, using abortion to attract female interest in the larger Communist goal of proletarian liberation. This strategy was partially successful. Yet the KPD's insistence on linking the fight for legal abortion "more than ever" to all other social, cultural, economic, and political issues, as well as its continuing refusal to invoke the less melodramatic issue of birth control, hampered its ability to retain the support of previously unorganized women politicized in 1931. Women could back the abortion struggle because it was concrete and directly relevant; sweeping calls for social revolution were too abstract, too frightening.[130]

KPD materials continued to question prevailing sexual mores in 1932. They explained how the USSR had reordered domestic relations by making marriage a loving union between materially secure equals. While divorce was easily obtainable, child support was strictly regulated and rape punished more severely there than in the capitalist West. Maria Reese scorned prurient *Spiessbürger* assumptions that Soviet reforms had opened the floodgates of promiscuity—the free Soviet woman scorned all who would see her as a sexual object. Bourgeois morality was also skewered in a pamphlet satirizing new swimsuit regulations at German beaches, a public decency measure that actually drew more attention to female genitalia than the swimsuits had. The KPD also noted that among the foes of "cultural Bolshevism" were a Nazi who ran a strip joint and Hugenberg, whose papers ran advertisements for massage parlors. These exposés posited a new sexual ethics that liberated bodies not in the name of decadent individualism but in the name of a healthy egalitarianism that would render "sex appeal" a superfluous commodity.[131]

While the KPD aimed to debunk essentialist views of femininity, these views still marked its propaganda. Women's appeals often portrayed the worker—now unemployed or on strike—as male, while women were paired with children in pieces discussing poverty or abortion.[132] A page from the 1932 party calendar conveys the largely unchallenged assumption that housework was women's work. Above the caption "Common life—common struggle!" sits a proletarian husband with his party newspaper, casting a stern glance at his wife, who has to read it over his shoulder while she cooks. The text proclaims that marriage should be a private and public partnership, but the image reflects the reality that doubly burdened women had less time for politics than their husbands. Furthermore, Wilhelm Reich's accompanying text blames capitalism for proletarian sexual dysfunction: the double burden destroys the working woman's ability to appear "sexually enticing for her husband." Physically spent, she cannot give him what he desires after his day of work, fueling the alcoholism and domestic violence that would only vanish with true socialism. Perhaps the proletarian cause could use some sex appeal after all.[133]

The political violence that marked 1932 was not just a backdrop of the campaigns; it permeated them, leaving its stamp on the language of mass appeals. How did this translate in appeals to women? It was a cherished convention that women were by nature pacifistic (despite women's proportionally strong support for the militaristic DNVP). Operating under this assumption, parties crafted appeals playing to female desires for peace and stability. In 1932 this dovetailed neatly into all parties' campaigns against the NSDAP, which had stolen the KPD's title of most violent political movement. For its part, the NSDAP worked to defuse its volatile image, arguably with less success than it had in other areas such as women's rights or religion.

The SPD, particularly in women's appeals, spotlighted Nazi violence, linking it to the destruction of families and presenting it as the polar opposite of the SPD's own constructive work to expand welfare. Curbing attacks on the KPD, it blasted NSDAP claims to respect mothers, arguing that Nazi thuggishness comprised the grossest insult to these givers of life. SPD propaganda routinely used pictures of the grieving families of workers murdered by the SA, displaying widows with young children to evoke outrage and solidarity. One piece claimed that a Nazi "scoundrel" wrote a letter to the mother of one of his victims crowing about his deed. The "stupid goats" incident was invoked in at least three women's flyers and one poster as "the summit of Nazi cruelty." Materials reminded women of the myriad costs of war, arguing that the NSDAP would unleash new ones because "war is fascism's first ideal." A Nazi state would reduce women to "war mothers" forced to teach the children they bore each year to worship the gun. Until they had the power to wage war abroad, the Nazis would continue their "murder plague" on German soil, sparing not even women. Unlike those of the KPD, SPD appeals to women did not counsel physical retaliation; only Iron Front propaganda designed for a youth audience hinted at this. Instead, women's propaganda banked on an innate female pacifism, combined with horror at the loss of reproductive and economic rights, to retaliate against fascism at the ballot box.[134]

The KPD generated sharper attacks, using vivid examples of the violence intrinsic to Nazism. Several pieces recounted a 1919 case in which

Killinger, then a Freikorpsman, ordered a Communist woman whipped "until there was no white spot left on her back." A July 1932 women's flyer, "Hitler Bandits with Whips and Pistols against Working-Class Girl!," reported that a twenty-year-old girl was shot and beaten senseless for distributing KPD flyers (see Figure 5.3). The piece, which also informed women and mothers of the dozens killed since the lifting of the SA ban, juxtaposes an image of the girl in happier days with a whip to show the true face of Nazism. Unlike other appeals in which the denunciation of fascism was so broad as to reduce the NSDAP to just another manifestation of capitalism, this piece explodes Nazi claims to honor German women largely by trading on female stereotypes. It refers to the victim as a "defenseless girl" and invokes SA attacks involving children to play to women's maternal instinct and desire for protection. Elsewhere a party memo ordered that propaganda cure women of their fascination for strapping, uniformed SA men, restating the KPD view of women as irrational, unreliable political actors.[135]

While the KPD acknowledged certain female stereotypes, its addiction to *Kampf* precluded acceptance of women's supposed pacifism. In fact, its 1932 appeals to them, as to all groups, were drenched in violence. They still urged women to join the struggle against the system, churning up images of a "looming catastrophe." Guided by the social fascism model, which in part predicted new imperialist wars as overproduction forced capitalist nations to seek new markets, all KPD agitation posited a brewing war against Russia and highlighted Japanese aggression against the Chinese. Women's materials, for their part, illustrated international atrocities against women and children with graphic descriptions of bombings, germ warfare, and rape. These were intended to generate solidarity and expose capitalist aims, which the KPD told women they abetted with their work in arms factories and their clinging pacifism. It is doubtful whether most women, particularly during the depression, could identify with victims of a distant conflict. However, they could relate to tales of state brutality at home, which KPD materials provided in abundance. In one piece, Tina Modotti asked whose fatherland was being defended when police clubbed striking husbands and sons. A Women's Day flyer urged policemen's wives to stop their men from attacking their "comrades of fate" and protect people, not capital. The KPD tried to link common scenes from proletarian life to a broad, brutal complex of capitalist "fascization," as in a flyer comparing the monthly food budget for police dogs with declining state spending on child nutrition. But women's experience got

Wehrloses Mädchen
aus Berlin mit Peitsche und Re-
volverschuß niedergestreckt

Der berüchtigte Führer des SA.-
Sturms 92, Schur, hat am 14. Juli. abends
die 20jährige Bankangestellte und Anti-
faschistin Erika Eckert im Hause
Schillerring 31. überfallen, als sie Flugblätter durch die Türen der Wohnungen
steckte. Mit der hier photographierten Nil-
pferdpeitsche hat der braune Hund die Wehr-
lose geschlagen und aus seinem Revolver
gezieltes Feuer auf sie eröffnet. Erika Eckert
brach mit einem schweren Ober-
schenkelschuß bewußtlos zusammen.

Hitlerbandit
mit Peitsche und
Pistole gegen
Arbeitermädchen!

Diese bestialische Tat entlarvt die scheinheiligen
Phrasen der Hitlerpartei. Der „Angriff" vom
1. Juli 1932 wagt noch zu schreiben:

„Die Hochachtung, die der Nationalsozialismus
der deutschen Frau und Mutter entgegenbringt,
verbietet es von selbst jedem Nationalsozialisten,
in beleidigender Weise über die deutsche Frau sich
zu äußern . . ."

Fast kein Tag vergeht, an dem nicht die Nazis
arbeitende Frauen in der gemeinsten und nieder-
trächtigsten Weise beleidigen und sie mit ihren
Mordwerkzeugen terrorisieren.

In Ohlau in Schlesien, wo die Nazis ein furcht-
bares Blutbad anrichteten, schossen sie in einer

figure 5.3
"Defenseless Girl
from Berlin Laid
Low with Whip
and Gunshots.
. . . Hitler Bandits
with Whips and
Pistols against
Working-Class
Girl!" (KPD,
July 1932)
(Landesarchiv
Berlin)

lost in the call for class war. Contact with the NSDAP made the KPD less attuned than ever to women's qualms about violence, equating proletarian struggle with armed struggle.[136]

Liberal women also warned against Nazi violence, struggling to uphold feminists' faith in progress over savagery.[137] While these women saw women's rights as synonymous with progress, concerns with rights were eclipsed in 1932 women's propaganda by the extremist threat to maternity, family, and culture. A flyer authorized by Lüders and signed by over one hundred women from the DSP and other organizations made an open call by "[us] women as mothers, daughters, and sisters" to end the "disgraceful civil war" German men had unleashed. The piece, with a circulation of 100,000,[138] cried, Did we bury our husbands, sons, and brothers on foreign soil during the war so our youths could be slaughtered at home? DSP materials emphasized specific cases of Nazi brutality but also condemned the destructive alliance of "swastika and Soviet star." Lüders's flyer named no guilty parties but presented women with images of a *Brüderkampf* (literally, war of brothers) that threatened national unity, friendship, and family life.[139] DVP women's flyers injected a strong nationalism into this formula, arguing that women's cultural mission was at risk. Women were praised for resisting the Left; now they had to reject Hitler's "socialism of destruction" by strengthening the "national circle" that defended German freedom.[140]

Violence, like religion, was used by the DNVP in 1932 to contrast its solid conservatism with the volatility of the NSDAP. Aware that rising numbers of its female supporters were gravitating toward Hitler, the DNVP tried to persuade women of its own resolve by spotlighting its leader, Hugenberg. As one pamphlet put it, he could free Germany from need, build a strong army, defend faith and *Heimat*, and reduce the cost of living. Yet while it aped the Nazi stress on a Führer, the DNVP demanded a more traditional authority, a restored monarchy. One women's appeal obliquely cast Hitler as a dangerous ruffian, arguing that while Germany needed a strong head of state, he must be independent of the masses, called to rule by right alone. Not only was mob rule distasteful and rowdy, but a November appeal also implied that Hitler's movement was dishonest. It quoted Prussian NSDAP faction leader Wilhelm Kube as saying, "If we have to ally with the devil's grandmother to get to power, we will," followed by the caption, "One changes fashion—why not convictions?" This piece visually links Nazi opportunism to clichés of female fickleness by depicting the devil's grandmother (who represents the Center Party) discarding her SPD mantle for one emblazoned with a swastika. This piece of anti-Center propaganda also meshes Conservative fears of the irrational masses with deep anxieties about female caprice, precisely at a time when balloting revealed the softness of women's loyalty to the DNVP. While the DNVP never openly accused women of treachery, this appeal is the DNVP's first to betray anger and suspicion that women were not suited for serious politics.[141]

How did NSDAP appeals respond to these warning bells? The much ballyhooed "stupid goats" scene in the Prussian Landtag was, not surprisingly, quashed, though Goebbels attempted a rebuttal, stating that party delegates would swear under oath that the episode never occurred. Such "lies," he wrote in *Der Angriff*, did not jibe with national socialism's "deep respect for mothers" and "defenders of the fatherland" and could only have been invented by slackers without a fatherland who "degraded" women with abortion propaganda.[142] Elsewhere, women's flyers tried to shift focus away from German streets to the world stage, one plainly stating that in power the NSDAP would not start "senseless" wars. But this was undermined by other rants against the "disgraceful peace" of Versailles and other treaties. A flyer entitled "Women Want Peace" pledged to "annihilate" class war at home, while a *Völkischer Beobachter* appeal told women that Hitler would rid Germany of "traitors and pacifists." Others, asserting that civil war was already here, tried to sway women with images of the "martyrs of Marxist blood terror," including a mother and her young son. Elsbeth Zander's November appeal ordered women not to retreat from battle at the last minute "as in 1918" but to avenge the fallen by helping the NSDAP to victory.[143] The overall effect of such appeals did little to conceal Nazi aggression, which in fact only grew more visible as the movement peaked that summer. Hitler's August declaration of support for the Potempa brownshirts who murdered a Communist before his mother's own eyes repelled many voters otherwise attracted to the NSDAP. Could propaganda resorting to insults have reassured any mother concerned about the escalating climate of civil war? Despite NSDAP attempts to soften its image in 1932, its rough edges were still visible enough to unsettle bourgeois protest voters, especially many women previously alienated by its brawling masculinity. But if this image still gave particularly Catholic and Socialist women pause, for the over 6 million women who voted NSDAP in July 1932 (the peak of its Weimar popularity), such concerns were overridden by antisystem sentiment.

How did the Nazi challenge affect the position of female activists, still delegated to the work of mobilizing women supporters, within parties? Did revived attention to women voters in 1932 restore them to the position they held during the first months of suffrage? Or did concerns about the loss of more reliable (that is, male) constituencies perpetuate women's lack of clout within their respective parties?

Within the NSDAP, women had never been involved in crafting appeals for any audience, except for occasional pieces in the party press. This was the job of the NSDAP Propaganda Directorate (Reichspropagandaleitung) and part of the "purely political" side of party work. Female activists' role in mobilization was strictly one of dissemination. More important, in the party's view, they were to provide aid to "civilian" party members and SA men, many of whom were unemployed. This included cooking meals for men campaigning and marching, collecting donations for families of slain party members or "political prisoners," and sewing uniforms for needy Nazis. In other words, women's domestic skills were deployed to help sustain the privileged political work of men.[144]

Jill Stephenson and Claudia Koonz have each documented the often tense relationship between female activists and party leaders prior to Hitler's coming to power. Some women opposed the 1931 merger of all women's groups into the NSF, itself subordinated to male leadership. Some also criticized the party for curbing their political activities. Anna Heimersdorf wrote party leaders that she did not consider politics harmful to femininity, while embattled NSF chair Elsbeth Zander argued (in vain) in the autumn of 1932 that women candidates could enhance the NSDAP's image among female voters. But ultimately, these women did not contest the movement's larger goals or its emphasis on female sacrifice applied to the "proper" spheres of culture, social work, or the domestic economy. Their devotion to fascism prevented them from mounting a serious challenge to the NSDAP's masculine leadership principle.[145]

In contrast to its Nazi rivals' aggressive attempt to mobilize women for rightist politics, the DNVP had beaten a retreat. Both the amount and content of women's appeals issued in this period indicate party disarray. The few materials the DNVP produced during Weimar's busiest election year lacked a strong message to women beyond the standard Conservative shibboleths of Christian nationalism transmitted through maternity. As the NSDAP snapped up female votes with the "family values" message the DNVP had pushed for years, the DNVP seemed at a loss as to how to respond. In the few extant party records, there is no evidence of concern or strategizing on how to stop Nazi inroads. Sketchy accounts of the 1931 party conference and executive meetings suggest that when organizational matters were discussed, the focus was more on mobilizing youth or workers than on mobilizing women. When female activists did speak at such gatherings, they addressed ostensibly nongendered issues such as "the German East."[146] While nationalism was a key issue for mobilizing conservative women, why did the DNVP lack a more concerted strategy at a time when its vote was unraveling? The August 1932 transfer of a Reichstag seat won by one of Germany's most prominent female conservatives, Paula Müller-Otfried—one of only three DNVP women elected in July—to a man who had recently defected from the DVP indicates disregard for the interests of Protestant women, a core DNVP constituency that respected Müller-Otfried's leadership.[147] While the DNVP's aura of Prussian stability may have held the allegiance of those too frightened by the Nazi alternative, clearly it had not been enough to prevent the defection of a large portion of its female vote to the NSDAP.[148]

Like the DNVP, the Center Party did not drastically alter its modus operandi regarding women in response to the NSDAP challenge. Almost no women's appeals appeared outside the party press in 1932; those that did were limited in scope to familiar emphases on family and religion. Even the hot issue of abortion was missing from election-year propaganda, unlike earlier years when the Center was the only non-Marxist party to broach the subject. In the absence of records from the national organization, it is difficult to know the extent of the concern expressed in *Das Zentrum* that "radical" family members often made it difficult for pro-Center women to cast their votes.[149] But the Center's abstention from 1932's war of political symbols and its reliance on tested tropes reflecting its view of female interests and nature implies confidence in Catholic women's continued loyalty. Organizationally, the Center suffered no dramatic resignations by key women, who remained active politicians and writers, as evidenced by the steady stream of writings in *Germania*'s women's page. Its focus on the spiritual made women indispensable to the Center's political vision. The party spoke to many women's longing for a Christian community rooted in law, welfare state capitalism, and clear gender roles. Catholic women responded to the message that female centrism constituted Germany's salvation as they had in the past, making the Center's vote the most stable in Weimar.

If anxiousness over women's support rarely surfaced in Center writings, the opposite holds for the DVP, whose women (men did not deign to comment on "women's issues") remained preoccupied with what they saw as female voters' stubborn resistance to politics. They anguished over proposals to alter franchise requirements or establish a women's party, neither of which went anywhere. Both published and internal writings convey fear that violence would scare bourgeois women from the polls. One piece even implied that female apathy was to blame for the current political chaos, the flip side of the argument that their influence modulated the tone of public discourse.[150]

But if women in the outside world were behaving badly, DVP women maintained through Weimar's last days that gender relations within the party were harmonious. Charlotte Gerwitt claimed in October 1932 that while other bourgeois parties tried to lure women at the last minute with patronizing paeans to the eternal feminine, hers alone made a sustained effort to help women make informed political decisions. Another wrote that, unlike the NSDAP, the DVP valued women's selfless activism, which explained their loyalty.[151] But the reality of continued indifference to women at major meetings, plus the fact that supporters were jumping ship, lends these accounts the air of wishful thinking. Martha Schwarz's boast that Elsa Matz's election to the Reichstag in July proved that the DVP cared less about quantity than quality came from the party with the consistently lowest percentage of female delegates.[152] DVP women were not forthcoming about the loss of two of their own to the DNVP, Lotte Garnich and former women's section leader Clara Mende. Garnich's defection was shrugged off as the act of one who had long since lost her following. Mende's split appeared amicable, although an internal memo noted that she had been critical of the DVP since it failed to reinstate her on the national ballot. Despite women's writings to the contrary, the DVP still downplayed the importance of female candidates. This only worsened as it desperately sought personalities with wide appeal; women were largely unknowns. Mende's fate typifies women's lack of leverage within the party that tried to mobilize female voters with warnings that their political influence was about to be squelched.[153]

If men in the NSDAP, DNVP, Center, and DVP saw the mobilization of female support as women's work, the KPD still aspired to make this the task of the entire movement. Thälmann and leaders at all levels prodded men to prove their Bolshevism by including women in all plans. But reports by both women and men in internal files and the party journal furnished no shortage of cases of women being overlooked or undervalued.[154] The KPD tried to combat what Clara Zetkin diagnosed as an inability to reach working-class women by promoting *Weg der Frau*, intervening in rent strikes, and paying more heed to women in small factories, white-collar jobs, and unemployment lines.[155] Women were not immune to radicalization in this heated season, and the KPD did attract some who were politicized by abortion rallies, the depression, or rising Nazism, when it conducted street actions with concrete objectives. Yet the KPD's growth during Weimar's last years came largely from male, not female, recruits. The prime sites of agitation remained large factories and delegate congresses, which bypassed women not already converted to the cause.

Similarly, the content of agitation still emphasized class war and social fascism, while the party pulled back organizationally from the one theme that did move proletarian women, abortion, fearful that the power of this cross-class gender issue could not be contained.[156] Even when the KPD message was delivered in the melodramatic style that women supposedly preferred, female audiences did not respond with their votes to hyperbole that positioned them as helplessly maternal victims of capitalism.[157] Ultimately, the KPD remained suspicious both of women's socially conservative bread-and-butter concerns and of their unwillingness to subsume gender interests to class, even when mobilized. A 1932 poster that called women to free themselves by breaking the chains of capital also reminded them to remember Rosa Luxemburg, a woman who placed class at the summit of her concerns.[158]

The SPD also strove to reconcile female voters' class and gender concerns. Tactically, its war on fascism continued its shift away from entertainment to more substantive forms of women's agitation. Alarmed that women constituted a growing slice of NSDAP voters, men and women at the 1931 party conference questioned how women could back such an unregenerate *Männerpartei*. Käthe Kern blamed the depression for heightening desires for a golden past, which Nazi propaganda exploited. She urged that SPD materials avoid sentimentality and promote female involvement in class struggle. (Struggle imagery did in fact mark SPD women's appeals in this period, even if images of female victimhood were never far from those of resistance.) Although disputes had rocked the party conferences of the 1920s, in 1931 there was general agreement that the SPD must extend more support to female activists in light of the fascist threat and the strains the economy placed on their time. Indeed, that year saw a flurry of activity in the form of over 1,500 Iron Front rallies and the brief but intense campaign against paragraph 218. But street campaigns never overshadowed the belief that women's activism best belonged in Parliament or the welfare office. While the SPD's vision had its limits, many female contemporaries accepted the SPD as a progressive party. By 1931 female membership increased to 230,331 (23 percent of all members), and the gender gap in the SPD vote had been eliminated, something the KPD was never able to achieve.[159]

This upbeat news, however, could not disguise the fact that women were still far from equal within the SPD, as illustrated most painfully by its parliamentary flipflops on abortion and double earners. Many SPD women were involved in the campaign for legal abortion—the party's 1931 vote against the KPD bill for full decriminalization was made largely against the will of its female delegates. Owing to the deep recrimination within the Left during Weimar, the SPD's vote could be interpreted as representing anti-KPD rather than antifeminist sentiment.[160] Its actions concerning the 1932 law against married *Beamtinnen*, however, cannot be explained away so easily. Its disregard of constitutional equality was purely an attempt to appease male voters at women's expense, based on the common misconception that women were less loyal and hence less valuable constituents. No party conference was held in 1932 to gauge the vote's impact on gender relations within party, but historians have argued that it split the SPD along gender lines.[161] There was little female delegates could do, their influence and numbers waning as the party's overall vote slid. Conditions in 1932 did not offer a hospitable forum to debate women's rights when the rule of law itself was in jeopardy. Despite talk of equal rights and comradeliness, the republic's crisis was another pretext for giving women's issues short shrift.

The party most devastated by the conditions attending the republic's demise was the left liberal DSP. Consumed with its own survival, it seemed to be actively disowning its former stance as the "party of women." The party that had produced over forty women's flyers for the 1919 National Assembly race produced barely one-tenth that in 1932 due to lack of funds and lack of interest. Party guidelines issued after its 1931 reincorporation failed even to mention women.[162] That same restructuring put longtime chair Gertrude Wittstock out of a job by eliminating the women's committee; her successor in a demoted "women's section," Martha Dönhoff, resigned just before the July 1932 election, citing both personal reasons and a gloomy "assessment of the party's tactical situation." While these women publicly maintained the appearance of loyalty,[163] private papers reveal profound alienation and despair among female activists.[164]

The DSP treated shabbily its most dedicated advocate for women, Marie-Elisabeth Lüders. Despite continued formal membership in the party and its executive, Lüders became an unstinting critic. Never comfortable with the party's rightward drift after 1930 and deeply stung by its failure to protect her Reichstag seat, she blasted the Young German Order as antiwoman.[165] While her rage at the DSP's betrayal on the *Beamtinnen* law expressed itself in criticism of women's tendency to give in "so that we are ultimately seen as pliable objects of men,"[166] she publicly stated at the December 1931 party conference that active male hostility had under-mined women's influence in the party. By late 1932, Lüders joined the group around August Wolff that demanded that the DSP dissolve itself or else they would resign.[167] Party leaders met her criticisms by backing a restructuring proposal that excluded her from the group assigned to reassess strategy, with Heinrich Landahl tossing in the barb that "the pre-vious women's leadership has failed."[168] Lüders still garnered respect from women and men, both inside and outside the party. One female student wrote party leaders that placing Lüders in another unwinnable ballot slot proved that the DSP did not stand up for women—she and many like her would now vote Center.[169] Lüders's fate symbolized the end of a trajec-tory the DDP began in 1919, in which female citizenship and defense of women's rights moved from the spotlight to the shadows. Just like the cartoon Hitler in Lüders's 1932 flyer, the DSP finally edged the modern woman out of its political picture.

In 1932's war of political symbols, the battle lines were drawn by the NSDAP. Its all-out campaign to win female votes also set the terms of debate over "women's issues." Unlike those of previous years, when this Nazi gospel of *Kampf* against the Weimar system conveyed only unfet-tered machismo, 1932 appeals aimed to win women by transforming bru-tality into resolve, misogyny into brotherly concern, and antimodernism into a noble fight against cultural enemies. The party strove to include women in its vision of a new order, as in a poster for the presidential race depicting a unified *Volk*, arms raised in the Hitler salute. Three fig-ures in the crowd are female; significantly, one is a peasant and another a girl in pigtails.[170] These women's appeals projected widespread desire for a return to stability and traditional roles with only a slight nod to the de-mands of modern life. Historians have shown how the NSDAP ascended by tapping the protest vote with negative campaigning. To win women, it presented feminism as an utter failure that threw them unprotected into a maelstrom of economic, political, and social competition with men. It stressed the same commitment to church, children, and charity as tradi-tional bourgeois parties, only now, the NSDAP argued, it alone could give these female domains the protection they needed. After three years of economic depression, when crisis seemed to have become a permanent condition, voters responded to those who proposed most convincingly to neaten the tangled borders between the sexes. At a time when the streets teemed with political warfare and women themselves hit the pavement as strikers or abortion protesters, the appeal of promises to restore women's right to be stay-at-home wives and mothers was great.

Else Brökelschen-Kemper, a DVP activist, wrote in late 1932 that women were attracted to the NSDAP because it addressed their desire for marriage and motherhood, their doubts that work could bring happiness, and their inability to see themselves in a new female type that appeared unfeminine and immoral.[171] Battling against this current, opponents in every party left of the DNVP exhorted women to realize that Nazi promises merely camouflaged plans to enslave maternity to breeding schemes and war machines, to toss women who needed and deserved jobs out of work, and to pervert German culture to suit the dictates of a crass racial materialism. The SPD, most directly responsible for female suffrage, joined the liberals in urging women to see that their very rights as citizens were at risk, while the KPD stressed the fascist threat to life and limb.

The NSDAP's intensified effort to win female votes paid off by July 1932. Where votes were tabulated by sex, women surpassed men's nationwide percentage of Nazi votes for the first time.[172] Yet, as Childers has shown, this support ran along confessional and class lines. Protestant women seem to have overcome their misgivings about the party more so than Catholic women. Working women also remained immune to Nazism's appeal. Such fragmentary and belated support disputes the thesis that female votes brought Hitler to power. Instead it reveals that women's voting allegiances had finally undergone the same shifts as men's.

Several factors combined to make the NSDAP the largest party, including its organization and, most important, its lack of association in the public mind with the hated Weimar system. The parties of the Left and center made credible arguments that women would lose their ability to influence a hypermasculine politics. But the times were not kind to rational arguments or moderate gestures. In the end, these parties were either too closely linked to Weimar, too bankrupt, too class-based, or too fractured for their case about Nazism's catastrophic consequences for German culture, freedom, family, and civility to spoil the NSDAP's broad appeal. With the exception of the sizable number of female voters who backed the SPD and the Center, women eventually went the same way as men in the great debate over whether or not Weimar was worth saving. While the Nazis did not directly attain power through an election, the fact that parties that openly opposed the republic held a firm majority did not bode well for German democracy. The parties of the republic urged women to "remain the backbone of the state that you've built and that they want to tear from your hands!"[173] By this time, however, few Germans felt compelled to save a system they associated not with democratic rights but with economic ruin.

Conclusion

:

Women and the Language of Weimar Politics

On 3 June 1932 a demoralized Marie-Elisabeth Lüders wrote a memo to the DSP women's committee lamenting women's lack of political clout: "While party discipline is necessary, women should not confuse this (as we have often done) with continual surrender and subordination, which ultimately causes men to view us merely as compliant objects, 'assistants' they can magnanimously consult when the moment suits them."[1] She went on to fault women's concentration in the less political areas of social welfare and culture for their inability to assert sustained political influence. Lüders, by this point, had witnessed the erosion of married women's right to work, the failed campaign to legalize abortion and contraception, and the rise of the misogynist Nazi movement. In light of Weimar's demonstrable failure to realize fully equal rights for women, it would be easy to conclude that suffrage had had no significant impact, an assessment heard in other countries after the enacting of female suffrage.[2] But this begs the question of how to measure impact. If we consider the impact women's enfranchisement had on discourse, a field whose prescriptions had real effects on lived experience, it becomes clear that women's presence did alter the everyday language of Weimar politics, injecting into it new themes, preoccupations, and even forms. Propaganda constructing women as political actors did not just prescribe roles for them; it was also implicated in Weimar's bitter battles over the legitimacy of the welfare state and the republic itself.

The proclamation of female suffrage in November 1918 produced a seismic shift in German politics, creating roughly 21 million new women voters, compared to 19 million men. Fear over how women would vote compounded already acute anxieties produced by the dislocations of war and industrialization. Parties reacted to the numerical imbalance in the electorate by producing a high number of appeals to female voters for Weimar's first elections. Addressing women as political actors for the first time, the parties concocted appeals born of a chaotic present filtered through notions of the eternal feminine. Consistently treating women as a group unified in its identity and interests, all parties assumed in 1919–20 that they could win the female vote by claiming support for constitutional equality, racing to claim that they had always been women's truest advocates while everyone else was just out to exploit them as "vote cattle." The National Assembly campaign also defined a set of women's issues that would endure throughout the Weimar era and resurface in West German political discourse. Female activists had a hand in this process, their power varying across time and party lines.

Women responded to their enfranchisement with a burst of activism and high turnout on election day. All was up for grabs in the optimistic, liminal year of 1919, as groups competed to define the nation, citizenship, and women's place in them. This cacophony of speech gradually dampened as sex-segregated balloting revealed that women were voting along the same class lines as men and responded most favorably to parties that stressed religion and culture, not female liberation. The election results met with comment across the political spectrum and profoundly impacted mobilization strategies vis-à-vis women. They persuaded all parties to devote more attention in each subsequent campaign to religious and cultural themes. Parties that already had these themes writ large in their programs, the Center and DNVP, heaved a sigh of relief, concluding that female suffrage was less of a threat than they had feared.

Elections reveal a political nation and offer a gauge of how participants in the political process make sense of social change.[3] The parties of Weimar Germany assumed that sexual difference was not only relevant but central to social and political relations. In Weimar propaganda, women's identification as women trumped all other identities they might bear, unlike men, whose gender identity was less obviously a subject of national debate. While the problems women faced were not completely unique—both sexes suffered in varying degrees from the effects of inflation, unemployment, and rationalization—women suffered a unique burden of characterization based on gender. They were treated rhetorically as what Jürgen Falter defines as a political subculture—a unified group with a consistent orientation capable of collective action—even though they exhibited little sense of common interest.[4] Assumptions about women emerged in the themes that propaganda constructing them repeatedly invoked: equal rights, culture, family, morality, religion, maternity, social welfare, women's work, pacifism, reproduction, and sexuality.

Only a few parties kept equality and suffrage as central motifs in their appeals. The SPD was one of them, taking credit in every election for the passage of female suffrage, sometimes even in appeals for mixed-sex audiences, to illustrate its vision of a just society. The KPD was the most militant in demanding gender equality as part of its overall goals, but it shouted its demands in a language of revolution too violent to attract wide female support.

Alone among the bourgeois parties, the DDP showcased a commitment to constitutional and legal equality in its women's propaganda, attempting to win female support with a new language of citizenship. The DDP entered Weimar politics as the only party openly to embrace feminism as a movement and an idea. The feminist notables who crafted DDP women's appeals appear to have had considerable creative latitude in early campaigns. But in postwar Germany, as in other European nations, feminism was a dirty word connoting selfish particularism at a time when the supposed attainment of emancipation should have laid old grievances to rest.[5] Mindful of this, DDP women activists infused propaganda with the moderate feminist argument that suffrage was good not just for women but also for the community. The common good—reified in all parties' propaganda—was identified with woman by virtue of her role as culture bearer and her "natural" propensity for self-sacrifice. Using citizenship as an integrative practice, DDP propaganda justified its extension to women by locating it within the family and the social, as well as the political sphere. This discourse aimed to mend the postwar rupture between the sexes by arguing that the benefits women's new rights would bring to the individual family could heal the wounded national family too. This "party of women" message did not yield a flood of female votes after 1920, much to the disappointment of DDP leaders. (The DDP's association with economic crisis also played a large role, as women also voted their pocketbooks.) The party, whose embrace of feminism was as much an opportunistic attempt to capitalize on its relationship to women's movement leaders as a profession of genuine egalitarianism, subsequently redirected the focus of women's appeals from equal rights to cultural themes and domesticity as the site of female citizenship. Moderate feminists within the DDP, such as Helene Lange and Gertrud Bäumer, were key here, as they had long hoped to anchor notions of female "cultural achievement" (*Kulturleistung*) capable of transforming a patriarchal society. The failure of this throws into relief the limits of bourgeois feminism's appeal to women voters during Weimar and its inability to transcend the women's realm or profoundly shape the parties' general development. Even the attempt of DDP women activists to articulate the liberal possibilities of a maternalist, essentialist femininity was squelched by 1932. The DDP's bid to construct a new female citizen, just like its broad attempt to create a republican language of politics, was buried under the weight of Weimar's persistent crises.

The DDP was not alone in identifying women's interests with those of the collective—in all partisan propaganda women's right to political activity was justified by their service to the community, whether defined as the nation, the race, Christianity, or the proletariat. Supporters of women's political rights maintained that women brought a humanizing, moderating tone to an aggressively male public arena, an argument made more vociferously as rising extremism in the early 1930s threatened to extinguish that influence. The NSDAP, for its part, altered the terms of debate. Its materials deployed citizenship as a divisive discourse, characterizing equality as a fraud that had robbed women of their right to master their maternal domain. Responding to critics from the KPD to the DVP that a Third Reich would reduce women to maidservants, the NSDAP promised women "emancipation from emancipation," drawing on established conservative discourses that linked the republic with the destruction of marriage, family, and culture. In the depression-era context of yet another economic disaster that rocked the nation to its core, this negative campaigning helped yield the breakthrough with female voters the NSDAP sought. The Nazis' success reaffirms the argument that the parties most likely to do well with women voters were those that pledged to defend traditional female territory, not those that vowed to chart new terrain.

Party discourses on the meanings of women's rights reveal the ways abiding constructions of woman as the repository of national virtue were translated into the language of politics. While other groups, such as the peasantry, could also be portrayed as personifying national virtue, appeals to them always invoked those groups' material and economic interests; women were routinely depicted as hovering above worldly concerns. This assumption about women became especially salient in discourses about the moral decline that both Left and Right agreed had infected postwar Germany. The identification of woman with morality was easily translated into propaganda stressing her indispensability to the project of national reconstruction, an enterprise to which she brought motherly love and selflessness. The DVP and DNVP posited woman as the source of a nationalistic cultural renewal; the Center viewed her as the font of religious revival and a bulwark against materialism throughout the 1920s and again with the rise of the "crass pagan materialists" in the NSDAP. The DDP was less alarmist but still posited women as agents of social reconciliation. Even the SPD depicted women as elevating the tone of public discourse, while KPD propaganda bore Engelsian notions of women as the true bearers of a moral future.[6]

Morality was folded into the larger complex of culture, which women's appeals routinely put forth in the guise of religion. The Center and DNVP, whose materials across the board blamed secularism for Weimar's immorality and chaos, horrified women with visions of schools in which Lenin's teachings replaced those of Jesus. These two parties, whose ties to the Catholic and Evangelical churches put their religious credentials beyond reproach, profited from women's tendency to vote their religion, though the DNVP failed to keep Protestant women from defecting to the NSDAP after 1929. Religion forced other parties to rethink the ways they appealed to female voters. The liberal DVP struggled to defend both secularization and Christian culture. The DDP, which advocated separation of church and state, tried to skirt religion altogether in its women's appeals and devised no effective retort to criticism of its cooperation with the "irreligious" SPD. The SPD and KPD were hurt by their atheist ethos and their stubborn tendency to mock clergymen as oppressors of women and workers. Indeed, it was only after the SPD muted its anticlericalism that its female vote rose. Similarly, the NSDAP only made headway with women after suppressing its pagan aura in the early 1930s with appeals that attacked the godless Weimar system and emphasized family values. It would appear that women's enfranchisement did indeed confessionalize German politics (as the DVP's forebears had feared), something that future research comparing religion in political discourse from the Kaiserreich through the postwar era could more definitively chart.

Maternity also attained new political significance during Weimar, quickly becoming pivotal to all parties' construction of the female voter. While the political woman ideally possessed a cool head, it was her warm, maternal heart that guided her political choices. This was the line particularly of the bourgeois and confessional parties, whose appeals depicted marriage as the summit of culture and the source of women's freedom. The Center and DNVP never wavered from the view that religion, marriage, and motherhood defined female interests and nature, while the NSDAP proclaimed woman's most basic right the right to motherhood. The mother was also a central image in leftist appeals. The KPD's madonnas of misery literally embodied capitalist injustice. SPD propaganda depicted maternal suffering, although it also used happy mothers and children as advertisements for the welfare state, particularly in 1925–28. The DDP's dominant female poster image evolved from the feminist notable into the mother whose body literally bridged the gap between farm and factory (see Figure Con.1).[7] Even the New Woman was transformed into a mother by 1930.

This discourse on maternity made the welfare state central particularly in appeals to women, who had been inextricably linked with social issues since the nineteenth century. All parties saw welfare as women's province, the arena for "organized motherliness" and advocacy for mothers and children. Even the KPD, whose women's appeals blasted welfare in its current form as a revisionist swindle, tagged social administration as a female domain in its visions of a Communist future. Nearly all parties invoked the basic need for *Mutterschutz*, even as they disagreed on its form.[8] The DVP hoped to attract bourgeois women with promises to break the "Socialist monopoly" on welfare and stressed private philanthropy. The KPD pointed to revolution and direct action as the way to get benefits, deferring the solution to daily problems to a socialist utopia. The SPD

figure con.1
"For Unity, Progress, People's Community! Vote List 6. State Party" (DSP, 1930) (Hoover Institution)

put welfare at the heart of both its domestic agenda and its agitation, portraying itself over the course of the 1920s as the force behind all advances in this field. Its pragmatism, combined with a clearer definition of women's interests around bread-and-butter issues, seems to have made the SPD more palatable to women, who were more likely to be religious and politically moderate. Just as the "women's issues" of religion and domesticity formed the heart of the Center's overall agenda, "the social" defined the SPD, enhancing its allure for female voters as the republic wore on.

Female activists, charged by their respective parties with creating propaganda for women, were instrumental in bringing this language into Weimar politics. Both Socialist and bourgeois feminists had long assigned similar social meanings to maternity and worked to insert women's concerns into formal politics in ways that recognized their rights but acknowledged their difference.[9] Excluded from formal politics before 1908, they had made the social their domain; after enfranchisement, female legislators' activities bore most fruit in the field of social policy. But because woman's identification with social issues could serve both emancipatory and regressive ends—male politicians happily let women relegate themselves to this area—historians will continue to debate whether this strategy empowered or ghettoized women and their concerns. Lüders's own negative assessment of this tactic in 1932 came only after years of believing that women could feminize politics through social work.

As propaganda depicted women as the embodiment of the social sphere, it also used their bodies to represent the national body (*Volkskörper*) in decline and in revival. The SPD, DDP, and Center, assuming that women's childbearing function made them innate pacifists, appealed to them as agents of peace both in the home and in public life. Others saw that same maternal body as the reason to oppose forcefully what they saw as an emasculating republic, such as the female activists in the DNVP who appealed to women as warriors for a Christian fatherland (a discourse later appropriated by the NSDAP). The KPD, for its part, urged women to join the war against the capitalist republic that perpetuated the enslavement of proletarian bodies; it wanted women cadres for the revolution but was branded, like the NSDAP, a brawling *Männerpartei* whose destructiveness alienated women.

Reproduction and sexuality constituted another set of women's issues that were part of Weimar's intense rhetorical struggle to control women's bodies. KPD and, to a lesser extent, SPD appeals used female bodies spent by repeated childbearing as the ultimate symbols of victimization under bourgeois capitalist morality. Their campaign propaganda displayed support for legal abortion, even before the issue exploded on the national scene in 1931, as a matter of reproductive choice and economic survival. Only the Center picked up the gauntlet, its appeals doggedly opposing abortion on moral and eugenic grounds; liberal and DNVP campaigns completely avoided the issue. The KPD alone made reproductive rights a demand in materials for all audiences,[10] yet this stance was ultimately guided by the desire to win the female support that had eluded the party.

As with other topics of concern to women workers and mothers, the KPD used abortion as a dramatic example of gender oppression to mobilize women for larger class-based goals.

All parties' appeals reveal widespread concern over the state of the nation's "stock" and the falling birth rate. They pledged to help women enjoy the blessings of motherhood, portrayed as the culmination of female existence, with the Left emphasizing voluntary maternity. The parties' views were refracted through different moral prisms, from the Left's vision of a socialist order that would free women from sexual commodification and repeated pregnancies to Center and Right demands for a return to Christian morality and neatly defined gender roles. One point on which all agreed, however, was that Nazi eugenics schemes constituted a grave threat to both female dignity and the sanctity of motherhood. Appeals from every party left of the DNVP exhorted women in the portentous year of 1932 to see that Nazi promises to restore their "right to be mothers" camouflaged odious racial designs that would degrade women to "baby machines."

Sexuality divorced from maternity did not appear favorably in any party's appeals. A scantily clad female body invariably symbolized the triumph of desire over the rationality women had to exhibit if they wished to be taken seriously as political actors. This body was also shorthand for female treachery to nation or class (nudity had no presence in the German political vocabulary until after the sexual revolution of the 1960s).[11] KPD imagery in particular ascribed traitorous potential to female sexuality; even though it blasted the hypocrisies of bourgeois morality, it praised the new Soviet morality not of Alexandra Kollontai but the abstemious Lenin. The German Left, in fact, was at pains to distance itself from "free love." SPD appeals concealed the party's links to the sex reform movement and strove to associate the party with family and industriousness by linking Nazis and Communists to deviant or promiscuous sexuality. Rightist appeals, for their part, translated the erosion of male authority precipitated by the war and Weimar's economic realignments into narratives of sexual chaos. Linking discourses of sex and race, Conservative and *völkisch* propaganda used images of guileless, virginal maidens defiled by Africans or Jews to symbolize national defeat in the early 1920s. Even after the NSDAP modulated its usage of such sexually charged imagery, by blasting the Weimar system it articulated widespread desires to return to a mythical past of gender transparency and stability that won rising support as Germany's economic and political prospects darkened.

These rhetorical deployments of the female body reveal another aspect of how women's presence altered German political discourse, namely its forms. Melodramatic appeals relied upon exaggerated expressions of sentiment to display what various parties saw as an intolerable political order. As Eve Rosenhaft argues, melodrama is a political language belonging to parties of radical opposition because it unmasks the true workings of society in morally loaded terms.[12] In Weimar, the KPD, DNVP, and the NSDAP appropriated this language, using women's bodies as the ultimate symbols of victimization—of the proletariat or of the nation itself.

The New Woman, who served German popular culture as a nodal point of discourses about sexuality, reproduction, mass society, and politics, barely surfaced in the language of Weimar politics, existing more as a charged absence than a literal presence. Only the SPD attempted to represent her, while the DDP/DSP transformed her into a mother by 1930. The SPD's 1928 poster depicting the New Woman as a comrade in the people's community could be read as an indication of the party's groping toward the cross-class *Volkspartei* status it would attain in West Germany in the 1960s. It also constitutes an attempt to infuse the New Woman with the attributes of seriousness and maturity she lacked in popular media portrayals. But this attempt was fleeting, as the New Woman was too loaded with sexual connotations to be a viable political image. For their part, the young, single females who lived New Womanhood tended to avoid formal politics, literally fashioning their identities elsewhere through consumption, mass culture, and work.

Women's identities as workers were acknowledged by all parties, whose appeals tried to show how they were defending working women's interests. Simultaneously, appeals expressed all parties' dissatisfaction with the current state of women's work, with the Center and DNVP all but rejecting female employment outside the home. To a greater or lesser degree, the parties all defined women primarily by their domestic roles, while the worker was implicitly male. Such assumptions informed arguments against women's work, which met with rising approval in periods of economic crisis. Appeals from the KPD to the DVP routinely pledged support for women's right to work, but only the KPD openly blasted attempts to curb it, backing up that stance by voting against the 1932 law dismissing married female civil servants. Appeals by others, such as the DDP/DSP and SPD, lukewarmly defended married women's right to work, while in practice supporting laws that curtailed it. The silence of those right of the DDP indicates their agreement that woman's place was not in the workforce; in fact, by the late 1920s, working women faded from appeals by bourgeois and confessional parties. In contrast, the attention lavished on housewives by parties across the spectrum—including the KPD, though its courting had a different aim—indicates a rising recognition of their economic function. It also makes plain the resurgent view that homemaking constituted women's truest occupation. Instead of the New Woman, Weimar parties were more prone to embrace the New Objectivity of the rationalized household, which gave domesticity luster at a time when many feared women would abandon it for single independence.

Clearly, propaganda depicted female workers differently from males. To women, economic issues were embedded in the language of culture, as in 1924, when the Weimar coalition parties urged women to foster peace in the home to aid national economic recovery. Even the DDP, the only nonsocialist party to create appeals for specific female occupational groups, invoked the fate of the nation and children in materials for career women more likely to be single or childless. The working woman could not escape her gender, unlike the man, whose gender was rhetorically invisible in appeals to his occupational interests. Party propaganda consistently depicted working women as more intuitively attuned to moral and cultural questions, unlike men, who acted politically on the basis of rational choice and concrete economic interest. Discourses on women, work, interests, and the economy furnish further examples of how voting itself was represented in highly gendered terms.

The ways in which parties appealed to female voters reveal not only their assumptions about women but also their own visions of the social and political order. Their prescriptive portrayals of woman simultaneously described themselves. For example, the central theme of DDP campaigns to women during the 1920s was woman's duty to use her role as "center of the family" to anchor democratic culture in the home and foster social harmony—the same task the DDP, as the "party of the middle," envisioned for itself in German political life. Because all parties assumed that women were primarily interested in issues of culture, their appeals to women allowed them to discuss their own cultural mission, which gave women an expanded public role, albeit one circumscribed within limits dictated by "female nature." The parties' construction of fixed, unitary identities for women mirrored Germans' search for stability in a republic that lurched from crisis to crisis.

Just as the parties' prescriptive portrayals of women should not be read in isolation from their portrayals of other groups or their overall political platforms, we cannot assume that Weimar's female voters evaluated parties solely on the basis of their message to women. For example, the KPD never won the votes of most women, who were convinced it would destroy the family just as it aimed to destroy the state. Similarly, women abandoned both liberal parties, whose associations with failed economic policies overrode any message they could devise. The DVP epitomized bourgeois respectability and individualism within an organic social model, yet its government role chained it to policies that hurt the middle classes. Regarding women, its propaganda struggled to hit a range of notes, supporting "reasonable" feminist demands for equal legal and work opportunities while portraying work as infinitely less satisfying than motherhood. Its appeals played to female desires for social, political, and economic stability, yet the party was implicated in a regime increasingly seen as a source of chaos and personal ruin. While the DVP's commitments to nationalism and Christianity initially endeared it to many women, its association with an unpopular government and lack of a strong identity could not prevent those votes from slipping away.

If women's rights are defined as equal access to sites of political and economic power free of limits based on gender, then it can be argued that female voters did not favor parties that supported women's rights. This study does not dispute that parties that defined women's role along traditional lines were more successful in attracting female votes than those that portrayed women in unconventional or revolutionary ways. However, if we take Weimar contemporaries' definition of what constituted women's issues—culture, religion, and social welfare—then it appears that female voters did respond positively to parties that had women's issues writ large in their propaganda and their agendas as a whole. We have seen how the SPD's increased emphasis on the delivery of tangible welfare services combined with the rise of the more radical KPD to help narrow the party's gender gap throughout the 1920s. Large numbers of female voters also trusted the Center—indeed, their support gave that party Weimar's highest voter retention rate (along with the SPD),[13] which in turn gave the Center the strength to act as a linchpin of both the Prussian coalition and every national government during Weimar.

Political language aimed at women backs up the classic Weimar periodization (crisis, relative stability, crisis, and collapse), while continuities in party women's frustration and disappointment at their lack of clout cut across it. The parties quickly accommodated themselves to women's presence, setting them off to work in women's committees and incorporating what were assumed to be their interests into party rhetoric. But, in Germany as elsewhere, just because electoral politics had ceased to be a male monopoly did not mean it had ceased to be male-dominated. The only women appointed to powerful party committees were those like Gertrud Bäumer who transcended being seen as representatives of women. Most female activists were relegated to *Frauenausschusse* with practically no sway over broader party policy. Men blocked female activists' agendas less through outright hostility than through subtle strategies of neglect or accommodation to limited change; they were amenable to funding special party journals for women but not to restructuring the party organization to make it more welcoming.

Female activists routinely complained of being treated like an afterthought to the work of party politics. The gender rifts that opened up in every party (except the DNVP, though this may be simply a lack of source evidence) were papered over both in propaganda and in internal discussions not least by female activists at pains to demonstrate their loyalty. While women were not the only group to feel used by the parties, their disappointment sank even deeper under the weight of expectations about what enfranchisement could bring. They had truly hoped to feminize national political life, installing women's unique needs and interests at the heart of a state that guaranteed their rights. While their invocation of female nature was intended to anchor women's influence within the state, it could easily be used to present women's concerns as particularistic, effectively undercutting their power outside a separate female sphere. One tangible effect of this discourse manifested itself in the parties' growing reluctance to "waste" ballot slots on women after 1920. Propaganda was based on assumptions that women were politically unreliable, and it reinforced those same assumptions.

This reluctance was also informed by discourses across the political spectrum that routinely portrayed women as the potential spoilers of each group's vision through their ignorance, apathy, or irrationality—the gendered version of the stab in the back myth. This is but one way that political discourses impacted women's lived experience—fewer female politicians meant less chance that women's concerns would be heard in legislatures. Public discourses on women's role, of which propaganda was a major part, produced a climate in which the PAV could pass or abortion reform fail despite 1931's massive protests. While discourses on Weimar's moral decline did not produce the rising popularity of the

NSDAP, Nazism's rise is certainly unthinkable without the preparation of this ground. Did women's presence feminize Weimar politics? It certainly introduced women's issues and bodies into political language in ways not before seen. Male critics often complained, particularly in 1932, that politics had been hijacked by the irrational moment, a female attribute that had now supposedly infected men. But Weimar politics were not feminized to the degree female activists would have liked, as Lüders's 1932 memorandum shows. Women's role in Weimar's discursive conflicts shows that they were not without the power to articulate, prescribe, or refashion identities for women. But their power to do so was ultimately dependent upon structures controlled by men.[14] The potential impact of women's enfranchisement, already short-circuited by Weimar's economic crises, was foreclosed in 1933 and would have to await the reemergence of democracy on German soil after 1945 for its full realization.

Party propaganda furnished a major part of women's visibility in Weimar. However the specifics of difference were elaborated at the time, they all came to rest on notions of woman's uniqueness. While the political parties in Weimar Germany viciously fought each other on many fronts, each represented women as vessels containing what that group hoped to find. Woman was the font of new life and healing balm. She was the source of inspiration to husbands, brothers, and sons fighting for revolution or fascism or democracy. She was the wellspring of national custom from which future generations could draw. She embodied unparalleled virtue and frightening depths of vice. A vessel is by nature passive; the active woman became an exceptional figure in propaganda representations, even those produced by the KPD, whose appeals for women to join the revolutionary struggle were outweighed by those stocked with women too downtrodden to fight. Such passivity had not always dominated political discourse regarding women, particularly in Weimar's early elections, during which propaganda exuded an optimism that women could bring decisive change and transform the nation. By the 1930s this hope had all but expired. Political language paints by necessity in broad strokes. Some parties, such as the SPD and DDP, used more colors than others to render women as symbols of wealth and poverty, vice and virtue, loyalty and betrayal, but however the parties chose to portray them, their model was always eternally feminine.

ABBREVIATIONS

Publications

AIZ	*Arbeiter-Illustrierte-Zeitung*
BT	*Berliner Tageblatt*
DAZ	*Deutsche Allgemeine Zeitung*
RF	*Rote Fahne*
VB	*Völkischer Beobachter*

Archives

BA	Bundesarchiv, Koblenz
BA Berlin	Bundesarchiv, Berlin
BA ZSg	Bundesarchiv, Koblenz, Zeitgeschichtliche Sammlung
GStA	Geheimes Staatsarchiv Preußischer Kulturbesitz, Berlin
HLA	Helene Lange Archiv, Landesarchiv, Berlin
Hoover	Hoover Institution Archives, Stanford University, Stanford, Calif.
LA	Landesarchiv, Berlin
NL	Nachlass (personal papers)
NSDAP/HA	NSDAP Hauptarchiv
SAPMO-BA	Stiftung Archiv der Parteien und Massenorganisationen der ehemaligen DDR im Bundesarchiv, Berlin, Zentrales Parteiarchiv

INTRODUCTION

1 For example, see Boak, "Women in Weimar Germany" and "'Our Last Hope.'"
   On women in the Nazi movement, see Koonz, "Some Political Implications
   of Separatism," and Stephenson, *Nazi Organisation of Women*. On women and
   socialism, see Thönnessen, *Emancipation of Women*, and Pore, *Conflict of Interest*. On women in the Communist Party, see Kontos, *Partei kämpft wie ein
   Mann!* A recent work exploring mobilization on the Right is Scheck, "German
   Conservatism."

2 Films were also used as party propaganda throughout Weimar—the DDP
   produced a campaign short as early as 1919—but are beyond the scope of this
   study.

3 Childers summarizes Nazi distribution methods in "Social Language of Politics," 343–44. The methods outlined in a DVP handbook, "Gegen den schwarz-
   rot-goldenen Block!" (in BA ZSg 1-42/14 [2]), were largely shared by other
   parties.

4 Posters blossomed as a political medium only after the 1918 lifting of an 1850
   Prussian law banning parties' use of illustrated posters; see Janusch, *Plakative
   Propaganda der SPD*, i.

5 These are *Rote Fahne* (organ of the KPD), *Vorwärts* (the SPD daily), *Berliner Tageblatt* (left liberal, aimed at the business and intellectual communities), *Germania*
   (Berlin's Catholic paper), *Deutsche Allgemeine Zeitung* (nationalist with DVP
   leanings), *Völkischer Beobachter* (the Nazi daily), and two boulevard papers, *Welt
   am Abend* (popular with working-class readers) and *8-Uhr Abendblatt* (read by
   both the middle and working classes).

6 On the crisis of German modernity, see Peukert, *Weimar Republic*. On Weimar-
   era propaganda, see Paul, *Aufstand der Bilder*, 16–25, 57–58.

7 Jones, *Languages of Class*; Sewell, *Work and Revolution in France*.

8 See his "Social Language of Politics" and "Languages of Liberalism."

9 Canning, "Gender and the Politics of Class Formation"; Weitz, *Creating German
   Communism*, 188–232.

10 These definitions of politics are from Scott, "On Language, Gender, and
   Working-Class History," 4. See also her *Gender and the Politics of History*.

11 Eve Rosenhaft has most recently made the call for such a metanarrative; see
   "Women, Gender, and the Limits of Political History," 149.

12 For details, see Clemens, *Menschenrechte*, 70–101.

13 Bremme, *Politische Rolle der Frau*; Boak, "'Our Last Hope'"; Falter, Lindenberger, and Schumann, *Wahlen und Abstimmungen*. The BDF opposed sex-
   segregated balloting, fearing that results could be manipulated by antisuffrage
   forces; see BDF to the interior minister, 6 February 1925, in HLA BDF/52-238
   [4] 239 [1]. Their fears about the secrecy of the ballot were well founded—
   procedure had routinely been violated during Wilhelmine elections; see
   Anderson, "Voter, Junker, *Landrat*, Priest," 1454.

14 Voter profiles culled from Bremme, *Politische Rolle der Frau*, 28–38, 51.

15 Peterson, "Politics of Working-Class Women."

16 Bremme, *Politische Rolle der Frau*, 69–74; Falter, Lindenberger, and Schumann,
   Wahlen und Abstimmungen, table 1.6.1.1. Helen Boak, in "Our Last Hope," argues

that the NSDAP won the female vote earlier than most studies suggest; see chapter 5 of this study.

17 Additional votes accrued to the party's national slate; see Childers, *Nazi Voter*, 42.

18 See ibid., 15–49; Bessel, "Formation and Dissolution of a German National Electorate"; and Fritzsche, *Rehearsals for Fascism*, 40.

19 Childers, "Social Language of Politics."

20 After an exhaustive survey of the archives with the largest holdings of Weimar party propaganda, I estimate that, on average, one of every eight to ten appeals was aimed directly at women. This figure does not include the many appeals addressed to both male and female voters.

21 The extent of parties' archival holdings varies. At least partial records of conferences exist for all parties in this study. The Bundesarchiv has extensive correspondence of the DVP, DDP, and KPD; the DNVP's archive is incomplete and not very revealing. The NSDAP Hauptarchiv contains that party's records, plus DDP records seized after 1933. Much of the SPD and KPD correspondence and directives has been published. The least material survives for the Center, whose archive was destroyed in 1942.

22 See Fairbairn, *Democracy in the Undemocratic State*, 38.

23 On these parties' Weimar origins, see Jones, *German Liberalism*, 18–27, and Hartenstein, *Anfänge der Deutschen Volkspartei*, 59–66, 92–105. On social motherhood, see Allen, *Feminism and Motherhood*; Stoehr, "Organisierte Mütterlichkeit"; and Clemens, *Menschenrechte*.

24 Bremme, *Politische Rolle der Frau*, 124 (table 39); Boak, "Women in Weimar Politics"; Koonz, "Conflicting Allegiances."

25 Else Wex wrote in 1929 that much of the work of the bourgeois women's movement had been taken over by women in Parliament. Perhaps this explains why the feminist movement waned—there was less of a need for it. See *Staatsbürgerliche Arbeit deutscher Frauen*, 114.

26 Clemens, *Menschenrechte*, 85–88.

27 See Boak, "Women in Weimar Politics." For contrasting views, see Usborne, *Politics of the Body*, 38–40, and Kaplan, *Making of the Jewish Middle Class*, 192–226. Recent studies that rethink the implications of women's identification with the social include Allen, *Feminism and Motherhood*, 3–11, and Hong, "World War I and the German Welfare State."

28 Bridenthal first advanced this thesis in 1973; it appeared most recently in Bridenthal and Koonz, "Beyond Kinder, Küche, Kirche."

29 Evans, *Feminist Movement in Germany*; Greven-Aschoff, *Die bürgerliche Frauenbewegung in Deutschland*.

30 Boak, "Women in Weimar Germany." In *Nazi Voter*, Childers raises the notion that women did not base their political self-identity primarily on gender, but he does not develop it.

31 See Grossmann, *Reforming Sex*, "Abortion and Economic Crisis," "*Girlkultur*," and "New Woman and the Rationalization of Sexuality." See also Usborne, *Politics of the Body*.

32 For example, see Bridenthal, "Organized Rural Women," and Scheck, "German Conservatism." Allen's *Feminism and Motherhood* and Reagin's *German*

Women's Movement also address this set of issues, though their focus is largely pre-Weimar.

33 *DAZ*, 16 August 1931. The author, identified only as "M.E.," is clearly male.

34 Kent, *Making Peace*, especially chap. 5; Roberts, *Civilization without Sexes*. For Germany, see Petro, *Joyless Streets*; Ankum, *Women in the Metropolis*; and Lavin, *Cut with the Kitchen Knife*.

35 On women and the First World War, see Daniel, *War from Within*, and Davis, *Home Fires Burning*.

36 For example, Larry Jones's otherwise exhaustive history of the liberal parties, *German Liberalism and the Dissolution of the Weimar Party System*, says little about women's place in them. Jones, Margaret Anderson, and Brett Fairbairn are among those now writing histories of German electoral politics that stress the meanings of voting and call for more attention to gender. See also Kühne, "Historische Wahlforschung," 63–67.

37 For more on this idea of political culture, see Lynn Hunt, *Politics, Culture, and Class in the French Revolution*, and her introduction to *New Cultural History*.

38 Canning, "Feminist History after the Linguistic Turn"; Clemens, *Menschenrechte*, 1–2.

39 On the contingencies of the category "women" in history, see Riley, *"Am I That Name?"*

CHAPTER ONE

1 On the concept of *Plakatkrieg*, see Paul, *Aufstand der Bilder*, 150.

2 Susan Kingsley Kent uses this phrase for Britain; the concept was also invoked by German observers. See Kent, *Making Peace*, 100–102; and Bessel, "'Eine nicht allzu große Beunruhigung.'"

3 Several nonparty organizations published instructional flyers for women. For example, see "Frauen-Merkblatt für die Wahl zur National-Versammlung," Hoover GSC/3; a piece by the Deutscher Prov.-Frauenrat, "10 Gebote für deutsche Wählerinnen!," encouraged women to elect parties with female candidates, Hoover Moenkemöller Coll. 31/209.

4 Morath at 12 April 1919 meeting of DVP Zentralvorstand, BA R45 II/34.

5 For a sample of party documents outlining the functions of the women's committees, see "Organisations- und Arbeitsplan für die Frauenarbeit im Rahmen der Deutschen Demokratischen Partei," 1925, BA R45 III/33, and "Grundsätze für die Zusammensetzung und Tätigkeit der örtlichen Frauenausschüsse," DVP, BA NL Dingeldey, folder 19.

6 Advertising agencies offered their services as well; for examples, see DVP file in BA Berlin 60 Vo 1/53112/7. It is often impossible to tell precisely who wrote an appeal—this study cites authors in every case where their names are given. All parties considered their women's committees responsible for women's propaganda.

7 These counts were tallied from the archival collections listed in the bibliography. They include materials for national, state, communal, and some regional races. Figures for the Center include appeals issued by the KFD.

8 On SPD organization, see *Handbuch für Ortsvereine.*

9 Fricke et al., *Lexikon zur Parteigeschichte.*

10 The DDP program for the National Assembly elections supported female suffrage; an end to gender discriminatory laws; equal education, opportunities, and positions for male and female workers; and welfare for women and child workers to strengthen national health (BA ZSg 1-27/19 [2]). "Der weibliche Wähler," a women's committee flyer for this election, defined women as "nicht nur Hausmütter, Gattinnen, Töchter, Arbeitskräfte, Angestellte, Gehilfinnen, Dienstboten, Mägde, sondern ihr alle habt eine neue Würde und Pflicht erhalten und ihr seid Staatsbürger!," in GStA/XII.HA/IV 128.

11 On social motherhood, see Clemens, *Menschenrechte*, 78–84, and Allen, *Feminism and Motherhood*, 3–4.

12 It appeared in eleven flyers expressly for women in 1919; it was not used in material for mixed or male audiences. Larry Eugene Jones estimates that one-fourth of all DDP literature in January 1919 was aimed at women; see his *German Liberalism*, 22. A DNVP memo noted that the DDP, "because of its financial resources, is making by far the strongest propaganda" ("Die neuen Parteien," *Deutscher Frauenbund—Bundesschrift*, December 1918, BA Berlin 60 Vo 2/485).

13 Bäumer had in fact been on the Progressive Party executive committee since 1911. On Lüders and Zahn-Harnack's wartime service, see Daniel, *War from Within*, 75–77.

14 Childers, "Languages of Liberalism," 326.

15 See, for example, "Wahl-Aufruf der Deutschen Volkspartei in Bayern (Deutsche Demokratische Partei)," 1919, BA ZSg 1-27/19 (2); "Wähler und Wählerinnen von Teltow," 1919, BA ZSg 1-27/19; and Friedrich Naumann's National Assembly flyer, "Demokratie und Frau," Hoover Moenkemöller Coll. 31/201.

16 "Deutsche! Halt! rufen wir Frauen," BA ZSg 1-27/20 (3); "Die Deutsche Demokratische Partei ist die Partei der Frauen," BA ZSg 1-27/19 (1). Both were National Assembly flyers.

17 "Deutsche Frauen!," National Assembly flyer, GStA/XII.HA/IV 128, emphasis in original.

18 Katharina v. Mayer, in "Die Organisierung der Frauen" (*Niederschrift über die Tagung der Parteisekretäre der DDP, 17.–18. Mai 1919*, in NSDAP/HA 38/743), states that women are striving to participate in political and party life, not to dominate but to become integrated into these structures. See also Clemens, *Menschenrechte*, for details on earlier feminist debates.

19 "Der weiblicher Wähler," National Assembly flyer, GStA/XII.HA/IV 128. See also "Das Wahlrecht," 1919 women's committee flyer, BA ZSg 1-27/19 (2).

20 On violations of electoral procedure during the Kaiserreich, see Anderson, "Voter, Junker, *Landrat*, Priest," 1454.

21 See the following women's committee flyers: "Die Demokratie und die Frauen!," 1919, BA ZSg 1-27/5, and "An die weiblichen Angestellten," 1919, BA ZSg 1-27/19. See also "Was heißt deutscher Volksstaat?," National Assembly flyer, GStA/XII.HA/IV 128.

22 "Was tut not," poster for 12 January 1919 Stuttgart communal election, and "Leitsatze der DDP für Angestellte & Arbeiter," 1919, both GStA/XII.HA/IV

128; "An alle Beamte im Reichs-, Staats-, und Gemeindedienst," 1919, GStA/XII.HA/IV 123.

23 "Die weibliche Angestellte in Handel und Industrie wählt frei von jedem Gewissenszwang die Deutsche Demokratische Partei," women's committee flyer, January 1919, BA ZSg 1-27/19 (1). Another women's committee flyer for local female leaders, "Wie gewinne ich berufstätige Frauen?," listed ways to reach specific types of female workers (in Hoover Moenkemöller Coll. 31/201). Roughly half of all DDP women's flyers in 1918–20 either were directly pitched to working women or mentioned women's work in the text (these targeted middle-class women; no serious attempt to reach working-class women was made).

24 For an example, see "Beamte und Lehrer! Männer und Frauen!," 1919, GStA/XII.HA/IV 128. The *Lexikon zur Parteigeschichte*, an East German encyclopedia, reports that the party's main slogans for 1919 were "for free democracy" and "against socialism and Bolshevism."

25 "An die weiblichen Angestellten," 1918 flyer, BA ZSg 1-27/19 (2); "Deutsche Frauen!," "Die Frau aus Haus und Beruf," and a women's committee flyer, "Das Wahlrecht," all January 1919, GStA/XII.HA/IV 128; "An alle Frauen und Mädchen!," January 1919 flyer, GStA/XII.HA/IV 384. "Frauen Berlins," an October 1920 leaflet in GStA/XII.HA/IV 131, asked, "Who refuses to hire women experts who don't count themselves among the Left radicals? . . . the red majority."

26 "Die 'Kommunisierung' der Frauen," *BT*, 23 April 1919. This myth was also propagated by the Center (see below) and the Society to Combat Bolshevism. A Society flyer, in fact, listed provisions of the "actual" decree, such as which women were communalized and how often a man could "use the people's property." See "Deutsche Frauen! Ahnt ihr, womit euch der Bolshewismus und Spartakismus bedroht?," in Hoover GSC/19/223.

27 "An die weiblichen Angestellten," January 1919, BA ZSg 1-27/19 (1).

28 The BDF discussed, but quickly dismissed, the idea in 1918; see Scheck, "German Conservatism," 43.

29 "Die 'Frauenliste': berechtigte Proteste," *BT*, 15 June 1920.

30 For women's flyers, see "Wir demokratischen Frauen," women's committee, January 1919, BA ZSg 1-27/19 (2); "An alle Frauen und Mädchen!"; and "Frauen Berlins," October 1920, GStA/XII.HA/IV 131.

31 "Deutsche Männer und Frauen!," January 1919 Prussian flyer, GStA/XII.HA/IV 128.

32 Electoral law mandated that preliminary election results be reported no later than 4:00 P.M. the day after balloting. Thus, estimated results of the National Assembly elections were known within days. However, mistakes in tabulating votes by sex and age group meant exact results did not appear for several months. See "Die Wahlen zur verfassunggebenden [*sic*] Deutschen Nationalversammlung," *Vierteljahrshefte zur Statistik des Deutschen Reiches* (1919).

33 See "Die DDP—eine Partei des sozialen Ausgleichs," a June 1920 flyer profiling top DDP candidates, Lüders being the only woman, in GStA/XII.HA/IV 130; "Unsere Kandidatinnen Agnes von Harnack . . . ," January 1919 Prussian flyer, GStA/XII.HA/IV 123; and "Warum gehören die Frauen in die Deutsche

demokratische Partei?," women's committee flyer by Helene Lange, n.d., LA 240/1785/48. See also Wobbe, "Die Frauenbewegung ist keine Parteisache."

34 "Was tut not."

35 "Demokratische Frauen," women's committee flyer, January 1919, BA ZSg 1-27/19 (1).

36 *Protokolle der Sitzungen der Nationalversammlung*, 72nd meeting, 1 August 1919 (Bd. 329), and 84th meeting, 20 August 1919 (Bd. 329).

37 A government flyer, "An die Fabrikarbeiterinnen!," states this plainly: "If you have a provider . . . , do not stay in your job or seek a new one. You have enough to do at home. Those not absolutely dependent on a job may not take one away from someone who is. Adding to the unemployment of those who need work endangers your security" (Hoover GSC/7).

38 "Warum gehören die Frauen in die DDP?"

39 "Frauen Neuköllns!," women's committee flyer, October 1920 Berlin election, LA 240/1024/27.

40 See Turner, "Contemporary Problems in the Theory of Citizenship," 5.

41 "Für den Wahltag," National Assembly election flyer, BA ZSg 1-27/19 (2).

42 "Deutscher Familienvater!," January 1919 flyer, LA 240/1024/32.

43 Salomon's authorship of this flyer is named in a DDP Reichsgeschäftsstelle memo of 13 December 1918 (NSDAP/HA 36/722). For more on Salomon, see Allen, *Feminism and Motherhood*, 206–12; Kaplan, *Making of the Jewish Middle Class*, 211–19; and Schmidt-Waldherr, *Emanzipation durch Professionalisierung?*, 169.

44 Dr. Kahl, quoted in *Flugschriften der DVP* (1920); Anna-Lise Schellwitz-Ultzen, "Die Frau im neuen Deutschland," BA ZSg 1-42/1; "Rede von Frl. Oberlehrerin Julie Velde, gehalten auf der 1. Nationalversammlung der DVP in Frankfurt," 1919, BA ZSg 1-42/7 [1].

45 See these National Assembly campaign flyers: "Die 14 Punkte: Was will die DVP?," LA 240/2381/27; "Die 10 Gebote der DVP!," BA ZSg 1-42/7 (2); and "Für Recht und Freiheit!," LA 240/2381/32. I found four flyers for this campaign entitled "Was will die DVP?"—all list women's equality among general demands.

46 See *Sachstimme*, DVP party organ in Saxony, June 1920 election edition, and an untitled flyer from 1920 depicting a kiosk covered with posters reading "Socialist Soviet Republic," "strike . . . murder," "Gala Ball," "Democratization," "Naked dancing" (accompanied by a picture of naked women), "stolen auto," "break in," and "two pounds of potatoes." Its caption reads: "Was uns der Umsturz hat errungen! / Die Säule kundet's frech und frei! / Doch diese Schande wird bezwungen / Wählst Du die Deutsche Volkspartei!" Both items in BA ZSg 1-42/7.

47 Childers, "Languages of Liberalism," 335.

48 See "Frauen und Mädchen Schleswig-Holsteins!," which, after claiming to support gender equality and religious freedom alongside catechetical instruction in schools, claimed, "No other party has introduced such a women's program [*Frauen-Programm*]" (in BA ZSg 1-42/7).

49 "An die deutschen Wählerinnen!," National Assembly flyer, BA ZSg 1-42/7 (2); "Frauen Gross-Berlins!" and "Wählt die DVP!," flyers for the October 1920

Berlin election, both GStA/XII.HA/IV 161; "Deutsche Frauen und Mädchen in Stadt und Land," National Assembly flyer, BA ZSg 1-42/7 (2); "Wer seine . . . Religion und Schule vor dem asiatischen Einfluss behueten . . . will," June 1920 flyer, GStA/XII.HA/IV 161. See also Hartenstein, *Anfänge der Deutschen Volkspartei*, 204.

50 This line was inherited from the DVP's forebears, the National Liberals. See Fairbairn, "Interpreting Wilhelmine Elections," 35.

51 "Was trennt uns von der DDP?," likely early 1919, LA 240/243/182.

52 On pastors, see Pyta, *Dorfgemeinschaft und Parteipolitik*, 288. On support from the Evangelical Women's League, see Baumann, *Protestantismus und Frauenemanzipation*, 263, and Scheck, "German Conservatism," 43.

53 The flight of women to the SPD never materialized, though this statement reveals the deep fear among defenders of the old regime in the early Weimar era. See "An die deutschen Wählerinnen!," and "Unsere Stimme für Heimat, Treue und Glauben! Ein Bauer an unsere Landfrauen," 1919 flyer, GStA/XII.HA/IV 158.

54 Mende, "Die Deutsche Volkspartei zur Frauenfrage," 1919, BA ZSg 1-42/1 (5). In late 1918, Mende wavered over whether to join the DVP or DDP. See also "Agitationsarbeit," *Frauenrundschau* section of *Nachrichtenblatt*, 20 May 1920.

55 "Frauen Gross-Berlins!," in GStA/XII.HA/IV 161.

56 Mende, "Die Deutsche Volkspartei zur Frauenfrage," 1919 pamphlet, BA ZSg 1-42/1.

57 Soldiers, in contrast, were provided with prostitutes and prophylactics. On gender and the war, see Daniel, *War from Within*.

58 See "Wie wählen die weiblichen Angestellten?," 1920, LA 240/1024/71; "Frauen vor!," BA ZSg 1-42/7; "Die 10 Gebote der DVP!"; "Was will die DVP?," 1919 flyer, LA 240/1024/41; and Mende, "Die Deutsche Volkspartei zur Frauenfrage."

59 "Wie stärken wir Frauen die deutsche Volkskraft? Rede von Frl. Dr. Marie Bernays auf der Leipziger Parteitag," LA 240/1024/124. See also Mende, "Die Deutsche Volkspartei zur Frauenfrage," and "Deutsche Frauen, wahret Eure heiligsten Güter," women's committee flyer for the National Assembly election, BA ZSg 1-42/7 (2).

60 For example, I found twenty-seven flyers from 1919 that mentioned women in some way; of these, only ten were addressed explicitly and solely to women.

61 See 12 April 1919 *Vorstand* meeting, in BA R45 II/34; Margarete Faehre, "Was erwartet die Deutsche Volkspartei von den Frauen?," *Deutscher Volksboter*, 25 January 1920; Stropp, "Wahlmüdigkeit?," *Frauenrundschau* section of *Nachrichtenblatt*, 20 May 1920; and "Die Nationalliberalen waren für das Stimmrecht," *Frauenrundschau* section of *Nachrichtenblatt*, 17 June 1920.

62 See also Marie Bernays, "Widersprüche und Unklarheiten im Frauenberufsleben," in *Frauenrundschau* section of *Nachrichtenblatt*, 29 January 1920.

63 "Nach der Schlacht," women's section of *Berliner Stimmen*, 20 June 1920.

64 For details, see Hartenstein, *Anfänge der Deutschen Volkspartei*, 215–23.

65 Clara Mende, "Nach der Schlacht," *Die Frau in der Politik*, 20 June 1920.

66 Emma Stropp, *Nachrichtenblatt*, 20 May 1920.

67 *Flugschriften der DVP* (1920).

68 Mathilde Drechsler Hohlt, "Wege und Ziele weiblicher Politik," *Frauen-*

rundschau section of *Nachrichtenblatt*, 5 August 1920; Käte Rahmlow's reply in ibid., 19 August 1920.

69 Morsey, *Deutsche Zentrumspartei*, 289.

70 "Wer hat den Frauen das Wahlrecht gebracht?," *Germania*, 18 January 1919; Marianne Weber, "Die Frau in der Zentrumspartei," *Mitteilungen der deutschen Zentrumspartei* 7 (16 February 1920): 99–102. On the history of the Catholic women's movement, see Breuer, *Frauenbewegung im Katholizismus*, and Kall, *Katholische Frauenbewegung*, 264–336. By comparison, church leaders in France ended opposition to female suffrage in 1919 for the same reasons as the Center; see Offen, "Women, Citizenship, and Suffrage," 161.

71 Augustinus, *Sozialismus und die Würde der Frau.*

72 Breuer, *Frauenbewegung im Katholizismus*, 212–16.

73 Ibid., 101.

74 See the following National Assembly flyers: "Junge Wählerin!," BA ZSg 1-108/9; "Katholische Deutsche Frau! Dein Volk ruft dich!," KFD flyer, BA ZSg 1-108/9; and "Die Wahlpflicht," KFD flyer, GStA/XII.HA/IV 278. See also Hedwig Dransfeld, "Frauen, die nicht zur Wahlurne kamen," *Germania*, 24 January 1919.

75 "Frauentum und Wahlrecht," *Germania*, 5 June 1920.

76 For example, see "An die Beamtenschaft Gross-Berlin," National Assembly flyer, GStA/XII.HA/IV 128.

77 "Wer hat den Frauen das Wahlrecht gebracht?"; "Frauenfrage auf dem Partei-tag," *Germania*, 22 January 1920; "Frauen, Wählerinnen! Christliche Frauen!," National Assembly flyer, GStA/XII.HA/IV 107. The Center, in fact, established its own quotas for women on ballots in 1920.

78 "Christliche Frauen!," June 1920 Berlin election flyer, Hoover GSC/3/5A/1.

79 "Junge Wählerin!"; "Frauen, Wählerinnen! Christliche Frauen!"

80 "Deutsche Frauen!," National Assembly election flyer, LA 240/1875/41.

81 For example, see "Frauen, Wählerinnen! Christliche Frauen!" Articles on women's work frequently appeared in *Germania*—their tone matches that of the flyers discussed here. The phrase "equal wages" never appeared in flyers, though it did appear once in a *Germania* article of 6 December 1919.

82 "Arbeitende Frauen u. Mädchen, was gibt Euch das Zentrum?," 1919, BA ZSg 1-108/8 (10). See also "Junggesellin von heute," *Frauenwelt* section of *Germania*, 6 December 1919, and Christine Teusch, "Frauenarbeit," *Germania*, 17 April 1919.

83 Quote in Usborne, *Politics of the Body*, 65.

84 Boak, "Women in Weimar Politics," 383–84. See also "Die aufsichtsreichen Kandidaten der Zentrumspartei," *Mitteilungen der deutschen Zentrumspartei*, 1 June 1920. On the founding of the women's committee, see chapter 2.

85 See Deutsche Zentrumspartei, *Erste Reichsparteitag des Zentrums*, afternoon session, 21 January 1920. The day after this exchange, an unsigned report on Dransfeld's speech in *Germania* omitted the women's criticisms. On the Center's failure to incorporate the KFD, see Breuer, *Frauenbewegung im Katholizismus*, 212–16.

86 Morsey, *Deutsche Zentrumspartei*, 319–25. After the 1920 election, 4.9 percent of Center Reichstag delegates were female, as compared to 9.0 percent for the

DDP, 11.5 percent for the SPD, 4.6 percent for the DNVP, and 4.8 for the DVP, according to figures from Boak, "Women in Weimar Politics," table 1.

87 Frevert puts female membership in these Catholic organizations at over 1.6 million; see *Women in German History*, 173.

88 Liebe, *Deutschnationale Volkspartei*, 17–19.

89 On the links between the Evangelical Women's League and the DNVP, see Scheck, "German Conservatism"; Reagin, *German Women's Movement*, 203–5, 234; and Kaufmann, *Frauen zwischen Aufbruch und Reaktion*, 47–57.

90 I found thirty-eight DNVP flyers for women produced between late 1918 and 1920, compared to thirty-six from the DDP and ten from the DVP. On organizational links, see 1919 memo on "Organisation," BA Berlin 60 Vo 2/45121/1.

91 Pyta, *Dorfgemeinschaft und Parteipolitik*, 292.

92 *Korrespondenz der DNVP*, 11 February 1919, denounced a petition drive conducted in the party's name to have woman suffrage revoked. See also Graef to Reichsfrauenausschuss, 10 February 1919, in BA Berlin 60 Vo 2/485.

93 *Ziele der DNVP*.

94 "Deutschnationale Frauenpolitik: Richtlinien der Deutschnationalen Volkspartei für Frauenfragen," 1919 flyer, BA ZSg 1-44/8. See also these National Assembly flyers: "Für die Hausfrau!," GStA/XII.HA/IV 177, and "Das verwandelte Deutschland und die Frauen," 1919, BA ZSg 1-44/11. *Stichworte und Winke für deutschnational Diskussionsredner* (1918) told speakers to counter criticism of conservative antisuffragism by arguing (untruthfully) that the DNVP had more women at the top of its electoral lists than any other party, even the SPD.

95 Liebe, *Die deutschnationale Volkspartei*, 19. On the objections of party leader Count Westarp to populist language, see Fritzsche, "Breakdown or Breakthrough?," 320.

96 "Das verwandelte Deutschland und die Frauen"; "Eiserne Blätter—Zum Frauenstimmrecht," GStA/XII.HA/IV 177. See also Baumann, *Protestantismus und Frauenemanzipation*, 258–62.

97 "Einigkeit," in *Frauennummer* of *Korrespondenz der DNVP*, 29 November 1919.

98 "Und was sagen die Frauen?," June 1920 flyer, BA ZSg 1-44/8.

99 "Frauen und Mütter deutscher Offiziere und Unteroffiziere," undated flyer (likely January 1919), GStA/XII.HA/IV 175; "Deutsche Frauen euch ruft die DNVP," postcard (likely National Assembly election), GStA/XII.HA/IV 195; M. Schiele, "Flugblatt der DNVP," National Assembly flyer, GStA/XII.HA/IV 177; "Das verwandelte Deutschland und die Frauen."

100 Allen, *Feminism and Motherhood*, 11.

101 "Was wünschest Du deutsche Frau?," undated flyer, BA ZSg 1-44/11. See also the following in *Korrespondenz der DNVP*: "Frauenkundgebung für die Ostmark," 21 June 1919; "Kundgebung deutscher Frauen gegen den Schmachfrieden," 2 July 1919; and "Tagung des Reichsfrauenausschusses," 12 July 1919.

102 Leonore Ripke-Kühn, "Frau und Politik," *Frauennummer* of *Korrespondenz der DNVP*, 13 December 1919. See also Scheck, "German Conservatism," 52.

103 "Wie wähle ich? 3 Fragen—12 Antworten aus Berliner Blättern," National Assembly flyer, LA 240/2381/11. See also the following in *Korrespondenz der DNVP*: "Demokratischer Stimmenfang bei den Frauen," 27 May 1920; "'Die Partei der Frauen,'" 20 February 1919; and "Frauen als Wähler," 11 June 1920.

For general appeals, see "Das Rückgrät des deutschen Volkes ist der Mittelstand!" and "Deutsche Jugend!," both 1919, GStA XII.HA/IV 177.

104 For women's flyers, see "Naumberger Briefe: An die Landfrauen," 1919, BA ZSg 1-44/8, and "An die deutschen Wählerinnen!," 1919, LA 240/1785/67. For occupational groups, see National Assembly flyers in GStA XII.HA/IV 177: "Aufruf! An alle wahlberechtigten Angehörigen des kaufmännischen und gewerblichen Mittelstandes!," "Für die Industriearbeiter—Was haben wir von einer sozialistischen Regierung zu erwarten?," and "Für den Bauern und ländlichen Arbeiterstand. . . ."

105 "Deine Kirche, der Religionsunterricht Deiner Kinder ist in Gefahr!," National Assembly flyer, GStA XII.HA/IV 177.

106 "Fräulein Frau," Korrespondenz der DNVP, 19 July 1919; "Wie wähle ich? Bürger und Bauer! Frauen und Jungfrauen!," January 1919 Prussian flyer, GStA/XII.HA/IV 178; "Die Frauen sollen dem Bolshewismus zum Siege verhelfen!," Korrespondenz der DNVP, 18 August 1920; Koss, Das wahre Gesicht des Bolshewismus; "An die deutschen Wählerinnen!," National Assembly flyer, LA 240/1785/67; "Deutschnationale Frauenpolitik."

107 For details on the occupation, see Nelson, "'Black Horror on the Rhine.'" On the DNVP's Reichstag protest, which was joined by all government parties except the USPD, see Lebzelter, "Die 'Schwarze Schmach,'" 38–39.

108 For examples, see "Notruf wider die schwarze Schmach!," undated pamphlet published by the Fichte-Bund in several languages, Hoover Franz Coll. 1/44, and "Helft! Helft!," published by the Deutscher Notbund, Hoover Mueller-Graeff Coll. box 3.

109 "Deutsche Männer und Frauen," BA ZSg 1-44/8.

110 "Zum 9. November 1919," BA ZSg 1-44/11.

111 Scheck, "German Conservatism," 50.

112 For women's flyers, see "An alle Frauen," January 1919, BA ZSg 1-44/11; "An die deutschen Wählerinnen!"; "Die Partei der Frauen," Korrespondenz der DNVP, 13 February 1919; "Wie wähle ich?"; "Deutsche Frauen!," June 1920, BA ZSg 1-44/8; and "Fräulein Frau." For general flyers, see "Deutsche Wähler und Wählerinnen!," June 1920, GStA/XII.HA/IV 181, and "Eure jetzigen Führer," January 1919, LA 240/2381/12. In addition to caricaturing Jewish and non-Jewish Socialists and Democrats, this last piece depicts feminist Anita Augspurg as an old hag.

113 "Nationales Manifest der Deutschnationalen Volkspartei," GStA/XII.HA/IV 175; "Staats- und Gemeinde-Beamten, Beamtinnen und Angestellte!," LA 240/1785/62.

114 "Deutsche Frauen im kaufmännischen Beruf!," n.d., BA ZSg 1-44/11. For sample appeals to occupational groups, see "Aufruf von Angehörigen freier Berufe der DNVP" and "Was ist ein Beamter?," both 1919, GStA XII.HA/IV 177.

115 "Was wünschest Du, deutsche Frau?," in BA ZSg 1-44/11; "Haufrauen! Mütter!," in Hoover Loesch Coll. 2/28; "An alle Frauen."

116 Memo of Berufsständischer Reichsausschuss der DNVP, 23 May 1919, in BA Berlin 60 Vo 2/45121/1.

117 This type of work had become so unpopular that, throughout 1919, labor ex-

changes reported great demand for domestic servants, even at a time when female unemployment was high because of demobilization. See Bessel, "Unemployment and Demobilisation."

118 "Häusliche Angestellte!" and "Heimarbeiterinnen, warum mußt Ihr wählen?," 1919 flyers, GStA/XII.HA/IV 177; "Darf die Heimarbeit abgeschafft werden?," *Korrespondenz der DNVP*, 1 February 1919. On conflict between housewives and domestic workers, see Bridenthal, "Professional Housewives" and "Organized Rural Women," 386–97.

119 "An die Frauen." See also comments made by the Berlin women in "Bericht über die Tagung des Landesfrauenausschusses des Wahlkreises Teltow-Beeskow-Storkow-Charlottenburg" and "Ausbildung der Frauenpflichten," in *Deutsches Wollen: Mitteilungen der DNVP* (Berlin), 10 January 1920.

120 Foellmer, *Zwei Jahre politisches Frauenwahlrecht*; Prillip, *Die deutschnationale Frau*; "Nach den Wahlen," *Frauennummer* of *Korrespondenz der DNVP*, 12 June 1920.

121 "Die erste Frauenrede in der Nationalversammlung," *Korrespondenz der DNVP*, 20 February 1919. Ironically, Juchasz was criticized by women of the USPD for speaking as a "German woman" rather than a good comrade.

122 Liebe, *Deutschnationale Volkspartei*, 65. An early memo declared that no Jew, even a converted one, could ever be admitted to the party; see "Deutschnationale Volkspartei. Der Name der Partei . . . ," in BA Berlin 60 Vo 2/45121/1.

123 See "Zum Austritt der Abgeordnete Anna von Gierke," 29 May 1920, and "Stadtverordnetenwahl," 12 June 1920, both in *Frauennummer* of *Korrespondenz der DNVP*.

124 A minor flap did arise over whether the women's committee had jurisdiction over girls in the DNVP Youth League (see Erich Hammer to Frauenausschuss, 28 February 1919, in BA Berlin 60 Vo 2/485). Otherwise, party files paint a picture of harmony in local organizations. For example, Johanna Meissner's 14 March 1919 letter to Margarete Behm asked whether Ortsgruppe Steglitz could forego forming a separate women's group because women were already so well integrated into the local that a women's unit would only splinter united forces. See BA Berlin 60 Vo 2/485–87.

125 For women's views, see "Zwei Jahre in der Partei," 4 December 1920, and "Frauenlisten und Frauenparteien," 18 October 1919, both in *Frauennummer* of *Korrespondenz der DNVP*. See also Scheck, "German Conservatism."

126 Bremme, *Politische Rolle der Frau*, 72.

127 This number includes materials specific to Berlin, Prussia, Breslau, and Westphalia, found in the major national collections listed in the bibliography. Regional flyers from other parties did not surface as often in these collections.

128 The SPD's July 1919 motion that article 109 of the constitution state that the sexes had equal rights was watered down by the assembly to read that men and women had equal rights "in principle."

129 For women's flyers, see "Wo sind die Frauen?," December 1918, GStA/XII.HA/IV 52/58; "Frauenrechte in der Republik," likely 1920, LA 240/1024/1; and "Auf zur Gemeindewahl!" and "Arbeiter, Frauen, Mitbürger von Steglitz!," February 1919 Berlin election, both GStA/XII.HA/IV 55. For flyers to mixed-sex audiences, see "Wähler und Wählerinnen!," 1919, BA ZSg 1-90/58; and "Richtet! Wahlet!," "Wer stimmt am 6. Juni für die SPD?," and "Volksgenossen

und—Genossinnen!," all June 1920, BA ZSg 1-90/58. "Rührt Euch!," a January 1919 campaign magazine, puts particular emphasis on the symbolism of female suffrage as a new beginning; in GStA XII.HA/IV 53.

130   Quoted in Fairbairn, *Democracy in the Undemocratic State*, 212.

131   "Wo sind die Frauen?"; "Preußenwahl!," January 1919 flyer, GStA/XII.HA/IV 54.

132   A National Assembly election flyer to soldiers also attacked the "European re-action" and its annexationist demands for dragging out the war; see "Soldaten, Kameraden!," in GStA XII.HA/IV 53.

133   "Die Religion ist in Gefahr!," June 1920 flyer, BA ZSg 1-90/58; "Frauen und Mädchen! Paßt auf!," January 1919 flyer, GStA/XII.HA/IV 53; Schreiber, in SPD, *Protokoll* (1919), 491.

134   Private household service, however, remained unregulated, which would cause continued bitter battles over these employees' rights throughout Weimar. See Bridenthal, "Class Struggle around the Hearth." For relevant SPD propaganda, see "Landtagswähler!," 1919 Prussian flyer, GStA/XII.HA/IV 54; *Handbuch für Sozialdemokratische Wähler* (1920); "Frauen und Mädchen! Reichstagswähler-innen!," June 1920, BA ZSg 1-90/58; "Hausangestellte auf zur Wahl!," 1919 flyer, GStA/XII.HA/IV 56; and "Frauen und Mädchen, Wählerinnen!," National Assembly flyer, BA ZSg 1-90/58. For comparable language, see "An die Beamten in öffentlichen Diensten!," National Assembly flyer, GStA XII.HA/IV 53.

135   "Frauen Berlins, seid wach!," National Assembly flyer, GStA/XII.HA/IV 53. This is the only direct reference to Marxist theory of women's emancipation I found in SPD literature from this period.

136   "Frauen! Daß Ihr wählen dürft . . . ," June 1920 flyer, and "Wie werden die Frauen wählen?," in *Wählerzeitung für Jedermann* (January 1919), both BA ZSg 1-90/58; "Preußenwahl!"

137   H. Lehmann, "Bürgerliche Frauen und die Politik," *Vorwärts*, 28 September 1919.

138   "Wacht endlich auf!," June 1920 poster, LA 240/2381/59; "Ich weiss, daß Du . . . ," undated flyer, BA ZSg 1-90/18; "Frauen: der Tag ist da!," National Assembly flyer, GStA/XII.HA/IV 53; "Frauen, denkt daran!," Munich National Assembly flyer, GStA/XII.HA/IV 56; *Wählerzeitung für Jedermann*.

139   See these National Assembly flyers: "Frauen und Mädchen im Wahlkampf!," GStA/XII.HA/IV 53, and "Sozialdemokratie und Nationalversammlung," LA 240/1785/2. The SPD could make this claim only when women's voting pref-erences were still unknown. It soon became clear that the parties who gained most from women's vote were not about to abolish it.

140   "Arbeiter! Bürger! Soldaten! Wähler und Wählerinnen des Kreises Teltow-Beeskow-Storkow-Charlottenburg!," January 1919, GStA/XII.HA/IV 53; "Frauen und Mädchen, Wählerinnen!"; *Wählerzeitung für Jedermann*; "Die Frauen und die Wahlen zur Gesetzgebung," National Assembly flyer, BA ZSg 1-90/58.

141   "Ich weiss, daß Du . . ."; "Gemeindewähler!," February 1919 flyer, GStA/XII.HA/IV 55; "Frauen, seid auf der Hut!," December 1918 flyer, GStA/XII.HA/IV 52/4.

142   Poster first used in late January 1919 Prussian elections; see "Mutter! Denk an

mich! Wähle sozialdemokratisch!," in GStA/XII.HA/IV 54. Another version is in Hoover Moenkemöller Coll. 31/204. On the SPD's turn to a "more readable" realistic style, see Weinstein, *The End of Expressionism*, 38.

143 Gertrud Zucker, "Frau und die Gemeindepolitik," *Vorwärts*, 20 February 1919. Neither Louise Schroeder's 1920 Reichstag bill to legalize abortion nor Adele Schreiber's call at the 1919 women's party conference for state-funded birth control clinics was mentioned in published campaign literature.

144 Usborne, *Politics of the Body*, 46.

145 Steinkopf, "Die Beamtin als uneheliche Mutter," *Vorwärts*, 13 June 1920; Schütze, "Beamtin als uneheliche Mutter," *Vorwärts*, 25 June 1920; Schroeder in *Bericht über die Tätigkeit der sozialdemokratischen Reichstagsfraktion 1920–21*; Schreiber at 1920 SPD conference, in SPD, *Protokoll* (1919), 491.

146 Lebzelter, "Die 'Schwarze Schmach,'" 39. The SPD, to its credit, never used this in campaign materials.

147 "Eine bürgerliche Frau über Bebel," *Vorwärts*, 25 February 1920.

148 "Frauen! Schützt Eure Religion!," 1919 flyer, BA ZSg 1-65/64; "Frauen! Mädchen!," 1919 flyer from Westphalia, GStA/XII.HA/IV 56; "Heraus aus dem Zentrums-Turm!," National Assembly flyer, GStA XII.HA/IV 53; "Die Religion ist in Gefahr!"

149 "Frauen, Religion, Politik!," January 1919, GStA/XII.HA/IV 53; "Frauen, seid auf der Hut!"; "Frauen! Schützt Eure Religion!"; "Die Religion ist in Gefahr!"; "Heraus aus dem Zentrums-Turm!"

150 "Die Religion ist in Gefahr!"; "Frauen, Religion, Politik!"

151 Bourgeois observers also noticed this and thanked women for thwarting a Socialist majority; see Elly Heuß-Knapp, "Die Reichstagswahlen und die Frauen," *DAZ*, 3 June 1920. Bremme put women's share of the SPD vote at 5–10 percent behind men's before 1930; see *Politische Rolle der Frau*, 71–73.

152 "Wo sind die Frauen?"; "Frauen, Religion, Politik!"; *Handbuch für sozialdemokratischen Wähler* (1920).

153 Bohm-Schuch at *Parteiausschuss* meeting, 4 May 1920; Grünberg and Juchasz in SPD, *Protokoll* (1919), 25–26, 62–63.

154 See the above-mentioned interpellation women delegates presented to the National Assembly; see also Margarete Pfirrmann, "Gleichberechtigung der Frau?," *Vorwärts*, 5 April 1919.

155 "Frauenfragen," *Deutschnationales Rüstzeug* 29/30.

156 For examples, see "Wähler und Wählerinnen von Birkenwerder!," March 1919, GStA/XII.HA/IV 81, and "Wähler und Wählerinnen!," 1919 poster, BA ZSg 1-91/14.

157 For example, see "Wen wählen wir am 6. Juni?," 1920 flyer, BA ZSg 1-91/15, and Kurt Kerlöw-Löwenstein, "Die Revolutionierung der Frau," *Die Kämpferin*, 13 November 1919.

158 "An die Frauen und Mädchen des arbeitenden Volkes!," National Assembly flyer, LA 240/1785/5.

159 Ibid. See also Mathilde Wurm's comments in USPD, *Protokoll* (30 November–6 December 1919), 511–21, and "Aufgaben der Frauenkonferenz," *Freiheit*, 29 November 1919.

160 "Frauen des arbeitenden Volkes!" and "Verbrecher am deutschen Volke," both June 1920 flyers, BA ZSg 1-91/15.

161 "Das Liebeswerben um die Frau!," June 1920, Hoover Franz Coll. box 1, emphasis in original.

162 Marie Hartung, "Das Ewig-Weibliche in der Politik," *Die Kämpferin*, 16 October 1919.

163 "An die arbeitende Bevölkerung!," June 1920 Berlin flyer, LA 240/1964/5; *Handbuch der Wähler der USPD* (1920), 122–28. See also Luise Zietz, "Die Frauen im Reichsparlament," 29 April 1920, and Hans Hackmack, "Wahlmosaik," 8 July 1920, both in *Die Kämpferin*.

164 "Arbeiter, Arbeiterinnen!," 1919 flyer, BA ZSg 1-91/14. See also Luise Zietz, quoted in USPD, *Protokoll* (30 November–6 December 1919), 469.

165 "Frauen! Arbeiterinnen und weibliche Angestellte!," June 1920, GStA/XII.HA/IV 81; "Und was sagst Du?," June 1920, BA ZSg 1-91/15.

166 "Frauen des arbeitenden Volkes!" The reference to women's bodies may also be alluding to reproductive politics, which were surprisingly absent from USPD literature, despite legislation the USPD introduced in July 1920 to repeal all penal code articles outlawing abortion. See Usborne, *Politics of the Body*, 217.

167 Luise Zietz, "Willst Du arm und unfrei bleiben?," 1920 pamphlet, BA ZSg 1-91/4 (7); "Die Pfaffenherrschaft über die Volkshochschule," n.d., BA ZSg 1-91/20; "Das Weib schweige in der Gemeinde!," June 1920, BA ZSg 1-91/15; Toni Sender, "Die Frauen und das Rätesystem," 1920 pamphlet, BA ZSg 1-91/12 (2).

168 Keinath, quoted in USPD, *Protokoll* (30 November–6 December 1919), 472.

169 Ibid., 518–21, 526–28.

170 See "Frauen! Mädchen! Arbeiterinnen!," n.d., BA ZSg 1-91/20; "Aktionsprogramm der USPD," in USPD, *Protokoll* (30 November–6 December 1919); Bertha Braunthal, "Die Berufsorganisation der Hausfrau," *Die Kämpferin*, 13 May 1920; Sender, "Die Frauen und das Rätesystem."

171 Sender, "Die Frauen und das Rätesystem."

172 "Und was sagst Du?"; "Das Recht auf Mutterschaft," *Die Kämpferin*, 11 January 1920; Bertha Braunthal, "Unsere Reichsfrauenkonferenz," *Kommunistische Rundschau* 5 (1920).

173 Keinath, quoted in USPD, *Protokoll* (30 November–6 December 1919), 472; see also Genossin Reichheim's comments in ibid., 475.

174 See also Bremme, *Politische Rolle der Frau*, 110, which says that numbers from Cologne put women at 40 percent of USPD voters.

175 Braunthal, "Berufsorganisation der Hausfrau." Braunthal took this fire with her when she defected to the KPD, a party that periodically lashed out at women for not "seeing the light."

176 See "Sieg der Frauen: Wahlen in Deutsch-Österreich," *Freiheit*, 26 October 1920; Mathilde Wurm, "Nicht reif genug!," *Aus der Frauenbewegung* in *Freiheit*, 8 December 1918; "Wahlmosaik"; "An die Frauen," *Freiheit*, 17 November 1918; and Hanna Hertz, "Die Entwicklung des Frauenwahlrechts," *Die Kämpferin*, 13 May 1920.

177 Marie Wackwitz, quoted in USPD, *Protokoll* (30 November–6 December 1919), 93.

178 USPD, *Protokoll* (October 1920); Braunthal, "Die Frauen vor der Entscheidung," *Kommunistische Rundschau* 2 (1920).

179 For example, Kücki Kaneko in *Die Kämpferin*, 23 December 1920, wryly joked that "a woman who has a life of her own and expresses it is moody and unfeminine—an oddity!"

180 See Kontos, *Partei kämpft wie ein Mann!*

181 Female membership in the SPD went from 66,000 to 207,000 in this period, while the USPD's doubled to 135,464 by late 1920. Female socialist trade union membership, including white-collar workers, went from 442,957 to over 1.7 million. See Frevert, *Women in German History*, 168–74.

182 Usborne, *Politics of the Body*, 74.

CHAPTER TWO

1 Jones, "In the Shadow of Stabilization," 21–41; Childers, "Inflation, Stabilization and Political Realignment," 409–31.

2 "Der Wahltag in Berlin," *Deutsche Tageszeitung*, 8 December 1924.

3 For contemporary observations, see "Der Mann ist der Haupt der Familie," 15 January 1924; "Die Frau als Verführerin—Aus der Praxis unserer Gerichte," 17 November 1924; and "Ist das Heiraten schon erschwinglich?," 8 February 1924, all in *8-Uhr Abendblatt*.

4 See DDP, *Material zum Wahlkampf Reichstagswahl 1924*, and various Reichsgeschäftsstelle memos in NSDAP/HA 36/721. Jones and Childers have both argued for this view of the DDP as party of class reconciliation.

5 Where votes were tabulated by sex, 4.1 percent of female and 4.3 percent of male voters chose the DDP in May 1924. In December, these figures were 6.2 and 6.4 percent, respectively. See Falter, Lindenberger, and Schumann, *Wahlen und Abstimmungen*, table 1.6.1.1. See also Jones, *German Liberalism*, 77, 174–81.

6 Reproduced in Hessisches Landesmuseum, *Politische Plakate der Weimarer Republik*, 122.

7 "Ein Brief," May 1924 flyer, GStA/XII.HA/IV 134.

8 "13 Millionen Deutsche Hausfrauen sind stimmberechtigt!," GStA/XII.HA/IV 133.

9 See "Frauen auf zur Wahl," *Reichstagswahlzeitung für Gross-Berlin 2*, and "Beamtinnen! Lehrerinnen!," May 1924 flyer, both GStA/XII.HA/IV 134.

10 "Die DNVP," *Materialien zur demokratischen Politik* 68:10–11; "Frauen, wollt ihr neuen wirtschaftlichen Wirrwarr vermeiden?," *BT*, 2 May 1924. The *BT*, whose relationship with the DDP was troubled from the start, was in May not so much pro-DDP as anti-Right. Panic over the radical Right's strong showing drew the *BT* closer to the DDP in December.

11 "Krieg oder Frieden?," May 1924 flyer, GStA/XII.HA/IV 62. Evidence suggests that the SPD also used this flyer.

12 Lüders, quoted in "Appell an die Frauen: Eine Kundgebung demokratischer Staatsbürgerinnen," *BT*, 3 May 1924.

13 "Germany's Rebirth through Democracy" was the theme of the DDP's most recent recruiting week, held in 1922. See BA R45 III/45 on DDP *Werbewochen*.

14 "Ein Brief."

15 For sample appeals to entrepreneurs and workers, see "An das deutsche Unternehmertum!" and "An die deutschen Arbeitnehmer!," both reprinted in *Mitteilungen der deutschen Zentrumspartei*, November 1924, GStA/XII.HA/IV 111.

16 "Frauen auf zur Wahl," *Reichstagswahlzeitung für Groß-Berlin* 2 (1924): 5, in GStA/XII.HA/IV 134.

17 Clemens, *Menschenrechte*, 20.

18 See Beckmann's comments in *Bericht über die Verhandlungen des 5. Parteitages der D.D.P.*, 61.

19 "Appell an die Frauen" and "Beamtinnen! Lehrerinnen!"

20 For the May election I found nine pieces specifically for women, including three appeals in the *BT* and two from *Wahlzeitungen*, which carried appeals to several groups. In December this figure was thirteen. Add to these totals the main women's pamphlet, "Betrachtungen einer werktätigen Frau" (BA ZSg 1-27/18 [6]), which was used all year. Anton Erkelenz, in "Leitfaden für Wahlorganisatoren und Wahlwerber" (GStA/XII.HA/III 15), also admonished the party not to slack off in its efforts to win the female voter.

21 "An alle Frauen!," 1924, GStA/XII.HA/IV 135; "Deutsche Frau, wählt demokratisch!," *BT*, 2 December 1924. On the women's party, see Frevert, *Women in German History*, 201, and Freda Marie Gräfin zu Dohna, "Demokratische Reichsfrauentag," *BT*, 8 August 1924.

22 Childers, "Languages of Liberalism," 339.

23 "Der demokratische Reichsfrauentag"; "Die Wählerin" supplement of issues 1–3 of *Der Wähler*, GStA/XII.HA/IV 135; Agnes von Zahn-Harnack's comments at the November 1924 party congress, in NSDAP/HA 37/738.

24 In mid-1924 DDP leaders opposed participation in any government that included the DNVP. See Frye, *Liberal Democrats*, 228.

25 See "Eine Rede Gertrud Bäumers: Demokratische Frauenkundgebung," *BT*, 27 November 1924; Lenka von Körber, "Pflicht der Mütter: Die Gefahren der völkischen Agitation," *BT*, 30 November 1924, and "Appell an die Frauen: Wahlrede in Chemnitz," *BT*, 27 November 1924; "Die Frauen und die schwarz-weiss-rot Parteien," December 1924, GStA/XII.HA/IV 135; and "Deutsche Frau, wählt demokratisch!" A DDP functionary argued that women were easy to mobilize for "anti-Semitic and emotion-based trends," which was weakening DDP efforts; see DDP Sekretariat Anneberg to Erkelenz, 13 January 1923, BA NL Erkelenz, folder 125.

26 "An alle Frauen!"

27 "Betrachtungen einer werktätigen Frau."

28 See "Deutsche Frau, wählt demokratisch!" and "Betrachtungen einer werktätigen Frau."

29 "Beamte, Beamtinnen!," GStA/XII.HA/IV 135; "Die Wählerin," *Der Wähler 3*, LA 240/1964/21.

30 "Eine Rede Gertrud Bäumers."

31 "Leitfaden für Wahlorganisatoren."

32 Paul, *Aufstand der Bilder*, 25. For an overview of liberal propaganda, see Möller, "Die sich selbst bewusste Massenbeeinflussung."

33 "Briefe einer berufstätigen Frau" in "Deutsche Frauenstimmen," LA 240/1941/

13. A 1921 flyer, "An die deutschen Frauen," expressed this as creating peace in the "great German *Vaterhaus.*"

34 Katharina von Meyer, "Die Organisierung der Frauen," speech at the May 1919 meeting of the party secretariat, in NSDAP/HA 38/743.

35 "Eindrücke eines Mannes vor der Eisenacher Frauentagung," *Der Demokrat,* 21 July 1921.

36 See, for example, "Entrechtete Beamtinnen," *Der Demokrat,* 23 December 1920, and "Die Rechtspflege und die Frauen," *Materialien zur demokratischen Politik* 58 (1921).

37 *Bericht über die Verhandlungen des 3. Parteitages der D.D.P., 1921.*

38 "Beamtenfragen. Die Wahrheit über den Personal-Abbau Verordnung," *Materialien zur demokratischen Politik* 93 (1924).

39 Schneider, *Deutsche Demokratische Partei,* 63–65; Frye, *Liberal Democrats,* 87–101. On party financing, see Fricke et al., *Lexikon zur Parteiengeschichte,* entry on the DDP. For an example of pressure from economic interest groups for more consideration, especially in candidate selection, see Rundschreiben der Demokratischen Bauernbund, BA NL Erkelenz, folder 111.

40 Bremme, *Politische Rolle der Frau,* 127.

41 For figures, see this chapter, note 6. Party membership plummeted from around 900,000 in 1919 to 209,530 in 1922 and 131,794 in 1925.

42 "Leitfaden für Wahlorganisatoren"; Stephan, "Plan einer demokratischen Werbewoche," 1925, BA R45 III/45.

43 See, for example, a Reichsgeschäftsstelle memo from 17 October 1924 on the suspension of several propaganda items, in NSDAP/HA 36/721.

44 See the April 1924 Parteitag discussion of the upcoming election and "Schlagworte für den Wahlkampf," December 1924, GStA/XII.HA/IV 135.

45 Childers, "Languages of Liberalism," 333. For a flyer representing this theme, see "An alle deutsche Männer und Frauen!," in GStA/XII.HA/IV 165.

46 It fell from 3.9 million votes in June 1920 to 2.6 million, all the more alarming in comparison to the 2.5 million won by splinter parties.

47 On the DVP's 1924 campaigns, see Jones, *German Liberalism,* 174, 216–57.

48 March 1924 report on Landesfrauenausschuss meeting in BA NL Dingeldey, folder 19. In the republic's early years, Dingeldey was chair of the DVP in Hessen.

49 "An die Frauen Berlins! Was hat die DVP getan, seitdem sie in der Regierung ist?," December 1924, LA 240/1941/8.

50 "Mein lieber Mann und ich," 1924, BA ZSg 1-42/7 (3); "Hausfrauen!," May 1924, GStA/XII.HA/IV 165; "An die Frauen Berlins!"

51 "Wählerinnen, habt Ihr schon vergessen?," 1924, BA ZSg 1-42/7 (3). Flyers for occupational groups include "Handwerker und Gewerbetreibende!" and "Kaufmännischer und gewerblicher Mittelstand!," both GStA/XII.HA/IV 165.

52 "Die Kulturfragen in der DVP," 1924 pamphlet, GStA/XII.HA/III 16; *Wahlhandbuch 1924,* BA ZSg 1-42/14 (4); "Das junge Mädchen," *DAZ,* 1 January 1924; Hannah Boehmer, "Neue Wege und Ziele unsere Jungmädchenwelt," *Berliner Stimmen,* 1 July 1924; "Die Frauen und die DVP," 1924, BA ZSg 1-42/7 (3). On the Home Economics Aid, see Landesverband Hessen to Frauenausschüsse, n.d.

(likely late 1920), BA NL Dingeldey, folder 19. On the housewives' movement, see Bridenthal, "Professional Housewives."

53   E. Fries, "Frauen-Berufe: Berufsfreudigkeit. Das Taylorsystem," *Korrespondenz Frauenpresse* 17 (2 September 1924); *Wahlhandbuch 1924.*

54   "Die Rechtsstellug der Ehefrau und der ehelichen Mutter," 1921, BA ZSg 1-42/1.

55   "An die Frauen Berlins! Frauen Berlins heraus!," in LA 240/1941/7.

56   See also a 1921 flyer, "An Preußens Frauen!," in which an image depicts women donating their hair and other valuables for the 1813 Wars of Liberation, with the caption: "Einst brachten die Frauen ihr Höchstes dar / Gebt jetzt nur die Stimme, nicht Euer Haar." In LA 240/1024/74.

57   Dr. Hanna Schwab, "Frau und Beruf," *DAZ,* 25 January 1924. The *DAZ,* while not officially an organ of the DVP, stood close to the party and was a mouthpiece for many of its politicians.

58   "Mein lieber Mann und ich"; "Welche Partei wählt der deutsche Beamte?," 4 May 1924, GStA/XII.HA/IV 165.

59   C. Mothander, "Eine Mutter," *DAZ,* 2 September 1924.

60   *Berliner Stimmen,* 5 December 1924; "Die Partei der Privatangestellten national und sozial ist die DVP!," December 1924, LA 240/1964/42.

61   "Die weibliche Angestellte sagt: Ich wähle immer DVP," 1924, BA ZSg 1-42/7 (3).

62   "Die Frauen und die DVP"; *Wahlhandbuch 1924.*

63   See "Beamtenpolitik" and "Die Frauen in der Politik der Deutschen Volkspartei," both 1924, GStA/XII.HA/III 16.

64   Dr. L., "Der Leser hat das Wort— . . . und die deutschen Frauen?," *DAZ,* 17 November 1924; "Die Frau in der Gemeinde," *Archiv der DVP,* 15 March 1924; "Die Frauen in der Politik der Deutschen Volkspartei."

65   *Frauen* section of *Berliner Stimmen* 9 (September 1924). See also "Aus der Arbeit unser Frauen," *Berliner Stimmen,* 20 March 1924.

66   "Die Frauen und die DVP"; "Deutsche Frauen! Deutsche Mütter!," May 1924, BA ZSg 1-42/7 (3); "An die Frauen Berlins! Was hat die DVP getan?"; *Wahlhandbuch 1924*; "Deutsche Mütter! Deutsche Frauen! Es ist höchste Zeit . . . ," 1921 Prussian election flyer, BA ZSg 1-42/7 (1). For a general appeal, see "An alle deutsche Männer und Frauen!"

67   For example, see A. Mayer, "Die Frauen und der Wahlkampf," *Berliner Stimmen,* 18 November 1924.

68   "An Preußens Frauen!" German agitation paid off in the next two years, as American and British groups—including feminist organizations—joined in condemning France on this issue. See Nelson, "'Black Horror on the Rhine,'" 620, and Whittick, *Woman into Citizen,* 73.

69   See *Wahlhandbuch 1924* and "Die Frauen in der Politik der Deutschen Volkspartei," which argued that it was not the blacks themselves who were to blame but the government that put them there. On the occupation and withdrawal of troops, see Lebzelter, "Die 'Schwarze Schmach.'"

70   "Mein lieber Mann und ich."

71   The daily press was full of stories about women smoking. For an example, see

Paulus, "Wenn Frauen rauchen: Schicklich und unschicklich," *DAZ*, 7 April 1924.

72 *Berliner Stimmen*, 17 December 1924; "Um was geht es am Sonntag?," *DAZ*, 2 December 1924.

73 "Wie wählen die Frauen," *Archiv der DVP*, 15 March 1924; "Die Frauen in der Politik der Deutschen Volkspartei"; "Wir alle wählen Deutsche Volkspartei," undated postcard, GStA/XII.HA/IV 170.

74 See BA R45 II/36 file on 1921 meetings of Zentralvorstand, which is full of requests from various occupational groups for seats on this key committee.

75 H. Margis, "Volksparteiliche Frauen in den neuen Parlamenten," *Berliner Stimmen*, 17 December 1924.

76 "Die staatsbewußte Frau," *DAZ*, 16 March 1924.

77 For example, see Dingeldey to Marie Mueller, 7 November 1921, BA NL Dingeldey, folder 19.

78 Anna Mayer, "Frauen und Wahlrecht," *Berliner Stimmen*, 17 April 1924.

79 See BA NL Kardorff-Oheimb, folders 18 and 21. See also two *8-Uhr Abendblatt* articles by and about her: "Wohin treiben wir?" (25 October 1924) and "Frau Katharina von Oheimb" (26 February 1924). In 1921 she was the only woman on the influential business committee. There was some dispute over whether her 1925 exit was voluntary (as she claimed) or whether she was ejected (as the party claimed); see "Frau Oheimb und die DVP," *Deutsche Zeitung*, 15 March 1925. She later married DVP bigwig Siegfried von Kardorff but never recouped her standing within the party.

80 Mayer, "Frauen und Wahlrecht"; "An die Frauen Berlins! Frauen Berlins heraus!"; "An die Frauen Berlins! Was hat die DVP getan?"

81 Frauenabteilung der Reichsgeschäftsstelle, "Winke für Frauenausschüsse," 1921, BA ZSg 1-42/1.

82 See 26 May 1922 memo from DVP Wahlkreis Geschäftsstelle Frankfurt/Oder to DVP Reichsgeschäftsstelle, BA R45 II/56, and Dingeldey to Tilla de Weerth regarding her resignation as Vorsitzende of the local Frauenausschuss, 5 April 1921, BA NL Dingeldey, folder 19.

83 For example, BA NL Kardorff-Oheimb, folder 19a, documents a rift between Oheimb and women's committee leader Elsa Matz; a 5 April 1921 letter from Dingeldey to de Weerth mentions some women's offense at seating arrangements at an official dinner. Personal conflicts likely provoked de Weerth's resignation; see 6 July 1920 notes on a memo for women's committees, BA NL Dingeldey, folder 19. Gertrud Büss blamed women's jealousy and need for male respect for their lack of authority; "Frauenkandidaturen," *Berliner Stimmen*, 24 December 1924.

84 "Die Frauen in der Politik der Deutschen Volkspartei," 22.

85 It polled 3.9 million votes, a slight gain from June 1920, which made it the third largest party. For 1924 campaign strategy, see Ruppert, *Im Dienst*, 53–61, 85–92.

86 Ibid., 89–90. See also Morsey and Ruppert, *Protokolle der Reichstagsfraktion* 1:59. Already in October 1920 Labor Minister Braun argued for a message to unify the Catholic milieu, noting that without the female vote, the party would be in dire straits.

87 See Kaufmann, "Vom Vaterland zum Mutterland," 254–79.

88 Hedwig Dransfeld, "Weshalb wählen wir Frauen Zentrum?," December 1924 flyer, GStA/XII.HA/IV 112; M. R. Junemann, "An die Frauen," *Germania*, 23 April 1924.

89 "Deutsche Frauen! Tut Eure Pflicht am 4. Mai," May 1924 flyer, GStA/XII.HA/IV 112.

90 "Zur Mitte, ihr Frauen!," appeal in *Germania*, 7 December 1924.

91 *Zweite Reichsparteitag des Zentrums*, 86. This was reflected in the attitude of Helene Weber, Reichstag delegate and adviser to the Prussian Welfare Ministry, who saw herself as a bridge builder, not a bureaucrat; Rieden, "Helene Weber," 124.

92 H. Dransfeld, "Die Frauenbeiräte des Zentrums," *Germania*, 7 March 1924; Junemann, "An die Frauen."

93 "Der Kampf gegen den §218," *Germania*, 20 May 1924.

94 "Für Freiheit und Recht! Gegen den Kulturkampf!," December 1924, LA 240/1962/20. This flyer contradicts Ruppert's claim that the Center limited attacks on this score to the NSDAP, KPD, and DNVP. See Ruppert, *Im Dienst*, 91.

95 "Deutsche Frauen! Tut Eure Pflicht am 4. Mai"; "Die Stunde der Frauen," *Germania*, 4 May 1924; Junemann, "An die Frauen"; "Wähler und Wählerinnen! Warum wählen wir?," December 1924 flyer, GStA/XII.HA/IV 112; M. R. Junemann, "Staatsbürgerin!," *Germania*, 4 December 1924.

96 W. Müller-Hermsdorf, "Zehn Gebote für Ehefrauen," *Germania*, 29 June 1924. These were taken from a sermon delivered by one Red Bustard in Cleveland, Ohio. See also Breuer, *Frauenbewegung im Katholizismus*, 105–10.

97 M. Timpe, "Die junge Akademikerin," *Germania*, 15 May 1924.

98 Morsey and Ruppert, *Protokolle der Reichstagsfraktion* 1:575.

99 See Schreiber, *Zentrum und deutsche Politik*; Dr. Hertha Eisenschmidt, "Lohnabbau und Frauenarbeit," *Germania*, 6 January 1924; and Julie Ermler, "Zum Beamtenabbau der Frauen," *Germania*, 19 February 1924.

100 See *Frauenrundschau* section of *Das Zentrum*, 15 February 1921, 1 June 1921, 1 July 1921, and 15 January 1922.

101 *Zweite Reichsparteitag des Zentrums*, 54–60.

102 In her December 1924 flyer, "Weshalb wählen wir Frauen Zentrum?," Dransfeld argued it was women's task to preserve "social peace" within the party. On the undesirability of "humanist" feminism, see *Frauenrundschau* section of *Das Zentrum*, 1 October 1921.

103 Dransfeld, "Weshalb wählen wir Frauen Zentrum?," and Junemann, "Staatsbürgerin!"

104 "Zur Mitte, ihr Frauen!"

105 In only two of six applicable districts did women get safe spots. To avoid a repeat of 1920, when the party with the strongest female support sent only three women to the Reichstag, Dransfeld and Weber were put on the Reich list in May 1924. See Ruppert, *Im Dienst*, 56–57.

106 See Dransfeld's two *Germania* articles on the subject, "Die Frauenmandate des Zentrums," 25 March 1924, and "Die Frauenbeiräte des Zentrums."

107 Junemann, "An die Frauen."

108 The index entry for "women" in the 1924 handbook reads, "see 'family.'"

109 In May, the SPD polled just over 6 million votes, merely 300,000 above the DNVP. The KPD vote jumped from 589,454 in June 1920 to 3.69 million in May 1924, indicating a serious erosion of working-class support for the SPD. Female defections, however, were more likely to appear as support for the Center, DNVP, or abstention. See Falter, Lindenberger, and Schumann, *Wahlen und Abstimmungen*, tables 1.3.1.1 and 1.6.1.1.

110 Contrast this with a 1924 memo that called campaigning "from man to man in factory and apartment block" most effective. SPD Referentenmaterial 1924–30, SAPMO-BA II/145/20.

111 "Das teure Brot," June 1924 flyer for housewives' demonstration, GStA/XII.HA/IV 61.

112 "Hier Überschüss, dort Mangel," BA ZSg 1-90/59; "Das Blatt der Frau: Zur Reichstagswahl 4. Mai 1924," GStA/XII.HA/IV 62; "Denkt an die Zeit," May 1924, BA ZSg 1-90/59; "Öffentliche Frauen-Kundgebung," December 1924, GStA/XII.HA/IV 63.

113 Clara Bohm-Schuch, "Die Frau in der Politik," *Handbuch für Sozialdemokratische Wähler*, and *Vorwärts*, 4 April 1924; "Krieg oder Frieden?" and "Deutsche Frauen!," both May 1924, GStA/XII.HA/IV 62; "Inflation oder stabilisierte Wirtschaft?," GStA/XII.HA/IV 61; "Amtliche Kochrezepte für Kohlrübenspeisen!," May 1924, BA ZSg 1-90/59.

114 "In letzter Stunde," October 1921 Berlin flyer, LA 240/1881/11. "Deutschnationalen gegen das Frauenwahlrecht," *Nachrichten für die Funktionäre*, February 1921, depicts a fictional DNVP man who cannot believe women were "stupid enough to vote for us."

115 "Vor der Wahl/Nach der Wahl," cartoon in *Vorwärts*'s "Die Wählerin" supplement, 2 April 1924.

116 See, for example, *7. Dezember* 4, whose cover depicts two generals and an enormously fat woman bedecked with swastikas praying to a drunken Bavarian God before an altar also made of swastikas.

117 "Warum wähle ich nicht Völkisch?," May 1924, BA ZSg 1-90/59. See also "Die Frau entscheidet!," May 1924, BA ZSg 1-90/59; "Die Frau am Wahltag: Ein letzter Ruf an die Wählerinnen!," *Vorwärts*, 3 May 1924; "Frauen, vergeßt nicht!!" and "Arbeiterfrau, Du hast zuviel Geld!," both December 1924, GStA/XII.HA/IV 63; and "Wer gab den Frauen die politische Gleichberechtigung?," BA ZSg 1-90/18.

118 "Frauen und Kommunisten," *Die Wählerin*, December 1924, GStA/XII.HA/IV 63.

119 "Besudelung Rosa Luxemburgs," May 1924, BA ZSg 1-90/59; "Kommunistische Bläserchor," December 1924, GStA/XII.HA/IV 63; "Diese 'angestrengte' Parlamentstätigkeit . . . ," December 1924, Hoover Franz Coll. box 1.

120 "Diese Frau in Samt und Seide . . . ," Staatsarchiv Hamburg 224/49 (2).

121 "Bebel mahnt—wählt Liste 1," May 1924, BA ZSg 1-90/59.

122 See *Bericht über die Tätigkeit der Sozial-Demokratischen Reichstagsfraktion 1921–22*; *Handbuch für Sozial-Demokratische Wähler 1924*; *Die Sozial Demokratie im Reichstag 1924*; and Anna Blos, "Wie sollen Ehefrauen wählen?," *Vorwärts*, 1 May 1924.

123 A 1924 flyer, "Die Sozialdemokratie ist der Sammelpunkt aller Hand- und Kopfarbeiter!," BA ZSg 1-90/18, illustrates this strategy visually. It depicts six

figures—a peasant, civil servant, factory worker, white-collar worker, female white-collar employee, and mother—walking on different paths that all lead to the SPD. For an example of a flyer to other workers, see "An die Beamten der Schutzpolizei!," in GStA/XII.HA/IV 62.

124 "Das Blatt der Frau"; "Heraus! Ihr Frauen vom Lande!" and "Verkäuferinnen, Büroangestellte, Stenotypistinnen!!!," October 1924, both BA ZSg 1-90/18; "Beamtenprogramm der SPD, Beschlossen auf dem Berliner Parteitag 1924" and "Liebe Kollegin!," December 1924, both GStA/XII.HA/IV 61; "Geehrtes Fräulein!," December 1924, GStA/XII.HA/IV 63; "Heimarbeiterinnen und der 7. Dezember," *7. Dezember* 4; "Hausfrauen!! Mütter!!," October 1924, BA ZSg 1-90/18; Adolf Braun, "Die Arbeiterinnen und die Gewerkschaften," 1923 pamphlet, BA ZSg 1-90/18 [2].

125 See "Das Fräulein an der Schreibmaschine," 18 September 1924, and a series of reports and readers' letters, "Frauenschicksal!," which ran in *Vorwärts* on 23 November, 30 November, and 13 December 1924.

126 "Der Frauen Schicksal ist beklagenswert," *Vorwärts*, 29 June 1924. The belief that American men helped out more, doing such jobs as taking out the garbage, was widespread.

127 "Um 4 oder um 6. Die Arbeiterfrauen haben zu entscheiden," *7. Dezember* 4; "Not lehrt denken. Bekenntnis einer Wahlfaulen," *7. Dezember* 3; "Das 'Wirtschaftsgeld' der Hausfrau," *7. Dezember* 1; "Hausfrauen!! Mütter!!"; "So wählt . . . ," December 1924, GStA/XII.HA/IV 63; Braun, "Die Arbeiterinnen und die Gewerkschaften."

128 Usborne, *Politics of the Body*, 166.

129 "Fort mit §218! Ein Nachwort zum Prozeß Heiser," front page, 20 May 1924; "§218 und die Frauen: Nachwort zum Heiser-Prozeß—Ein Mahnwort an die Frauen," 8 October 1924; and M., "Nur nicht Mutter werden!," 7 February 1924, all in *Vorwärts*.

130 "Recht oder Pflicht zur Mutterschaft," *Vorwärts*, 29 May 1924.

131 "Das Mutterrecht der Beamtin," *Frauenstimme* of *Vorwärts*, 21 August 1924. See also "Oh! Diese Republik!," May 1924, BA ZSg 1-90/59, and "Das Blatt der Frau."

132 See "Kapitalismus und Prostitution," 26 November 1924, and Dr. H. Scherm, "Gebärzwang oder?," 10 July 1924, both in *Vorwärts*'s *Frauenstimme*, and "Schutz dem gefährdeten Weib: aus der Arbeit der Frauenhilfsstelle am Polizeipräsidium," *Vorwärts*, 23 December 1924.

133 C. Bohm-Schuch, "Unser Kampf für Mutter und Kind," *Vorwärts*, 30 April 1924.

134 Contrast Britain, where no party openly addressed birth control. Pugh, "Impact of Women's Enfranchisement," 323.

135 Usborne, *Politics of the Body*, 114.

136 For negative examples of female behavior, see "Oh! Diese Republik!"; "Not lehrt denken"; "Frauen denkt nach und handelt!," April 1924, BA ZSg 1-90/59; and "Ich wähle nicht!," in "Die Wählerin," *Vorwärts*, 16 April 1924. See also "Unsere Frauenagitation," *Nachrichten für die Funktionäre*, January 1922.

137 Hagemann, *Frauenalltag und Männerpolitik*, 537.

138 The SPD published a weekly *Vorwärts* supplement, "Die Wählerin," during

both campaigns, held at least two major women's rallies in June and December, and produced at least twenty-two flyers specifically for women in 1924.

139 Hagemann, *Frauenalltag und Männerpolitik*, 637. The proportion of SPD delegates who were female hovered around 12 percent during Weimar, a figure much higher than any other party, except the KPD, whose totals fluctuated wildly until settling around 14 percent in the early 1930s. Boak, "Women in Weimar Politics," 373.

140 Bohm-Schuch, "Die Frau in der Politik."

141 See protocols of the June 1924 women's conference in SPD, *Sozialdemokratischer Parteitag 1924*, 219–47.

142 For examples, see "Not lehrt denken," and Luise Weidner, "Die Frauenbewegung," in *Frauenwelt* section of *Vorwärts*, 24 January 1924.

143 "Die Abstimmung der Frauen," *Nachrichten für die Funktionäre*, March 1922.

144 This came from the Hamburg SPD women. Hagemann, *Frauenalltag und Männerpolitik*, 541.

145 This strategy fit in well with increasingly lenient public attitudes about abortion. For example, the popular nonpartisan *8-Uhr Abendblatt* argued that no matter one's views, this issue could no longer be swept under the rug because twenty women a day died from illegal abortions. See "Täglich 20 Tote infolge Fruchtabtreibung," *8-Uhr Abendblatt*, 7 January 1924.

146 See circular 1, 1919, of the women's section for a list of flyers produced that year, in SAPMO-BA I/2/701/14. See also "Achtung! Handlungsgehilfinnen und -gehilfen!," 17 February 1919, GStA/XII.HA/IV 86.

147 H. Sturm, "Frauenagitation," 31 October 1920, SAPMO-BA I/2/707/87.

148 See "Frauen und Mädchen des Proletariats!" and "Werktätige Frauen! Frauen aus Fabrik und Kontor!," in GStA/XII.HA/IV 87.

149 "Was ist des Arbeiters Lage?," Berlin-Bibliothek poster collection. See also "Jetzt ist's genug!," 1920, GStA/XII.HA/IV 87.

150 Weitz reaches similar conclusions after analyzing images from the *Arbeiter-Illustrierte-Zeitung*; see his *Creating German Communism*, 188–232.

151 "Die Rede des Ziegelbrenner: Die Welt-Revolution beginnt," January 1919, GStA/XII.HA/IV 84; "Werktätige Frauen!"; Sturm, "Frauenagitation."

152 "Frauen der Arbeiterklasse!," 1921, BA ZSg 1-65/64; "Instruktion zur Arbeit unter den Arbeiterinnen," SAPMO-BA I/2/701/16; *KPD Taschenkalender 1923*.

153 Contrary to Usborne's claim that the KPD did not address the issue of birth control until 1924, a 15 June 1923 meeting of the women's section favored promoting birth control as an alternative to abortion (SAPMO-BA I/2/701/9). See also Usborne, *Politics of the Body*, 114.

154 On confusion over women's role, see FRS meeting protocol, 15 June 1923, SAPMO-BA I/2/701/9. On women as "politically uninterested," see "Vom Unterhaltungsteil in der kommunistischen Zeitung," *Parteiarbeiter*, 1 July 1923. For FRS strategy and complaints about lack of support, see "Arbeitsplan für das FRS für die Zeit September–Dezember 1923," SAPMO-BA I/2/701/11, and FRS reports to the party central, July and October 1922, June 1923, SAPMO-BA I/2/701/12.

155 Weitz, *Creating German Communism*, 90.

156 On the factory strategy, see "Die nächsten Aufgaben der Partei," 1 June 1923, and "Neue Wege der Frauen-Propaganda," 15 June 1923, both in *Parteiarbeiter*. This is a central theme of Silvia Kontos's study of KPD women's policy, *Die Partei kämpft wie ein Mann!* See also Weitz, *Creating German Communism*, 100–131.

157 "Proletarische Frauen!," in Hoover Franz Coll. box 1.

158 "An die deutsche Beamtenschaft!," BA ZSg 1-65/62. See also "Arbeiterfrauen! Deutschland bricht zusammen . . . ," GStA/XII.HA/IV 88.

159 There was always a rhetorical tension between the feminist slogan the KPD used to mobilize female support for legal abortion—"Your body belongs to you!"—and the need to see the abortion laws as part of the larger complex of "class justice." See Usborne, *Politics of the Body*, 162–68, and Grossmann, *Reforming Sex*, chap. 4.

160 *RF*, 1 May 1924.

161 L. Korpus, "Zum Kampftag der Frauen," and "Demonstration der Berliner Frauen vor dem Reichstag," *RF*, 8 March 1924; M. Riesbeck, "Brief einer Proletarierin," *RF*, 9 April 1924.

162 The KPD won 3.69 million votes in May 1924. Where votes were tabulated according to sex, women were less than 40 percent of all KPD voters, the lowest of any major party. See Falter, Lindenberger, and Schumann, *Wahlen und Abstimmungen*, tables 1.3.1.1 and 1.6.1.1.

163 L. Konrad, "Wie gewinnen wir die Arbeiterinnen für die Revolution?," *Parteiarbeiter*, 10 March 1924.

164 Memo of 9 February 1924 (addressee illegible), BA Berlin 15.07 St12/83. See also FRS reports to the party central, August–September 1921 and May 1922, SAPMO-BA I/2/701/12.

165 See, for example, the FRS April 1924 report in SAPMO-BA I/2/701/12.

166 Braunthal to the KPD Central, Reich Election Committee, 1 March 1924, SAPMO-BA I/2/701/30.

167 FRS report, January–February 1924, SAPMO-BA I/2/701/12; FRS circular 2, 8 March 1924, SAPMO-BA I/2/701/14. Clara Zetkin's correspondence reveals her to be sympathetic to these complaints; see letters exchanged 23 December 1923, 23 February 1924, and 11 March 1924 with a female functionary in Saxony named "Alma," SAPMO BA NL Zetkin, FBS 265/16042/100.

168 "Annemarie" (Braunthal) to Zetkin, 21 March 1924, SAPMO-BA I/2/701/30.

169 *Bericht über den 9. Parteitag der KPD*, 64/30–33, 195–96.

170 Zetkin remained a respected figure, but her actual power diminished after she left the party central in 1921; Kontos, *Partei kämpft wie ein Mann!*, 55–56. Braunthal's letter is in SAPMO-BA I/2/701/30.

171 See the following *RF* articles: "Was geht das Sachverständigengutachten die Frauen an?," 25 June 1924; "Die Peitsche saust!," 3 October 1924 ("Die Kommunistin" section); "Was Arbeiterfrauen kaufen—und was sie nicht kaufen können," 7 October 1924.

172 "Die Kommunistin," *RF*, 12 September 1924; "Moralische Initiative in Rußland," *Welt am Abend*, 10 June 1924.

173 "Die Liebe geben und Geld nehmen. Was sie waren und wie sie wurden: Bilder

aus dem Sumpf der Spießermoral," *RF*, 8 May 1924; "Was wird mit den Abtrei-bungsparagraphen?," 6 June 1924, and "Fort mit dem §218!," 14 June 1924, both in *Welt am Abend*.

174 The more independent *Welt am Abend* revealed cases of KPD/SPD cooperation in the field. Compare *RF*'s "Nieder mit dem Mordparagraph 218!" (30 Septem-ber 1924) with *Welt am Abend*'s "Wir brauchen Soldaten: Deutsch-völkische Versammlung über 218" (28 June 1924). *Welt*'s owner, Willi Münzenberg, a Communist, often ran afoul of KPD chieftains who objected to his indepen-dent spirit. It is worth noting that his newspapers were more popular with working-class readers than the dreary *RF*. See Surmann, *Die Münzenberg-Legende*.

175 Reichskommissar für Überwachung der öffentlichen Ordnung, "Ausschnitt aus der Bericht Stuttgart . . . vom 30 August 1924," BA Berlin 15.07 St12/83.

176 "Referentenmaterial: Disposition für eine Wahlrede im Reichstagswahlkampf Herbst 1924," GStA/XII.HA/IV 91. This piece still used the name of Noske, the SPD "bloodhound" who used Freikorps brutally to put down the Janu-ary 1919 Spartacist uprising, to denote the SPD, indicating the intensity of fratricidal hatred on the German Left.

177 "Proletarische Kinder in Dreck und Schande!," *RF*, 27 November 1924. The piece assumed that venereal disease could be spread by poor hygiene and physical proximity, which, by deemphasizing sexual transmission as a cause, allows the infected to appear as innocent victims of social conditions. Com-pare Engelstein on early-twentieth-century Russia, "Morality and the Wooden Spoon."

178 *RF*, 15 November 1924.

179 "Die arbeitenden Frauen haben das Wort," *Die Kommunistin*, November 1924.

180 Untitled booklet, 1924, GStA/XII.HA/IV 89.

181 *Welt am Abend*, not *RF*, offered a more constructive solution to the housework problem. An article on a "truly liberated" woman showed her husband and children helping with the housework to allow her time for political activity; see "Arbeitszeit der Hausfrau," 22 November 1924.

182 "Tatsachen!," December 1924, GStA/XII.HA/IV 89.

183 "Das sozial-demokratische Wahlgeschäft" and "Keine Arbeiterfrau wählt So-zialdemokraten!," both 28 November 1924; "Die politische Gleichberechtigung der Frau und die Reichstagswahl: das Steckenpferd der Sozialdemokraten," 15 November 1924; "Nichtwähler und Frauen! An die Front!," 3 December 1924, all in *RF*.

184 It had lost nearly 1 million votes since May, while the SPD gained over 1.8 million.

185 Women's section report on the December 1924 campaign, SAPMO-BA I/2/701/30.

186 See women's section meeting of 15 and 19 December 1924, SAPMO-BA I/2/701/9.

187 Weitz, *Creating German Communism*, 151.

188 See "National-Sozialistische Freiheitsbewegung Deutschlands Vereinigte Völk-ische Liste: Allgemeine Grundsätzliche Richtlinien," LA 240/1941/19, and "Deutsch-Völkische Freiheitspartei. Allgemeine, grundsätzliche Richtlinien,"

GStA/XII.HA/IV 211. See also Koonz, *Mothers in the Fatherland*, 57, and Schmidt-Waldherr, *Emanzipation durch Professionalisierung?*, 28.

189   "Beamte! Beamtinnen! Angestellte! Pensionäre!," May 1924, GStA/XII.HA/IV 211; G. Feder, "Des Weibes Kulturtat," *VB*, 9 December 1920; "Frauen-studium—Frauenberuf," *VB*, 15 July 1920.

190   "Die Zehn Gebote," NSDAP, *Taschen-Jahrbuch* (1924); "Deutsche Frau!," n.d., Hoover GSC/13/117; Feder, "Des Weibes Kulturtat."

191   "Wo sind unsere Töchter?," n.d., Hoover Franz Coll. box 2; untitled flyer, 1921, Hoover GSC/14/129.

192   "Wer schuf die Zwangswirtschaft? hat aber nie angestanden!," 1923, Hoover Loesch Coll. 3/38; "Deutsche Frau!"

193   "Deutsche Frauen!," 1924, Hoover GSC/13/117; "Deutschland," n.d., Hoover Mueller-Graeff Coll. box 3.

194   "Die Religion ist in Gefahr!," 1924, NSDAP/HA 42/869.

195   Liebe, *Deutschnationale Volkspartei*, 95.

196   See the December 1924 flyer entitled "Arbeiter!," which also addresses nu-merous occupations, and "Kunstler! Geistesarbeiter!," both GStA/XII.HA/IV 188.

197   "Deutsche Hausfrau!," May 1924, GStA/XII.HA/IV 187; "Deutsche Hausfrau!," December 1924 poster, BA ZSg 1-44/9.

198   "Deutsche Arbeiterfrauen!," BA ZSg 1-44/11.

199   "Die Deutschnationalen und die Angestellten," *Deutschnationales Rüstzeug* 8; "Die Stellungnahme der DNVP zu den Goldgehaltern und zum Abbau des Berufsbeamtentums!," BA ZSg 1-44/11. "Beamte, was taten die Deutsch-nationalen für Euch!," GStA/XII.HA/IV 187, boasts of securing a "wife supplement" for married civil servants.

200   "Beamtinnen und weibliche Angestellte aller Berufe!," May 1924, GStA/XII.HA/IV 187; "Kolleginnen in Handels-, Industrie- und sonstigen Büros," December 1924, GStA/XII.HA/IV 188; "Die Frau in Familie und Staat," *Deutschnationales Rüstzeug* 7.

201   For details, see Bridenthal, "Class Struggle around the Hearth," 246–50.

202   See "Deutsche Schwestern!," May 1924, GStA/XII.HA/IV 187; "Die Frau in Familie und Staat"; and Behm, quoted in *Führer durch den Reichsparteitag der DNVP, 1924*. For an appeal to doctors, see "Deutsche Ärzte, Zahnärtzte, Apotheker und Tierärzte!," December 1924, GStA/XII.HA/IV 188.

203   "Deutsche Frauen und Mädchen!," May 1924, BA ZSg 1-44/9. For this lan-guage in appeals to other groups, see "Kommilitoninnen, Kommilitonen!" and "Kunstler und Geistesarbeiter!," December 1924, both GStA/XII/HA.IV 188. On the Dawes Plan, see "Deutsche Frauen! Welchen Weg wollt ihr gehen!?," May 1924, GStA/XII.HA/IV 187. Anti-Dawes language disappears in December.

204   Scheck, "German Conservatism," 50; Reagin, *German Women's Movement*, 223.

205   "Wir deutsche Frauen in Stadt und Land . . ." and "An die weiblichen Haus-angestellten!," both May 1924, GStA/XII.HA/IV 187.

206   "Wir Landfrauen wissen genau . . . ," May 1924, GStA/XII.HA/IV 187; "An die weiblichen Hausangestellten!"

207   "Arbeiter, auf ein Wort!," 1924, LA 240/1076/18.

208 "Die Falschspieler!," May 1924, BA ZSg 1-44/9. See also "An die weiblichen Hausangestellten!" and "Deutsche Frauen!"

209 "Was uns die Republik bescherte!" and "Denkt nach, ihr deutsche Frauen!," both December 1924, BA ZSg 1-44/9.

210 "Deutsche Arbeiterfrauen!" and "Die Frau in Familie und Staat."

211 "Wir wissen, was wir am 4. Mai zu tun haben, wir deutsche Frauen!" and "Frauen!," both May 1924, GStA/XII.HA/IV 187; "Deutsche Schwestern!"; "Arbeiter!," December 1924, GStA/XII.HA/IV 188.

212 See "Deutsche Erzieher!" and "Landlehrer, wo sitzt Euer wahrer Freund?," both December 1924, GStA/XII.HA/IV 188.

213 See "Wir wissen" and "Die Frau in Familie und Staat."

214 In May, 4 of its 106 delegates elected were women; in December it was 5 of 103—the lowest percentage of female representation of any party except the NSDAP. See Boak, "Women in Weimar Politics," table 1.

215 Only reports for the 1920 and 1929 party conferences exist. These yield little information on this issue, as the conferences were intended mainly as pompous shows of party unity. Internal publications, too, seem more like a place to present the accepted party line than a forum for debate.

216 Scheck, "German Conservatism," 48.

217 This is how they are profiled in "Deine Reichstagskandidaten!," December 1924, BA ZSg 1-44/9.

218 "Vorwärts zur Wahl!," December 1924, GStA/XII.HA/IV 188.

CHAPTER THREE

1 Childers, *Nazi Voter*, 127–47.

2 In February 1926, 21.4 percent of all union members were unemployed.

3 In the 1907 census, white-collar women comprised 5 percent of all women working; in 1925 they were 12.6 percent. For detailed analysis of the census, see Rosa Kempf's 1931 study, *Die deutsche Frau nach der Volkszählung.*

4 Petro, *Joyless Streets*, 69.

5 Ostwald, in *Sittengeschichte der Inflation*, 7–8, traces this back to the hyperinflation.

6 Female participation fell steadily from the unusually high peak of the 1919 election until 1930 (as did male turnout). Bremme calculates from available statistics that female turnout lagged, on average, 5–10 percent behind male. See *Politische Rolle der Frau*, 28–31.

7 The Sunday outing was immortalized in the 1929 film *Menschen am Sonntag.* Many essays in *Mein Arbeitstag—Mein Wochenende* note how anticipation of a Sunday *Ausflug* helped working-class women get through the week.

8 This constituted an increase of 5 percent. The 1925 census reported that 35.6 percent of women had paid employment; 55 percent of them worked in agriculture or family businesses, though that figure was falling. See Kempf, *Die deutsche Frau nach der Volkszählung*; Bridenthal and Koonz, "Beyond *Kinder, Küche, Kirche*"; and Frevert, *Women in German History*, 185.

9 Usborne, *Politics of the Body*, 91–93; Grossmann, "New Woman"; Hong, *Welfare, Modernity, and the Weimar State*, 27.

10 For details, see Usborne, *Politics of the Body*, chap. 4.

11 See Hausen, "Mother's Day."

12 "Wahlkampf," *Germania*, 10 May 1928.

13 This was also stressed in the section on women in an official party history released that year; see Lipinski, *Sozialdemokratie von ihren Anfängen bis zur Gegenwart* 2:229–32.

14 "Frauen! Auf zur Präsidentenwahl!," March 1925, BA ZSg 1-90/19; "Die Wählerin," April 1925, GStA/XII.HA/IV 66/2.

15 "Beamte, denkt daran!," *Vorwärts*, 17 May 1928.

16 "Liebe Else!," Hoover GSC/33; "Frauen, merkt auf!," BA ZSg 1-90/23; "Die Wählerin," May 1928, GStA XII.HA/IV 73; "Frauen Berlins!," November 1928, Hoover GSC/5; Minna Todenhagen, "Dem Gedanken des Tages," *Vorwärts*, 27 March 1927. For appeals to general audiences, see "Sie ziehen an einem Strick!," May 1928, BA ZSg 1-90/23, and "Wohin treiben wir?," 1927 Werbewoche circular, GStA/XII.HA/IV 71. On SPD conceptions of democracy, see Harsch, *German Social Democracy*, 9–11, 171.

17 In Hoover Poster Coll. GE 1715. I thank Jeff Fear for sharing his insights on this poster.

18 "Du, deutsche Jugend . . . ," 1928, BA ZSg 1-27/20 (2).

19 "3 Fragen an die Frauen," 1928, BA ZSg 1-27/19 (6).

20 See "3 Fragen"; "Postbeamtinnen!," 1928, GStA/XII.HA/IV 142; M.-E. Lüders, "Farbe bekennen!," *BT*, 18 May 1928; and "Programm der Deutschen Demokratischen Partei," in *Organisations-Handbuch der DDP*. Otto-Peters's argument that women deserved rights both because they were human beings and because they possessed particular "female" strengths, which could promote freedom and humanity in both the family and the public sphere, informs this imagery. See Clemens, *Menschenrechte*, 17.

21 Paul, *Aufstand der Bilder*, 84. For 1928 campaign themes, see NSDAP/HA 3/82. For a sample general appeal, see "An das ganze schaffende Deutschland!," *VB*, 15 May 1928.

22 "Wehrt Euch gegen die wahre Beherrscher Deutschlands!," 1928, Hoover GSC/33. See also Graf Westarp, "Zehn Jahre republikanische Unfreiheit: Das Verbrechen vom 9. November und seine Folgen," 1928, BA ZSg 1-44/6 (12).

23 In Berlin and Leipzig women comprised about 59 percent of the DNVP vote; in Catholic areas less than half; see Bremme, *Politische Rolle der Frau*, table 24. Where votes were counted by sex, 13.3 percent of all women and 10.1 percent of men voted DNVP; see Falter, Lindenberger, and Schumann, *Wahlen und Abstimmungen*, table 1.6.1.1. The 200,000-strong Evangelical Women's Association (VEFD) remained a DNVP ally and booster; on this alliance in this period, see Kaufmann, *Frauen zwischen Aufbruch und Reaktion*, 59–72. DVP women resented this, as it violated the VEFD's official neutrality; see DVP Reichsgeschäftsstelle Wahlbrief 6 (5 May 1928), "Parteipolitik in der Frauenbewegung," BA Berlin 60 Vo 1/53169/224.

24 "Dr. Marie Elisabeth Lüders für die Befreiung der Frau!," May 1928, GStA

XII.HA/IV 142; "Frauen denkt daran!," 1928, BA ZSg 1-27/19 (5). See also "Hausfrau—merk' auf!," 1928, BA ZSg 1-27/19 (6); "An die Klein-Rentner," May 1928, GStA/XII.HA/IV 142; and "Der letzter Appell," May 1928, Hoover GSC/33. For appeals to other groups, see "Landvolk in Not!," "Deutsche Angestellte!," and "Mittelstandspolitik!," all 1928, GStA/XII.HA/IV 142. The DDP had slid from over 5.6 million votes in January 1919 to 1.5 million in May 1928; see Falter, Lindenberger, and Schumann, *Wahlen und Abstimmungen*, table 1.3.1.1.

25 Crew, "Ambiguities of Modernity," 338.

26 For details, see "Die Sozial-Demokratie im Wahlkampf 1928," BA ZSg 1-90/23.

27 Harsch says that by 1928 between one-quarter and one-third of SPD voters were nonproletarians; see *German Social Democracy*, 29.

28 For voting statistics, see Falter, Lindenberger, and Schumann, *Wahlen und Abstimmungen*, table 1.6.1.1. It is worth remembering that the national total does not always match the total numbers given when votes are tabulated by sex because not all electoral districts kept sex-specific tallies. SPD, *Jahrbuch* (1928), put national female membership at 198,771 at the end of 1928, up 17,230 from the previous year. This made women 21.2 percent of total party membership.

29 "Beamte! Parteigenossen!," 1928 flyer, GStA XII.HA/IV 73.

30 For examples, see "Wer soll da hinein?," 1928 pamphlet, Hoover GSC/33; "Die Wählerin," March 1925, GStA/XII.HA/IV 66/1; "2 1/2 Millionen Frauen-überschuss in Deutschland," October 1926 Saxon Landtag election, Hoover GSC/28.

31 "Und wie wohnst Du?," BA ZSg 1-90/18; "Frauen, merkt auf!"

32 Weitz, *Creating German Communism*, 110.

33 In Hoover GSC/33.

34 Catholic and white-collar women were seen as particularly susceptible to "cultural" issues; see ZK Sekretariat–Frauen "Kursusdisposition," memo, 15 August 1928, BA-SAPMO I/2/701/21. For more discussion of women's interests, see "Wie gewinnen wir die Betriebsarbeiterin," *Parteiarbeiter*, December 1927, and protocol of women's section meeting, 13 January 1925, SAPMO-BA I/2/701/9.

35 "Frauenstimme: Aufklärung zum Volksentscheid," LA 240/2088/250; "Frauen-welt: Sonderflugblatt zur Volksentscheid," "Mutter! Die Fürsten prassen!," and "Schloß Oels in Schlesien," all GStA/XII.HA/IV 69; "Milliarden den Fürsten—uns tut Not!," poster, GStA/XII.HA/IV 70.

36 Reproduced in Hessisches Landesmuseum, *Politische Plakate der Weimarer Republik*, 72. A similar message appears in a general 1928 flyer, "Wer *muss* sozialistisch wählen?," in BA ZSg 1-90/23, which addresses several groups who are all encouraged to vote SPD "for the sake of the children."

37 "Die Wählerin"; "Frauenstimme," *Vorwärts*, 12 May 1928; "Wer soll da hinein?" Military spending came back to haunt the SPD when it discovered that several of its cabinet members later in 1928 raised no objection to a new battleship; see Kolb, *Weimar Republic*, 78.

38 "Arbeiterinnen! Hausfrauen!," April 1925, GStA/XII.HA/IV 94; "Frauen, denkt an den 'Retter'!," *RF*, 30 September 1927; "Brotverteuerung . . . ," May 1928, GStA/XII.HA/IV 100.

39 "Frauen, Mütter deutscher Volksgenossen!" and "An alle Frauen!," both BA ZSg 1-108/9. While Marx's share of the vote roughly matched the percentage

of Catholic women in the electorate (33.4), 57.9 percent of women overall voted for Hindenburg in 1925, compared to 54.1 percent of men. See Falter, Lindenberger, and Schumann, *Wahlen und Abstimmungen*, table 1.6.1.2.

40   "An alle Frauen!," April 1925, Staatsarchiv Hamburg; "Der Wahlaufruf des preussischen Zentrums," *Germania*, 24 April 1928.

41   The Barmat brothers were businessmen who profited handsomely during the inflation; their close ties to several SPD officials, including President Ebert, aroused suspicion. For details, see Friedrich, *Before the Deluge*, 199–201. The SPD in 1928 responded by including "government reform" in its list of demands.

42   "Das Tagewerk der Bonzen," 1928, BA ZSg 1-44/11; "Wehrt euch gegen die wahren Beherrscher Deutschlands!"

43   "Von Frauen an Frauen!," October 1925 Berlin election, GStA XII.HA/IV 190; Evangelische Frauenverband Berlins, "Wen wählt die christliche Frau?," April 1925, LA 240/1962/23; "Deutsche Frauen!," 1926, GStA/XII.HA/IV 191.

44   Reagin, *German Women's Movement*, 210.

45   Hong, *Welfare, Modernity, and the Weimar State*, 36.

46   See "Wen wählt die christliche Frau?"; "Deutsche Frauen!," *Deutschnationales Rüstzeug* 1C; "Deutsche Arbeiterin! Deutsche Arbeiterfrau!," 1928, BA ZSg 1-44/11; and "Von Frauen an Frauen!"

47   Childers, "Languages of Liberalism," 334.

48   "Frauenkundgebungen für Hindenburg," *Berliner Stimmen*, 25 April 1925. Stresemann had deep reservations about Hindenburg's candidacy and endorsed him only at the last minute. The women's endorsement, however, sounded quite enthusiastic, betraying a difference of opinion within the party along gender lines.

49   Dr. Wildebrandt, "Die Staatsangehörigkeit der Frau," *Berliner Stimmen*, 9 May 1925. See also the following in *Berliner Stimmen*: "Reichsfrauentagung der DVP in Jena," December 1926; "Mitteilungen," 1 April 1926; "Reichsfrauenausschuß," October 1926; and Mende, "Politische Wünsche zum Neuen Jahr," January 1928. See also *Wahlhandbuch 1928*, 414–42, and "Der Wahlaufruf der Deutschen Volkspartei," *DAZ*, 23 April 1928.

50   See "2 1/2 Millionen Frauenüberschuss," and *Die Sozialdemokratie im Reichstage 1925*, 222.

51   "Wer *muss* sozialistisch wählen?"; "Frauen an die Front!," poster, Hoover GSC/33.

52   Else Scheibenhuber, in SPD, *Sozialdemokratischer Parteitag 1925*, 168; Marie Juchasz, "Die Frau und die Sozialdemokratie," *Vorwärts*, 6 November 1927. This also appears in Sozialdemokratischer Landtagsfraktion, *Referentenmaterial für die Wahl zum Preußischen Landtag 1928*, 56.

53   For examples, see *Arbeiter-Taschenkalender* (1925); "Die werktätige Frau an die Wahlfront!," *RF*, 29 April 1928; and *Der Reichstag 1924–1928*, 485.

54   While this message found little resonance during the relative stability of the mid-1920s, nagging unemployment fed a stream of support that slowly helped the KPD in 1928 gain over half a million votes since December 1924.

55   SPD, *Sozialdemokratischer Parteitag 1927*, 327.

56   "Beamte! Parteigenossen!"

57 "Frauen, merkt auf!"

58 "Richtlinien für die Arbeit unter den Frauen," 12.

59 "Zur internationalen Frauenwoche," *Parteiarbeiter*, February 1928.

60 "Arbeiterinnen! Hausfrauen!"; "Arbeiterinnen und Hausfrauen!," Hoover GSC/11/91.

61 "Die Frauen an die Soldaten," 1925, GStA/XII.HA/IV 94.

62 The page in question is 3 December, in Hoover GSC/21/217.

63 See the DNVP program in *Politischer Almanach 1926*; *Deutschnationales Rüstzeug* 1C; and "Deutsche Arbeiterin!"

64 See "Der Reichs-Vertretertag des Deutschen Frauenordens," *VB*, 25 October 1927; "Volk und Mütter," *VB*, 27 March 1927; "Über Frauenberufe," *VB*, 25 March 1927; and Walter Bobe, "Die Aufgaben der Frauenwelt in der N.S.D.A.P.," *VB*, 18 June 1927.

65 "An die Adresse der Wählerin," *Frauenwelt* section of *Germania*, 13 May 1928.

66 "Was wir wollen!," October 1925, GStA/XII.HA/IV 114; *Politisches Jahrbuch 1925*, 377–81, in BA ZSg 1-108/22; "Frauenwelt," *Germania*, 22 April 1928.

67 *Politisches Jahrbuch 1925*.

68 See "Postbeamtinnen!"; "Dr. Marie Elisabeth Lüders"; Gertrud Wittstock, "Demokratische politische Frauenarbeit," *Materialien zur Demokratischen Politik 143* (1928); and *Frauenarbeit in der DDP*, 7.

69 Membership—and the dues it yielded—hit new lows, falling from roughly 900,000 in 1919, to 131,794 in 1925, to 116,873 in 1927; see Fricke et al., *Lexikon zur Parteiengeschichte*, entry on the DDP. See also Jones, *German Liberalism*, 294–302.

70 See "Dr. Marie Elisabeth Lüders"; "Postbeamtinnen!"; and Wittstock, "Demokratische politische Frauenarbeit." "Der letzter Appell" contains candidate profiles.

71 "Der Gross-Berliner Wähler," October 1925, LA 240/2381/177; "Reichsfrauentagung."

72 "Die weibliche Angestellte sagt: Ich wähle immer DVP . . . ," May 1928, BA ZSg 1-42/8. The image of female white-collar worker as bridge between "the working masses and powerful capital" also appeared in "Mitteilungen," *Berliner Stimmen*, 1 April 1926. Compare "Deutsche Studenten, Kommilitonen!" and "Deutscher Mittelstand!," both 1928, GStA/XII.HA/IV 169.

73 The writer praised a new generation of women who refused to see work as a substitute for disappointments elsewhere: "We need women who innerly embrace work as models for the next generation—not only girls but young men—so they learn to work in harmony . . . on the task of renewing the German spirit" (M. Steffann, "Lebensgestaltung der berufstätigen Frau," *Berliner Stimmen*, December 1926).

74 "Deutsche Frauen wählt!," May 1928, GStA/XII.HA/IV 169; "Frauen Berlins!," October 1925, GStA/XII.HA/IV 167; Anny Kulesza on women and education in *Deutscher Aufbau*, BA ZSg 1-42/14 [6].

75 Else Frobenius, "An die Frauen," *DAZ*, 16 May 1928; "Einladung zu einer Öffentlichen Frauenkundgebung," May 1928, BA ZSg 1-42/8; Anni Klingspor obituary, *Berliner Stimmen*, 1 July 1926.

76 *Wahlhandbuch 1928*, 437–40.

77 Schmidt-Waldherr, *Emanzipation durch Professionalisierung?*, 205.

78 "Achtung Hausfrauen!," October 1925, GStA/XII.HA/IV 167; Frobenius, "An die Frauen"; *Wahlhandbuch 1928*, 414–23; "Was muß die Hausfrau über die Teuerung, ihre Ursachen und ihre Bekämpfung wissen?," *Merkblätter für die Parteiarbeit*, December 1925. The BDF, which many DVP women still belonged to, also encouraged women to rationalize housework to provide more time for politics; see Schmidt-Waldherr, *Emanzipation durch Professionalisierung?*, 178.

79 "Frauen denkt daran!"; "Hausfrau, merk' auf!" On women and logic, see "Vernunft muss siegen" and "An die deutsche Frauen," both April 1925, GStA XII.HA/IV 139.

80 See the following in *Vorwärts*: "Die neue Familie," 3 April 1927, and "Die Frau und die Technik," 4 November 1927. Minna Todenhagen notes technology's negative impact on unemployment in "Dem Gedanken des Tages."

81 "Die neue Familie."

82 "Wahlkampf," *Germania*, 10 May 1928.

83 Synopsis taken from Weiss, *Der nationale Wille*, 204–7.

84 Ruppert, *Im Dienst am Staat*, 321. See also motions adopted at the fourth Reich party conference (November 1925) in *Offizieller Bericht* and "An die Adresse der Wählerin." On Center policies and their relationship to the Catholic milieu, see Rosenhaft, "Women, Gender, and the Limits of Political History," 157.

85 "Für Freiheit und Recht! Gegen den Kulturkampf!," May 1928, Hoover GSC/30/100; "Wähler und Wählerinnen!," Hoover GSC/33; "10 Gebote," *Germania*, 19 May 1928.

86 "Wen wählt die christliche Frau?"; "Von Frauen an Frauen!" See also "Bürger und Bürgerinnen!," October 1925 Berlin election, GStA/XII.HA/IV 190.

87 "Das Wahlprogramm der Deutschnationalen," *DAZ*, 19 April 1928; "Was muß der Wähler für den 20. Mai wissen?," 1928, GStA/XII.HA/IV 192; "Die Sozialdemokratie: Sozialdemokratie zu Kultur- und Frauenfragen," *Deutschnationales Rüstzeug* 1C (1928), BA ZSg 1-44/10; Westarp, "Zehn Jahre republikanische Unfreiheit."

88 "Von Frauen an Frauen!"; "Die Sozialdemokratie."

89 M. von Tiling, "Wir Frauen und die christliche Schule," BA ZSg 1-44/6 (13); "Deutschnationale Volkspartei in der Reichstagswahl (1928)," Hoover GSC/30; Westarp, "Zehn Jahre republikanische Unfreiheit." For posters, see "Wir halten fest am Wort Gottes!," 1928, Hoover GSC/33, and "Wir halten fest am Gebet!," Hoover Mueller-Graeff Coll. box 3. The Schulgesetz was also the focus of the national DNVP women's conference in 1925.

90 "Der Wahlaufruf der Deutschen Volkspartei"; *Wahlhandbuch 1928*, 419.

91 *Preußen-politik 1925–28*, BA ZSg 1-42/14 (5); *Berliner Stimmen*, 25 October 1925, 2; "Frauen Berlins!"

92 "Frauen Berlins!"; "Was geht uns Frauen den 20. Mai an?," 1928, BA ZSg 1-42/8.

93 "Was geht uns Frauen den 20. Mai an?"

94 G. Rageota, "Mutterschaft oder persönliche Freiheit," *BT*, 16 May 1928.

95 Poster reprinted in Hessisches Landesmuseum, *Politische Plakate der Weimarer Republik*, 123.

96 "Die nationalen Aufgaben der Frau," 1928 *Werbewoche* essay, NSDAP/HA 38/753.

97 "Die sozial-demokratische Partei," *Materialien zur Demokratischen Politik 139* (1928); "3 Fragen."

98 Erkelenz, "Demokratische Partei und Presse," December 1926, GStA/XII.HA/ IV 141.

99 Bäumer, *Die Frau in der Krise der Kultur.* Bäumer was a major force behind the antismut law, as was the BDF.

100 A total of 491 Reichstag seats were open in May 1928. In December 1924, the DDP won 6.3 percent of all votes cast; in 1928 this shrank to 4.8 percent, a 21.7 percent loss. In areas where votes were tallied by sex, the DDP's male and female shares were now equal. See Falter, Lindenberger, and Schumann, *Wahlen und Abstimmungen*, tables 1.3.1.1, 1.3.1.3, and 1.6.1.1.

101 For example, see "An das ganze schaffende Deutschland!"

102 "Wo bleiben die Frauenvereine?," *VB*, 27/28 February 1927; "Ehe und freie Liebe in Sowjetrussland," *VB*, 18 March 1927; "Vernichtung der Frauenehre in Sowjetjudäa," *VB*, 30 September 1927.

103 "Der Blutrausch des Bolshewismus," in Hoover GSC/14/129. See also "Die Stadt der Unehelichen," *VB*, 29 September 1927; "Amerikatollheit," *VB*, 18 March 1927; and "Der Geburtenrückgang in Deutschland," *VB*, 5 April 1928.

104 "Man ziehe die Priester aus den Parlamenten," *VB*, early March 1928; "Der Geburtenrückgang in Deutschland"; Dr. phil. Reche, "Sterilisierung Minderwertiger?," *VB*, 6/7 February 1927.

105 Gerhard Paul notes that the NSDAP tried to tone down its anti-Semitism (*Aufstand der Bilder*, 87). While many broadly circulated materials were less inflammatory, those who wrote the items discussed did not always get the message.

106 See Käthe Schirmacher's speech, in which she blasted the "bolshevizing" effects of French *Negermoral* and predicted that the coming world war being prepared by "Wall Street and Moscow" would pit white against black, in *Führer durch den Reichsparteitag der DNVP 1926.*

107 SPD, *Jahrbuch* (1927); "Frauen, merkt auf!"

108 The SPD's Freethinker organization had 600,000 members by the late 1920s; see Lösche and Walter, "Zur Organisationskultur," 513. Mathilde Wurm at the 1925 women's conference called Catholicism a danger for every liberationist movement (SPD, *Protokoll* [1925], 352), while Erich Mäder at the 1927 party conference blasted any softening toward religion as a violation of the spirit of Bebel and Marx (SPD, *Protokoll* [1927], 68). Toni Pfülf, however, at the 1927 women's conference, warned the party to use tact so as not to alienate the many religious proletarian women (SPD, *Protokoll* [1927], 323).

109 "Die werktätige Frau an die Wahlfront!"; "Was will der Rote Frauen- und Mädchenbund?," *RF*, 11 February 1928; "Arbeiterin, was geht dich die Politik an?," 1927, BA ZSg 1-65/14.

110 "Deutsche Frauen und Mädchen!," May 1928, GStA/XII.HA/IV 72; Todenhagen, "Dem Gedanken des Tages."

111 See Meyer-Renschhausen, "Bremen Morality Scandal." For a leftist perspective, see "Rund um Kolomak: Veraltete Paragraphen einer verkrachten Zeit," *Welt am Abend*, 22 June 1927. The KPD and some SPD members objected to the 1927

law because it could potentially be used to harass the sex reform movement; see Grossmann, *Reforming Sex*, 11.

112 See the following articles in *Vorwärts*'s women's section, 1927: Dr. F. Dyren-furth, "Die gewaltsame Unterbrechung der Schwangerschaft," 13 October; "Wie wird Abtreibung gestraft?" and "Die neue Mutterschaft," 1 September; A. Faust, "Doppelte Moral," 7 July; "Ein Aufschrei der Not," 26 May; "Ge-burtenkontrolle und Ethik," 3 March; "Warum Sexualberatung?," 3 February; and "Bei den 'Abtreibern,'" 20 January.

113 "Die Frau in der Politik und Beruf," BA ZSg 1-90/23 (10). See also Saldern, "Modernization as Challenge," 99.

114 "Wir Mütter," in *Wahlauftakt 1928*, Hoover GSC/53; "Wir kämpfen für Mutter und Kind," Hoover GSC/5; Sozialdemokratischer Landtagsfraktion, *Referenten-material für die Wahl zum Preußischen Landtag 1928*, 57. The SPD had no single position on eugenics (Hong, *Welfare, Modernity, and the Weimar State*, 252); for various party pronouncements on eugenics, see Usborne, *Politics of the Body*, 58, 138.

115 Toni Breitscheid, "Einheit der Frauenbewegung?," *Vorwärts*'s women's page, 13 October 1927.

116 Dr. Rosenfeld argued at the 1927 party conference that homosexuality had always existed and that it made no sense to fight a "sickness" with illegality; see SPD, *Protokoll* (1927), 153.

117 L. Nagy, "Der Proletarier und seine Frau," *Vorwärts*, 2 February 1927.

118 "Die Frauen am 20. Mai: Frauenrecht—Frauenpflicht," *Vorwärts*, 13 May 1928.

119 "Wie mobilisieren wir die Frauen zum Kongress?," *Parteiarbeiter*, October 1926, 297–98.

120 "Arbeiterinnen und Hausfrauen!"; "Fort mit dem Abtreibungsparagraphen," Hoover Mueller-Graeff Coll. box 4.

121 Dr. K. Hiller, "Über Abtreibung, Sodomie und Ungezucht," *Welt am Abend*, 2 June 1927; RFMB Bundesleitung Abschrift, February 1928, BA Berlin 15.07 St12/91 Bd. 22; "Was will der Rote Frauen- und Mädchenbund?"; "Letzter Appell!," May 1928, GStA/XII.HA/IV 100.

122 "Die werktätige Frau an die Wahlfront!" See also "Proletarische Frauen!," October 1926 Saxon Landtag election, Hoover GSC/28, and "Referenten-material," 1926, BA ZSg 1-65/13.

123 Usborne, *Politics of the Body*, 162.

124 See Grossmann, *Reforming Sex*, especially chap. 4.

125 Usborne writes that the KPD did not officially suggest contraception as a way to prevent abortion until 1928 (*Politics of the Body*, 116), though articles on the subject did appear in *Rote Fahne* in 1927: "Madam wünscht keine Kinder," 16 March; "Sexualreform in der Sowjetunion," 28 October; and "Gegen den Gebärzwang," 15 July. As in so many other areas, *Welt am Abend* was far quicker to present reproduction in a less polemic, franker style to working-class readers.

126 "Wie wählten die Frauen?," *Parteiarbeiter*, July 1928.

127 "Um den §218 des R. Str. G. (Abtreibung)," *Zentrum—Politisches-Agitation Material* (1926).

128 "An die Adresse der Wählerin"; "Anträge und Entschliessungen," *Fünfte Reichs-parteitag des Zentrums*. Note that the 13 May 1928 women's section of *Germania* devoted three pages to Mother's Day. See also two posters from Hoover Mueller-Graeff Coll. box 4: "Sorgt für unsere Zukunft" and "Wer schützt Familie-Heimat-Arbeit?"

129 Brandt wrote "Die Sozialdemokratie"; see also "Deutsche Arbeiterin!" and "Das Tagewerk der Bonzen."

130 The DDP officially rejected abortion on demand but agreed with the reform bill because, as Lüders put it, "the severe laws" had not saved "the life of even one infant." See Usborne, *Politics of the Body*, 172.

131 A report on the Prussian party conference in *Berliner Stimmen*, June 1927, argued that current divorce law should only be expanded to include the mentally ill—other changes would not be in women's interest. The 1928 *Wahlhandbuch* said the DVP rejected abortion on ethical and medical grounds but approved of milder punishments for offenders.

132 "Für uns wählt Deutsche Volkspartei!," n.d., GStA/XII.HA/IV 170.

133 Petro, *Joyless Streets*, 127–32.

134 "Frau des schaffenden Volkes!," 1928, Hoover GSC/36; "Arbeiterin, was geht dich die Politik an?" See also the following 1927 *RF* pieces: "Wie werde ich schlank?," 29 January; "Wie werde ich schlank?," 6 February; "Wofür sie rationalisieren," 8 January; and "Die Mode der Dame," 21 September.

135 "Mannequinschule eröffnet Lehrgang," *RF*, 16 September 1927.

136 See the following *VB* pieces: "Erotische Reizkultur," 3 March 1928; Ernst Dombowski, "Tugend der deutschen Frau," 24 April 1927; and Edith Gräfin Salburg, "Die Entsittlichung der Frau durch die jüdische Mode," 18 June 1927.

137 On flyers using fashion, see "Ansprechende Flugblätter für die Frauen," October 1927, and "Wo ein Wille, da ein Weg," November 1928, both in *Parteiarbeiter*. The *RF* ad is in GStA XII.HA/IV 97. "Frau des schaffenden Volkes!"; "Arbeiterinnen! Arbeiterfrauen," May 1928, Hoover GSC/16/152.

138 For example, a DNVP flyer blasting SPD decadence also conveyed a negative image of the elegant, fashionable woman; see "Das Tagewerk der Bonzen."

139 The figure was actually closer to twenty. Party yearbooks list women's proportion of total party membership to be 15.8 percent in 1924, 21.2 percent in 1928, and 23 percent in 1931. See SPD, *Jahrbuch* (1924, 1928, 1931).

140 See "Nachwort zur Präsidentenwahl," *Die Genossin*, June/July 1925; Schneider, "Die deutsche Wählerin"; Siemsen, in Hagemann, *Frauenalltag und Männerpolitik*, 554; and "Wie wählen die Frauen?" See also Peterson, "Politics of Working-Class Women."

141 Janusch's study of SPD campaigns notes that in 1928 poster design, formerly left up to local groups, became centralized; over 3 million were distributed that year in large or postcard size. This was also the first SPD campaign to make extensive use of propaganda films. See *Plakative Propaganda der SPD*, 26–30.

142 Fabian, quoted in Hagemann, *Frauenalltag und Männerpolitik*, 541.

143 This attitude was replicated in *Die Genossin*; see November 1924 and December 1925 issues. It also marks the Berlin district's self-evaluation of its women's work; see *Jahresbericht 1925/1926*, 60–64. *Frauenwelt* was indeed a popular publication with rank-and-file women.

144 SPD, *Protokoll* (1927), 324.
145 See recap in *Die Genossin*, October 1925; SPD, *Jahrbuch* (1927), 190, also notes the glaring lack of women at the local level.
146 SPD, *Protokoll* (1925), 168.
147 Usborne, *Politics of the Body*, 50.
148 See Berlin police report of August 1925, BA Berlin 15.07 St12/83; "Abweisungen der Frauenabteilung: Auswertung der Bewegung für die Fürstenenteignung," SAPMO-BA I/2/701/14.
149 Arendt and Freigang, "Der Rote Frauen- und Mädchenbund," notes that RFMB membership peaked in 1927 at 25,000, surpassing total female membership in the KPD (16,200). See also Kontos, *Partei kämpft wie ein Mann!*, 60. On the RFMB's subsequent failure to expand, see Progress Report, Berlin Police Presidium, late February 1928, BA Berlin 15.07 St12/91 Bd. 21.
150 For female party membership, see Arendt, "Weibliche Mitglieder der KPD," table 1. In areas where votes were reported by sex in 1928, 20.3 percent of men and 15.5 percent of women voted KPD; see Falter, Lindenberger, and Schumann, *Wahlen und Abstimmungen*, table 1.6.1.1. Women comprised about 40 percent of the KPD vote, the lowest ratio during Weimar.
151 For general organizational developments in this period, see Weitz, *Creating German Communism*, 155–57, 171. The general line is also discussed in a 1925 women's strategy document by the KPD Zentrale, "Richtlinien für die Arbeit unter den Frauen," SAPMO-BA I/2/701/16.
152 See Weitz, *Creating German Communism*, 221.
153 "Arbeiterin, was geht dich die Politik an?," 20.
154 Sammelrundschreiben 42, 21 October 1927, SAPMO-BA I/2/701/14; RFMB Bundesleitung Abschrift, February 1928, BA Berlin 15.07 St12/91 Bd. 22.
155 See police report of October 1925, BA Berlin 15.07 St12/83.
156 "Partei in Not!," February 1926, and "Frauenzirkel im Grossbetrieb," May 1927, both in *Parteiarbeiter*; "Richtlinien für die Organisierung der Konferenzen werktätigen Frauen (endgültig)" and "Delegiertenkarte," both SAPMO-BA I/2/701/16. Canning describes similar "moments of inscription" among women in the German Textile Workers Union; see "Feminist History after the Linguistic Turn," 386.
157 "Abschrift aus der Anlage zu R.Ko.6575/25 II," BA Berlin 15.07 St12/83; "Frauenarbeit," November 1925, and "Zur internationalen Frauenwoche," February 1928, both in *Parteiarbeiter*.
158 See *Parteiarbeiter*: "In welche Zellen gehören die Frauen?," January 1926; "Winke für die Arbeit der Straßenzelle," March 1926; and "Der Betrieb ist die Grundlage der Parteiorganisation—nicht das Wohngebiet!," October 1927. See also 8 March 1926 report from the Reich Commissar of Public Order (Nr. 2043/26II—Berlin), BA Berlin 15.07 St12/83.
159 Rundschreiben der BL der KPD, Württemberg Abt. Frauen, 23 March 1926, BA Berlin 15.07 St12/83; 20 October 1926 letter to Politbüro, SAPMO-BA I/2/701/22; women's secretariat memo of 10 February 1927, SAPMO-BA I/2/701/14; "Tätigkeitsbericht der Frauenabteilung," April–June 1927, SAPMO-BA I/2/701/12; Halbe (Frauenabteilung) to the ZK, 24 January 1927, SAPMO-BA I/2/701/9.

160 "Wie eine Frauenveranstaltung organisiert werden muß," *Parteiarbeiter*, February 1928. For the damning memo, see "Zum Sammelrundschreiben Nr. 1, 1928: Arbeitsplan der Reichsfrauen-Abteilung," SAPMO-BA I/2/701/11.

161 For discussion of women's "illusions," see "Anweisungen an die Frauenabteilungen der K.L.," 25 May 1928, SAPMO-BA I/2/701/15. See also "Ausschnitt aus Lagebericht 9 Juni 1926 . . . Sitzung kommunistischer Frauenfunktionäre," 18 May 1926, BA Berlin 15.07 St12/83.

162 Checklist in Hoover Loesch Coll. SPD, *Jahrbuch* (1926), stated that of seven flyers for the 1926 communal elections, two were for women ("Die Frauen und die Gemeindewahlen" and "Das Frauenwahlrecht"); I was unable to locate these. The 1927 party conference briefly discussed the structure of the NSDAP women's organization.

163 Bobe, "Aufgaben der Frauenwelt."

164 Koonz, "Some Political Implications of Separatism."

165 Goebbels, quoted in "Reichs-Vertretertag des Deutschen Frauenordens." See also 1927 Parteitag report in NSDAP/HA 21/390.

166 In Hoover Mueller-Graeff Coll. box 3.

167 Bremme, *Politische Rolle der Frau*, 69.

168 Josef Traumann, in *Organisations-Handbuch für Zentrumswahler* (1925 ed.).

169 *Politisches Jahrbuch 1925*.

170 "Die Partei und der Reichsfrauenausschuß," *Unsere Partei*, 15 March 1927. This was this publication's only article on women in 1927.

171 Boak, "Women in Weimar Politics," 373.

172 Scheck, "German Conservatism," 49.

173 Jones, *German Liberalism*, 252, 291.

174 For the 1928 Reichstag election, I found no Center flyers produced solely for women, one from the DNVP, and three from the DVP.

175 Kempkes, *Deutscher Aufbau*, 22.

176 See protocol of Zentralvorstand meeting of 12 April 1919, BA R45 II/34. By 1929 Elsa Matz, chair of the Reichsfrauenausschuss, and Clara Mende, by virtue of her token membership in the *Vorstand*, were the only women on the executive, the true locus of power within the DVP.

177 See the following letters in BA R45 II/58: Matz to Kempkes, 19 February 1925; Reichsfrauenausschuss (Matz, Gertrud Wolf, and Alice Neven du Mont) to Vorstand/Stresemann, 15 December 1925; Magdeburger Frauenausschuss to Reichsfrauenausschuss, 23 November 1925; and protocols of executive (Geschäftsführender-Ausschuss) meetings, 27 January 1926 and 8 December 1927. On Stresemann addressing the Zentralvorstand as male, see protocol of meeting of 19 March 1927, in BA R45 II/42 (he does eventually slip into "meine Damen und Herren").

178 Hans Ehlermann, "Schriftenreihe für politische Werbung 1: der Wahlkampf 1928," GStA/XII.HA/IV 142.

179 "Die Frau und das Rathaus"; "Die Deutschnationale Volkspartei," *Materialien zur demokratischen Politik* 137 (1928).

180 Party chair Erich Koch-Weser openly justified the vote against equal rights for *Beamtinnen* as a tradeoff for the "greater goal" of overall salary reform for civil

servants; see Koch-Weser to DDP Reich Women's Organization, 21 December 1927, BA NL Lüders, 109.

181 Geysenheyner, quoted in *Frauenarbeit in der DDP*, 9–10; Lüders's critique found in a six-page memo of 6 June 1928 in BA NL Lüders, 109. See same folder for her memos dated 1 February and 1 March 1927 to Gertrud Wittstock documenting the effects of speaking tours to regional groups on her health and finances.

182 On this battle, see the following in BA NL Lüders, 109: memo Arbeitsgemeinschaft DDP Frauen von Potsdam II, 18 November 1927; protocol of Vorstand meeting, Frauenarbeitsausschuss Reichswahlbezirk Berlin, 23 November 1927; Frau E. Reiss to Lüders, 30 November 1927; Lüders to Herr Merten, 29 November 1927; Merten to Lüders, 3 December 1927; and Ilse von Huelsen-Reicke to Lüders, 15 December 1927.

183 "Die Berufsstellung der demokratischen Reichstagskandidaten," *Der Demokrat*, 10 May 1928.

184 See Ollendorf in *Frauenarbeit in der DDP*, 18. While only two of the twenty-five DDP Reichstag delegates elected in May 1928 were women, percentagewise the party still had more female representation than any other except the SPD and KPD.

185 See *Frauenarbeit in der DDP*, 22–23; Lüders, "Farbe bekennen!"

186 Childers, "Languages of Liberalism," 326.

187 Lüders, "Farbe bekennen!"

CHAPTER FOUR

1 Bridenthal and Koonz, "Introduction," 14–16.

2 Childers, *Nazi Voter*, 168.

3 Tatschmurat, "'Wir haben keinen Beruf,'" 22–29.

4 Soden, "'Hilft uns denn niemand?'"

5 Hausen, "Mother's Day."

6 "Busen und Hüften werden trotz alledem modern!," *8-Uhr Abendblatt*, 20 March 1930.

7 Fromm, *Working Class*, 148–62. Respondents were not limited to working-class men and women, despite the book's title.

8 Koonz, *Mothers in the Fatherland*, 106; Kardorff, *Brauchen wir eine Frauenpartei?*

9 Boak, "'Our Last Hope,'" 294.

10 For details, see Jones, *German Liberalism*, 385, and Childers, *Nazi Voter*, 139–52. On the reorganization of propaganda, see Paul, *Aufstand der Bilder*, 70–91.

11 Shively, "Party Identification."

12 There has been much debate on the degree to which women's allegiances were shifting to the NSDAP. Childers, in *Nazi Voter*, 188–89, sees the major breakthrough coming in 1932. Koonz stresses that by 1931 women were fewer than 50,000 of the NSDAP's 1 million members (*Mothers in the Fatherland*, 51–112). Boak, however, stresses the speed with which the female vote caught up to— and in some areas surpassed—the male NSDAP vote already by 1930 ("'Our

Last Hope'"). Considering how small the female NSDAP vote had previously been, except in isolated districts in Bavaria, any significant female shift to the party would show up as a high percentage increase. In areas where votes were tabulated by sex in 1930, 15.3 percent of women voted NSDAP, compared to 17.4 percent of men, a 12 percent difference according to Falter, Lindenberger, and Schumann, *Wahlen und Abstimmungen*, table 1.6.1.1.

13 See also Janusch, *Plakative Propaganda der SPD*, 91.

14 See *VB*, 14/15 September 1930.

15 "Pflicht und Arbeit unserer Schwestern," n.d., Hoover GSC/13/117.

16 "Des Muttertages Sinn," *VB*, 11/12 May 1930; "Der Sumpf," *VB*, 7/8 September 1930; "Die Entsittlichung des deutschen Volkes durch das Judentum," *VB*, 10/11 August 1930. See also Darré, "Marriage Laws and the Principles of Breeding," reprinted in *Weimar Republic Sourcebook*, 133–37.

17 "Weckruf Nr. 5," n.d., NSDAP/HA 71/1532.

18 "Stimmen aus dem Volke—Die weiblichen Angestellten," *VB*, 13 February 1930.

19 "Wählerinnen u. Wähler!," *VB*, 9 September 1930.

20 "Die 'Deutsche Staatspartei,'" *VB*, 1 August 1930.

21 On early Weimar *völkisch* discourse, see chapter 2. Alfred Rosenberg's *Myth of the Twentieth Century*, published in 1930, made this same argument about masculinity and femininity. Fears unleashed by the simultaneity of women's political and sexual emancipation were not confined to the NSDAP or even Germany; on Britain, for example, see Alberti, "Keeping the Candle Burning," 296.

22 "Erklärung," *Königshofener Zeitung*, 14 October 1930, NSDAP/HA 20A/1749.

23 The Center's vote fell only from 12.1 to 11.8 percent in 1930—numerically, it actually gained over 400,000 votes. See Falter, Lindenberger, and Schumann, *Wahlen und Abstimmungen*, tables 1.3.1.1 and 1.3.1.2.

24 "Arbeiterfrauen in der K.P.D.!," *VB*, 28 August 1930.

25 Jones, *German Liberalism*, 339–40.

26 Childers, *Nazi Voter*, 158.

27 Fifty percent of NSDAP voters in 1930 came from the DNVP; see Paul, *Aufstand der Bilder*, 93. See also Falter, Lindenberger, and Schumann, *Wahlen und Abstimmungen*, table 1.6.1.1. Compare with December 1924, in which 11.5 percent of women and 9.7 percent of men voted DNVP. Bremme shows that in Berlin, Frankfurt, and Leipzig the DNVP's gender gap widened in favor of women between 1928 and 1930; see *Politische Rolle der Frau*, table 24.

28 "An die deutschnationalen Frauen!," *Unsere Partei*, 6 August 1930, also published as DNVP flyer number 557.

29 "Ein zweites Sowjet-Sachsen gefällig?," in Hoover GSC/12.

30 "Was hat das Christentum zum Marxismus zu sagen?" This tract was a transcript of her speech at the 1929 party conference.

31 "Christliche Deutsche Männer und Frauen!," 1929 Saxon election, Hoover GSC/12.

32 Vorstand meeting, 8 April 1930, BA Berlin 60 Vo 2/45126/56. To Tiling's suggestion of more emphasis on Christianity in campaign slogans, Hugenberg recommends that "the men responsible for editorial changes" note this

(Müller-Otfried's name was then suggested by Käthe Schirmacher). Tiling wrote three major pamphlets between 1928 and 1930, while the few other existing women's materials have no attribution. On Tiling, see Kaufmann, *Frauen zwischen Aufbruch und Reaktion*, 72–76.

33 Tiling, *Konservativ oder Liberal?* See also Kaufmann, *Frauen zwischen Aufbruch und Reaktion*, 90–92.

34 See *Unsere Partei*, 1 September 1930, 1.

35 "Gesetze, welche die Hausfrauen in Stadt und Land angehen," *Deutschnationales Rüstzeug 22F* (1930). Bridenthal makes a similar argument about the term *Hausfrauenstand*; see "Organized Rural Women," 377.

36 See the following in *Unsere Partei*: "Margarete Behm," 1 May 1930; "Frau D. Müller-Otfried zum Gruss!," 15 June 1930; and "Käthe Schirmacher," 1 December 1930. On Schirmacher's early career, see Kaplan, *Making of the Jewish Middle Class*, 205; Clemens, *Menschenrechte*, 52–57; and Schmidt-Waldherr, *Emanzipation durch Professionalisierung?*, 164.

37 Konservative Volkspartei Reichsgeschäftsstelle to Alice Bensheimer of the BDF, 6 September 1930, in HLA BDF/52-239 [3]. On Hugenberg's plans, see Walker, "German Nationalist People's Party," 635, and Tormin, *Geschichte der deutschen Parteien*, 195. In terms of female candidates, the DNVP routinely had among the least.

38 This total includes votes won by the Center and its sister, the Bavarian People's Party.

39 Ruppert, *Im Dienst*, 357.

40 See the following 1930 appeals in *Germania*: "Drei Fragen an die Wähler," 7 September; "Zentrumsfrauen und Politik," 10 August; and "Der Wille zur Ordnung," 31 August, *Frauenwelt* section. See also Childers, *Nazi Voter*, 190.

41 Untitled flyer, LA 240/2088/81; "Die Zentrumspartei im Kampf," *Das Zentrum*, July/August 1930. See also "Um Staat und Volk!," *Frauenwelt* section of *Germania*, 7 September 1930, and "Die Frauen mahnen!," *Germania*, 14 September 1930.

42 Kaufmann, "Vom Vaterland zum Mutterland."

43 "Anträge und Entschliessungen," *Fünfte Reichsparteitag des Zentrums*; Morsey and Ruppert *Protokolle der Reichstagsfraktion* 2:246–47, 336.

44 Kaufmann, "Vom Vaterland zum Mutterland," 264.

45 "Große Frauen-Kundgebung," *Germania*, 4 September 1930; "Letzter Appell!," *Germania*, 14 September 1930.

46 "Die Frauen mahnen!"

47 *Das Zentrum*, for example, began in 1930 to increase its coverage of the NSDAP's ideology, history, and program.

48 "Was bedeutet die Strafrechtsreform?," *Das Zentrum*, July/August 1930. See also "An die Wählerinnen!," *Frauenwelt* section of *Germania*, 24 August 1930.

49 See the following in *Germania*'s *Frauenwelt* section: Helene Weber, "Führerinnen der Zentrumspartei," 14 September 1930; Helene Weber, "In letzter Stunde!," 7 September 1930; and Otto Mors, "Frauenaufgaben in der Politik," 10 August 1930. See also "Frauen zur Reichstagswahl," *Germania*, 3 September 1930, and "Drei Fragen an die Wähler."

50 "Letzter Appell!"; Weber, quoted in "Große Frauen-Kundgebung."

51 "An die Wählerinnen!"

52 See "An dich, katholische Frau!," *Frauenwelt* section of *Germania*, 31 August 1930.

53 "Nach der Wahl," *Frauenwelt* section of *Germania*, 21 September 1930. A 12 August 1930 letter from the Center to the BDF stated that its women's committee—not the party as a whole—would concern itself with finding more female candidates, but this appears to have yielded few tangible results; in HLA BDF/52-239 [2].

54 Kaufmann, "Vom Vaterland zum Mutterland," 271.

55 This lack of materials met with no comment in the party journal's discussion of women and the election's outcome; see "Die Betrachtung der Wahlergebnisse," *Das Zentrum*, November 1930. This journal ran a list of women's pamphlets prepared for the 1930 election: "Frauen und die Wahlen: Ein Wort an die deutschen Frauen von Luise Becher" and "Was die Hausfrauen wohl meinen (Plauderei)." I did not find copies of these.

56 "Katholische Frauen Berlins!," *Germania*, 11 September 1930; Pius XI, quoted in *Germania*, 14 September 1930.

57 The official report of the December 1928 party conference has no index entry for women, lists no women as speakers, and shows no discussion of women in the order of business. Strategy discussions in *Das Zentrum* also fail to mention mobilization among women: "Organisation und Werbung," April 1930, and "Die Betrachtung der Wahlergebnisse."

58 "An die Jungwählerinnen!," *Frauenwelt* section of *Germania*, 7 September 1930.

59 Where votes were counted by sex in 1930, 8.3 percent of women versus 5.2 percent of men voted Center or BVP. See Falter, Lindenberger, and Schumann, *Wahlen und Abstimmungen*, table 1.6.1.1.

60 For details, see Jones, *German Liberalism*, 330–43; Childers, *Nazi Voter*, 134–36; and Childers, "Languages of Liberalism," 349–50. The DDP was not officially dissolved until November 1930.

61 For example, in a series of postcards from this period spotlighting liberal personalities, Bäumer's read that all must believe in democracy as in Christ; in GStA/XII.HA/IV 144. These ideas had long been espoused by Bäumer; for a summary, see Wittrock, *Weiblichkeitsmythen*, 14–33. Wittrock considers Bäumer a protofascist.

62 For sample general appeals, see "Geschäftsleute, Frauen, Unternehmer und Arbeitnehmer, freie Berufe, Beamte!," BA ZSg 1-27/20 (2), and "Deutsche Volksgenossen!," GStA/XII.HA/IV 144. See also Childers, *Nazi Voter*, 154–55, and Jones, *German Liberalism*, 380–86.

63 "An die deutschen Frauen!," September 1930, LA 240/2088/89; "Frauen, ihr seid eine Macht!," *Wahlzeitung der DSP* 3.

64 "Keiner darf abseitsstehen!," 1930 paste-up sheet, and "Deutsche Jugend erwache!," both GStA/XII.HA/IV 145.

65 For a sample appeal to men, see "Sehr geehrter Herr!," September 1930, GStA/XII.HA/IV 145. For a sample general appeal, see "Nichtwähler!," BA ZSg 1-27/20 (2). For a general women's appeal, see "Frauen!," in GStA/XII.HA/IV 145.

66 "Frauen, ihr seid eine Macht!"

67 "Wählt Liste 6," GStA/XII.HA/IV 145 and Hoover Poster Collection. The Berlin firm is Lindemann and Lüdecke. This analysis is indebted to Canning, "Feminist History after the Linguistic Turn," 383–85.

68 "Hausfrauen und Mütter!," May 1929, Hoover GSC/28; "Frauenrecht und Frauendienst in der Gemeinde," November 1929, BA Berlin 15.07 67165-277.

69 "Sehr geehrte Frau!" and "Frauen aller Stände!," both GStA/XII.HA/IV 145.

70 "DSP Frauenkundgebung," September 1930, GStA/XII.HA/IV 145; "Die Frau, die unbedingt in den Landtag gehört [Else Ulich-Beil], schreibt an die Wählerinnen," June 1930 Saxon election, Hoover GSC/16/151; Else Fisch, "Liebe deutsche Mitbürgerin!," September 1930, GStA/XII.HA/IV 145. To compare discourse on radicalism to *Berufsgruppen*, see "Bauer in Not!" and "An alle Handwerker und Kaufleute!," in GStA/XII.HA/IV 145.

71 "Warum wählen die Frauen Liste 6?," Hoover Loesch Coll. 2/26.

72 "Ein offener Brief an Viele!," September 1930, GStA/XII.HA/IV 145.

73 "Jubiläumstagung in Berlin vom 17.–23. Juni 1929," NSDAP/HA 39/769; Offen, "Defining Feminism."

74 She was also a BDF point woman for youth issues and in 1929 addressed an audience of around 1,000 at a BDF forum entitled "Youth, Women, and the State"; see Harvey, "Serving the Volk," 209.

75 "Sehr geehrte Frau!," May 1929, Hoover GSC/28; "Hausfrauen und Mütter!"; "Frauenrecht und Frauendienst in der Gemeinde."

76 *Mitteilungen des Reichsfrauenausschuss*, 20 May 1930, BA ZSg 1-27/3.

77 This was also argued by Emma Ender and Alice Bernsheimer, "Beträchtliche Minderbewertung der Frauenarbeit in Reichs-, Länder-, und Kommunalver-waltungen," 1930, HLA BDF/55-248 [3] 249 [1].

78 *Mitteilungen des Reichsfrauenausschuss*, 11 April 1929; "Arbeitende Frau!," September 1930, BA ZSg 1-27/20 (2), emphasis in original; "An die berufstätigen Frauen," May 1929, Hoover GSC/28.

79 "Fürsorgebeamtinnen!" and "Kindergärtnerinnen!," both May 1929, Hoover GSC/28; "Geschäftsleute, Frauen, Unternehmer und Arbeitnehmer, freie Berufe, Beamte!," September 1930, BA ZSg 1-27/20 (2).

80 "Arbeitende Frau!"

81 On the Order's corporatism, see Harvey, "Serving the Volk," 215.

82 *Mitteilungen des Reichsfrauenausschuss*, June/July 1929, BA ZSg 1-27/3.

83 "Deutsche Volksgenossen!," 1930, GStA/XII.HA/IV 145.

84 From 1929, see "Frauenrecht und Frauendienst" and "Sehr geehrte Frau!" For the 1930 flyer, see "Warum wählen die Frauen Liste 6?"

85 For a general appeal, see "Nichtwähler!" For appeals to occupational groups, see "An alle Handwerker und Kaufleute!" and "Bauer in Not!" For appeals to women, see "Frauen, ihr seid eine Macht!," "Frauen aller Stände!," "Hausfrauen und Mütter!," and "Eine offene Brief an Viele!"

86 *Frauenarbeit in der DDP*, 18. Similar recurring complaints appear in the protocol of the DDP *Ortssitzung*, 17–18 September 1929, BA R45 III/29.

87 "Sehr geehrte Frau!" For more on Else Ulich-Beil, see Schmidt-Waldherr, *Emanzipation durch Professionalisierung?*, 25–26.

88 The SPD, in comparison, won 33. See Falter, Lindenberger, and Schumann, *Wahlen und Abstimmungen*, table 1.7.2.14.

89 Werner Stephan to BDF, 11 August 1930, HLA BDF/52-239 [3].

90 See her scathing six-page postmortem of the DDP's 1928 campaign, 6 June 1928, in BA NL Lüders, 109.

91 On Lüders's candidacy, see DDP *Vorstand* meetings of 10 July and 12 August 1930, NSDAP/HA 37/732. Lüders's immediate response can be gleaned from marks she made on a 23 September 1930 letter from the *Vorstand* notifying her of the loss of her seat. Consisting mostly of underlines and question marks, they indicate that she did not swallow the letter's statement of regret at her loss, which the party blamed on the "Unverstand der Wähler." In BA NL Lüders, 99. I am indebted to Larry Jones for his insights on Lüders's position within the changed DSP.

92 "Das kulturpolitische Manifest der DSP," GStA/XII.HA/IV 145.

93 Jones, "Generational Conflict."

94 This collapse of propaganda did not cause the party's collapse but reflected it. See Möller, "Die sich selbst bewusste Massenbeeinflussung," 14–15.

95 See 1930 poster, "Für Einigkeit, Fortschritt, Volksgemeinschaft!," whose central figure is a blonde woman with one arm raised in triumph. In GStA/XII.HA/IV 145.

96 The BDF's 1930 *Wahlaufruf* called for a defense of democracy. The poor showing of prodemocratic parties also stands as an index of the BDF's own weakness by this time.

97 "Wählt Deutsche Volkspartei!," September 1930, BA ZSg 1-42/8.

98 Jones, *German Liberalism*, 341, 367.

99 Ibid., 383–86. See also Matz at DVP Vorstand meeting, 24 August 1930, BA R45 II/47.

100 DVP cartoon strip, September 1930, BA ZSg 1-42/8.

101 Frau Hertwig-Bünger at the 4 July 1930 Zentralvorstand meeting, BA R45 II/46. For this study, no DVP materials for elections other than the 1930 Reichstag campaign were found.

102 "Die 5. Reichstagswahl ist Schicksalswahl!," BA ZSg 1-42/8. See p. 2 for the address to women.

103 Mayer, quoted in "Frauen zur Reichstagswahl," *Germania*, 3 September 1930. See also Else Matz, "Staatsbürgerliche Pflicht der Frau," *Berliner Stimmen*, 31 August 1930.

104 "Deutsche Frau Dein Volk ruft!" and "Wie wählt die evangelische Frau?," both GStA/XII.HA/IV 170; "Frauenfragen in der Wahlbewegung," *Sondermaterial für den Wahlkampf 1930*, BA ZSg 1-42/4; "Die 5. Reichstagswahl ist Schicksalswahl!"

105 "Frauenfragen in der Wahlbewegung"; "Wie wählt die evangelische Frau?" These materials' blatant disregard of Catholic women's views illuminates the religious cleavage that marked Weimar political culture.

106 "Frauenfragen in der Wahlbewegung."

107 "Wähler wach einmal auf!," BA ZSg 1-42/8, warns against "Marxists and anti-Semites." For the threat to the Reich, see "Du bist in Gefahr," 1930, BA ZSg 1-42/8. On dance halls, see *Wahlwecker*, 14 September 1930, LA 240/2088/85.

108 "Stichworte für den Wahlkampf 1930," BA ZSg 1-42/4; "Frauenfragen in der Wahlbewegung"; "Deutsche Frau Dein Volk ruft!" See also the following

articles in *Berliner Stimmen*: "Frauen im Wahlkampf," 17 August 1930; "Staat, Gesellschaft und Familie," 4 May 1929; "Mitarbeit der Frau in der Politik," 18 May 1929; and "Ehe oder Kamderschaftsehe?," 9 March 1929.

109 See the *Berliner Stimmen* piece "Mitarbeit der Frau in der Politik" and the pamphlet "Frauenfragen in der Wahlbewegung."

110 "Frauenfragen in der Wahlbewegung"; *Wahlwecker*; "Was erwarten die Frauen vom neuen Reichstag?"

111 "Mitarbeit der Frau in der Politik"; "Deutsche Frau Dein Volk ruft!"; "Einladung zur Frauentagung der Wahlkreisfrauenausschusse Berlin, Potsdam I und II der DVP," 14–17 May 1930, BA Berlin 60 Vo 1/53123/39. On the need to maintain optimism, see Marie Szagunn's comments at the 23 August 1930 meeting of the DVP Reichsausschuss, BA R45 II/32. See also "Königin-Luise-Bund und DVP," *Berliner Stimmen*, 27 October 1929, and Reagin, *German Women's Movement*, 235.

112 "Deutsche Frau Dein Volk ruft!"

113 For internal writings, see the following in *Berliner Stimmen*: Fräulein Dr. Wolf, 6 April 1930, 2; "Dies Academicus der Frau," 22 June 1930; and "Frauen am Himmel," 10 August 1930.

114 "Deutsche Frau Dein Volk ruft!"

115 Compare "Frauenfragen in der Wahlbewegung," and "Das neue Deutschland und die berufstätige Frau," *Berliner Stimmen*, 3 November 1929.

116 On female clerks, see "Frauenfragen in der Wahlbewegung." See also *Reichsklub der DVP Mitglieder-Verzeichnis* (1929), BA ZSg 1-42/14 [8]. For relevant *Berliner Stimmen* articles, see "Gehalt für die Hausfrau?," 15 December 1929; "Die Macht der Hausfrau," 15 December 1929; "Frauen in die Politik!," 18 May 1930; and "Ausstellung Berufsfrauen-Hausfrauen," 3 November 1928.

117 Langheld, "Die Frauen entscheiden die Wahl!," *DAZ*, 7 September 1930. See also Matz, "Staatsbürgerliche Pflicht der Frau," and "Frauen im Wahlkampf."

118 The paper was characterized as among those "largely representing our view" in the 1929 DVP *Addressen-Verzeichnis*, BA ZSg 1-42/14 [9].

119 "Die Frau von gestern und die von heute," *DAZ*, 7 September 1930, 1; "Kochtopf wichtiger als Wahlurne?," *8-Uhr Abendblatt*, 12 September 1930.

120 On gender comraderie, see "Wähler wach einmal auf!"; "Eine Frau im Handelsministerium," *Berliner Stimmen*, 14 September 1929; and list of Berlin candidates in *Berliner Stimmen*, 17 August 1930. For DVP crowd shots, see "Wählt Deutsche Volkspartei!" For activities of the Reichsklub, see its *Mitglieder-Verzeichnis 1929*. See also August 1930 letter to BDF in HLA BDF/52-239 [3].

121 See Zentralvorstand meeting of 24 August 1930, BA R45 II/47. The DVP's desire to recruit youth is invoked repeatedly in meetings throughout 1930; the DVP was also courting the Young German Order, which ultimately cast its lot with the DDP. See protocols of DVP Reichsgeschäftsstelle, 1930, BA R45 II/32, and Jones, "Generational Conflict," 362.

122 See comments by Alice Neven-Dumont and Frau Hertwig-Bünger at Zentralvorstand meeting of 24 August 1930, BA R45 II/47.

123 The women's organization is practically invisible in the files of the Geschäftsführende Ausschuss and Zentralvorstand in BA R45 II. On the selection of

Clara Mende's replacement for the "woman's chair" on the central committee,
see meeting protocol of 14 December 1929, BA R45 II/44.

124 Garnich, "Frau und Politik," 11 May 1930, and Schwarz, "Frauen und politischer
Zeitgeist," 12 January 1930, both in *Berliner Stimmen*.

125 K. von Kardorff, "Brauchen wir eine Frauenpartei?," *8-Uhr Abendblatt*, 23 January 1930. See also her 1931 pamphlet of the same name.

126 L. Garnich, "Frauenlisten?," *Berliner Stimmen*, 10 November 1928.

127 "Mitarbeit der Frau in der Politik."

128 Harsch, *German Social Democracy*, 63–64.

129 On the Sklarek affair, a corruption scandal that brought down the SPD mayor
of Berlin, see Friedrich, *Before the Deluge*, 359. Harsch traces the case's anti-
Semitic angle, exploited by both the Right and the KPD (*German Social
Democracy*, 69–70).

130 While roughly one in ten of these votes went to the NSDAP, the KPD benefited most, jumping from 10 to 13 percent overall in 1930.

131 For illustrations, see Janusch, *Plakative Propaganda der SPD*, 110–25.

132 Wurms, "Gleichberechtigt, aber 'zur linken Hand,'" 46; Duverger, *Political Role
of Women*, 54.

133 "Wo findet die berufstätige Frau Verständnis für ihre schwere Lage?," 1930
flyer signed "the women of the SPD," Hoover GSC/36; "Landfrau auch du
mußt wählen," 1930, Hoover GSC/5. See also "Internationaler Frauentag: Mit
uns die Zukunft," n.d., Hoover GSC/20/204, and "Arbeitermädel her zu uns,"
n.d., Hoover GSC/5. For sample general appeals, see "Warum 9 Millionen
Wähler?," 1928, Hoover GSC/14/127; "Arbeiter! Wählt Eure Partei," undated
poster, Hoover Mueller-Graeff Coll. box 4; "Wählt Liste 1," September 1930,
GStA/XII.HA/IV 77; and *Rote Wahlpost* (Danzig), 1930, BA ZSg 1-90/41.

134 "Internationaler Frauentag."

135 "Frau! Schwester! Kampfgenossin! Arbeitskollegin!," n.d., Hoover GSC/5/1.

136 "Internationaler Frauentag"; "Wo findet die berufstätige Frau?"; "Landfrau";
"Arbeiterinnen! Angestellte!," 1930, BA ZSg 1-90/41; "Kommunisten auf dem
Frauenfang," *Der Kämpfer*, 25 February 1929. On the link between social
welfare and the creation of a *Volksgemeinschaft*, see Crew, "Ambiguities of
Modernity," 328.

137 "Die Frau in Politik und Beruf," BA ZSg 1-90/23 (10); SPD, *Protokoll* (1929),
221.

138 SPD, *Protokoll* (1929), 220–32, 244–45.

139 "Halt! Hausfrauen," 1930, Hoover GSC/36; "Wer verteuert Dir das Leben?," 1930
pamphlet, SAPMO-BA II/145/20; "Liebe Volksgenossin!," 1929 Saxon Landtag
flyer, Hoover GSC/25.

140 The SPD women's bureau argued that women were especially interested in
"questions that directly touch their lives" ("Bericht des Frauenbureaus," SPD,
Protokoll [1929]).

141 On female Socialists' work to create recognition of female *Eigenart* within
organized labor, see Canning, "Gender and the Politics of Class Formation,"
761–66. For appeals to housewives, see "Ein Wort an die Frauen," 1930, BA ZSg
1-90/41; "Halt! Hausfrauen"; and "Wer verteuert Dir das Leben?"

142 "Mutter, Deine Stimme entscheidet unsere Zukunft!," n.d., Hoover Mueller-

Graeff Coll. box 4; "Wo steht der Feind?," 1930, BA ZSg 1-90/41; "Liebe Volksgenossin!"

143 "Unser Weg über den proletarischer Prenzlauer Berg," Berlin 1929, LA 240/ 2127/13; "Die städtische Eheberatungsstelle?," 1929 poster, Hoover GSC/16/151. The fact that one of these was not just for women weakens Cornelie Usborne's argument that reproduction was treated strictly as a women's issue. See also "Berliner Volksblatt: Frauen entscheiden!," 1930, GStA/XII.HA/IV 77, and "Halt! Hausfrauen."

144 "Wo findet die berufstätige Frau?"; "Warum 9 Millionen Wähler?"; "Arbeiterinnen- und Mütterschutz in Gefahr!," 1929, BA ZSg 1-90/18; SPD, *Protokoll* (1929), 232; SPD, *Jahrbuch* (1929), 121, in which Severing declared that the party's motto must be "foster and protect voluntary motherhood." See also Usborne, *Politics of the Body*, 57–58, and Canning, "Feminist History," 385.

145 Westfalen, in "Frauenbewegung," SPD, *Jahrbuch* (1929).

146 "Wo steht der Feind?" and "Wer verteuert Dir das Leben?"

147 "Mütter und Frauen! 5 Tote," 1930, LA 240/2381/90; "Viehische Roheit an einer wehrlosen Frau" and "Von Killinger wirbt um die Wählerstimmen, er ist Landtagskandidat," June 1930 posters, Hoover GSC/14/130. Another flyer on this incident was produced in 1930, "Frauen, so geht's euch im Dritten Reich!," but seems to have been more widely used after the election; see SPD, *Jahrbuch* (1930), 217.

148 See SPD, *Jahrbuch* (1929). Written with the benefit of hindsight, the 1930 yearbook claimed that women worked especially hard in the 1930 campaign because of the Nazi threat to their rights.

149 "Sehr geehrtes Fräulein," May 1929, Hoover GSC/28; "Internationaler Frauen- tag."

150 For example, see "Wählen? Ja! Ja! Ja!," in which a housewife "sees the light" after a series of encounters, in BA ZSg 1-90/41.

151 "Zehn Jahre Frauenwahlrecht," *Sozialdemokratische Korrespondenz*, July 1929. Unfortunately, this piece bears no author credit.

152 For example, see "Die Betriebsrätewahlen," *Vorwärts*, 30 March 1930.

153 For this debate, see SPD, *Protokoll* (1929), 220–45. See also Hagemann, *Frauen- alltag und Männerpolitik*, 542–46, 631.

154 Quoted in Hagemann, *Frauenalltag und Männerpolitik*, 545–47.

155 Boak, "'Our Last Hope,'" 292; Peterson, "Politics of Working-Class Women."

156 On social fascism, see Rosenhaft, *Beating the Fascists?*, 31–33.

157 "Anweisungen an die Frauenabteilungen der Reichstags-Wahlkampagne," July 1930, SAPMO-BA I/2/701/15.

158 Arendt, "Weibliche Mitglieder der KPD," table 1.

159 On its limited successes in this period, see Weitz, *Creating German Communism*, 223–24.

160 See "Infomations-material über Sowjetmilitarismus," October 1928, SAPMO- BA I/145/19. *Sturmtempo* quote from "Anweisungen an die Frauenabteilungen."

161 See Harsch, *German Social Democracy*, 46–50. The decision was vehemently opposed by the vast majority of Social Democrats.

162 For posters, see "Arbeiterinnen! Um gleichen Lohn bei gleicher Arbeit," 1930, Hoover GSC/16/151, and "Denkt daran!," 1929, Hoover GSC/28. See also the

flyer "Die Satten gegen die Hungernden," 1930 and 1932, BA ZSg 1-65/64.
For examples from the party journal, see *Parteiarbeiter's Arbeit unter den Frauen*
section, October 1928 and June–August 1929.

163 For a sample flyer, see "Wo ist der Ausweg aus Hunger und Not?," 1930, Hoover
GSC/36. On anti-SPD tactics and the acknowledgment that women preferred
less warlike language, see "Arbeit der SPD unten den Frauen in Deutschland
und anderen Europäischen Ländern," June 1930, SAPMO-BA I/2/701/37.

164 Overlach, in KPD, *Protokoll* (1929); "Das wahre Gesicht der SPD: Ein Wort an
die SPD Arbeiter von Maria Reese, ehemalige SPD Reichstags-Abgeordnete,"
1930, BA ZSg 1-65/25; "Wo ist der Ausweg?"; "Welt-Frauenstimmrechts-
Kongress oder Kampfwoche gegen die bürgerliche Frauenbewegung?," *Arbeit
unter den Frauen* section of *Parteiarbeiter*, June 1929.

165 "Frauenschicksale—Eine tuberkulöse Familie," *Welt am Abend*, 3 September
1930; "Welt-Frauenstimmrechts-Kongress?"

166 "Werktätige Frauen—So darf es nicht bleiben," September 1930, Hoover
GSC/36; "Werktätige Frauen und Mädchen!," 1930 Saxon poster, Hoover
GSC/16/151; "Referentenmaterial für den Reichstagswahlkampf 1930," BA ZSg
1-65/25.

167 For flyers, see "Arbeiter! Arbeiterinnen!," September 1930, BA ZSg 1-65/62;
"Werktätige Frauen—So darf es nicht bleiben"; and "Jeder Gewerkschaftler
liest 'Die Rote Fahne,'" 1930, GStA/XII.HA/IV 102. For anti-Catholic strategy,
see "Arbeitsplan für April und Mai 1930," SAPMO-BA I/2/701/11, and "Zen-
trumswahlerfolg und seine Lehren für die Partei," *Parteiarbeiter*, January 1930.
Kulturkampf quote from *Programm der Kommunistischen Internationale 6. Welt-
kongress* (1928), 109–10.

168 "Werktätige Frauen—so darf es nicht bleiben."

169 "Schluß mit der Volks-Ausplünderung!," n.d., BA ZSg 1-65/65; "Denkt daran!";
"Wo ist der Ausweg?"; "Das wahre Gesicht der SPD"; "Wohin führt der Weg?,"
1930 women's pamphlet, BA ZSg 1-65/25.

170 For KPD policy on housewives, see Kontos, *Partei kämpft wie ein Mann!*, 131–49.

171 "Schluß mit der Volks-Ausplünderung!"; "Arbeiterfrauen! Warum ist Hunger
und Elend so gross?," n.d., Hoover GSC/12; "Arbeiter, Angestellte, Beamte,
Hausfrau!," September 1930, GStA/XII.HA/IV 102.

172 "Die Arbeiterfrauen nicht vernachlässigen!," *Arbeit unter den Frauen* section of
Parteiarbeiter, March 1930.

173 "Werktätige Frauen—so darf es nicht bleiben"; KPD, *Handbuch der kommunistischen Reichstagsfraktion: 21 Monate Hermann Müller Regierung*, 393–406. This
pronatalism would constitute a tension in the gathering movement against
paragraph 218; see Grossmann, *Reforming Sex*, 92–95.

174 "Alle Frauen und Mädchen protestieren am 7. Dezember gegen die Justizsch-
mach," 1929 poster, Hoover GSC/16/151; "Todesstrafe für Abtreibung," 1930
sticker, BA ZSg 1-65/64; "Arbeiter! Arbeiterinnen!"; "Wo ist der Ausweg?";
"Werktätige Frauen—so darf es nicht bleiben."

175 Weitz, *Creating German Communism*, 219; Usborne, *Politics of the Body*, 116–17.

176 In *Referentenmaterial für den Reichstagswahlkampf 1930*, KPD speakers are urged to
criticize this Nazi "militarization of women."

177 "Straße frei am 1. Mai!," 1929, LA 240/2127/6; Weitz, *Creating German Commu-

nism, 205–32. On female participation in street conflict, see Rosenhaft, *Beating the Fascists?*, 151–54.

178 For example, see "Der Frauenorganisator im Betrieb," *Parteiarbeiter*, May 1930.

179 "Freiheit die sie meinen," Saxony 1930, Hoover Mueller-Graeff Coll. box 4.

180 For examples, see *Parteiarbeiter*, September 1928 and June 1930. On the delegate movement, see Kontos, *Partei kämpft wie ein Mann!*, 75–78.

181 The IAH fell under the umbrella of Willi Münzenberg, whose popular *Arbeiter-Illustrierte-Zeitung* was also edited by a woman. The *AIZ* often presented a richer view of proletarian gender relations, as in a 1927 article urging husbands to help with the housework; see "Mehr Freizeit für die werktätige Frau," *AIZ* 41 (1927). See also Kontos, *Partei kämpft wie ein Mann!*, 69–71.

182 Official policy stated that every third candidate had to be female; the 1929 Berlin election was the only instance where this policy was met.

183 "Rote Vertrauensleute auch in Arbeiterinnenbetrieben," *Arbeit unter den Frauen* section of *Parteiarbeiter*, October 1929.

184 Where votes were tabulated by sex, 24 percent of men versus 18.1 percent of women voted KPD in 1930; thus, women continued to constitute only about 40 percent of KPD voters. See Falter, Lindenberger, and Schumann, *Wahlen und Abstimmungen*, table 1.6.1.1.

185 On particularism versus individualism and citizenship, see Turner, "Contemporary Problems in the Theory of Citizenship," 4–6.

186 Jones, "Generational Conflict," 365.

CHAPTER FIVE

1 Paul, "Krieg der Symbole," 28.

2 This was Weimar's most visual election year: 20 percent of campaign posters were pictorial, double the figure for the previous thirteen years. See ibid., 27, and Paul, *Aufstand der Bilder*, 152.

3 See Kolb, *Weimar Republic*, 96–126, and Peukert, *Weimar Republic*, 251–67.

4 Frevert says the BDF made no protest in *Women in German History*, 198. But its archives contain a letter protesting the law on the grounds that "a great deal of [our world's] decline . . . stems from the fact that it is an all-male world"— female work alongside men would help remedy this malaise; see "Zum Abbau der weiblichen Beamten in Preussen," HLA BDF/53-242 [1]. See also "Frauenarbeit und Wirtschaftskrise: Erklärung des Bundes deutscher Frauenvereine," *Frankfurter Zeitung*, 29 April 1931, reprinted as "Women's Work and Economic Crisis," in *Weimar Republic Sourcebook*, 212–13. Fears that the law would promote divorce and unwed cohabitation appear in Lüders, *Fürchte Dich Nicht*, 104.

5 Quoted in Kaufmann, "Vom Vaterland zum Mutterland," 263–64.

6 M. D., "§218," *Germania*, 19 April 1931.

7 On the 1931 protests, see Grossmann, "Abortion and Economic Crisis" and *Reforming Sex*, 78–106. Abortion's illegality makes statistics unreliable; contemporaries agreed on the figure of 1 million abortions, but mortality rates were hotly debated. On the female mob as emblem of modernity, see Huyssen, "Mass Culture as Woman."

8 Tschachotin, "Technik der politischen Propaganda," 425.

9 Kerbs, "Die illustrierte Presse," reprints some examples on pp. 78–87.

10 See Childers, *Nazi Voter*, 193–95, and Paul, *Aufstand der Bilder*, especially sections 3 and 4. On the Harzburg Front, see Leopold, *Alfred Hugenberg*, 88–125.

11 See Childers, "Limits of National Socialist Mobilization."

12 Helen Boak details those areas, particularly parts of Bavaria, where the NSDAP or *völkisch* block did do well with women prior to the early 1930s; see "'Our Last Hope.'"

13 "Hitler sagt über die deutsche Frau . . . ," *VB*, 6 April 1932.

14 Stephenson, *Nazi Organisation of Women*, 50–64; Childers, *Nazi Voter*, 198, 259. See also BA Berlin 15.01-26125 on the NSF's growth.

15 H. Passow, "Die propagandistische Erfassung und Bearbeitung der Frau," *Unser Wille und Weg* 11 (November 1932); G. Diehl, "Deutsche Frauen, erwacht!," *VB*, 24 April 1932. See also "Der kommende Wahlkampf und die Mitwirkung der Frau," *VB*, 27 March 1932.

16 Boak, "'Our Last Hope,'" 297.

17 Childers, *Nazi Voter*, 206–7; Tormin, *Geschichte der deutschen Parteien*, 197; Leopold, *Alfred Hugenberg*, 88, 118–25.

18 *Unsere Partei* lists materials produced for July: three pamphlets and no special flyers for women (I did find one, however). The same list appeared for the November election. See "Wahlkampfmaterial," 15 June 1932.

19 Childers, *Nazi Voter*, 260–61; Winkler, "Abschied von Weimar," 11–26.

20 L. Becher, "Frauenparolen," *Frauenwelt* section of *Germania*, 6 November 1932. A July 1932 campaign memo lists eight flyers produced for that election for peasants, *Mittelstand*, blue- and white-collar employees, the unemployed, women, youth, and the "politically uncommitted"; see Childers, "Languages of Liberalism," 346. See also Paul, "Krieg der Symbole," 29.

21 "Deutsche Frauen!," July 1932 flyer, BA ZSg 1-108/8; H. Weber, "Politische Entscheidungsstunde," *Frauenwelt* section of *Germania*, 10 July 1932.

22 "Kameraden, jetzt gilt's!," July 1932, BA ZSg 1-108/8.

23 Boak argues that the share of the female vote going to the Center and Bavarian People's Party gradually fell during Weimar, although women in Catholic areas still preferred them to any other through 1932. See "'Our Last Hope,'" 291.

24 The NSDAP used uncannily similar images of this male giant, as documented in Paul, *Aufstand der Bilder*, illus. 45–52.

25 Bodek, "Communist Music in the Streets," 278.

26 "Einheitsfrontaktion," Hoover Mueller-Graeff Coll. box 3.

27 On female membership, see Arendt, "Weibliche Mitglieder der KPD," table 1. Women remained 15 percent of all KPD members. On *Weg der Frau*, see Surmann, *Die Münzenberg-Legende*, 200–206.

28 On the strategy toward women, see Rundschreiben 27, 10 November 1930, SAPMO-BA II/145/20; SPD, *Jahrbuch* (1931), 122–32; and *Nationalsozialismus und Frauenfragen: Material zur Information und Bekämpfung*, 1932, BA ZSg 1-90/43.

29 Paul, "Krieg der Symbole," 52–54.

30 In Arnold, *Anschläge: 220 politische Plakate*, plate 110.

31 For flyers to general audiences, see "Dumme werden gesucht!," "Adolf Hitler ist schuld," and "Kriegsbeschädigte, Arbeitslose, Invaliden, Unfallrentner, Wit-

wen!," all July, BA ZSg 1-90/45, and *Reichstagswahl 31. Juli 1932: Rededisposition und Referentenmaterial*, BA ZSg 1-90/43 (20). For sample women's flyers, see "Frauen und Mütter!," November 1932, reprinted in Childers, *Nazi Voter*, 289; "Frauen aufgepasst!," July 1932 pamphlet, BA ZSg 1-90/18; "Liebe Schwester Emilie!," "Mütter, Frauen, Mädchen," and "Hoetens Frau Schmitz!," all July, BA ZSg 1-90/45; "Arbeiterinnen! Angestellte! Mütter! Frauen!," April Prussian election, LA 240/2088/121; "Frauen, wollt Ihr das?," "Werte Frau!," and "Diktatur oder Parlament?," all presidential election, BA ZSg 1-90/44; and "Sehr geehrte Frau," *Werbematerial: Mappe I* (1931), BA ZSg 1-90/41.

32 DVP Wahlkampfleitung Gross-Berlin Pressestelle, 29 October 1932, BA Berlin 60 Vo 1/53122/36.

33 DVP 1931 program published in *Handbuch des öffentlichen Lebens*, 447–48.

34 See Childers, "Languages of Liberalism," 351–55, and Jones, *German Liberalism*, 417–18, 454. BA R45 II/17 details negotiations between the DVP and DNVP for a combined Reich list in July and November—the DNVP got the top twelve candidate spots, while the DVP had to settle for spots thirteen through twenty.

35 These issues are summarized in a July 1932 flyer, "Bürgerinnen!," BA ZSg 1-42/8.

36 I found only three flyers from 1932; two women's pamphlets appeared in 1931.

37 See 27 November 1930 memo from Potsdam district 1 on recruitment, BA Berlin 60 Vo 1/53123/39; Wahlkampfleitung Gross-Berlin, 29 October 1932; and Elsa Matz to Schwertfeger, 18 February 1933, in BA NL Schwertfeger. Thanks to Larry Eugene Jones for bringing this to my attention.

38 Möller, "Die sich selbst bewusste Massenbeeinflussung," 17.

39 On the DSP in this period, see Childers, "Languages of Liberalism," 355, and *Nazi Voter*, 202–6; and Jones, *German Liberalism*, 401–2, 442–60.

40 Several such posters whose authorship cannot be determined are in Hoover Mueller-Graeff Coll. box 3.

41 "Die Frauen und das Wahlergebnis," *Mitteilungen des Reichsfrauenausschuss* 10 (20 October 1930), NSDAP/HA 39/772.

42 Passow, "Propagandistische Fassung und Bearbeitung der Frau."

43 Rosenberg, "Die deutsche Frau im Kampf um ihr Recht," *VB*, 5 November 1932; "Adolf Hitler spricht zu den nat.-soz. Frauentag," *VB*, 5 October 1932; "Grundsätze und organisatorische Richtlinien der National-sozialistischen Frauenschaft," NSDAP/HA 13/254; German Women's Order, "Deutsche Frauen Deutsche Madchen!," February 1931, BA Berlin 15.01-26125/29; "Wie sie lügen!," July 1932 flyer, Hoover GSC/5 (early version in NSDAP/HA 15/289).

44 "Hindenburgwähler!," April 1932, LA 240/2381/154.

45 Passow wrote that propaganda must educate women to buy German and avoid department stores, but this did not surface in the electoral materials I found. See also "Die kommende Wahlkampf und die Mitwirkung der Frau."

46 *Rednerinformation* 3/4; "Grundsätze und organisatorische Richtlinien"; "Die Frau ist entrechtet," March 1932 flyer design, NSDAP/HA 15/287.

47 "Die Frau ist entrechtet!"

48 "Frauen im Dritten Reich," April flyer design, NSDAP/HA 15/288.

49 DNVP program, reprinted in *Weimar Republic Sourcebook*, 348–52.

50 "Warum sind wir Frauen deutschnational?," *Unsere Partei*, 5 April 1932;

"Deutsche Frauen, Volk und Staat rufen Euch!," *Unsere Partei*, 8 July 1932 (also printed as a flyer). For 1931 writings, see U. Scheidel, "Warum sind wir Frauen deutschnational?," 15 January 1931, and Elisabeth Spohr, "Die deutsche Frau und das Buch," 15 March 1931, both in *Unsere Partei*, and "Wer gehört in die DNVP?," 1931 leaflet, BA ZSg 1-44/11.

51 "Ein ernstes Wort an deutschen Frauen und Mädchen," 1932 pamphlet, BA ZSg 1-44/7.

52 Schmidt-Waldherr, *Emanzipation durch Professionalisierung?*, 92–93.

53 "Ins Dritte Reich: Zitate nationaler Männer," n.d., NSDAP/HA 39/772.

54 "Deutsche Frauen, Staatsbürgerinnen!," July 1932, BA ZSg 1-27/20 (3). On DDP languages of citizenship, see Childers, "Languages of Liberalism."

55 "Deutschland von Morgen: Freiheitlich-nationales Blatt," July 1932 flyer (likely Prussia), LA 240/834/9.

56 "Hallo—wir alle wählen," April Prussian Landtag pamphlet, Hoover GSC/5; "Frauen, so geht's euch im 3. Reich!," September 1930, BA ZSg 1-90/41; "Arbeiterinnen! Angestellte!," April Prussian Landtag flyer, LA 240/2088/121; "Frauen aufgepasst!"; "Mütter, Frauen, Mädchen"; "Liebe Schwester Emilie!" On Toni Sender, see "Frauenehre vor Gericht," *Vorwärts*, 11 August 1932, and Sender, *Autobiography of a German Rebel*, 294–97.

57 The incident appears in the following SPD materials, all July 1932: "Hort es! Ihr Frauen und Madchen!," poster in Hoover Mueller-Graeff Coll. box 4; "'Ihr dummen Ziegen, dafür werden Eure Söhne Euch ja gemacht!,'" "Ihr dummen Ziegen—Wer ist gemeint?," "Preussen wird Hitler geopfert!," "Dumme werden gesucht!," and "Wollt ihr das?," all BA ZSg 1-90/45; "Deutschland von Morgen: Freiheitlich-nationales Blatt." See also *AIZ*, 31 July 1932.

58 Slang, "Weibchen und Weiber im 'Dritten Reich,'" *AIZ*, 17 July 1932; "Deutschland erwacht!," April 1932 (publisher unclear), LA 240/2074/23; "Frauen der arbeitenden Klasse!," April 1932, BA ZSg 1-65/65; "Amnestie!," 1932, Hoover GSC/5; "Arbeitende Frauen und Mädchen!," July 1932, LA 240/2088/141; "Antifaschistinnen!," July 1932 armband, BA ZSg 1-65/65; "Offener Brief an alle Kampfbundkameraden und Kampfbundkameradinnen!," 1932, GStA/XII.HA/ IV 198.

59 Kulesza, "Frauenfragen der Gegenwart"; "Unterschiedliche Einstellung nationaler Führer zur politischen Betätigung der Frau," *Frauenrundschau*, 7 January 1932; "Drei Fragen hinter der Tür!," July 1932, BA ZSg 1-42/8.

60 For examples, see "Weshalb Zentrum?," *Frauenwelt* section of *Germania*, 24 April 1932, and "Kulturpolitische Forderungen des Zentrums," *Das Zentrum*, October–November 1932.

61 "Die Frauen der Zentrumsliste" and Christl Pech, "Die Frau und die Parteien," *Germania*, 17 April 1932; "Deutschland ruft uns!," 24 July 1932; "Es geht in diesem Wahlkampf," *Frauenwelt* section of *Germania*, 30 October 1932; "Die Frauen rufen," *Germania*, 30 July 1932.

62 Matz, "Schwarz-brauner Block und die Frauen," *Frauenrundschau*, 4 May 1932.

63 J. Lange, "Um das Frauenwahlrecht," 21 April 1932, and Ingeborg Feth, "Politische Frauenwille in nationalem Liberalismus," 22 June 1932, both in *Frauenrundschau*.

64 Kulesza, "Frauenfragen der Gegenwart"; "Bürgerinnen!"

65 A. von Kulesza, "Frauengedanken über den National-Sozialismus," *Frauen-rundschau*, 2 November 1932; DVP, "Wissen Sie schon—Frau Hilter?"

66 "Nationaler Selbstmord: Ein Ruf an die Frauen," *Demokratischer Zeitungsdienst*, 20 July 1932, *Frauenbeilage*. It is not known if any newspaper picked up the piece, written for the party's press service.

67 Lüders, "Deutsche! Halt! rufen wir Frauen," July 1932 flyer, BA ZSg 1-27/20 (3).

68 "Die berufstätige Frau wählt Adolf Hitler!," *VB*, 13/14 March 1932. This begs the question of whether women who *wanted* to work deserved protection; presumably, they did not. See also "Adolf Hitler soll die Frauen aus Beruf und Stellung jagen," April flyer design, NSDAP/HA 15/288.

69 "Frauen wehrt Euch!," July 1932, BA ZSg 1-90/45; "Frauen, wollt Ihr das?"; "Hallo—wir alle wählen"; "Arbeiterinnen! Angestellte!"; "Liebe Schwester Emilie!"

70 For text of the statement, see "Kampf der Hetze gegen die arbeitende Frau!," *Sozialdemokratisches Parteikorrespondenz*, June 1931.

71 Untitled flyer design, November 1932, BA ZSg 1-65/63. See also "Die Frau im 'Dritten Reich,'" 1931 pamphlet, BA ZSg 1-65/73 (13); "Mein Erlebnis als Frauendelegierte in Berlin," 1930–31 pamphlet, BA ZSg 1-65/25; "Eine ernste Frage steht vor uns Frauen," November 1932, BA ZSg 1-65/63; and "Frauen der arbeitenden Klasse!"

72 For internal writings, see "Bearbeitung der Betriebe mit weiblichen Ar-beitern und Angestellten," *Arbeit unter den Frauen* section of *Parteiarbeiter*, June 1931; "Richtlinien für die Arbeit den werktätigen Frauen," 1931, SAPMO-BA I/2/701/16; and "Arbeitsplan für die Arbeit der Partei unter den Frauen (Mai–Juni 1931)," SAPMO-BA I/2/701/11. Published materials include "Die Frau im 'Dritten Reich'"; "Kapitalismus ist Krieg—Frauen kämpft für den Frieden," 1932, Hoover GSC; "1,3 Millionen Frauen finden Arbeit," 1931, BA ZSg 1-65/65; Maria Reese, "An der Front des roten Aufbaus," 1932 pamphlet, BA ZSg 1-65/27; "14. Jahrestag der Russischen Revolution," October 1931, BA ZSg 1-65/73; and "Frauen des arbeitenden Volkes auf Euch kommt es an!," November 1932 pamphlet, Hoover GSC.

73 This is the tone of many women textile workers' writings in *Mein Arbeitstag—Mein Wochenende*. Mason argues that the high rate of young women who left the workforce and applied for marriage loans during the recovery of 1933–34 implies that many were glad not to have to work; see "Women in Germany," 1.

74 "Adolf Hitler soll die Frauen aus Beruf und Stellung jagen."

75 "Frauen im Dritten Reich"; "Adolf Hitler will die Frauen aus Beruf und Stellung jagen," April 1932, LA 240/2088/68; "Frauen der Arbeit"; "Hindenburg-wähler!" See also Childers, *Nazi Voter*, 239.

76 "Deutsche Frauen," July flyer design, NSDAP/HA 15/289, emphasis in original.

77 "Koburg: Nationalsozialismus in der Praxis," 1932, LA 240/2087/19.

78 See "Hausfrauen! Mütter!," 1932, Hoover Loesch Coll. 2/28; "Warum müßen wir Frauen deutschnational sein?," BA ZSg 1-44/7.

79 On the evolution of this legislation, including Helene Weber's key role, see Morsey and Ruppert, *Protokolle der Reichstagsfraktion* 2:508, 550.

80 "Weshalb Zentrum?"; "Die Frauen der Zentrumsliste"; "Das hohere Mädchen-

schulwesen," *Das Zentrum*, October–November 1932; *Das Zentrum*, December 1930 issue.

81 I found three that directly addressed single women's right to work: "National-sozialisten und aktuelle Beamtenfragen," Prussian flyer, April 1932, GStA/ XII.HA/IV 198; "Adolf Hitler will die Frauen aus Beruf und Stellung jagen"; and "Wie sie lügen!" See also Elsbeth Zander, "Die deutsche Frau wählt nationalsozialistisch!," *VB*, 30 July 1932.

82 Koonz, *Mothers in the Fatherland*, discusses the latitude women activists possessed before Hitler's coming to power.

83 "Adolf Hitler: Mein Programm!," April 1932, BA Berlin 15.01-26068; "Natio-nalsozialismus und Frauentum," *Rednerinformation* 3/4; Elsbeth Unverricht, "Die Frau im Beruf wählt nationalsozialistisch!," *VB*, 2 November 1932; "Frauen! Millionen Männer ohne Arbeit," poster in Hoover Mueller-Graeff Coll. box 3.

84 "Frauen aufgepasst!"; "Frauen wehrt Euch!"; "Was geht dich der Marxismus an?," 1931 pamphlet, BA ZSg 1-90/42 (15).

85 "Bürgerinnen!"; Kulesza, "Frauenfragen der Gegenwart"; "Drei Fragen hinter der Tür!"; "Entwürfe für Inserate," 1932, BA ZSg 1-42/8; "Kann die berufstätige Frau Hitler wählen?," *Frauenrundschau*, 24 March 1932.

86 "Nationalsozialisten und aktuelle Beamtenfragen"; "Beamte erwacht!," GStA/ XII.HA/IV 213.

87 On *Beamtinnen*, see Kulesza, "Frauenfragen der Gegenwart." See also the following in *Frauenrundschau*: Lotte Garnich, "Krise und Frauenberufsarbeit," 4 February 1932; "Zusammenarbeit von Mann und Frau im Beruf," 1 December 1932; Elisabeth Schwarzhaupt, "Die Stellung der NS zur Frau," 6 April 1932; I. Feth, "Die Vollimmatrikulation der Frau in Gefahr!," 2 June 1932.

88 DSP Reichsfrauenausschuss memo, 16 May 1931, NSDAP/HA 40/788; proto-col of DSP organizational conference proceedings, 5–6 December 1931, NSDAP/HA 39/775.

89 "Deutsche Frauen, Staatsbürgerinnen!"; "An die Beamten und Angestellten Groß-Hamburgs!," July 1932, BA ZSg 1-27/20 (3).

90 "Werte Frau." A 1931 pamphlet dodged SPD complicity in the postwar de-mobilization of female labor by telling speakers to argue that it was Brüning, not Severing, who fought for a renewed PAV; see "Referentenmaterial für Beamtenfragen," BA ZSg 1-90/42 (4). In December 1930, the SPD wrote a bill to reduce "Schwarzarbeit" and "double earners," but without gender-coded language; see SPD, *Jahrbuch* (1931), 100–101. On female party membership, see Lösche and Walter, "Zur Organisationskultur," 526.

91 Fromm survey quoted in Nolan, *Visions of Modernity*, 223. For anti-SPD strategy, see Frauenabteilung memo, 30 June 1932, SAPMO-BA I/2/701/15; "Arbeitsplan für die Arbeit der Partei unter den Frauen (April–Mai 1931)," SAPMO-BA I/2/701/11; and "Richtlinien für die Arbeit unter den werktätigen Frauen."

92 Childers, *Nazi Voter*, 243.

93 "Mobilmachung gegen den Staat," July 1932, Hoover Loesch Coll. 3/31. See also Childers, *Nazi Voter*, 258–61.

94 "Bürgerinnen!"; "Drei Fragen hinter der Tür!"; Kulesza, "Frauengedanken über

den National-Sozialismus." On the cultural threat of Bolshevism, see Boelitz, *Grundsätzliches zur Kulturlage*.

95   "Frauen, wollt Ihr das?"; "Frauen aufgepasst!"; "Ihr dummen Ziegen, dafür werden Eure Söhne Euch ja gemacht!" On Hitler and the clergy, see cover of *Sozialistische Aktion: Blätter zur Reichstagswahl*, 22 October 1932, BA ZSg 1-90/45.

96   "Deutsche Frauen, Volk und Staat rufen Euch!"

97   Leopold, *Alfred Hugenberg*, 118 n. 85, notes this failed attempt to win Catholics. For appeals, see *Unsere Partei*, 15 April 1932, and "Kampf den Gottesleugnern," *Unsere Partei*, 5 April 1932.

98   "Warum sind wir Frauen deutschnational?"

99   It issued a steady stream of articles in its journal about how to respond to Nazi misrepresentations of the Center's alliances with the SPD; for an example, see *Das Zentrum*, November 1930.

100   For Nazi appeals, see "Deutsche Katholiken hört!," July 1932, NSDAP/HA 15/289; "Adolf Hitler ist romhörig!," April 1932, NSDAP/HA 15/288; "Katholische Männer und Frauen!," March flyer design, NSDAP/HA 15/287; "Wie sie lügen!"; and "Millionen bauen, Millionen vertrauen, Millionen hoffen auf Adolf Hitler," *Flammenwerfer*, June 1932, in LA 240/2087/27.

101   "Anweisungen der Frauenabteilung des ZK," 18 February 1932, SAPMO-BA I/2/701/15; 30 June 1932 Frauenabteilung memo.

102   "Religion, Ehe, Familie" and "Unser tägliches Brot gib uns heute," both 1932 pamphlets, Hoover GSC; "Die Frau im 'Dritten Reich.'" On "refined torture," see "Unsere Arbeit unter den Zentrums-frauen," 1932 report, SAPMO-BA I/2/701/33.

103   "Demagogen um den §218," *Unsere Partei*, 1 May 1931.

104   "Warum sind wir Frauen deutschnational?"

105   What little discussion of sexual morality, urban "degeneracy," and abortion did appear was relegated largely to *Unsere Partei*; see 1931 issues of 15 January, 1 May, and 1 October.

106   *Rednerinformation* 5 (April 1932).

107   Rosenberg, "Die deutsche Frau im Kampf um ihr Recht."

108   "Katholische Männer und Frauen!"

109   "Wie sie lügen!" A sketch exists for a March flyer intended to dispel rumors that Magda Goebbels was a wealthy Jew and that Josef Goebbels had had an affair with an "evil whore and cocaine dealer" known to have Jewish lovers. I never saw a printed flyer of this and suspect none was made. See "Sie lügen! Sie lügen!," NSDAP/HA 15/287.

110   "Demagogen um den §218."

111   "Warum müßen wir Frauen deutschnational sein?"

112   This includes longtime DNVP activists such as Leonore Kühn. On the National Opposition, see Schmidt-Waldherr, *Emanzipation durch Professionalisierung?*, 27, 122–28.

113   "Mütter merkt auf!," *Der Angriff*, n.d., Hoover Loesch Coll. 3/32; "Frauen aufgepaßt!," *Roter Adler*, July 1932, GStA/XII.HA/IV 198.

114   "Frauenelend unter dem Sowjetstern: 218 —Was eine Rußlandfahrerin erzählt," *Deutschland Erwache!*, 17 July 1932, in GStA/XII.HA/IV 198. Agitators were

urged to use reports of former Communists who had traveled to Russia to discredit the KPD; see *Rednerinformation* 10 (28 September 1932).

115 Diehl, "Deutsche Frauen, erwacht!"; Rosenberg, "Die deutsche Frau im Kampf um ihr Recht."

116 For example, see "Alkoholismus und 'freie Liebe' in Sowjetrußland," *Frauenwelt* section of *Germania*, 31 July 1932.

117 "Was denkt der Nationalsozialismus über Ehe und Familie?," BA ZSg 1-108/9; "Katholiken, die Augen auf!," April 1932, BA ZSg 1-108/8.

118 Usborne, *Politics of the Body*, 176.

119 "Katholiken, die Augen auf!"; "Antworten Sie, Herr Hitler!," 1932, BA ZSg 1-108/8; "Nationalsozialismus und Frau," *Das Zentrum*, February 1932; *Das Zentrum*, December 1930 issue on Nazi cultural policy.

120 Schwarzhaupt, "Die Stellung der NS zur Frau"; "Drei Fragen hinter der Tür"; "Bürgerinnen!"; "Das Frauen Bildnis im Wandel der Zeiten," *Berliner Stimmen*, 2 November 1930; *Aktions-Programm der DVP*, 1931, BA ZSg 1-42/4. On abortion, see "Volksgesundheit und §218," *Berliner Stimmen*, 24 May 1931, the only DVP mention of abortion found in this period. On the BDF and abortion, see Grossmann, *Reforming Sex*, 89.

121 SPD, *Protokoll* (1931), 259.

122 "Frauen aufgepasst!"; "Arbeiterinnen! Angestellte!"; "Frauen marschieren!," *Berliner Volksblatt*, 19 April 1931.

123 Serialization began 27 August 1932; for readers' letters, see "Gilgi ist keine von uns," *Vorwärts*, 18 October 1932. See also Frevert, "Kunstseidene Glanz," 18.

124 *Nationalsozialistische Lügen: Worte und Taten der national-sozialistische Reichstagsfraktion* 22, BA ZSg 1-90/42 (6). See also "Hoch die Vielweiberei!," cartoon in *Vorwärts*, 27 January 1931.

125 "Eine Frage an die Mütter—Für's Röhmische III. Reich?," *Volks-Bote: Wahlsondernummer der SPD Groß-Stettin*, November 1932, BA ZSg 1-90/45. On Nazi "sexual crimes," including homosexuality and prostitution, see "Der braune Sumpf der Nazi-Hauptquartier," *Welt am Abend*, 11 March 1932. The SPD press had a history of this kind of exposé, "outing" Röhm in 1930 and industrial heir Fritz Krupp in 1902; on Krupp, see Fairbairn, *Democracy in the Undemocratic State*, 211.

126 The phrase "healthy popular feeling" comes from Peukert, *Inside Nazi Germany*, 219.

127 Grossmann, *Reforming Sex*, 104.

128 For an example of the commonly used 1932 image of militant youths, see "Jungwahler, entscheide dich!," July 1932, BA ZSg 1-90/45. An image of the *Proletarierin* as a breast-feeding mother is found on the cover of *Vorwärts*'s *Volk und Zeit* supplement, 21 June 1931.

129 A 1931 memo demanded exposure of the "hidden agenda" of SPD satellite organizations. Among those listed were groups that stressed greater availability of birth control; see "Arbeitsplan . . . April–Mai 1931" and "Arbeitsplan . . . Mai–Juni 1931." For appeals, see *Zwei Jahre Brüning Diktator*, 195; "Frauen des arbeitenden Volkes"; "Eine ernste Frage"; and "Arbeitende Frauen und Mädchen!"

130 Kontos, *Partei kämpft wie ein Mann!*, 87–90; Weitz, *Creating German Communism*,

219; Grossmann, *Reforming Sex*, 78–106. On the KPD and contraception, see Usborne, *Politics of the Body*, 116. For sample flyers, see "Amnestie!," and "An die Frauen, Mütter und Bräute der Polizeibeamten!," March 1932, BA ZSg 1-65/65. For posters, see Hoover Mueller-Graeff Coll. box 4.

131 See "15 Jahre Befreiung der Frau," November 1932 pamphlet, and "Von Zwickeln und Muckern," 1932 pamphlet, both Hoover GSC; "Religion, Ehe, Familie"; and Reese, "An der Front des roten Aufbaus."

132 See, for example, "Eine ernste Frage."

133 *Arbeiter Kalender 1932*, 21–22. Grossmann reproduces this page in *Reforming Sex*.

134 On violence, see "Arbeiterinnen! Angestellte!" and "Frauen aufgepasst!" For "stupid goats" references, see "Wollt ihr das?"; "Ihr dummen Ziegen, dafür werden Eure Söhne Euch ja gemacht!"; "Ihr dummen Ziegen—Wer ist gemeint? Frauen liest!"; and "Hort es! Ihr Frauen und Madchen!" For general appeals, see "Die 'Front der Nationalen Opposition' von Harzburg," July 1932, BA ZSg 1-90/41, and "Preussen wird Hitler geopfert!" On women and the welfare state, see "Hallo—wir alle wählen."

135 On Killinger (likely Manfred von Killinger, though no first name was ever specified), see "Deutschland erwacht!" For Nazi atrocity flyers, see "Hitlerbandit mit Peitsche und Pistole gegen Arbeitermädchen!," July 1932, LA 240/2087/28; "Arbeitende Frauen und Mädchen!"; and "Eine Mutter ruft!," 1932, BA ZSg 1-65/65. On women's attraction to Nazism, see "Faschistische Frauenorganisationen 1931–32," SAPMO-BA I/2/701/38.

136 "Kapitalismus ist Krieg—Frauen kämpft für den Frieden!"; "Krieg!," March 1932, Hoover GSC/5; Tina Modotti, "5.000.000 Witwen, 10.000.000 Waisen," November 1932, Hoover GSC; "An die Frauen, Mütter und Bräute der Polizeibeamten!"; "Wo Kommunisten regieren!," 1932, LA 240/1875/64. On the KPD cult of violence, see Rosenhaft, *Beating the Fascists?*, especially chap. 2.

137 For a comparison with British liberal feminist languages of progress, see Rendall, "Citizenship, Culture, and Civilization," 141.

138 Circulation figure in Reichhold to Lüders, 21 July 1932, BA NL Lüders, 99. This figure is in line with the average circulation of major party fliers in 1932.

139 Lüders, "Deutsche! Halt! rufen wir Frauen."

140 DVP, "Wissen Sie schon—Frau Hilter?"; "Entwürfe für Inserate"; "Hindenburg bleibt unser Reichspräsident," 10 March 1932, and "National-politische Frauenarbeit," 13 April 1932, both in *Frauenrundschau*.

141 "Mit des Teufels Großmutter . . . ," NSDAP/HA 41/837; *Unsere Partei*, 24 October 1932, also referred to "Das Zentrum, die Urgroßmutter des Satans." On women's voting in 1932, see Bremme, *Politische Rolle der Frau*, 74–75. On the *Führerprinzip*, see "Ein ernstes Wort an die Frauen und Mädchen." On monarchy, see "Warum sind wir Frauen deutschnational?"

142 "Mütter merkt auf!"

143 Zander, "Deutsche Frauen—Nationalsozialistinnen!," *VB*, 30/31 October 1932; "Frauen der Arbeit"; "Frauen, Ihr wollt frieden!," July 1932 flyer mock-up, NSDAP/HA 15/289; Zander, "Die deutsche Frau wählt nationalsozialistisch!"; "N.S.-Bilder vom Tage: Opfer roten Mordterrors!," *VB*, 1 November 1932, whose caption reads, "German mother, we will never forget your child!"

144 On female activity at election time, see Mitteilungen 22 des Landeskriminal-

polizeiamts (Ia) Berlin, 15 November 1932, BA Berlin 15.01-26125/124. See also Stephenson, *Nazi Organisation of Women*.

145 Heimersdorf to the Reichsleitung, August 1931, NSDAP/HA 13/254. See Stephenson, *Nazi Organisation of Women*, 65–74, on friction within the NSF.

146 Outlines of 1931 Parteitag and 18 September 1931 *Vorstand* meetings in BA Berlin 60 Vo 2/45126/57.

147 Martha Schwarz, in the DVP women's press, questioned why the DNVP "let" Müller resign her seat and suspected that she was forced. See "Frauen im neuen Reichstag," *Frauenrundschau*, 31 August 1932.

148 This is based on material in Childers, *Nazi Voter*, 260–61, and Boak, "'Our Last Hope,'" 299, which both posit the shifting loyalties of Protestant women.

149 "Die Betrachtung der Wahlergebnisse," *Das Zentrum*, November 1930.

150 "Bürgerinnen!"; Lange, "Um das Frauenwahlrecht"; Kulesza, "Frauenfragen der Gegenwart"; Elsa Matz, "Gefahren einer Frauenpartei," *DAZ*, 1 October 1931.

151 Gerwitt, "Frauenstimmen im Wahlkampf," 20 October 1932, and "Die volksparteiliche Frauen stehen treu zur Partei," 4 March 1932, both in *Frauenrundschau*. This hymn to female loyalty was written before voters utterly abandoned the DVP in July 1932. For more optimism, see Elsa Matz's reports on her autumn 1932 speaking tour, BA Berlin 60 Vo 1/53121/35.

152 This excludes the NSDAP. It lost its crown in July 1932 but only because it was reduced to seven seats, lending its lone woman greater statistical weight. See Boak, "Women in Weimar Politics," table 1, and Schwarz, "Die Frauen im Reichstag," *Frauenrundschau*, 5 August 1932.

153 On Mende, see Liesel Hapke letter, 17 November 1932, BA Berlin 60 Vo 1/53122/36, and memo, 20 February 1933, BA Berlin 60 Vo 1/53169/225. On candidate selection, see DVP memo, 10 June 1932, BA Berlin 60 Vo 1/53169/225.

154 *Arbeit unter den Frauen* section of *Parteiarbeiter*, October 1930, January 1931, March 1931, January 1932, February 1932; Thälmann to Central Committee, "Vorwärts unter dem Banner der Komintern," 14 May 1931, BA ZSg 1-65/73; "Sonderrundschreiben über die Arbeit der Partei unter den Frauen," 30 March 1931, SAPMO-BA I/2/701/15.

155 Zetkin, in "Der AIZ-Kolporteur," October 1931, BA ZSg 1-65/65. Similar instructions appear in women's section memos to cell leaders, 2 July 1931 and 18 March 1932, SAPMO-BA I/2/701/15. See also "Bearbeitung der Betriebe mit weiblichen Arbeitern und Angestellten," and "Halbjahresplan der Frauenabt. der ZK November 1931–März 1932," SAPMO-BA I/2/701/11.

156 On backpedaling on abortion, see Grossmann, *Reforming Sex*, 92–95.

157 On melodrama, see Petro, *Joyless Streets*, 127, and Rosenhaft, "Women, Gender, and the Limits of Political History," 162–63.

158 In Hoover Mueller-Graeff Coll. box 3.

159 On women voting NSDAP, see "Frauen für das Hakenkreuz," *Sozialdemokratisches Parteikorrespondenz*, January 1931, and SPD, *Protokoll* (1931), 150, 248–52. On rallies, see Wurms, "Gleichberechtigt, aber 'zur linken Hand,'" 46. For criticism of SPD reformism, see Hagemann, *Frauenalltag und Männerpolitik*, 545–49. For membership figures, see SPD, *Jahrbuch* (1931), 122.

160 See Wickert, *Unsere Erwählten* 1:198–99, on the fate of this resolution.

161 Usborne, *Politics of the Body*, 57.

162 "Richtlinien der Deutschen Staatspartei," 1931, NSDAP/HA 40/783.

163 *Mitteilungen des Reichsfrauenausschuss*, 17 September and 20 October 1930; November 1930 Parteitag protocol, NSDAP/HA 37/742. Wittstock even wrote that organizational forms were less important than women's "willingness to work and sacrifice"; see Reichsfrauenausschuss Rundschreiben, 27 November 1930, NSDAP/HA 40/787.

164 Lüders's papers (BA NL) document this collapse. Problems with propaganda and organization are cited in a 2 April 1931 report from DSP Kreisgruppe Essen, folder 100, and Lüders's report of March 1931, folder 272. On Wittstock, see Edelheim and Scheffen to Höpker-Aschoff, 4 November 1930, and Höpker-Aschoff to Zentral-Frauenarbeitsausschuss der DDP, 7 November 1930, both folder 99. See also Dönhoff to Lüders, 23 June 1932, folder 99.

165 Protokoll über die Sitzung der DDP, 27 September 1930, NSDAP/HA 37/732. Others expressed regret over her absence in the Reichstag, including Bäumer (November 1930 conference, NSDAP/HA 37/742) and Dönhoff (Protokoll über die Sitzung des Vorstandes, 16 October 1930, NSDAP/HA 37/732).

166 Lüders to DSP Abteilung Frauen, 3 June 1932, BA NL Lüders, folder 99.

167 I thank Larry Jones for this information.

168 See protocol of DSP executive meeting, 11 September 1932, BA R45 III/50.

169 Anne Marie Meiners to DSP Vorstand, 19 July 1932, BA NL Lüders, folder 99.

170 "Das ganze Volk sagt am 10. April JA!," 1932 poster, GStA/XII.HA/IV 215.

171 "Reaktion?," *Frauenrundschau*, 8 December 1932.

172 Childers, *Nazi Voter*, 260.

173 "Deutschland von Morgen: Freiheitlich-nationales Blatt."

CONCLUSION

1 Lüders to DSP Abteilung Frauen, 3 June 1932, BA NL Lüders, folder 99.

2 For British comments that female suffrage had been "a flop," see Pugh, "Impact of Women's Enfranchisement," 313.

3 Fairbairn, *Democracy in the Undemocratic State*, 7.

4 Falter, "Social Bases of Political Cleavages," 371–72.

5 For comparison on the difficulties of promoting a feminist agenda in postwar Britain, see Riley, *"Am I That Name?,"* 13, 59, and Alberti, "Keeping the Candle Burning."

6 On Friedrich Engels, see Riley, *"Am I That Name?,"* 47.

7 Compare the female images in a DDP poster from the January 1919 Prussian election, "Bürgerinnen wählt am 26. Januar!," which depicts four feminists dressed in prewar garb (Hoover Mueller-Graeff Coll. box 3), with a 1930 poster, "Für Einigkeit, Fortschritt, Volksgemeinschaft!" (GStA/XII.HA/IV 145).

8 This was consistent with their broad acceptance of some kind of state welfare policy by 1920. See Hong, *Welfare, Modernity, and the Weimar State*, 34.

9 Canning, "Gender and the Politics of Class Formation," 761.

10 Many SPD activists also desired this, but because legal abortion was never official party policy, the issue was not always prominently displayed in propaganda.

11 For examples of the West German CDU's use of naked or barely clothed women in posters from the 1970s, see Langguth, *Politik und Plakat*.

12 Rosenhaft, "Women, Gender, and the Limits of Political History," 165–69.

13 Falter, "Social Bases of Political Cleavages," 380.

14 Mouffe, "Feminism, Citizenship and Radical Democratic Politics."

PRIMARY SOURCES

Archival Materials

Bundesarchiv, Berlin (BA Berlin)
    Records of the Deutsche Volkspartei (60 Vo 1)
    Records of the Deutschnationale Volkspartei (60 Vo 2)
    Reichskommissar für Überwachung der öffentlichen Ordnung (15.07)
    Reichsministerium des Innern (15.01)
Bundesarchiv, Koblenz (BA)
    Nachlass Eduard Dingeldey
    Nachlass Anton Erkelenz
    Nachlass Katharina von Kardorff-Oheimb
    Nachlass Marie-Elisabeth Lüders
    Nachlass Schwertfeger
    Records of the Deutsche Demokratische Partei (R45 III)
    Records of the Deutsche Volkspartei (R45 II)
    Zeitgeschichtliche Sammlung (ZSg) 1
        27 DDP/DSP
        42 DVP
        44 DNVP
        65 KPD
        90 SPD
        91 USPD
        108 Zentrum
Geheimes Staatsarchiv Preußischer Kulturbesitz, Berlin (GStA)
    Hauptabteilung (HA) XII
    III Flugschriften
        2 DNVP
        8, 15 DDP
        16 DVP
    IV Plakate und Flugblätter seit 1878
        52–79 SPD

81 USPD

84–102 KPD

107–14, 278 Zentrum

122–45 DDP/DSP

157–70 DVP

175–95 DNVP

198–215 NSDAP

390 Breslau

Hoover Institution Archives, Stanford University, Stanford, Calif.

Rudolf Franz Collection

Loesch Collection

Moenkemöller Collection

Mueller-Graeff Poster Collection

Poster Collection (GE slides — Germany)

Weimar Republic Collection (GSC)

Landesarchiv, Berlin (LA)

Helene Lange Archiv (HLA), records of the Bund deutscher Frauenvereine

Repatorien 240 Wahlangelegenheiten

Acc. 243, 966, 1024, 1076, 1747, 1785, 1875, 1881, 1941, 1962, 1964, 2087, 2088,
2127, 2381

NSDAP Hauptarchiv (NSDAP/HA)

Reel 3, folder 82 NSDAP

Reel 13, folder 254 NSDAP

Reel 15, folders 287–89 NSDAP

Reel 20A, folder 1749 NSDAP

Reel 21, folder 390 NSDAP

Reel 36, folder 721 DDP

Reel 37, folders 732–42 DDP/DSP

Reel 38, folders 743, 753 DDP

Reel 39, folders 769–75 DDP

Reel 40, folders 783–88 DSP

Reel 41, folder 837 DNVP

Reel 42, folder 869 NSDAP

Reel 71, folder 1532 NSDAP

Staatsarchiv Hamburg, folder 224

Stiftung Archiv der Parteien und Massenorganisationen der ehemaligen DDR im
Bundesarchiv, Berlin, Zentrales Parteiarchiv (SAPMO-BA)

Correspondence of KPD Women's Secretariat, I/2/701, I/2/707

Nachlass Clara Zetkin

SPD Referentenmaterial, II/145

Published Party Conferences

Deutsche Demokratische Partei, Reichsgeschäftsstelle, ed. *Bericht über die
Verhandlungen des 1. Parteitages der Deutschen Demokratischen Partei, Berlin, den 19.
bis 22. Juli 1919.* Berlin, [1919].

———. *Bericht über die Verhandlungen des 2. Parteitages der Deutschen Demokratischen Partei, Nürnberg, den 11. bis 14. Dezember 1920.* Berlin, [1921].

———. *Bericht über die Verhandlungen des 3. Parteitages der Deutschen Demokratischen Partei, Bremen, den 12. bis 14. November 1921.* Berlin, [1921].

———. *Bericht über die Verhandlungen des 4. Parteitages der Deutschen Demokratischen Partei, Elberfeld, den 9. bis 10. Oktober 1922.* Berlin, [1922].

———. *Bericht über die Verhandlungen des 5. Parteitages der Deutschen Demokratischen Partei, Weimar, den 5. bis 6. April 1924.* Berlin, [1924].

Deutsche Volkspartei. *Bericht über den 1. Parteitag der DVP, 13. April 1919 in Jena.* Berlin, [1919].

Deutsche Zentrumspartei. *Erste Reichsparteitag des Zentrums: Offizieller Bericht (Berlin, 19. bis 22. Januar 1920).* Berlin, [1920].

———. *Zweite Reichsparteitag des Zentrums: Offizieller Bericht (Berlin, 15. bis 17. Januar 1922).* Berlin, [1922].

———. *Vierte Reichsparteitag des Zentrums: Offizieller Bericht (Cassel, 16. bis 17. November 1925).* Berlin, [1926].

———. *Fünfte Reichsparteitag des Zentrums: Offizieller Bericht (Köln, 8. bis 9. Dezember 1928).* Berlin, [1929].

Deutschnationale Volkspartei. *Führer durch den Reichsparteitag der DNVP in Hamburg, 30. März bis 2. April 1924.* Berlin, [1924].

———. *Führer durch den Reichsparteitag der DNVP in Köln, vom 8. bis 11. September 1926.* Berlin, [1927].

Kommunistische Partei Deutschlands. *Protokoll des 12. Parteitages (Wedding, 9. bis 16. Juni 1929).* Berlin, [1929].

Sozialdemokratische Partei Deutschlands. *Protokoll über die Verhandlungen des Parteitages der Sozialdemokratischen Partei, Weimar, den 10. bis 15. Juni 1919, sowie Bericht über die 7. Frauenkonferenz.* Berlin, 1919.

———. *Protokoll über die Verhandlungen des Parteitages der Sozialdemokratischen Partei, Weimar, 1922.* Berlin, 1922.

———. *Sozialdemokratischer Parteitag 1924: Protokoll mit dem Bericht der Frauenkonferenz.* Berlin, 1924.

———. *Sozialdemokratischer Parteitag 1925 in Heidelberg: Protokoll mit dem Bericht der Frauenkonferenz.* Berlin, 1925.

———. *Sozialdemokratischer Parteitag 1927 in Kiel (22. bis 27. Mai): Protokoll mit dem Bericht der Frauenkonferenz.* Berlin, 1927.

———. *Sozialdemokratischer Parteitag 1929 in Magdeburg: Protokoll.* Berlin, 1927.

———. *Sozialdemokratischer Parteitag 1931 in Leipzig (31. Mai bis 5. Juni): Protokoll.* Berlin, 1927.

Unabhängige Sozialdemokratische Partei Deutschlands. *Protokoll über die Verhandlungen des außerordentlichen Parteitages vom 12. bis 17. Oktober 1920 in Halle.* Berlin, [1920].

———. *Protokoll über die Verhandlungen des außerordentlichen Parteitages vom 30. November bis 6. Dezember 1919 in Leipzig. Mit Protokoll der Reichsfrauenkonferenz der U.S.P.* Berlin, [1920].

Berlin Newspapers

8-Uhr Abendblatt
Arbeiter-Illustrierte-Zeitung
Berliner Tageblatt
Deutsche Allgemeine Zeitung
Freiheit
Germania
Rote Fahne
Völkischer Beobachter
Vorwärts; *Vorwärts-Almanach*
Welt am Abend

Party Periodicals

Archiv der Deutschen Volkspartei
Berliner Stimmen: Zeitschrift für Politik (DVP)
Der Demokrat: Mitteilungen aus der Deutschen Demokratischen Partei
Demokratische Partei-Korrespondenz
Demokratischer Zeitungsdienst: Frauenbeilage
Der deutsche Demokrat: Nachrichtenblatt der DDP Berlin, Bezirk 19
Deutscher Volksboter: Wochenschrift für Politik und Wirtschaft
Deutschnationales Rüstzeug
Frauenrundschau: Beilage zur Nationalliberal Korrespondenz
Die Frau in der Politik: Monatbeilage der "Deutschen Stimmen"
Die Gleichheit
Die Kämpferin
Kommunistische Rundschau
Korrespondenz der DNVP
Materialien zur Demokratischen Politik
Merkblätter für die Parteiarbeit (DVP)
Mitteilungen der deutschen Zentrumspartei
Mitteilungen des Reichsfrauenausschuss der DDP
Mitteilungsblatt der Vereinigten Sozialdemokratischen Partei Deutschlands
Nachrichtenblatt Nationalliberale Korrespondenz: Wochenausgabe des Pressedienstes der DVP
Nachrichten für die Funktionäre (SPD)
Der Parteiarbeiter (KPD)
Rednerinformation (NSDAP)
7. Dezember (SPD, 1924)
Sozial-Demokratisches Parteikorrespondenz
Unsere Partei (DNVP)
Wahlzeitung der Deutschen Staatspartei
Das Zentrum: Mitteilungsblatt der deutschen Zentrumspartei

Other Contemporary Published Sources

Arnold, F. *Anschläge: 220 politische Plakate als Dokumente der deutschen Geschichte 1900–1980.* Munich, 1985.

Augustinus. *Der Sozialismus und die Würde der Frau.* Flugschriften der preussischen Zentrumspartei Nr. 3. Berlin, 1919.

Bäumer, Gertrud. *Die Frau in der Krise der Kultur.* Berlin, 1926.

Boelitz, Otto. *Grundsätzliches zur Kulturlage der Gegenwart.* Berlin, 1931.

Deutsche Demokratische Partei. *Frauenarbeit in der Deutschen Demokratischen Partei: Bericht über die Verhandlungen der Reichsfrauentagung der deutschen demokratischen Partei Dresden, 21. bis 23. September 1928.* Berlin, 1928.

———. *Leitfaden für Wahlorganisatoren und Wahlwerber.* Berlin, 1924.

———. *Material zum Wahlkampf Reichstagswahl 1924—Rededisposition.* Berlin, 1924.

———. *Organisations-Handbuch der DDP.* Berlin, 1926.

Deutsche Volkspartei. *Flugschriften der DVP—Reden aus der Nationalversammlung.* Berlin, 1920.

———. "Wissen Sie schon—Frau Hilter?" *Flugschriften der Deutschen Volkspartei* 78 (1931).

Deutsche Zentrumspartei. *Politische Agitations-Material.* 1926.

Deutschnationale Volkspartei. *Jahrbuch der DNVP.* 1921.

———. *Stichworte und Winke für deutsch-nationale Diskussionsredner.* 1918.

———. *Ziele der DNVP.* 1918.

Foellmer, Emma. *Zwei Jahre politisches Frauenwahlrecht.* Berlin, 1920.

Fromm, Erich. *The Working Class in Weimar Germany: A Psychological and Sociological Study.* Translated by Barbara Weinberger, edited by Wolfgang Bonss. Cambridge: Harvard University Press, 1984.

Handbuch des öffentlichen Lebens. Edited by Maximilian Müller-Jabusch. Leipzig: Verlag K. F. Koehler, 1931.

Hessisches Landesmuseum Darmstadt. *Politische Plakate der Weimarer Republik 1918–1933.* Darmstadt, 1980.

Kardorff, Katharina von. *Brauchen wir eine Frauenpartei?* Berlin, 1931.

Kempf, Rosa. *Die deutsche Frau nach der Volks-, Berufs- und Betriebzählung von 1925.* Mannheim, 1931.

Kempkes, A., ed. *Deutscher Aufbau: Nationalliberale Arbeit der Deutschen Volkspartei.* Berlin, 1927.

Kommunistische Partei Deutschlands. *Arbeiter Kalender.* 1932.

———. *Arbeiter-Taschenkalender.* 1925.

———. *Handbuch der kommunistischen Reichstagsfraktion: 21 Monate Hermann Müller Regierung.* Berlin, 1930.

———. *KPD Taschenkalender.* 1923.

———. *Der Reichstag 1924–1928: 4 Jahre kapitalistische Klassenpolitik. Handbuch der kommunistischen Reichstagsfraktion.* Berlin, 1928.

———. *Zwei Jahre Brüning Diktator: Handbuch der kommunistischen Reichstagsfraktion.* Berlin, 1932.

Koss, Henning von. *Das wahre Gesicht des Bolshewismus.* 1919.

Kulesza, Anny von. "Frauenfragen der Gegenwart." *Flugschriften der Deutschen Volkspartei* 79 (1931).

Lipinski, Richard. *Die Sozialdemokratie von ihren Anfängen bis zur Gegenwart: Eine gedrängte Darstellung.* Vol. 2. Berlin: J. H. W. Dietz, 1928.

Lüders, Marie-Elisabeth. *Fürchte Dich Nicht: Persönliches und Politisches aus mehr als 80 Jahren, 1878–1962.* Cologne: Westdeutscher Verlag, 1963.

Mein Arbeitstag—Mein Wochenende: 150 Berichte von Textilarbeiterinnen. Compiled and edited by the Deutscher Textilarbeiter-Verband. Berlin: Textilpraxis Verlag, 1930.

Morsey, Rudolf, and Karsten Ruppert, eds. *Protokolle der Reichstagsfraktion der deutschen Zentrumspartei.* 2 vols. Mainz: Matthias-Grunewald-Verlag, 1981.

Nationalsozialistische Deutsche Arbeiterpartei. *Taschen-Jahrbuch der deutschen National-sozialisten.* 1924, 1926, 1929, 1931.

Ostwald, Hans. *Sittengeschichte der Inflation: Ein Kulturdokument aus den Jahren des Marksturzes.* Berlin: Neufeld und Henius, 1931.

Politischer Almanach. 1925–30.

Prillip, Beda. *Die deutschnationale Frau und die Fragen der Gegenwart.* 1919.

Protokolle der Sitzungen der Nationalversammlung.

Revolutionäre Programme: Programme der deutschen und russischen revolutionären Arbeiterparteien und der Kommunistischen Internationale. Mannheim: Sendler, 1975.

Schneider, Max. "Die deutschen Wahlerinnen." *Gesellschaft* 4 (1927).

———. "Frauen an die Wahlurne: 14 Jahre Frauenwahlrecht in Deutschland." *Gesellschaft* 10 (1933).

Schreiber, Georg. *Zentrum und deutsche Politik: Ein Handbuch zu den Dezemberwahlen 1924.* 1924.

Sender, Toni. *Autobiography of a German Rebel.* New York: Vanguard, 1939.

Sozialdemokratische Partei Deutschlands. *Bericht über die Tätigkeit der Sozial-Demokratischen Reichstagsfraktion 1920–21.* Berlin, 1921.

———. *Bericht über die Tätigkeit der Sozialdemokratischen Reichstagsfraktion 1921–22.* Berlin, 1922.

———. *Handbuch für die Ortsvereine: Eine Anweisung für die Erledigung der Aufgaben der Ortsvereine.* Berlin, 1930.

———. *Handbuch für Sozial-Demokratischen Wähler.* Berlin, 1924.

———. *Das Heidelberg Programm.* Berlin, 1925.

———. *Jahrbuch der Sozial-Demokratie.* 1926–31.

———. *Die Sozialdemokratie im Reichstage 1925.* Berlin, [1926].

Sozialdemokratische Partei Deutschlands, Bezirksverband Berlin. *Jahresbericht 1925/ 1926.* Berlin, 1927.

Sozialdemokratischer Landtagsfraktion. *Referentenmaterial für die Wahl zum Preußischen Landtag 1928.*

Stampfer, Friedrich, ed. *Das Goerlitzer Programm.* Berlin, 1922.

Tergit, Gabriele. *Etwas Seltenes Überhaupt: Erinnerungen.* Frankfurt, 1983.

Tiling, Margarete von. *Konservativ oder Liberal? Zukunft oder Untergang?* Berlin, 1930.

———. *Wir Frauen und die christliche Schule.* 1928.

Treue, Wolfgang. *Deutsche Parteiprogramme seit 1861.* Göttingen: Musterschmidt, 1954.

Tschachotin, Sergei. "Die Technik der politischen Propaganda." *Sozialistische Monatshefte* 38, no. 75 (1932): 425–31.

Unabhängige Sozialdemokratische Partei. *Handbuch der Wähler der USPD.* Berlin, 1920.

Vierteljahrshefte zur Statistik des Deutschen Reiches—1. Ergänzungsheft. Berlin, 1919.

Weimar Republic Sourcebook. Edited and compiled by Anton Kaes, Martin Jay, and
Edward Dimendberg. Berkeley: University of California Press, 1994.
Weiss, Max, ed. *Der nationale Wille: Werden und Wirken der Deutschnationalen
Volkspartei 1918–1928*. Essen: Deutsche Vertriebsstelle Rhein und Ruhr, 1928.
Wex, Else. *Staatsbürgerliche Arbeit deutscher Frauen, 1865–1928*. Berlin, 1929.

SECONDARY SOURCES

Alberti, Johanna. "Keeping the Candle Burning: Some British Feminists between
Two Wars." In *Suffrage and Beyond: International Feminist Perspectives*, edited by
Caroline Daley and Melanie Nolan, 295–312. New York: New York University
Press, 1994.
Allen, Ann Taylor. *Feminism and Motherhood in Germany, 1800–1914*. New Brunswick:
Rutgers University Press, 1991.
Anderson, Margaret Lavinia. "Voter, Junker, *Landrat*, Priest: The Old Authorities
and the New Franchise in Imperial Germany." *American Historical Review* 98, no. 5
(December 1993): 1448–74.
Ankum, Katharina von, ed. *Women in the Metropolis: Gender and Modernity in Weimar
Culture*. Berkeley: University of California Press, 1997.
Arendt, Hans-Jürgen. "Die kommunistische Frauenpresse in Deutschland 1917 bis
1933." *Beiträge zur Geschichte der Arbeiterbewegung* 29 (1987): 78–88.
———. "Weibliche Mitglieder der KPD in der Weimarer Republik—zahlenmäßige
Stärke und soziale Stellung." *Beiträge zur Geschichte der Arbeiterbewegung* 19 (1977):
652–60.
Arendt, Hans-Jürgen, and Werner Freigang. "Der Rote Frauen- und
Mädchenbund—die revolutionäre deutsche Frauenorganisation in der Weimarer
Republik." *Beiträge zur Geschichte der Arbeiterbewegung* 21 (1979): 249–58.
Baumann, Ursula. *Protestantismus und Frauenemanzipation in Deutschland 1850 bis 1920*.
Frankfurt: Campus Verlag, 1992.
Bessel, Richard. "'Eine nicht allzu große Beunruhigung des Arbeitsmarktes':
Frauenarbeit und Demobilmachung in Deutschland nach dem Ersten
Weltkrieg." *Geschichte und Gesellschaft* 9 (1983): 211–29.
———. "The Formation and Dissolution of a German National Electorate from
Kaiserreich to Third Reich." In *Elections, Mass Politics, and Social Change in Modern
Germany*, edited by Larry Eugene Jones and James Retallack, 399–418.
Cambridge: Cambridge University Press, 1992.
———. "Unemployment and Demobilisation in Germany after the First World
War." In *The German Unemployed*, edited by Richard J. Evans and Dick Geary,
23–43. London: Croom Helm, 1987.
Boak, Helen. "'Our Last Hope': Women's Votes for Hitler—A Reappraisal." *German
Studies Review* 12 (1989): 289–310.
———. "Women in Weimar Germany: The *Frauenfrage* and the Female Vote." In
Social Change and Political Development in the Weimar Republic, edited by Richard
Bessel and E. J. Feuchtwanger, 155–73. London: Croom Helm, 1981.
———. "Women in Weimar Politics." *European History Quarterly* 20 (1990): 369–99.
Bodek, Richard. "Communist Music in the Streets: Politics and Perceptions in

Berlin at the End of the Weimar Republic." In *Elections, Mass Politics, and Social Change in Modern Germany*, edited by Larry Eugene Jones and James Retallack, 267–85. Cambridge: Cambridge University Press, 1992.

Bremme, Gabriele. *Die Politische Rolle der Frau in Deutschland*. Göttingen: Vandenhoeck und Rupprecht, 1956.

Breuer, Gisela. *Frauenbewegung im Katholizismus: Der Katholische Frauenbund 1903–18*. Frankfurt: Campus Verlag, 1998.

Bridenthal, Renate. "Class Struggle around the Hearth: Women and Domestic Service in the Weimar Republic." In *Towards the Holocaust: The Social and Economic Collapse of the Weimar Republic*, edited by Michael N. Dobkowski and Isidor Wallimann, 243–64. Westport, Conn.: Greenwood Press, 1983.

———. "Organized Rural Women and the Conservative Mobilization of the German Countryside in the Weimar Republic." In *Between Reform, Reaction, and Resistance: Studies in the History of German Conservatism from 1789 to 1945*, edited by Larry Eugene Jones and James Retallack, 375–405. Providence: Berghahn, 1993.

———. "Professional Housewives: Stepsisters of the Women's Movement." In *When Biology Became Destiny: Women in Weimar and Nazi Germany*, edited by Renate Bridenthal, Atina Grossmann, and Marian Kaplan, 153–73. New York: Monthly Review Press, 1984.

Bridenthal, Renate, and Claudia Koonz. "Beyond *Kinder, Küche, Kirche*: Weimar Women in Politics and Work." In *When Biology Became Destiny: Women in Weimar and Nazi Germany*, edited by Renate Bridenthal, Atina Grossmann, and Marian Kaplan, 33–65. New York: Monthly Review Press, 1984.

———. "Introduction: Women in Weimar and Nazi Germany." In *When Biology Became Destiny: Women in Weimar and Nazi Germany*, edited by Renate Bridenthal, Atina Grossmann, and Marian Kaplan, 1–29. New York: Monthly Review Press, 1984.

Canning, Kathleen. "Feminist History after the Linguistic Turn: Historicizing Discourse and Experience." *Signs* 19, no. 2 (Winter 1994): 368–404.

———. "Gender and the Politics of Class Formation: Rethinking German Labor History." *American Historical Review* 97, no. 3 (June 1992): 736–68.

Childers, Thomas. "Inflation, Stabilization and Political Realignment in Germany, 1924–28." In *Die Deutsche Inflation: Eine Zwischenbilanz*, edited by Gerald Feldman, Carl-Ludwig Holtfrerich, Gerhard A. Ritter, and Peter-Christian Witt, 409–31. Berlin: De Gruyter, 1982.

———. "Languages of Liberalism: Liberal Political Discourse in the Weimar Republic." In *In Search of a Liberal Germany*, edited by Konrad Jarausch and Larry Eugene Jones, 323–59. London: Berg, 1990.

———. "The Limits of National Socialist Mobilization." In *The Formation of the Nazi Constituency*, edited by Thomas Childers, 232–59. London: Croom Helm, 1986.

———. *The Nazi Voter: The Social Foundations of Fascism in Germany, 1919–1933*. Chapel Hill: University of North Carolina Press, 1983.

———. "The Social Language of Politics in Germany: The Sociology of Political Discourse in the Weimar Republic." *American History Review* 95 (April 1990): 331–57.

Clemens, Bärbel. *"Menschenrechte haben kein Geschlecht"*: *Zum Politikverständnis der bürgerlichen Frauenbewegung.* Pfaffenweiler: Centaurus, 1988.

Crew, David. "The Ambiguities of Modernity: Welfare and the German State from Wilhelm to Hitler." In *Society, Culture, and the State in Germany, 1870–1930*, edited by Geoff Eley, 319–44. Ann Arbor: University of Michigan Press, 1996.

Daniel, Ute. *The War from Within: German Working-Class Women in the First World War.* Translated by Margaret Ries. Oxford: Berg, 1997.

Davis, Belinda. *Home Fires Burning: Food, Politics, and Everyday Life in World War I Berlin.* Chapel Hill: University of North Carolina Press, 2000.

Duverger, Maurice. *The Political Role of Women.* Paris: UNESCO, 1955.

Engelstein, Laura. "Morality and the Wooden Spoon: Russian Doctors View Syphilis, Social Class and Sexual Behavior, 1890–1905." In *The Making of the Modern Body*, edited by Thomas Laqueur and Catherine Gallagher, 169–208. Berkeley: University of California Press, 1987.

Evans, Richard. *The Feminist Movement in Germany 1894-1933.* Beverly Hills: Sage, 1976.

Fairbairn, Brett. *Democracy in the Undemocratic State: The German Reichstag Elections of 1898 and 1903.* Toronto: University of Toronto Press, 1997.

———. "Interpreting Wilhelmine Elections: National Issues, Fairness Issues, and Electoral Mobilization." In *Elections, Mass Politics, and Social Change in Modern Germany*, edited by Larry Eugene Jones and James Retallack, 17–47. Cambridge: Cambridge University Press, 1992.

Falter, Jürgen. "The Social Bases of Political Cleavages in the Weimar Republic, 1919–1933." In *Elections, Mass Politics, and Social Change in Modern Germany*, edited by Larry Eugene Jones and James Retallack, 371–97. Cambridge: Cambridge University Press, 1992.

Falter, Jürgen, Thomas Lindenberger, and Siegfried Schumann. *Wahlen und Abstimmungen in der Weimarer Republik: Materialien zum Wahlverhalten 1919-1933.* Munich: Beck, 1986.

Frevert, Ute. "Kunstseidene Glanz: Weibliche Angestellte." In *Hart und Zart: Frauenleben 1920-1970*, 15–21. Berlin: Elefanten Press, 1990.

———. *Women in German History: From Bourgeois Emancipation to Sexual Liberation.* New York: Berg, 1989.

Fricke, Dieter, Werner Fritsch, Herbert Gottwald, Siegfried Schmidt, and Manfred Weissbecker, eds. *Lexikon zur Parteiengeschichte: Die bürgerlichen und kleinbürgerlichen Parteien und Verbände in Deutschland 1789-1945.* Leipzig: VEB Bibliographisches Institut, 1986.

Friedrich, Otto. *Before the Deluge.* New York: Avon, 1972.

Fritzsche, Peter. "Breakdown or Breakthrough?: Conservatives and the November Revolution." In *Between Reform, Reaction, and Resistance: Studies in the History of German Conservatism from 1789 to 1945*, edited by Larry Eugene Jones and James Retallack, 299–328. Providence and Oxford: Berghahn, 1993.

———. *Rehearsals for Fascism: Populism and Political Mobilization in Weimar Germany.* New York: Oxford University Press, 1990.

Frye, Bruce B. *Liberal Democrats in the Weimar Republic: The History of the German Democratic Party and the German State Party.* Carbondale: Southern Illinois University Press, 1985.

Greven-Aschoff, Barbara. *Die bürgerliche Frauenbewegung in Deutschland 1894–1933*. Göttingen: Vandenhoeck and Rupprecht, 1981.

Grossmann, Atina. "Abortion and Economic Crisis: The 1931 Campaign against Paragraph 218." In *When Biology Became Destiny: Women in Weimar and Nazi Germany*, edited by Renate Bridenthal, Atina Grossmann, and Marian Kaplan, 66–86. New York: Monthly Review Press, 1984.

———. "*Girlkultur*, or a Thoroughly Rationalized Female: A New Woman in Weimar Germany?" In *Women and Culture and Politics: A Century of Change*, edited by Judith Friedlander, Blanche W. Cook, Alice Kessler-Harris, and Carroll Smith-Rosenberg, 62–80. Bloomington: Indiana University Press, 1986.

———. "The New Woman and the Rationalization of Sexuality in Weimar Germany." In *Powers of Desire: The Politics of Sexuality*, edited by Ann Snitow, Christine Stansell, and Sharon Thompson, 153–71. New York: Monthly Review Press, 1983.

———. *Reforming Sex: The German Movement for Birth Control and Abortion Reform, 1920–1950*. New York: Oxford University Press, 1995.

Hagemann, Karin. *Frauenalltag und Männerpolitik: Alltagsleben und gesellschaftliches Handeln von Arbeiterfrauen in der Weimarer Republik*. Bonn: J. H. W. Dietz, 1990.

Harsch, Donna. *German Social Democracy and the Rise of Nazism*. Chapel Hill: University of North Carolina Press, 1993.

Hartenstein, Wolfgang. *Die Anfänge der Deutschen Volkspartei 1918–1920*. Düsseldorf, 1962.

Harvey, Elizabeth. "Serving the Volk, Saving the Nation: Women in the Youth Movement and the Public Sphere in Weimar Germany." In *Elections, Mass Politics, and Social Change in Modern Germany*, edited by Larry Eugene Jones and James Retallack, 201–21. Cambridge: Cambridge University Press, 1992.

Hausen, Karin. "Mother's Day in the Weimar Republic." In *When Biology Became Destiny: Women in Weimar and Nazi Germany*, edited by Renate Bridenthal, Atina Grossmann, and Marian Kaplan, 131–52. New York: Monthly Review Press, 1984.

Hong, Young-Sun. *Welfare, Modernity, and the Weimar State, 1919–1933*. Princeton: Princeton University Press, 1998.

———. "World War I and the German Welfare State: Gender, Religion, and the Paradoxes of Maternity." In *Society, Culture, and the State in Germany, 1870–1930*, edited by Geoff Eley, 345–69. Ann Arbor: University of Michigan Press, 1996.

Hunt, Lynn. *Politics, Culture, and Class in the French Revolution*. Berkeley: University of California Press, 1984.

———, ed. *The New Cultural History*. Berkeley: University of California Press, 1989.

Huyssen, Andreas. "Mass Culture as Woman: Modernism's Other." In *Studies in Entertainment: Critical Approaches to Mass Culture*, edited by Tania Modleski. Theories of Contemporary Culture 7:188–207. Bloomington: Indiana University Press, 1986.

Janusch, Daniela. *Die plakative Propaganda der Sozialdemokratischen Partei Deutschlands zu den Reichstagswahlen 1928 bis 1932*. Bochum: Studienverlag Dr. N. Brockmeyer, 1989.

Jones, Gareth Stedman. *Languages of Class: Studies in English Working Class History, 1832–1982*. Cambridge: Cambridge University Press, 1983.

Jones, Larry Eugene. "Generational Conflict and the Problem of Political

Mobilization in the Weimar Republic." In *Elections, Mass Politics, and Social Change in Modern Germany*, edited by Larry Eugene Jones and James Retallack, 347–69. Cambridge: Cambridge University Press, 1992.

———. *German Liberalism and the Dissolution of the Weimar Party System, 1918–1933*. Chapel Hill: University of North Carolina Press, 1988.

———. "In the Shadow of Stabilization: German Liberalism and the Legitimacy Crisis of the Weimar Party System, 1924–1930." In *Die Nachwirkungen der Inflation auf die deutsche Geschichte 1924–33*, edited by Gerald Feldman, 21–41. Munich: R. Oldenbourg, 1985.

Kall, Alfred. *Die katholische Frauenbewegung in Deutschland*. Paderborn: Schöningh, 1983.

Kaplan, Marion A. *The Making of the Jewish Middle Class: Women, Family, and Identity in Imperial Germany*. New York: Oxford University Press, 1991.

Kaufmann, Doris. *Frauen zwischen Aufbruch und Reaktion: Die Protestantische Frauenbewegung in der ersten Hälfte des 20. Jahrhunderts*. Munich: Piper, 1988.

———. "Vom Vaterland zum Mutterland: Frauen im katholischen Millieu der Weimarer Republik." In *Frauen suchen ihre Geschichte*, edited by Karin Hausen, 254–79. Munich: Beck, 1983.

Kent, Susan Kingsley. *Making Peace: The Reconstruction of Gender in Interwar Britain*. Princeton: Princeton University Press, 1993.

Kerbs, Diethart. "Die illustrierte Presse am Ende der Weimarer Republik." In *Berlin 1932: Das letzte Jahr der Weimarer Republik*, edited by Diethart Kerbs and Henrick Stahr, 68–89. Berlin: Edition Hentrich, 1992.

Kolb, Eberhard. *The Weimar Republic*. Translated by P. S. Falla. London: Unwin Hyman, 1988.

Kontos, Silvia. *Die Partei kämpft wie ein Mann! Frauenpolitik der KPD in der Weimarer Republik*. Frankfurt: Roter Stern, 1979.

Koonz, Claudia. "The Competition for Women's Lebensraum, 1928–1934." In *When Biology Became Destiny: Women in Weimar and Nazi Germany*, edited by Renate Bridenthal, Atina Grossmann, and Marian Kaplan, 199–236. New York: Monthly Review Press, 1984.

———. "Conflicting Allegiances: Political Ideology and Women Legislators in Weimar Germany." *Signs* 1 (1976): 663–83.

———. *Mothers in the Fatherland: Women, the Family, and Nazi Ideology, 1919–1945*. New York: St. Martin's Press, 1987.

———. "Some Political Implications of Separatism: German Women between Democracy and Nazism, 1928–1934." In *Women in Culture and Politics: A Century of Change*, edited by Judith Friedlander, Blance W. Cook, Alice Kessler-Harris, and Carroll Smith-Rosenberg, 269–85. Bloomington: Indiana University Press, 1986.

Kühne, Thomas. "Historische Wahlforschung in der Erweiterung." In *Modernisierung und Region im wilhelminischen Deutschland: Wahlen, Wahlrecht und politische Kultur*. Bielefeld: Verlag für Regionalgeschichte, 1995.

Langguth, Gerd, ed. *Politik und Plakat: 50 Jahre Plakatgeschichte am Beispiel der CDU*. Bonn: Bouvier Verlag, 1995.

Lavin, Maud. *Cut with the Kitchen Knife: The Weimar Photomontages of Hannah Höch*. New Haven: Yale University Press, 1993.

Lebzelter, Gisela. "Die 'Schwarze Schmach': Vorurteile—Propaganda—Mythos." *Geschichte und Gesellschaft* 11 (1985): 37–58.

Leopold, John A. *Alfred Hugenberg: The Radical Nationalist Campaign against the Weimar Republic.* New Haven: Yale University Press, 1977.

Liebe, Werner. *Die Deutschnationale Volkspartei 1918–1924.* Düsseldorf: Droste, 1956.

Lösche, Peter, and Franz Walter. "Zur Organisationskultur der sozialdemokratischen Arbeiterbewegung in der Weimarer Republik." *Geschichte und Gesellschaft* 15 (1989): 511–36.

Mason, Tim. "Women in Germany, 1925–1940: Family, Welfare, and Work." *History Workshop* 1 (1976): 74–113 and 2 (1976): 5–32.

Meyer-Renschhausen, Elisabeth. "The Bremen Morality Scandal." In *When Biology Became Destiny: Women in Weimar and Nazi Germany*, edited by Renate Bridenthal, Atina Grossmann, and Marian Kaplan, 87–108. New York: Monthly Review Press, 1984.

Möller, Frank. "Die sich selbst bewusste Massenbeeinflussung: Liberalismus und Propaganda." In *Propaganda in Deutschland: zur Geschichte der politischen Massenbeeinflussung im 20. Jahrhundert*, edited by Gerald Diesener and Rainer Gries, 3–22. Darmstadt: Primus-Verlag, 1996.

Morsey, Rudolf. *Die deutsche Zentrumspartei 1917–1923.* Düsseldorf: Droste, 1966.

Mouffe, Chantal. "Feminism, Citizenship and Radical Democratic Politics." In *Feminists Theorize the Political*, edited by Judith Butler and Joan Wallach Scott, 369–84. New York: Routledge, 1992.

Nelson, Keith L. "The 'Black Horror on the Rhine': Race as a Factor in Post–World War I Diplomacy." *Journal of Modern History* 42 (1970): 606–27.

Nolan, Mary. *Visions of Modernity: American Business and the Modernization of Germany.* New York: Oxford University Press, 1994.

Offen, Karen. "Defining Feminism: A Comparative Historical Approach." *Signs* 14, no. 1 (1988): 119–57.

———. "Women, Citizenship, and Suffrage with a French Twist, 1789–1993." In *Suffrage and Beyond: International Feminist Perspectives*, edited by Caroline Daley and Melanie Nolan, 151–70. New York: New York University Press, 1994.

Paul, Gerhard. *Aufstand der Bilder: Die NS-Propaganda vor 1933.* Bonn: J. H. W. Dietz, 1990.

———. "Krieg der Symbole: Formen und Inhalte des symbol-publizistischen Bürgerkrieges 1932." In *Berlin 1932: Das letzte Jahr der Weimarer Republik*, edited by Diethart Kerbs and Henrick Stahr, 27–55. Berlin: Edition Hentrich, 1992.

Peterson, Brian. "The Politics of Working-Class Women in the Weimar Republic." *Central European History* 10 (1977): 87–111.

Petro, Patrice. *Joyless Streets: Women and Melodramatic Representation in Weimar Germany.* Princeton: Princeton University Press, 1989.

Peukert, Detlev. *Inside Nazi Germany: Conformity, Opposition, and Racism in Everyday Life.* New Haven: Yale University Press, 1987.

———. *The Weimar Republic: The Crisis of Classical Modernity.* Translated by Richard Deveson. New York: Hill and Wang, 1992.

Pore, Renate. *A Conflict of Interest: Women in German Social Democracy 1919–1933.* Westport, Conn.: Greenwood Press, 1981.

Pugh, Martin. "The Impact of Women's Enfranchisement in Britain." In *Suffrage and*

Beyond: International Feminist Perspectives, edited by Caroline Daley and Melanie Nolan, 313–28. New York: New York University Press, 1994.

Pyta, Wolfram. *Dorfgemeinschaft und Parteipolitik 1918–1933: Die Verschränkung von Milieu und Parteien in den protestantischen Landgebieten Deutschlands in der Weimarer Republik*. Düsseldorf: Droste Verlag, 1996.

Reagin, Nancy R. *A German Women's Movement: Class and Gender in Hanover, 1880–1933*. Chapel Hill: University of North Carolina Press, 1995.

Rendall, Jane. "Citizenship, Culture, and Civilization: The Languages of British Suffragists, 1866–1874." In *Suffrage and Beyond: International Feminist Perspectives*, edited by Caroline Daley and Melanie Nolan, 127–50. New York: New York University Press, 1994.

Rieden, Charlotte. "Helene Weber als Gründerin der katholischen Schule für Sozialarbeit in Köln und als Sozialpolitikerin." In *Sozialarbeit und Soziale Reform: Zur Geschichte eines Berufs zwischen Frauenbewegung und öffentlicher Verwaltung*, edited by Rüdeger Baron, 110–43. Weinheim: Beltz Verlag, 1983.

Riley, Denise. *"Am I That Name?": Feminism and the Category of "Women" in History*. Minneapolis: University of Minnesota Press, 1988.

Roberts, Mary Louise. *Civilization without Sexes: Reconstructing Gender in Postwar France, 1917–1927*. Chicago: University of Chicago Press, 1994.

Rosenhaft, Eve. *Beating the Fascists?: The German Communists and Political Violence, 1929–1933*. Cambridge: Cambridge University Press, 1983.

———. "Women, Gender, and the Limits of Political History in an Age of 'Mass' Politics." In *Elections, Mass Politics, and Social Change in Modern Germany*, edited by Larry Eugene Jones and James Retallack, 149–73. Cambridge: Cambridge University Press, 1992.

Ruppert, Karsten. *Im Dienst am Staat von Weimar: Das Zentrum als regierende Partei in der Weimarer Demokratie 1923–1930*. Düsseldorf: Droste, 1992.

Saldern, Adelheid von. "Modernization as Challenge: Perceptions and Reactions of German Social Democratic Women." In *Women and Socialism/Socialism and Women: Europe between the Two World Wars*, edited by Helmut Gruber and Pamela Graves, 95–134. New York: Berghahn, 1998.

Scheck, Raffael. "German Conservatism and Female Political Activism in the Early Weimar Republic." *German History* 15, no. 1 (1997): 34–55.

Schmidt-Waldherr, Hiltraud. *Emanzipation durch Professionalisierung? Politische Strategien und Konflikte innerhalb der bürgerlichen Frauenbewegung während der Weimarer Republik und die Reaktion des bürgerlichen Antifeminismus und des Nationalsozialismus*. Frankfurt: Materialis Verlag, 1987.

Schneider, Werner. *Die Deutsche Demokratische Partei in der Weimarer Republik: 1924–1930*. Munich: Fink, 1978.

Scott, Joan W. *Gender and the Politics of History*. New York: Columbia University Press, 1986.

———. "On Language, Gender, and Working-Class History." *International Labour and Working Class History* 31 (Spring 1987): 1–13.

Sewell, William, Jr. *Work and Revolution in France: The Language of Labor from the Old Regime to 1848*. Cambridge: Cambridge University Press, 1980.

Shively, W. Phillips. "Party Identification, Party Choice, and Voting Stability: The

Weimar Case." *American Political Science Review* 66, no. 4 (December 1972): 1203–25.

Soden, Kristine von. "'Hilft uns denn niemand?' Zum Kampf gegen den §218." In *Hart und Zart: Frauenleben 1920–1970*, 83–93. Berlin: Elefanten Press, 1990.

Stephenson, Jill. *The Nazi Organisation of Women.* London: Croom Helm, 1981.

Stoehr, Irene. "'Organisierte Mütterlichkeit.' Zur Politik der deutschen Frauenbewegung um 1900." In *Frauen suchen ihre Geschichte*, edited by Karin Hausen, 225–53. Munich: Beck, 1983.

Surmann, Rolf. *Die Münzenberg-Legende: Zur Publizistik der revolutionären deutschen Arbeiterbewegung 1921–1933.* Cologne: Prometh Verlag, 1982.

Tatschmurat, Carmen. "'Wir haben keinen Beruf, wir haben Arbeit': Frauenarbeit in der Industrie der zwanziger Jahre." In *Hart und Zart: Frauenleben 1920–1970*, 22–29. Berlin: Elefanten Press, 1990.

Thönnessen, Werner. *The Emancipation of Women: The Rise and Decline of the Women's Movement in German Social Democracy.* London: Pluto Press, 1973.

Tormin, Walter. *Geschichte der deutschen Parteien seit 1848.* Stuttgart: Kohlhammer, 1966.

Turner, Bryan S. "Contemporary Problems in the Theory of Citizenship." In *Citizenship and Social Theory*, edited by Bryan S. Turner, 1–18. London: Sage, 1993.

Usborne, Cornelie. *The Politics of the Body in Weimar Germany: Women's Reproductive Rights and Duties.* Ann Arbor: University of Michigan Press, 1992.

Walker, D. P. "The German Nationalist People's Party: The Conservative Dilemma in the Weimar Republic." *Journal of Contemporary History* 14 (1979): 627–47.

Weinstein, Joan. *The End of Expressionism: Art and the November Revolution in Germany, 1918–1919.* Chicago: University of Chicago Press, 1990.

Weitz, Eric D. *Creating German Communism: From Popular Protests to Socialist State.* Princeton: Princeton University Press, 1997.

Whittick, Arnold. *Woman into Citizen.* Santa Barbara: ABC-Clio, 1979.

Wickert, Christl. *Unsere Erwählten: Sozialdemokratische Frauen im Deutschen Reichstag und im Preußischen Landtag 1919 bis 1933.* 2 vols. Göttingen: Sovec, 1986.

Winkler, Heinrich August. "Abschied von Weimar: Ein politisches Porträt des Jahres 1932." In *Berlin 1932: Das letzte Jahr der Weimarer Republik*, edited by Diethart Kerbs and Henrick Stahr, 11–26. Berlin: Edition Hentrich, 1992.

Wittrock, Christina. *Weiblichkeitsmythen: Das Frauenbild im Faschismus und seine Vorläufer in der Frauenbewegung der 20er Jahre.* Frankfurt: Sendler, 1985.

Wobbe, Theresa. "'Die Frauenbewegung ist keine Parteisache': Politische Positionen der Gemäßigten und Fortschrittlichen der bürgerlichen Frauenbewegung im Kaiserreich." *Feministische Studien* 5 (1986): 50–65.

Wurms, Renate. "Gleichberechtigt, aber 'zur linken Hand': Zur Frauenbewegung in der Weimarer Republik." In *Hart und Zart: Frauenleben 1920–1970*, 38–52. Berlin: Elefanten Press, 1990.

19–20, 30, 31, 42, 51, 65, 66, 91, 231,
  264, 270
—Presidential: 1932, 219–20, 224
—Reichstag: June 1920, 20, 35; May
  1924, 70, 75; December 1924, 71;
  May 1928, 120, 123, 166–67, 169–70;
  September 1930, 170, 172, 216–18;
  July 1932, 219, 226, 228; November
  1932, 219
Equality, female, 2, 11–12, 15–16, 43,
  60, 66, 72, 116, 123–24, 166–67, 172,
  179, 221–23, 230–38, 270–73, 280.
  See also Citizenship; Communist
  Party; German Democratic Party;
  German People's Party; National
  Socialist German Workers Party: and
  women's rights; Social Democratic
  Party
Erkelenz, Anton, 78, 80, 143, 186
Eugenics, 56, 147, 183, 205, 217, 250, 252,
  276, 277
Evangelical Women's League (VEFD),
  10, 42, 311 (n. 23)

Fabian, Dora, 153
Fashion, 122, 152–53, 167, 171
Feder, Gottfried, 234
Female activists, 7, 8, 9, 14, 16, 259, 281–
  82. *See also individual parties' women's
  organizations*
Female Civil Servants Law (*Beamtinnen-
  gesetz*) (1932), 244–46, 264, 278
Female "nature," 1, 7, 15–16, 30, 66, 183,
  207, 250, 272, 279–82 passim; as
  defined by bourgeois feminists, 24,
  190; in German People's Party propaganda, 33, 137, 196–97, 216, 230,
  237; and women's work, 115, 137, 179,
  197, 240, 246; and motherhood, 176,
  188
Feminism, 4, 11, 12, 61, 83, 238, 257, 276;
  in German Democratic Party propaganda, 24, 28, 75, 188, 190, 271; in
  German People's Party propaganda,
  33, 85, 230, 236; in German National

People's Party propaganda, 43, 233;
  in Nazi propaganda, 159, 265. *See also*
  Female "nature"; League of German
  Women's Associations; Women's
  movement
Fisch, Else, 188
Fischer, Ruth, 94–95
Frauenausschusse. See Women's Commit-
  tees
Frauenwelt, Die, 93, 98–99, 154
Frobenius, Else, 137
Froebisch, Frieda, 154
Fromm, Erich, 171, 246

Garnich, Lotte, 200, 262
German Defense and Offense League, 46
German Democratic Party (DDP), 2, 5–
  6, 10, 23–30, 37, 70, 72–80, 87, 120,
  126, 130, 138, 186–93, 271–82 passim;
  women's organization of, 9, 79–
  80, 164–66, 192–93; relationship of,
  to bourgeois feminism, 9, 272; and
  female citizenship, 15, 23–25, 29–30,
  79, 124, 165, 187, 234, 265, 271–72;
  and the republic, 15, 24, 26, 124, 142,
  193; and "party of women" slogan,
  24–25, 30, 32, 73, 76, 83, 124, 142,
  165, 190, 264, 272; and language of
  democracy, 24–25, 72, 74, 77–78,
  186; and women's work, 24–25, 78,
  136–37, 188, 222; anti-SPD propaganda of, 26–27, 40, 76–77; and
  religion, 27, 143, 273–74; and culture, 27–28, 75, 188–91 passim; as
  advocate of female equality, 30, 73,
  76, 136, 166–67, 187–88, 190, 265;
  in opponents' propaganda, 54, 105,
  140, 194; and abortion, 146, 150, 191,
  196; female candidates of, 164–65.
  See also Feminism; German National
  People's Party; German People's
  Party; German State Party
German National People's Party
  (DNVP), 2, 5–6, 16, 42–51, 70, 93,
  110–15, 119, 120, 143, 177–80, 186,

194, 201, 226, 255, 271–78 passim;
women's organization of, 10, 50–51,
110, 114, 160–62, 179–80, 260–61,
281; anti-Semitic propaganda of,
27, 45, 47–48, 74, 110–13, 125, 144,
226, 248, 249, 250; and women's
work, 43, 48, 111, 132, 134–35, 240,
244; female candidates of, 43, 161,
180; and nationalism, 44–45, 110,
112, 130, 140–41, 178, 226, 233, 273;
anti-SPD propaganda of, 45, 111–
13, 125–26, 130–31, 134, 140, 150, 179,
233, 248; anti-DDP propaganda of,
45, 112, 179, 233; and religion, 46, 51,
139–41, 166, 178, 247–48; and culture,
51, 113–15, 178, 233; in opponents'
propaganda, 73, 76, 87, 88, 193; and
abortion, 114, 250, 276; alliance of,
with NSDAP, 177, 180, 225; anticommunist propaganda of, 178, 226,
247–8; and motherhood, 179, 243;
anti-Nazi propaganda of, 179, 259.
See also Evangelical Women's League
(VEFD); Feminism
German National Shop Clerks Association (DHV), 111, 171
German People's Party (DVP), 2, 5–
6, 30–37, 70, 73, 76, 80–87, 119,
120, 143, 186, 193–201, 266, 274–80
passim; women's organization of, 9,
34–36, 86–87, 162–63, 198–200, 261–
62; relationship of, with bourgeois
feminism, 9, 198–99, 237, 280; anti-
SPD propaganda of, 31–32, 40, 82,
85, 141–42, 229; and religion, 31–
32, 84, 140–42, 150, 200, 229, 247,
258, 273; and female equality, 31–
32, 85, 131, 197; and culture, 32, 84,
194–95, 200; anti-DDP propaganda
of, 32, 85, 194; and women's work,
33–35, 82–83, 132, 137–38, 197, 243–
45; female candidates of, 35, 85–86,
163, 198–200, 262; and nationalism,
82, 84–85, 131, 141–42, 194–97, 200,
229–30, 258, 273; and abortion, 196;

and motherhood, 200, 252; anti-
Nazi propaganda of, 229–30, 236,
245, 247, 252, 272. *See also* Female
"nature"; Feminism; Housewives;
Morality; *Volksgemeinschaft*
German State Party (DSP), 186–93,
216, 238; and Jews, 186, 190; and
motherhood, 187, 193, 257; and New
Woman, 187–88, 234; anti-Nazi propaganda of, 191, 230–31, 234, 236,
245, 252, 257; female candidates
of, 192–93; women's organization
of, 230–31, 264–65, 269; and culture, 231, 238, 257. *See also* German
Democratic Party; *Volksgemeinschaft*
Gerwitt, Charlotte, 262
Gierke, Anna von, 50, 180
Goebbels, Joseph, 159, 173, 234, 238, 251,
259, 337 (n. 109)
Göring, Hermann, 219
Grünberg, Helene, 56, 58

Halbe, Erna, 104, 106, 157
Harnack, Agnes von. *See* Zahn-
Harnack, Agnes von
Harzburg Front. *See* German National
People's Party: alliance of, with
NSDAP
Heuss, Theodor, 230
Heymann, Lida Gustava, 10
Hiller, Kurt, 148
Hindenburg, Paul von, 119, 123, 129–31,
153, 160, 170, 220, 230–31
Hitler, Adolf, 107, 238, 252. *See also*
Hitler Putsch; National Socialist
German Workers Party
Hitler Putsch, 74, 107
Home workers, 48–49, 95–96, 111–12,
133–34, 179
Hommes-Knack, Edith, 207
Homosexuality, 147, 253
Housewives, 39, 49, 53, 66, 73, 105,
136, 179, 188, 216, 279; in German
People's Party appeals, 82–83, 137–
38, 197; in Social Democratic Party

People's Party; German State Party; Independent Social Democratic Party; National Socialist German Workers Party; Social Democratic Party

Women's list, 11, 27, 32, 35

Women's movement, 4, 16, 24–26, 73, 163, 200, 210, 271, 285 (n. 25). *See also* Feminism

Women's party, 10–11, 15, 32–33, 35, 49, 76, 91, 172, 200, 261

Women's suffrage, 13, 19, 23, 31, 35, 37–38, 43, 61, 72, 116, 175, 233–34, 270, 282, 312 (n. 28)

Women's work, 12–13, 16, 20, 63, 66–67, 120–21, 131–39, 171, 218, 271, 278–79; and right to work, 169, 191, 221–23, 238–46, 269. *See also* Center Party; Communist Party; Demobilization; Domestic Servants; Double earners; Female Civil Servants Law; Female "nature"; German Democratic Party; German National People's Party; German People's Party; Home workers; Housewives; National Socialist German Workers Party; Personnel Retrenchment Decree; Social Democratic Party

Women voters, 1, 14, 25, 66, 80; and support for conservative and religious parties, 4, 64, 109, 177, 185, 248, 270; general voting patterns of, 4–5, 121, 153, 172, 201, 214–15, 225, 259, 266, 280; criticisms of, 58, 184, 192, 197–98, 206, 217, 227, 261, 281

World War I, 2, 20, 33, 54, 57, 60, 66, 236

Wurm, Mathilde, 63, 64, 65, 316 (n. 108)

Young German Order, 175, 186, 191, 192, 264, 327 (n. 121)

Young Plan, 170, 172, 173, 177–78, 232, 239–40

Youth, 7, 21, 163, 173, 185, 187, 193, 204, 225

Zahn-Harnack, Agnes von, 24, 28, 142–43, 172

Zander, Elsbeth, 259, 260

Zetkin, Clara, 11, 104, 262

Ziegler, Anna, 63

Zietz, Luise, 63, 65